365 fISH

TEXT BY ANTAL VIDA
ILLUSTRATIONS BY TAMÁS KÓTAI

365 FISH

h.f.ullmann

© VINCE BOOKS 2006

English translation: Balázs Farkas, Balázs Kertész and Zsuzsa Láng

Translation revision: Bob Dent and Christopher Sullivan

Supervision: József Pekli

Coordination: Péter Teravágimov

Book design of the original edition: Móni Kaszta – www.arkasdesign.hu

Picture scanning: Pozitív Logika Grafikai Stúdió

© 2006 Tandem Verlag GmbH

h.f.ullmann is an imprint of Tandem Verlag GmbH

Original title: *365 Fish*

ISBN 978-3-8331-2070-1

© 2011 for the English edition: Tandem Verlag GmbH
h.f.ullmann is an imprint of Tandem Verlag GmbH

Cover design: Simone Sticker
Cover photo (background): © Getty Images Munich

Overall responsibility for production: h.f.ullmann publishing, Potsdam, Germany

Printed in China

ISBN 978-3-8331-5963-3

10 9 8 7 6 5 4 3 2 1
X IX VIII VII VI V IV III II I

If you would like to be informed about forthcoming h.f.ullmann titles, you can request our newsletter by visiting our website (**www.ullmann-publishing.com**) or by emailing us at:
newsletter@ullmann-publishing.com.
h.f.ullmann, Birkenstraße 10, 14469 Potsdam, Germany

{ introduction }

CONTENTS Introduction 6 | Fish 1–365 11 | Index 195

There are more species of fish living on earth than all other vertebrates together. At present we know of nearly 30,000 species of fish, but this number is increasing daily. Considering that the average depth of oceans, as the largest aquatic residences on earth, is about 4,000 metres, and considering also that we are familiar only with the top hundred metres or so, we can rightly suspect that there is much waiting to be discovered. These days we are aware of life at the deepest points of oceans, but we know only tiny details of the deep fauna. Not only deep seas but also tropical fresh waters are home to many unknown species. Thus it is very difficult to estimate the number of species of fish living on our planet. At present researchers, depending on their temperament, estimate the figure at between 50,000 and half a million. While mankind is searching for traces of life on Mars, more than 90 per cent of the fish species in oceans may still have to be discovered.

■ As far as we now know, life on earth emerged in seas and oceans. Consequently, every freshwater fish had a sea creature as its ancestor. Yet the boundary between salty sea water and fresh water was a real obstacle to the spread of life. The whole body surface of aquatic creatures is in an osmotic relationship with their outside world. The salt concentration tries to be in constant balance. Thus if a freshwater fish gets to the sea the water will stream out through its skin, while the reverse happens in the case of a sea fish in fresh water. In a different way we could say that a freshwater fish would dry out in sea water and a sea fish would bloat in fresh water. Therefore, only very few species of fish can get through the boundary between seas and rivers. The best-known of these are the eel, the sturgeon and the salmon. Before migration, these fish experience significant changes. This book will introduce both the sea and freshwater types of certain species.

■ Breeds of salmon well demonstrate the process of conquering fresh waters. Some live in the sea and swim up to the fresh water only in order to multiply, whereas populations of other breeds live in either the sea or fresh water isolated from one another, but some breeds have completely turned to a freshwater way of life.

■ The conquest of fresh waters is still taking place. For example, in European rivers even today there are some species which began their exodus to discover the interior of a continent only a few decades ago. The natural process is usually sparked off by a sudden increase in the population of a species in an estuary, but sometimes man also gives a hand. Newcomers often arrive in the 'new world' in the ballast water of ships. That was how a Black Sea species of goby 'invaded' the Danube at the Vienna International Port.

■ Since many species have economic significance, they were often introduced from other continents. Today this is legally regulated in most countries, but several native species of fish still suffer from the mistakes of the past. The newcomers often enjoy considerable advantages over the natives – they have left behind predatory enemies and the causes of their diseases, and they are still unknown in the food chain in their new place of residence. Therefore they are suddenly able to reach huge numbers while they squeeze out competitors more vulnerable from an ecological aspect. These competitors are usually the protected, endangered species.

- Certain species developed strategies which have helped them conquer enormous territories in a few centuries. The way the Eurasian silver crutian carp spread reveals a most surprising method. Their proliferation, called gynogenesis, involves the situation whereby the spreading silver crutian carp populations have, at the borderline, only female members, which are able to smuggle their spawn as odd-ones-out among related species' spawn at any time. Although these spawn are impregnated by the sperm of the alien species' males, the silver crutian carp eggs are only stimulated by the alien species' sperm to multiply. Genetic information cannot get inside the ovum. Thus, the offspring will not be hybrids but identical copies of the original fertile silver crutian carp female. As soon as an area is no longer considered a border region for the silver crutian carp, in that it has become stable among the fish, males begin to appear and the species will gradually return to its traditional way of proliferation. This strategy can result in a single fish being able to produce a new population wherever it finds itself in the world. This is how this species of fish is conquering the whole of Europe today.

- The case of coelacanths is a good example of the lack of exploration of the deep seas. These fish were thought to have become extinct several million years ago, at least until the 1930s when one, which was caught by fishermen of the Comoro islands in the Indian Ocean, was found at a fish market. In 1999 another coelacanth species generated excitement among scientists, but this time it came from the Celebes Sea, the mid-western basin of the Pacific Ocean. Both species live at a depth of only 100–200 metres, so we can only guess what else this depth may hide.

- The coelacanths are considered as the predecessors of terrestrial quadruped vertebrates, or tetrapods. Thus we primates actually originate from sea animals, too. However, our ancestors were not the first to step on land, for when the first fish-like creature slid clumsily on to the shore, it was already populated by billions of arthropods. This was exactly what might have tempted our first ancestors to dry land – the desire for tasty insects.

- There are still fish which stopped at this level of evolution. Mudskippers live in the mangrove swamps where they can move awkwardly only a few metres away from the water. Yet they are excellent at jumping and can catch insects in their flight. Conquering the mainland made fish perform tasks which the mudskipper could not do perfectly. The drying out of the external layer of the epithelium in the case of the eyes presents the gravest problem. The unfortunate mudskipper, which is regarded as a dead-end of evolution, tried to resolve it by storing some water in the socket under its eyes. It protects itself against drying out by strangely pulling in the eyeballs and bathing them in the water cavity. Of course, this is not a perfect solution, since a sudden unlucky movement results in the water spilling out and it has to go for water again. Eyelids could have presented a more effective solution, but the mudskipper 'did not think of that'.

- The other main problem is presented by breathing from the atmosphere. The mudskipper must jump back in the water from time to time. It seems to be drinking, but it only perfuses the water through its gills in order to get oxygen again. It was another fish that invented the organ called lungs. There are still fish in several continents which have lungs. The Australian lungfish can live even in stagnant waters where there is hardly any dissolved oxygen.

These animals come up to the surface for air a few times an hour, but cannot cope with complete desiccation. Yet the South American and African lungfish are able to survive the dry season without water in holes they themselves make. Then they are in hibernation and breathe only through their lungs.

■ The dry season presented a serious challenge for fish living in the tropical savannas. The isolated lakes found there have water only in the rainy season, when they are full of nourishment for fish. The fish had to grasp this opportunity at any price, therefore certain species evolved which only live for one season (a few months) while they grow up, are fertilised and multiply. The spawn survive the dry season at the bottom of the dried-out lakes and spawn maturation only begins with the effect of moisture. These killifish or live bearers are among to the most colourful freshwater fish.

■ The biggest problem for fish was to conquer the air. We have seen the mudskipper's hopeless version of conquering the mainland. Similarly, flying fishes did not become the acrobats of the air. Flying fishes live all over the world. They are able to glide above the water surface for some time, often sailing with their huge, butterfly-wing-like pectoral fins, but after a short flight they often fall into fishermen's boats.

■ If we are talking about near absurdities we must mention that there are fish living in the depths of the earth. Cave fish live in cave waters and are often completely blind. The Devils Hole pupfish lives exclusively in Devils Hole, Ash Meadows in Nye County, Nevada in North America. They occupy an area of about 20 square metres (!), thus populating the smallest area among the vertebrates.

■ And as we are talking about superlatives let us mention the tiniest vertebrate in the world, the eight-millimetre-long plainchin dreamarm, which is a representative of the anglerfish from the North Atlantic Ocean. The largest species of fish is the huge whale shark, a meek plankton-filtering king of the open oceans. Its length can reach 20 metres and it can weigh as much as 34 tonnes.

■ The age of fish can be defined relatively precisely. A pattern similar to the age-rings on trees can be found on their scales. In the case of species without scales, a thin section from the bones enables us to determine the age. A shortraker rockfish, caught on the shores of the Northeast Pacific Ocean in the United States, is the oldest known fish. Its proven age was 157 years.

■ Fish are also in a winning position among vertebrates with regard to fecundity. The greasy grouper populating the Indo Pacific Ocean produces no fewer than 340 million eggs. Fish have a relatively high number of offspring, nevertheless an increasing number of fish species have become endangered as a result of excessive fishing. The worst situation can be found along the sea shores of the developed countries, where fishing is most intensive and efficient. The artificial multiplication of seawater fish species is much more problematic than that of freshwater fish. The biological research into an economically significant freshwater fish species is so advanced that we are able to keep numbers at a suitable level by restocking. In the case of sea fish species, restrictive fishing is still the most successful.

■ Overfishing, however, is only one of a number of human activities which endanger the survival of the fish species on earth. The Red List of the IUCN (International Union for the Conservation of Nature) includes 816 threatened species of fish, and a further 654 are to be added. In addition to excessive fishing, the most significant sources of danger include environmental pollution, the regulation of rivers, the consequences of clearing tropical rain forests, the drainage of wetlands, the effects of dams and hydro-electric power stations, sea explosions, the consequences of the thinning ozone layer and global warming, angling, droughts and the expansion of deserts, and collections for aquaria and museums. The list is far from complete and neither is the future too promising. At present mankind clearly understands that freshwater stocks will represent the most important natural capital once oil resources are exhausted. However, the main losers will be creatures in water, as a result of the manipulation of these stocks.

- This book primarily introduces species which are economically significant. They are fished and caught or made into local  specialities. Three hundred and sixty-five species of fish are described out of the approximately 4,500 species which are fished. We have tried to represent all parts of the earth. Thus breeds of salmon from Siberia and fish from the Australian Great Barrier Reef can be found in the book.

- We have also tried to give the name of the fish in the language of the locations where it can be found. Of course, the multitude of languages is similar to that of fish, therefore we could not achieve perfection. Even so, 223 languages and dialects are included in this book, ranging from Alutiig in Alaska to Yoruba in Nigeria. (The key to abbreviations next to the names can be found at the end of the book.) One of the purposes of writing this work has been for the traveller to be able to use it in a restaurant or at a fish market anywhere in the world. Thus the text also includes information about how the respective fish is prepared traditionally. In the case of languages with a non-Latin script, for example Russian, Greek or Japanese, we have used the Latin transcription in order to facilitate use of the book.

- Preference was given to the so-called official, FAO (Food and Agriculture Organisation of the UN) names in world languages – for example English, Spanish, Portuguese or French, which are used all over the world. Not all species have FAO names at present, therefore some fish names can be found in the book in, for example, English in connection with Pakistan or Spanish with Mauritania.

- Unfortunately, there is not a single language in which the names of species do not change continually. You might think that  a name in Latin would be the sure means among the languages in the world. This is no longer so, unfortunately. The Latin nomenclature changes from year to year depending how a species is classified in the taxonomy of fish. There have been great changes in the past few years, even in the cases of well-known fish. This book uses Latin names in use at the beginning of 2006.

- Each entry indicates the fish family the species belongs to, both in Latin and English. This may help place the given fish in the multitude of species and it also shows which related species live on the earth. Ichthyology, the branch of zoology dealing with fish, divides fishes into six main categories as follows:

1. The single order of the category of hagfishes has only one family. The approximately 70 species included here live exclusively in the seas. Their body

is elongated, eel-like, covered with a slimy discharge, and they have no internal solid frame. They do not have twin fins, scales or jaws. The eyes are under the skin, therefore they are nearly completely blind. They are usually known as scavengers, since they drill themselves into the bodies of deceased fish, but they also often eat salt-water molluscs. They have no economic significance.

2. The only order of the lamprey category includes a single family. All the 42 known species have eyes only at a mature age. Seven pairs of gill openings can be seen on their eel-like, naked bodies. They have no twin fins or jaws. Their mouth is characteristically circular. With this they stick

to live animals, sucking on their bodily fluids. They occur both in fresh water and in the sea. Some of the species are rare and endangered, others are fished.

3. The category of shark and rays comprises 44 families of cartilaginous fish. This makes all together 1000 species, which have 5–7 pairs of gill openings on two sides of their head. The skin-covered fins have no rays and there are no scales on the body. The solid internal frame is of cartilaginous tissue. They are sea species nearly without exception. Their tail fin is characteristically asymmetrical. There are often large fangs in their well-developed jaws. They have no air-bladders. Several species play an economic role.

4. All the representatives of three families in the single order of the chimaera category live exclusively in the sea. There is a gill cover over four gill openings, but no spiracle opening. The skin in adults is naked. Males have a clasping organ on the head and the solid frame is built up of cartilaginous tissue. Several of their species can be found in the deep seas. At spawning the males fertilise the females internally with their abdominal process. Their economic importance is small.

5. The category of ray-finned fishes includes 45 orders, more than 90 per cent of the known fish species. The fins are usually supported by rays. Scales, if present, are ganoid, cycloid or ctenoid. Their internal frame is of real bone tissue. Nostrils are relatively high up on the head. Ray-finned fishes represent the largest variety among all the classes of fish. They occur in both fresh water and the sea. Species of the most economic significance belong to this category.

6. The category of lobe-finned fishes includes 3 orders, 4 families and 11 species. Paired fins form lobes or filaments. The tail is heterocercal. There is a double dorsal fin and there are cosmoid scales. The above-mentioned coelacanths and lungfishes are included here. They are generally rare and endangered species with no economic significance.

■ After this short course in ichthyology, let us see the selected 365 species of fish or, without going through, let us put this book in our travelling case and start off for the world. Without any doubt, we shall have the opportunity to use it wherever we may find ourselves in this incredibly colourful world.

{ fish 1-365 }

1 | Sea lamprey | Petromyzon marinus | PETROMYZONIDAE / LAMPREYS

Sea lamprey (En), Meerneunauge (D), Lamprea de mar (E), Lamproie marine (F), Lampreda di mare (I), Zeeprik (Nl) • Morska paklara (Cr), Havlampret (Da), Loimpre (Ga), Havniøye (N), Lampreia do mar (P), Morskaya minoga (R), Havsnejonöga (S), Merinahkiainen (SF)

Sea lamprey occur in the waters of the Atlantic Ocean stretching from Norway and Iceland to the Iberian Peninsula and the western region of the Mediterranean, but they are virtually absent from the eastern Mediterranean and the Black Sea. In the western region of the Atlantic they are abundant from Labrador to the northern strip of the Gulf of Mexico. In North America landlocked populations of sea lamprey are native to the Great Lakes, in the Finger Lakes, in Oneida Lake and Lake Champlain. The largest known body length of sea lamprey is 120 cm (47 in), the largest body weight being 2.5 kg (5.5 lb). The larvae live in the mud and feed on micro-organisms and detritus. Parasitic in habit, mature specimens living in the ocean attach themselves to other fish, feeding on their blood and flesh. To prevent the host animal's blood from coagulating, sea lamprey produce an anti-coagulant substance. The freshwater populations may cause serious depletion of other fish stocks, and often also cause inconvenience to holidaymakers by attaching themselves to humans. Exploitation of the sea lamprey stock is insignificant, in some areas it has been added to the list of protected species.

2 | Caspian lamprey | Caspiomyzon wagneri | PETROMYZONTIDAE / LAMPREYS

Caspian lamprey (En), Kaspiiskaya minoga (R)

An endemic species dwelling in the Caspian basin, Caspian lamprey inhabit the coastal waters and feeding rivers of the Caspian Sea. Lamprey in the Volga river have suffered serious depletion and today count as a rarity. The largest size they may attain is a body length of 55 cm (22 in), and weight of 200–250 g (7–9 oz). A non-parasitic species, intestines of Caspian lamprey have revealed only algae and water plants, However, they probably consume the remains of dead fish, too. Caspian lamprey also have the habit of attaching themselves to other fish, but only in order to change places. Before spawning the body decreases by 20–22%, and the fish dies soon after the spawning season. The meat of the fish is reported to be poisonous, special treatment of the meat is necessary before cooking. Before 1868 dried sea lamprey were primarily used as candles, or for obtaining oil. Only after this date was the fish used for human consumption. Nowadays it is held to be an extremely precious and palatable delicacy.

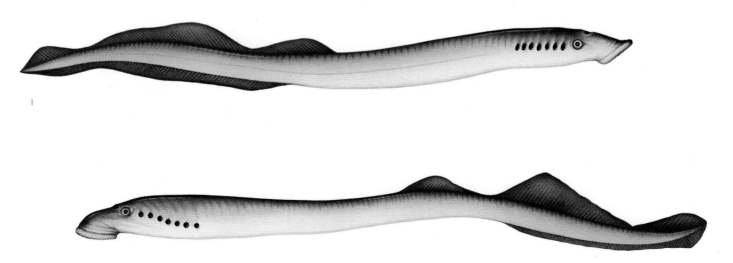

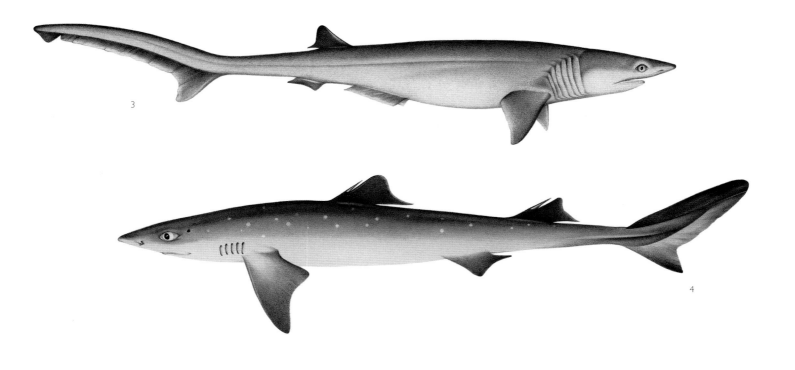

3 | **Sharpnose sevengill shark** | Heptranchias perlo | HEXANCHIDAE / COW SHARKS

Sharpnose sevengill shark (En), Perlon, Spitzkopf-Siebenkiemer (D), Cañabota bocadulce (E), Perlon (F), Squalo manzo (I), Spitssnuitzevenkieuwshaai (Nl) • Epta carcharias (Gr), Sheva-zim (Isr)

Distributed in all tropical seas, sharpnose sevengill sharks lead a hiding lifestyle. They attain a maximum length of about 1.5 m (60 in), and like the most ancient sharks, they have seven gills and a relatively large mouth on the lower part of the head. With its slender and elongated body of light blue or metallic blue colour, the sevengill shark is a handsome creature. It dwells a six thousand feet deep in the ocean, mostly living in the regions close to the sea bottom. Like the related species, they are predatory in habit, usually hunting in smaller groups. Fishermen working in the littoral zone (close to the coast) often catch sevengills, since they easily take live bait. In practice, sevengills are harmless to humans when in water; nevertheless, after landing they may cause unpleasant moments on board the fishing boat. Ovoviviparous, their young emerge from the yolk-sac right before its being extruded into the water. They produce about one or two dozen offspring, which at birth are 25–30 cm (10–12 in) long. The young start their life in the littoral zone, in waters six feet deep. Local fishermen often turn young sevengills into souvenirs to sell to tourists. The meat of sevengill sharks is considered of average quality, and is usually eaten pan-fried, especially in the summer.

4 | **Spiny dogfish, Piked dogfish** | Squalus acanthias | SQUALIDAE / DOGFISH SHARKS

Spiny dogfish (En), Dornhai (D), Mielga (E), Aiguillat commun (F), Spinarolo (I), Doornhaai (Nl) • Pighaj (Da), Stiktokentróni, skylópsaro (Gr), Háfur (Is), Qozan qetan (Isr), Piggha (N), Galhudo-malhado (P), Obyknovennaya kolyuchaya akula (R), Pigghaj (S), Piikkihai (SF), Mahmuzlu camgöz (Tr)

Named after the sharp spines in front of each of their two dorsal fins, spiny dogfish (also called spurdog or skittledog) is the shark species most frequently observed by swimmers and divers. Spiny dogfish are of small build, seldom reaching the body lengths of more than 1 m (39 in). In general they are not dangerous to man. However, this is not the case in reverse, fishermen being especially keen on bagging entire schools of spiny dogfish. One of those very rare shark species that like to form dense schools, spiny dogfish are distributed in nearly all seas of the world, except in Polar regions. It is not surprising, therefore, that an immense variety of dishes are prepared from dogfish. In western Europe shark-jelly is a highly appreciated delicacy, and so are the different aspic dishes of spiny dogfish roe. The meat of the fish is a staple food in tropical regions. Due to its relatively small size, the sun-dried and smoked meat of the spiny dogfish is easy to store – and to sell. The head of the spiny dogfish – only 15–30 cm (6–12 in) in diameter – would also make an ideal souvenir, since it really takes up very little space in one's suitcase.

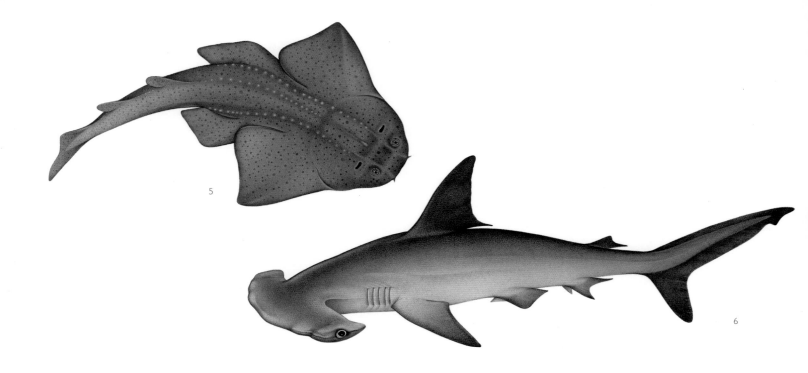

5 | Angelshark | Squatina squatina | SQUATINIDAE / ANGEL SHARKS

Angelshark (En), Europäischer Meerengel (D), Angelote (E), Ange de mer commun (F), Squadro, pesce angelo (I), Zee-engel (Nl) • Angelos, rína, vióli (Gr), Mak'akh (Isr), Xkatlu (Malt), Pei ange (Mon), Keler (Tr), Sfinn (Tun)

The close relationship between rays and sharks is perhaps best exemplified by this species. It is of interest to note that most of its local names throughout the entire Atlantic area are in some way derived from "angel", probably alluding to its wing-like pectoral and ventral fins. The colour of this shark is highly variable, from greenish brown to greyish, to match the tone of the sea bottom. It particularly likes coastal regions, and dives to a maximum depth of 50–100 m (150–300 ft). For its 1–2 m (40–80 in) length and 50–80 kg (100–160 lb) weight it is a favourite trophy. In cold seas, mainly in the Baltic area, it grows slowly, and its populations are decreasing. An ovoviviparous species, females give birth to between 10 and 25 young, which are 20–25 cm (8–10 in) long. The locomotion of angelsharks is entirely ray-like, and when circumstances permit, they also bury themselves into the mud. Their flesh is much praised by the British and North Americans, and is highly valued on markets. The "wings" are exported to the Far East, to serve as ingredients for famous vegetable soups.

6 | Scalloped hammerhead (shark) | Sphyrna lewini | SPHYRNIDAE / HAMMERHEAD SHARKS

Scalloped hammerhead (shark) (En), Gebuchteter Hammerhai, Bogenstirn-Hammerhai (D), Cornuda común (E), Requin-marteau halicorne (F), Pesce martello (I), Geschulpte hamerhaai (Nl) • Bronze hammerhead shark (En), Aka-shumokuzame (J), Yu bengkong (Mal)

One of the most widely distributed species of the small family of hammerhead sharks, it has been noted in almost all the warm seas of the world. Somewhat smaller than its relatives, it has a more muscular and stubbier build. Its common name – bronze – is attributed to the dark, shiny tone of its back and fins. It usually reaches 2–3 m (80–118 in) in length, and 100–200 kg (220–440 lb) in weight, and is considered particularly aggressive and capable of attacking humans. Its flattened, hammer-like head is of a fairly regular crescent shape, and the lidless eyes are located on its two ends. This species can also be distinguished by the fact that its pointed pectoral fins lie almost precisely below the rounded dorsal fin. The upper lobe of the caudal fin is very long, with one or two rounded notches below its tip. The bronze hammerhead likes "lifting", and follows its fleeing prey to several hundred metres deep. Most frequently caught by drag nets, it is sometimes hooked by anglers. Its flesh is rated as good, while its fins, deep-frozen and packed, are transported to Far Eastern markets.

7 | **Smooth hammerhead** | Sphyrna zygaena | SPHYRNIDAE / HAMMERHEAD SHARKS

Smooth hammerhead (En), Gemeiner Hammerhai, Glatter Hammerhai (D), Cornuda común, pez martillo (E), Requin-marteau commun (F), Pesce martello (I), Hamerhaai (Nl)

Distributed in all the oceans, smooth hammerheads are perhaps the best-known species of shark. They have heads that resemble double-headed hammers, with one eye on each stalk. The second dorsal fin is very small, with the large, elongated upper lobe of the caudal fin being used in manoeuvring. With lengths of 3–4 m (120–160 in), they belong among the large sharks. They travel around in all three large oceans of the planet, and like to hunt for schooling fish along the marine currents. They sometimes hunt in small groups, but mostly they are solitary in habit. They are of potential harm to humans; hundreds of attacks have been recorded. Viviparous, they give birth to a few dozen offspring about half a metre (20 in) long. When young, their heads are quite regular in shape, the "hammer" becoming larger with age and separating their eyes more and more. The meat of the hammerhead is highly appreciated in the catering industry, with big-game fishermen supplying the food market. The principal method for catching hammerheads is trolling. Chinese restaurants world-wide pay a generous price for the fins, an important ingredient of many a Chinese recipe.

8 | **Tope shark** | Galeorhinus galeus | TRIAKIDAE / HOUNDSHARKS

Tope shark (En), Hundshai (D), Cazón (E), Requin-hâ (F), Canesca (I), Ruwe haai (Nl) • Gråhaj (Da), Soupfin shark, school shark, vitamin shark, liver-oil shark, oil shark (En), Galéos drossitis (Gr), Gráháfur (Is), Karishan (Isr), Gråhai (N), Perna-de-moça (P), Seraya akula (R), Bethaj, gråhaj (S), Harmaahai (SF), Camgöz baligi (Tr)

With the exception of arctic seas, this species occurs almost everywhere. Its grey to brownish-grey ground colour is an adaptation to the coastal sandy-muddy bottom. Rapidly circling in these waters, it thus frightens benthic animals, mainly small flounders. On average it grows to approximately 1 m in length, though the largest specimens can reach nearly 2 m (80 in). In contrast to large sharks, the tope shark prefers hunting in groups, sometimes using the tactics of driving smaller schooling fish "into the corner". Although its triangular teeth can be dangerous when hooked, the soupfin shark has not been noted to attack humans. Specimens of approximately 50 kg (100 lb) are in high esteem on European markets, as huge fillets can be cut from this size. Offered in all major supermarkets, vitamin shark flesh is machine-cut according to the wishes of the customer. The somewhat tough material can be prepared like beef. The skin of the tope is rougher than that of other species of shark, and is used by furniture makers for polishing.

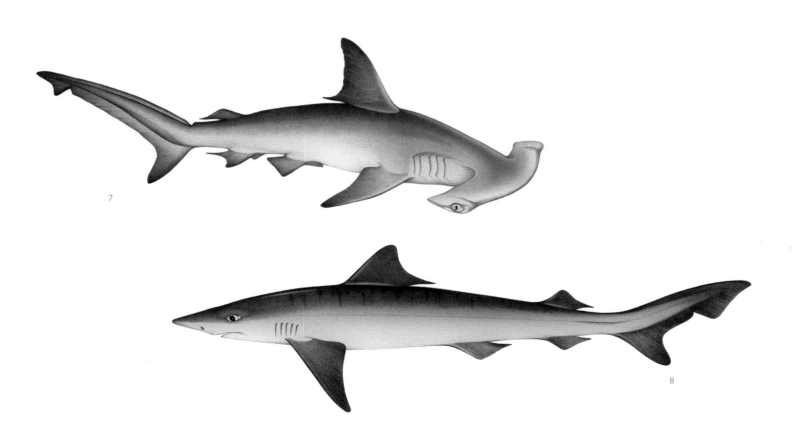

7

8

9 | Smooth dogfish, Dusky smooth-hound | Mustelus canis | TRIAKIDAE / HOUNDSHARKS

Smooth dogfish, Dusky smooth-hound (En), Punktierter Glatthai (D), Musola dentuda (E), Émissole douce (F), Palombo (I), Donkere toonhaai (Nl) • Akula amerikanskaya kuniya, sobachya akula (R)

A member of the relatively small-bodied hound shark family, smooth dogfish attain lengths of about 1–1.5 m (40–60 in). In spite of this size, they are totally harmless to humans, since they primarily feed on demersal invertebrates. Still, if they manage to acquire the leftovers of the prey caught by larger predators, they are not so picky as not to eat up the carrion. Smooth dogfish are mainly distributed in the Atlantic Ocean and the warmer marginal seas. They favour the shallower waters of the littoral zone. They have often been observed following ships and waiting for discarded leftovers. They can be recognised by their round caudal fins and their high forehead over the eyes. In addition to commercial fishing fleets, recreational fishermen also catch them successfully. Although the mouth of the smooth dogfish is small and furnished with tiny and dense teeth, the fish should be handled with utmost care. The meat of the smooth dogfish is considered to be of medium quality, proper spicing improving the taste considerably. It is a frequent catch in Central America, where slices of dogfish are salted and sun-dried, preserving the meat this way for several months.

10 | Smooth-hound | Mustelus mustelus | TRIAKIDAE / HOUNDSHARKS

Smooth-hound (En), Südlicher Glatthai (D), Musola (E), Émissole lisse (F), Palombo, palummu, nisseua, mussola, penn (I), Toornhaai, gladde haai (Nl) • Musola vera (Cat), Gray mouth dog (En), Galeos (Gr), Kerishon (Isr), Mazzola bla xewka, mazzola tat-tbajja, zaghrun (Malt), Kalb ibahr (Mor), Caçao, caneja (P), Köpek baligi (Tr), Ktat (Tun)

The best known and the first described species of hound shark (Triakidae family) occurs throughout the Atlantic, and its warm seas. It prefers coastal waters, avoiding rocky areas entirely. While the average specimen grows to a much smaller size, the smooth-hound can reach 250 cm (120 in) in length and 100 kg (200 lb) in weight. It is characterised by small teeth resembling those of skates, which help it to grind its main food: invertebrates buried in sand or mud, gastropods and crustaceans. While smooth-hounds are wholly harmless to humans, they frequently cause disturbance when appearing close to the shore. They are not bound to a certain area, and often migrate in the sea for considerable distances. Their reproduction is independent of seasons, which helps to explain why 30–50 cm (12–20 in) long young nearly always turn up in nets of fishermen. The flesh of this species is considered of medium quality, and can be cheaply purchased in markets. Along the West African coast and further inland it is consumed as slices dried in the sun.

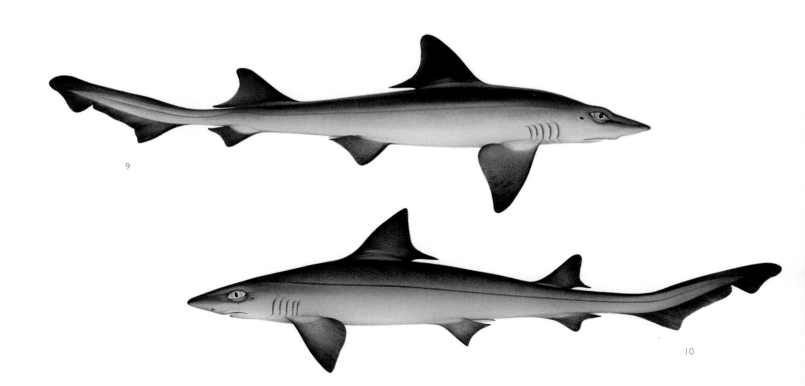

9

10

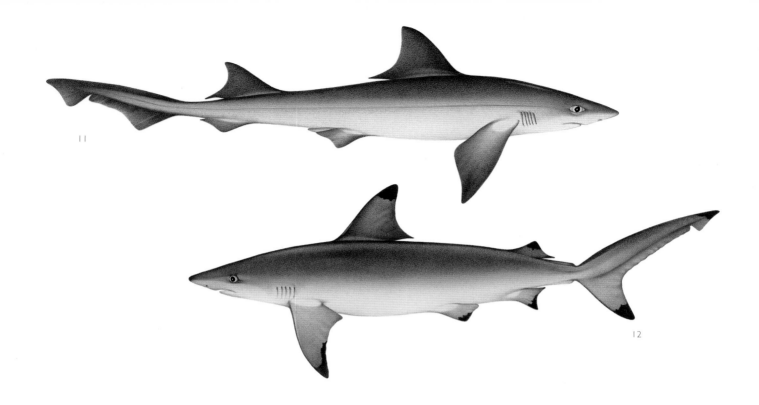

11 | **Narrownose smooth-hound, Patagonian smooth-hound** | Mustelus schmitti | TRIAKIDAE / HOUNDSHARKS

Narrownose smooth-hound, Patagonian smooth-hound (En), Argentinischer Glatthai (D), Patagonisk glathaj (Da), Gatuso (E), Émissole gatuso (F), Palombo atlantico (I), Smalsnuittoonhaai (Nl) • Patagonian smooth-hound (En), Cação-da-Patagónia (P)

Primarily an inhabitant of Atlantic waters, the barbeled hound shark can also be found in southern waters of the Pacific off South America. One of the smallest sharks, it grows to 80 cm (31 in) at most. Thanks to its slender, elongated body it can penetrate into extremely shallow water close to the shore, but it has also been caught in streams and canals emptying into the sea. Its characteristic, huge pectoral fins, which appear as if out-of-proportion, help it to move around in shallows. The dorsal fin is located halfway between the pectoral and the ventral fins, and the barbeled hound shark can often be seen while pursuing its prey into harbours. Its main food is small schooling fish, but it attacks nearly all small, bottom-dwelling organisms. In the vicinity of urban areas it also forages on organic debris. Its flesh is not much valued on the market, and is mostly locally consumed. A much more common sight are stuffed specimens of maximum 50 cm (20 in) length offered as souvenirs. Due to its high reproductive rate it is not protected, and is considered an abundant species everywhere.

12 | **Blacktip shark** | Carcharhinus limbatus | CARCHARHINIDAE / REQUIEM SHARKS

Blacktip shark (En), Schwarzspitzenhai (D), Tiburón macuira (E), Requin bordé, requin blanc (F), Squalo pinne nere (I), Zwartpunthaai (Nl) • Tubarão-de-pontas-negras (P)

The blacktip shark is a cosmopolitan species occurring world-wide in warm subtropical and tropical seas. Its name alludes to its black-tipped fins. It appears both in the open sea and along the coast, but consistently remains in the vicinity of the continental and island shelf. It is frequently found in river mouths, muddy bays, mangroves and lagoons, as well as along the margin of coral reefs. Its maximum size is 2.5 m (100 in) and 120–130 kg (265–287 lb). It hunts actively in open water, and preys on pelagic and bottom-dwelling fish, smaller sharks and rays, cephalopods and crustaceans. Although it seldom attacks humans, it can be dangerous when provoked and can cause serious damage. It often occurs in the catch of fishermen and coastal anglers. Its flesh is sold and eaten fresh, while its fins are made into sharkfin soup. Also its skin is put to use, and oil is pressed from its liver. Its populations are getting endangered.

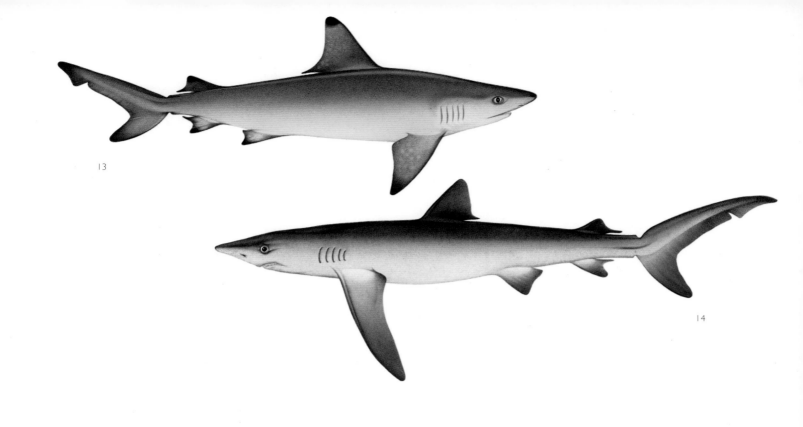

13 | **Blacktip reef shark** | Carcharhinus melanopterus | CARCHARHINIDAE / REQUIEM SHARKS

Blacktip reef shark (En), Schwarzspitzen-Riffhai (D), Tiburón de puntas negras (E), Requin pointes noires (F), Squalo pinne nere (I), Zwartpuntrifhaai (Nl) • Blacktip shark (Au, NZ), Tsumaguro (J), Yu sirip hitam, yu nipah (Mal), Buguing (Phi), Blackfin reef shark (US)

A member of the Carcharhinus genus, blacktip reef sharks dwell in the Indian and Pacific Oceans, from the Red Sea and the East African coasts to Hawaii. They have also became abundant in the eastern region of the Mediterranean by passing through the Suez Canal. A shark species of medium build, blacktip reef sharks average 2 m (79 in) in body length and may weigh about 70–80 kg (154–176 lb). They primarily inhabit shallow coastal waters in the regions around reefs and areas flooded with the tide, but occasionally they may occur in the open sea not far from the coast. They have been observed hunting in mangrove swamps, following a tidal flux. Although they sometimes intrude into freshwaters too, blacktip reef sharks never depart too far from the sea. Hunting in small groups or individually, their diet consists of fish, crustaceans, Cephalopodae and other molluscs. They may become aggressive with divers fishing with fish-spears and harpoons. A viviparous species, in blacktip reef sharks fertilization of the roe happens internally, the small sharks hatch in the body of the mother and only afterwards are the 2–4 offspring "delivered". In Eastern cuisine a great variety of recipes exist for preparing the fins: simmered in meat and soy gravy, or boiled to make the special shark-fin soup; fillets are generally roasted or pan-fried.

14 | **Blue shark** | Prionace glauca | CARCHARHINIDAE / GRAY SHARKS

Blue shark (En), Blauhai (D), Tiburón azul (E), Peau bleue (F), Verdesca (I), Blauwe haai (Nl) • Glafkokarcharias (Gr), Yoshikirizame (J), Guelha, tintureira (P), Akula sinyaya (R), Zarlacz blekitny (Pl), Pamuk baligi (Tr)

Quite a frequent type of shark, blue shark are of proportionate build, their colour being a beautiful marine blue. Adult specimens average 3–4 m (118–158 in) and 200–300 kg (440–660 lb) in size. A markedly bold and aggressive shark, the blue shark apparently has a conscious attraction for human company. In many regions blue shark have been observed to ascend larger rivers to attack swimmers in bights. They produce quite a large number of offspring with as many as a few dozen per female fish. Divers distinguish them from the much more peaceful mako shark by the disproportionately large upper lobe of the tailfin, which is at least three times as long as that of the mako. This distinguishing mark can save lives, especially in deeper oceans. In tropical waters blue shark are landed in high numbers by lining, since they devour all sorts of bleeding meat, fish and giant water-snails used as bait. The meat of the blue shark is sold at a very high price in the food market, although it is not an abundant item. Far Eastern cuisine mainly appreciates the fins of the blue shark, the fins having become so precious a delicacy that in these regions it often happens that blue shark meat is used as bait on hooks intended for blue sharks. The meat of the fish is by no means as precious as the fins, the fillet rather resembling veal of mediocre quality.

15 | **Shortfin mako** | Isurus oxyrinchus | LAMNIDAE / MACKEREL SHARKS

Shortfin mako (En), Mako, Kurzflossen-Mako (D), Marrajo dientuso (E), Taupe bleu (F), Squalo mako (I), Haringhaai (Nl) • Blue pointer (Au, NZ), Mako-haj, makrelhaj (Da), Mako shark, sharp-nosed mackerel shark (En), Rynchokarcharias (Gr), Aozame (J), Cheong-sang-a-ri (Kor), Dikburun (Tr)

Ranging through tropical and temperate seas of the earth, mako sharks are among the most beautiful sharks. They are light-blue, though appearing deep blue in the water, with contrasting white bellies. Their body is of a perfect torpedo shape, with a symmetrically lobed crescent-shaped tail – an unusual trait among sharks. They attain body lengths of 2–3 m (79–118 in) and may weigh several hundred kilograms. They prey on other fishes in smaller schools or individually. Mako sharks are also known by their peculiar habit of repeatedly leaping out of the water, a habit which has not been substantially explained. Thus in most cases when the leaping fish are observed the graceful show is not intended to impress potential prey. A relatively abundant species, mako shark are apparently stable in numbers. In contrast to their related species, they produce a high number of offspring, which may explain the peculiarly rich populations of mako shark. In addition, adult mako shark avoid the coastline, and thus human habitation. They are mostly landed by ocean-going fishing fleets, and the processed fillets and fins are marketed as food – chiefly in Japan.

16 | **Porbeagle** | Lamna nasus | LAMNIDAE / MACKEREL SHARKS

Porbeagle (En), Heringshai (D), Marrajo sardinero (E), Requin-taupe commun (F), Smeriglio (I), Haringhaai, neushaai (Nl) • Sildehaj (Da), Mackerel shark (En), Karcharías, skylópsaro (Gr), Hámeri (Is), Tubarão-sardo (P), Sillihai (SF)

Seldom does it happen, but it certainly does, that an animal is named after its prey. This is the case with the porbeagle, since in many languages it is called "herring shark", because fleets fishing for herring meet them most frequently. Thus, in seaside regions porbeagle is often served as food, especially as a cutlet. Porbeagle inhabit most oceans and seas. Nevertheless, it is mainly in the Northern Hemisphere that they are of higher commercial value. They average 2–3 m (79–118 in) in length, but their body is stockier, more robust than that of other sharks, thus often attaining a body weight of a tonne. Like the majority of sharks, the porbeagle is an ovoviviparous species (i.e. the egg hatches within the mother). The female porbeagle protects and nourishes 2–4 embryos in her oviduct, the offspring emerging from her body with body lengths of about 50 cm (20 in). In wintertime, porbeagle form small schools and start off in the direction of the Equator, since they do not like waters with temperatures below 20°C (68°F).

15

16

17 | Thresher shark, Thintail thresher | Alopias vulpinus | ALOPIIDAE / THRESHER SHARKS

Thresher shark, Thintail thresher (En), Fuchshai, Drescherhai (D), Zorro (E), Renard (F), Squalo volpe, pesce volpe (I), Voshaai (Nl) • Almindelig rævehaj (Da), Long-tailed thresher shark, fox shark (En), Aleposkylos (Gr), Skotthàfur (Isr), Onagazame, Mao-naga (J), Akula-lisitsa (R), Revehai (N), Tubarão-raposo (P), Rävhaj (S), Kettuhai (SF)

Easy to distinguish from the rest of the shark family by its extremely long heterocercal tail (i.e. a tail fin having two unequal lobes, the upper lobe being larger) which exceeds the entire length of the body, the names attached to the long-tailed thresher shark are in most languages related to this frighteningly efficient, multifunctional "weapon". Firstly, the fish uses its enormous caudal fin in hunting, thrashing the water to stun and frighten its prey. Secondly, the tail also helps the rest of this benthic wanderer. By applying the disproportionately large pectoral fins too, by extending them, the thresher shark assumes a quasi-pelagic (i.e. almost floating) position when sleeping. Sometimes it only assumes this position to spot some new, unsuspecting prey. Although a giant fish with its body length of 5–6 m (200–236 in), the thresher shark is not generally considered dangerous to people. However, dogs which have fallen into water, or large sea-birds resting afloat on the surface of the seas have been observed being captured by thresher sharks. Thresher shark are landed commercially for food, their meat being of medium quality. In the Far East their fins are highly prized, shark-fin soup being a popular dish. This great interest in the species is reflected in the decreasing number of thresher sharks in the Pacific Ocean.

18 | Bowmouth guitarfish | Rhina ancylostoma | RHINOBATIDAE / GUITARFISHES

Bowmouth guitarfish (En), Geigenrochen (D), Guitarra (E), Angelot (F), Pesce violino (I), Rondbekkegrog (Nl) • Shark ray, mud skate (En), Shinonome-sakatazame (J), Mog dag-su-gu-ri (Kor)

Closely related to rays and member of the Rhinobatidae family, bowmouth guitarfish inhabit the Indian Ocean and the western regions of the Pacific Ocean. They dwell in the area stretching from the Red Sea and the Persian Gulf to South Africa, in the east as far as Japan, Australia, the Philippines and Micronesia. A species of large build, bowmouth guitarfish may attain body lengths of 270 cm (106 in) and weights of 135 kg (300 lb). They generally prefer shallow waters, live at depths of 3–90 m (10–295 ft), over sand and mud bottoms, in the vicinity of reefs and wreckage. They very seldom occur in the midwater zone or near the surface. Predato in habit, they mainly feed on demersal crustaceans and molluscs. An ovoviviparous fish, after the interior fertilization of the roe the young guitarfish hatch in the body of the female, and afterwards the four offspring are born. The offspring are 45 cm (18 in) in length at birth. Bowmouth guitarfish are armed for defence with a row of large spines above the eyes and behind the head, which make them difficult to handle, and they may destroy the entire catch in the trawl. They are marketed for food fresh and salted-dried, but it is only the pectoral fins that are eaten. They can be seen in many marine aquarium shows.

17

18

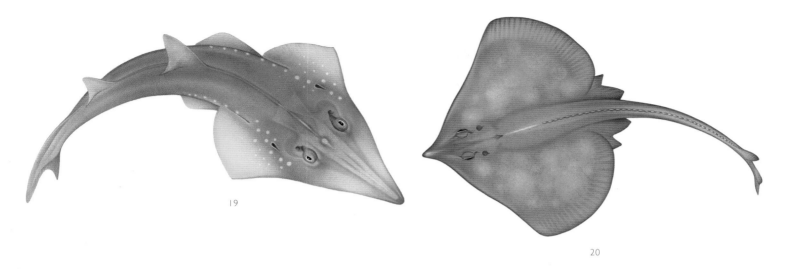

19

20

19 | **Giant guitarfish** | Rhynchobatus djiddensis | RHINOBATIDAE / GUITARFISHES

Giant guitarfish (En), Riesengeigenrochen (D), Pez cuna manchado (E), Poisson paille à pois (F) • White-spotted shovel-nosed ray (Au), Sorsor (Ban), Arado, sudsod (Bik), Pay par saa (HK), Pari, cucut biola (Ind), Tongari-sakatazame (J), Paitan (Kuy), Dong-su-gu-ri (Kor), Yu kemejan (Mal), Pating sudsod (Tag), White-spotted guitarfish (US)

A large bodied ray-like species of the Rhinobatidae family, giant guitarfish dwell in the western region of the Indian Ocean, in the Red Sea and in the tropical waters of the western region of the Indian Ocean. The biggest specimens may grow as large as 310 cm (122 in) and 230 kg (507 lb). They live in the vicinity of the coast at depths of 2–50 m (7–164 ft), also intruding into the shallow brackish waters of river estuaries. They enjoy a demersal lifestyle and live over sand and mud bottoms. Their diet mainly consists of bottom-dwelling crustaceans, shellfish and tiny fish. Fishermen use crabs and sardines as live bait for catching giant guitarfish. The male fish is usually 160 cm (63 in), the female 180 cm (70 in) at the time they become sexually mature. Fertilization happens internally, the roe evolve and hatch in the body of the female fish. Soon after hatching, usually four offspring are born, their size at birth being about 60 cm (24 in). Due to the very precious meat they yield, giant guitarfish are a very popular target of both commercial and recreational fishermen. Since the fins are highly valued in the Asian market, the stock is in danger of being overfished. The fins are used in soup or are fried.

20 | **Sydney skate** | Raja australis / Okamejei australis | RAJIDAE / RAYS

Sydney skate (En), Sydney-Rochen (D), Raya del Pacífico (E), Raie de Pacifique (F), Razza del pacifico (I), Sydneyrog (Nl) • Common skate, pommy skate (Au), Australian skate (En), Pari (Mal)

Related to rays, Sydney skate dwell in the western region of the Pacific Ocean. An endemic species, they are found exclusively in the tropical and subtropical waters around Australia. A small-bodied species, they may attain a maximum body length of 50–60 cm (20–24 in) with a weight of a few pounds. They prefer to stay in relatively shallow waters, not going deeper than 100–150 m (328–492 ft); they live over sand and mud bottoms, though occasionally intrude into the brackish waters of river estuaries. They feed on bottom-dwelling crustaceans and molluscs, catching their prey from hiding. They attain sexual maturity at body lengths of 40 cm (16 in). After the interior fertilization of the eggs, the roe evolve in a four-tipped sac in the female's body, and after hatching, they are "delivered". Due to their small size, commercial fishing of the species is not significant, but they are often caught in bottom trawls and they regularly occur in the catch of marine fishermen. As with the other rays, it is the meat of the wings that is used for food. The meat is marketed fresh or frozen, and is usually pan-fried or roasted.

21

22

21 | Common skate, Blue skate | Dipturus batis | RAJIDAE / RAYS

Common skate, Blue skate (En), Glattrochen (D), Raya noriega (E), Pocheteau gris (F), Razza bavosa (I), Vleet (Nl) • Skade (Da), Flapper skate, Common skate (En), Skata (Is), Glattrokke, storskate (N), Raia-oirega (P), Slätrocka (S), Silorausku (SF)

Distributed in the colder regions of the Atlantic Ocean, common skate are mainly abundant in the northwestern waters. Specimens 2–3 m (80–120 in) in length and 100–150 kg (220–330 lb) in weight are not a rarity. They belong to the so-called sharp-nosed group, the characteristic trait of which is that the wing-like fins widen only behind the eye line. The large mouth on the lower part of the head is furnished with several teeth lined in rows, about 40–50 in both jaws. They are predato in habit, and they descend to depths of several hundred feet. They characteristically encircle their prey from the rear and from above. Landed by commercial fishing fleets in great numbers, common skate are sometimes caught by recreational fishermen too. The meat of the fish is exceptionally flavoursome, hence it is used in a great variety of forms. Loss during the processing is also minimal, usually not exceeding 10–20% of the total weight of the animal. The customer should be cautious, though, because the names of canned skate may be misleading, the product may be sold to the unsuspecting customer as lobster meat. For its exceptionally high commercial value, the price of common skate is permanently on the increase.

22 | Big skate | Raja binoculata | RAJIDAE / RAYS

Big skate (En), Zweiaugenrochen (D), Raya (E), Raie du Pacifique (F), Razza (I), Grote rog (Nl) • Skate (Au), Pari (Mal)

A large-bodied species related to rays, big skate live in the northern region of the Pacific Ocean, from the Bering Strait, Glubokaya Harbour, Cape Navarin to the south up to the Gulf of California and the coasts of Mexico. The largest among the related species of the west coast of North America, they may grow as large as 250 cm (100 in) and 90–100 kg (200–220 lb). They live at depths of 3–800 m (10–2600 ft) over soft mud and sand bottoms. They spend most of the time buried in the sea bottom, waiting for their prey. They trap active prey by dropping down on it from above. In captivity, skate very quickly learn how to catch their prey by pressing them to the glass wall of the aquarium. The female is fertilized internally. They produce 1–7 eggs, or roe (in most cases 3–4), which the female deposits in oblong leathery cases, sometimes even as long as 30 cm (12 in). The protective case of the eggs hardens in contact with water and by the threads at the tip they attach to some hard base on the sea bottom. A regular catch of both commercial and recreational fishermen, they are usually released by the latter. Fishermen cut off the pectoral fins to sell them off as escallop meat. Marketed for food fresh and frozen, the meat of big skate is usually pan-fried or baked in the oven. They are also frequently seen in aquarium shows.

23 | Thornback ray | Raja clavata | RAJIDAE / RAYS

Thornback ray (En), Nagelrochen, Keulenrochen (D), Raya de clavos (E), Raie bouclée (F), Razza spinusa (I), Stekelrog (Nl) • Sømrokke (Da), Dröfnuskata (Is), Piggskate (N), Raia-pinta (P), Knaggrocka (S), Okarausku (SF)

The most widely distributed of rays in European waters, thornback rays may attain sizes as large as 1 m (40 in) and 20 kg (44 lb). They belong to the so-called round-nosed group, their body being usually wider than their length. They advance in water by large undulating movements of their wing-like pectoral fins, while steering with the caudal part. The name of the fish derives from the thorns lined up along the spine. The male fish has a special copulatory organ called a clasper. Several yellowish spots are scattered all over the brownish body, although specimens of lighter body colours have also been observed. Similarly to other rays, thornbacks have remarkable electric organs and in case of danger they defend themselves by administering electric shocks to enemies or prey. They feed over sand and mud bottoms, catching the animals stirred by their movements. With the mouth on the lower part of the head they very efficiently catch their prey; nevertheless, they also like to feed on detritus carried by marine currents, so they may be regarded as omnivorous. The meat of the thornback ray has been especially popular in the Baltic states, and there are traditional recipes for preserving this valued fish in both smoked and pickled form.

24 | Little skate | Leucoraja erinacea | RAJIDAE / RAYS

Little skate (En), Igelrochen (D), Raya de Canadá (E), Raie hérisson (F), Razza (I), Kleine rog (Nl) • Raia-de-verão (P), Igelkottsrocka (S), Hedgehog skate (US)

Mainly distributed in the coastal waters of the northern Atlantic, little skate attain body lengths of about 50 cm (20 in). They primarily feed on benthic invertebrate organisms and smaller fish. One of those few species of ray that are not distressed by the closeness of human habitations, they even enter ports and beaches where swimmers may be taken aback by the sudden reaction of some skate they accidentally step on. Known in a great number of countries, little skate are given various local names. Nevertheless, statistical and commercial data refer to the species as "Canadian" since this is where little skate are exploited to the greatest extent. The caudal section of the fish is long and slender, the length of it more or less equalling the overall length of the diamond-shaped body. Other characteristics include a round snout, and numerous dark, 1–2 cm (0.4–0.8 in) large spots scattered all over the rust-red or brown body. Similarly to related species, the eggs in little skate are fertilised internally. The male fish transfer sperm to the female by a copulatory organ, or clasper, which develops in the spawning season from the pelvic fin. The meat of little skate is of medium quality, yet nevertheless of high commercial value.

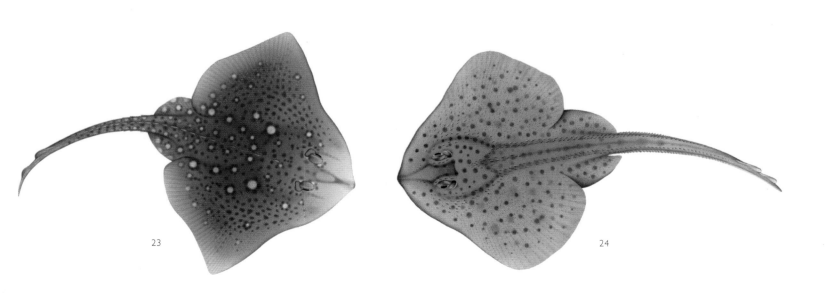

23   24

25 | **Honeycomb stingray** | Himantura uarnak | DASYATIDAE / STINGRAYS

Honeycomb stingray (En), Indoaustralischer Tüpfelrochen, Leopard-Stechrochen (D), Chupare oval (E), Pastenague léopard (F), Luipaardpijlstaartrog (Nl) • Heuningkoek-pylstert (Afr), Lokhmah ragtah (Ara), Coachwhip ray (Au), Katongganon (Ban), Bitoonan (Bik), Netmønstret piskerokke (Da), Long-tailed stingray, marbled ray, coachwhip ray (En), Imantoura (Gr), Hyomon-otome ei (J), Budang (Kuy), Burá alveolado (P), Manal thirukai (Tam), Tirpana baligi (Tr), Dahunan (Vis)

Related to rays, honeycomb stingrays dwell in the Indian Ocean and the western part of the Pacific, from the Red Sea to South Africa, in Polynesia, as far north as Taiwan, while in the south they are abundant around Australia. The tail of honeycomb stingray may be as long as three times its body length. The tail is armed with a medium-sized spine that causes serious, extremely painful wounds. A large-bodied species, larger specimens may attain body lengths of 200 cm (79 in) and weights of 120 kg (265 lb). It is very abundant by sandy beaches, in shallow waters of river estuaries and lagoons; they occur to depths of 50 m (164 ft), and they also dwell on sand-bottomed coral reefs. They also occasionally intrude into brackish waters and freshwaters. A predatory species, they feed on small fish, shellfish, crustaceans and worms. An ovoviviparous species, after internal fertilization the young ray stay in the body of the female fish until hatching, and they are born afterwards. The young are usually 3–5 in number and are 25–30 cm (10–12 in) long. Honeycomb stingray are fished in great numbers, since their meat is used in Eastern medical practices.

26 | **Danube sturgeon** | Acipenser gueldenstaedti | ACIPENSERIDAE / STURGEONS

Danube sturgeon (En), Waxdick, Russischer Stör (D), Esturión del Danubio (E), Esturgeon de Danube (F), Storione danubiano (I), Donausteur (Nl) • Essetra (Bul), Obična jesetra (Cr), Russian sturgeon, osetr (En), Vágótok (H), Osetr (R), Nisetru (Ru), Jeseter ruský (Slk), Rusmersini baligi (Tr)

A Eurasian cartilaginous ganoid, the Danube sturgeon has an armourlike set of scutes (bony plates) along the body. Very rare in the areas west of the Carpathians, Danube sturgeon are a protected species in most European countries, and at the lower flow of the Danube restrictions on methods of fishing and a harvest limit have been introduced. Similarly to other related species, they undertake migrations between freshwater and saltwater. In Russia, due to artificial closures of rivers by dams, large freshwater populations of Danube sturgeon have evolved. Of enormous size, the Danube sturgeon reach body lengths of about 3–4 m (120–160 in) and may weigh as much as 100 kg (220 lb). Their delicious meat and eggs, or roe, used for obtaining caviar, are highly prized. In around 20 countries, including the United States, Danube sturgeon are the subject of constant research in genetics and artificial breeding. Practically, they do not get marketed. In the catering industry one can hardly, if ever, come across dishes made of Danube sturgeon, though very expensive restaurants may be an exception to the rule.

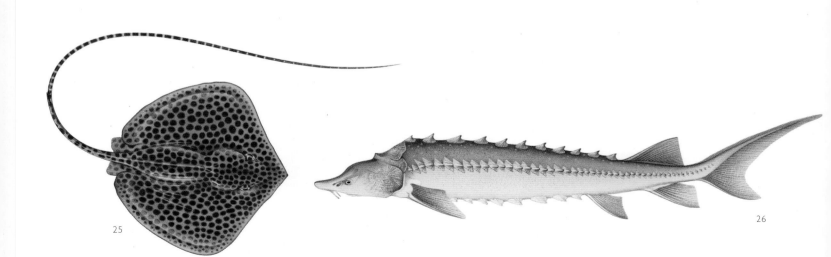

25

26

27 | Ship, Fringebarbel sturgeon | Acipenser nudiventris | ACIPENSERIDAE / STURGEONS

Ship, Fringebarbel sturgeon (En), Glattdick, Glattstör (D), Esturión barba de flecos (E), Esturgeon à barbillons frangés (F), Glatdick (I), Glatdicksteur (Nl) • Ship (Bul), Sim (Cr), Fringe-barbel sturgeon (En), Színtok, sima tok (H), Ship (R), Viza (Ru), Jeseter hladký (Slk), Síp balagi (Tr)

A migratory cartilaginous species, ship also have a variant permanently living in freshwater. Ship are considered very precious across Europe, the member states of the former Soviet Union being virtually the sole exporters of this highly prized fish. Some countries invest large amounts of money in breeding and rearing populations in artificial lake systems for reasons of genetic and environmental preservation. A species with a long life, ship reach a length of nearly 2 m (80 in) and may weigh 100 kg (220 lb), but they do not have a high tolerance for environmental degradation. In the Caucasus region and in the Caspian sea there are even fishing safaris organised with the target being the largest specimens of ship. The landing of such a trophy can be an unforgettable experience for those devoted to fishing.

28 | Atlantic sturgeon | Acipenser oxyrinchus | ACIPENSERIDAE / STURGEONS

Atlantic sturgeon (En), Atlantischer Stör (D), Esturión (E), Esturgeon noir (F), Stellato (I), Steur (Nl)

Members of the Acipenseridae family, Atlantic sturgeon inhabit the northwestern region of the Atlantic, from the Labrador peninsula to the northeast of Florida. Occasionally they may occur as far south as Bermuda and French Guiana. An enormous fish in build, Atlantic sturgeon may attain a maximum body length of 4 m (160 in) and weight of 300 kg (660 lb). The largest female specimen landed was recorded to be 430 cm (170 in) in length and 368 kg (811 lb) in weight. Atlantic sturgeon dwell in shallow waters over the continental shelf, migrating up rivers to spawn. Spawning migration starts in spring, but actual spawning begins in July. The roe (2.5 mm in diameter) are deposited on the river bed, where they attach to the bottom. The young may spend as much as four years in freshwater, afterwards migrating to the sea. The female fish attains sexual maturity in about 8–20 years, and spawns only every third or fourth year. Atlantic sturgeon feed on demersal worms, insect larvae and small fish. Due to the excellent, flavoursome and practically boneless meat of the fish, and to the roe that yields caviar of high quality, Atlantic sturgeon is a commercially extremely valued fish and the stock is widely exploited, though international commerce in the species is prohibited. The smoked meat of the fish is marketed for food.

29

30

29 | Sterlet | Acipenser ruthenus | ACIPENSERIDAE / STURGEONS

Sterlet (En, D, F, Nl, Da, N, S, Cze), Esterlete (E), Sterleto (I) • Chiga (Bu), Kečiga (Cr), Jeseter malý (Cze), Sterlet (Da), Kecsege (H), Sterljad (R), Jeseter malý (Slk)

A member of the Acipenseridae occurring in comparatively large numbers in central and eastern Europe. It is usually of a much smaller size than other species of the sturgeon family, and reaches only a few kilograms in weight and 40–70 cm (18–28 in) in length. Its genetic centre falls into European and Asian rivers flowing into the Black Sea. Rarely observed along the sea coast, it most commonly occurs in the lower sections of rivers. With its downward-oriented mouth it can take up benthic organisms and organic sediment from the water bottom. Its flesh is much sought after as a valuable delicacy, so its captive propagation and reproduction has been developed in recent decades, and is practised increasingly frequently. The amount of specimens of 0.5–1 kg (1–2 lb), involving masses raised in large fish factories working on the recycled water method, is constantly increasing on the markets. Also popular with anglers, the sterlet is restocked into rivers by angling clubs. Except for its migratory behaviour associated with spawning, it is comparatively faithful to its habitat. For its artificial propagation, circular tanks successfully used for housing other sturgeons are the best.

30 | Starry sturgeon | Acipenser stellatus | ACIPENSERIDAE / STURGEONS

Starry sturgeon (En), Sternhausen (D), Esturión estrellado (E), Esturgeon étoilé, sevruga (F), Storione stellato (I), Stersteur (Nl) • Pastruga (Bul, Cr), Sőregtok (H), Sevrjuga (R), Pastruga (Ru), Jeseter hviezdnatý, (Slk), Mersin baligi (Tr)

One of the rarest and extremely valuable species of the sturgeon family, the starry surgeon once inhabited most northern rivers of the Mediterranean basin and even the water system of the Danube. Nowadays it is virtually restricted to the region extending from the Black Sea to the Aral Sea. Being a species ascending rivers to spawn, populations of starry sturgeon have been adversely affected by the building of dams and reservoirs, coupled with environmental pollution. The oldest specimens are 1.5–2 m (60–80 in) long and weigh 50 kg (110 lb), but attain sexual maturity much earlier, when they weigh approximately 5–8 kg (11–18 lb). Although omnivorous, starry sturgeon chiefly appreciate demersal (bottom-dwelling) organisms and their larvae. Starry sturgeon are fished both by nets and by angling, their meat being highly appreciated. Along the Iranian coast of the Caspian Sea the eggs, or roe, of starry sturgeon are used as a source of caviar, and constant research is conducted in artificial breeding and rearing of their fry.

31 | Sturgeon | Acipenser sturio | ACIPENSERIDAE / STURGEONS

Sturgeon (En), Stör, Baltischer Stör (D), Esturión (E), Esturgeon d'Europe occidentale (F), Storione (I), Steur (Nl) • Atlantichka esetra (Bul), Atlantska jesetra (Cr), Stør (Da, N), Esturjão (P), Baltiyskiy osetr (R), Sip (Ru), Stör (S), Kolan baligi (Tr)

The common Old World sturgeon is the most widespread of the sturgeons. It reaches a length of 1–3 m (39–118 in) and may weigh 50–80 kg (110–176 lb). Marine and freshwater variants of the species have been observed in practically all parts of the northern hemisphere. Its anadromous feature, i.e. its habit of migrating up rivers from the sea to breed in fresh water, had been noted as early as Ancient Roman times, and it has been considered a most precious delicacy ever since. Its very palatable meat is easily conserved due to the high lipid content. Caviar obtained from its eggs, or roe, is also very precious. Therefore, it is logical that in many regions sturgeon are bred in lake fisheries and in cages suspended in large rivers or in the open sea. Large populations of sturgeon dwell most notably in Russia, in the water systems of the Volga and the Don rivers. In a natural environment, sturgeon lead a typically demersal (bottom-dwelling) way of life, mainly subsisting on lower organisms. Sturgeon fry are extremely vulnerable, thus their rearing in lake fisheries is difficult. This is why the young are preferably kept in intensive enclosures from where they are later released into natural waters.

32 | White sturgeon | Acipenser transmontanus | ACIPENSERIDAE / STURGEONS

White sturgeon (En), Weißer Stör (D), Esturión blanco (E), Esturgeon blanc (F), Storione bianco (I), Witte steur (Nl) • Esturjão-branco (P), Vit stör (S), Pacific sturgeon (US)

A member of the sturgeon family, white (Oregon or Sacramento) sturgeon occur along the northern stretch of the Pacific coast and are secretive in habit, typically hiding in the muddy or sand-bottom sea bed; they may grow to a length of 3–6 m (118–236 in) and weigh as much as half a ton (1100 lb). Schools ascending the feeding rivers of the Pacific have been observed both along the Asian and the North American coast. One of the earliest species to be artificially bred, white sturgeon are reared in intensive, automated factories, where the fish are kept in round pool systems, this being the chief method, for instance, in the United States. Nevertheless, nearly all countries engaged in cultivation of sturgeon have their own white sturgeon populations, thus its specimens of 3–10 kg (6.5–22 lb) are marketed world-wide. Exclusively freshwater populations of white sturgeon have also evolved, still, the most typical variants are those migrating, movements of which are facilitated in the United States by fluvial fish passages near dams, installed as prescribed by authorities.

31

32

33 | Beluga | Huso huso | ACIPENSERIDAE / STURGEONS

Beluga (En), Hausen (D), Beluga (E), Bélouga, grand esturgeon, huiron (F), Storione ladano (I), Huso, beluga (Nl) • Moruna (Bul, SC), Vyza (Cze), Viza (H), Beluga, kyrpy (R), Morun (Ru), Mersin morinasi (Tr)

Beluga live in the basin of the Caspian Sea and the Black Sea, sometimes occurring also in the Adriatic Sea. This is the largest species of sturgeon and also the largest freshwater species in Europe. Included in the Guinness Book of Records as the most expensive fish, beluga is considered an endangered species and is protected by law. International commerce of the fish is strictly prohibited. Specimens as large as 7–8 m (22–25 ft) long and 1500–2000 kg (3300–4400 lb) in weight used to be a usual catch in the past, but nowadays the largest size reported is around 5–6 m (16–19 ft). A bottom-dwelling predatory species, beluga feed on smaller fish. They ascend the feeding rivers to spawn, the journey often causing depletion of the stock because of barrages and dams built on the rivers. They are primarily used for obtaining the precious caviar from their roe, but beluga meat is also used as food. Marketed fresh, smoked or frozen beluga meat is extremely delicious, be it poached, sautéed or grilled. A hybrid of the female beluga and the male sterlet (Acipenser ruthenus) is artificially bred in large quantities, mainly for obtaining caviar.

34 | Longnose gar, Billfish | Lepisosteus osseus | LEPISOSTEIDAE / GARS

Longnose gar, Billfish (En), Langnasen-Knochenhecht (D), Catán pintado, pejelagarto pinto (E), Garpique longnez (F), Luccio alligatore (I), Langneus-beensnoek (Nl) • Gar-pike (En)

The Lepisosteidae family comprises the most ancient species, among them the species of the longnosed gar, or billfish. From a distance one would take them for pikes, since in both species the dorsal and anal fins are located toward the posterior part of an elongated, fusiform body. Local names refer to their forcep-like jaws, with the sharp teeth protruding on both sides of the beak. They primarily dwell in freshwaters of North and Central America, although populations have often been observed in the brackish waters of bays and swamps extending behind sandhills along the coast. Billfish may attain body lengths of 80–100 cm (30–39 in), a size that should make one cautious when children are taking diving lessons. However, they are not dangerous to people; they feed on smaller fishes abruptly attacked from hiding. Many think billfish to be monogamous, since in the spawning season the couples "see each other" for a very long time. They stick their roe to the sea bottom, and the eggs hatch in a few days. The larvae have a special adhesive organ at the end of the snout, by which they can hold on to seaweed to remain in a particular area until they attain the proper size of fry. Fillets of gar are usually sautéed, other parts are used in fish soups.

33

34

35 | Machete, Pacific ladyfish | Elops affinis | ELOPIDAE / LADY FISHES AND BONY FISHES

Machete, Pacific ladyfish (En), Pazifischer Frauenfisch (D), Malacho del Pacífico (E), Guinée-machète du Pacifique (F), Tarpone (I), Tienponder (Nl) • Pacific tenpounder (En), Yuk sor (HK), Bandeng lelaki (Ind), Kara-iwashi (J), Bandang, menangin (Mal), Bid-bid (Phi), Pla ta lüak (Thai)

Belonging to one of the earliest genera of teleost fishes (having complete bony skeletons), machete are the most widely distributed among the related species. Estimates show that the species has been observed both in fresh and salt waters over at least one third of the entire planet. As many as fifty countries can boast of having excavated machete fossils from the Cretaceous period. Their ancient origin is primarily confirmed by the skeleton of the fish, and also by their ability to use their swimbladder as an auxiliary respiratory organ when in extreme danger. Other anatomical traits include a jugular bone-plate and numerous tiny, sharp teeth densely covering the jaws and the roof of the mouth cavity. They travel in large groups, preying along the major marine currents. They are particularly attracted by moving waters, and this is how they occasionally travel upstream in larger rivers flowing into the ocean, sometimes even reaching as far as several hundred kilometres from the ocean. They average in size up to about 50 cm (20 in) and in weight a couple of pounds. Most local names attached to the species refer to the long and narrow build of the fish and the silvery scales covering the entire body. It is generally held to be a first class fish to fry, although the bones have to be carefully taken care of.

36 | Ladyfish | Elops saurus | ELOPIDAE / LADY FISHES AND BONY FISHES

Ladyfish (En), Frauenfisch, Atlantischer Tarpun (D), Malacho, banano, chiro (E), Guinée machète, tarpon banane (F), Tarpone (I), Tienponder (Nl) • Tenpounder (En), Fateixa (P)

One of the most abundant species of the family Elopidae, ladyfish, also called tenpounder, wander in large schools in the warm seas of the Atlantic. Local names are extremely varied and in most cases they totally differ from the species' Latin or Spanish name, which refer to the amphibian-like head of the fish. With long, elongated and slim body with large dorsal and caudal fins to aid them in harmonizing their movement, ladyfish are mostly found in the Carribean, where they occasionally occur in estuarine areas. They may reach a length of 1 m (40 in), but this length is accompanied by a weight of hardly a few pounds. Ladyfish fillets are exceptionally flavoursome, but the amount of meat obtained from the fish hardly ever exceeds half of its weight, thus processing is not profitable. Besides commercial fishing fleets, recreational fishermen also exploit the stock, since ladyfish take a great variety of bait. Younger specimens also intrude in mangrove marshes, where large numbers are easily caught by trapping.

37 | Tarpon | Megalops atlanticus | MEGALOPIDAE / TARPONS

Tarpon (En), Tarpun (D), Tarpón (E), Tarpon argenté, grande écaille (F), Tarpone (I), Tarpon (Nl) • Silver fish, silver king (En), Tarpão-do-Atlântico, Tainha-congo (P), Sabalo (US), Mell (Wol)

A widely known fish of the warmer parts of the Atlantic, tarpon can claim the high esteem of fishermen. Tarpon, attaining a size of about 1–2 m (39–79 in) and 100 kg (220 lb), involve a truly adventurous success when fished, since they fight until the very last second of their life, even on board the fishing boat. It may not seem fair that such a noble opponent should have such an ugly face – it has an amphibian-like head, and its meat is not very palatable either. Along the American and the Caribbean coast tarpon enter the mouths of rivers and move into the protected waters of shallow brackish bays behind mangrove forests. They frequently occur in the swamps of Florida and Louisiana, where they may easily get into trouble since they often get stranded with the turn of the tide. In the Gulf of Mexico and in the Caribbean, tarpon are used for preparing delicious dishes, based on traditional recipes dating back to the times of French and Spanish colonisation. Such traditional dishes have since been enriched, and exotic seasoning makes tarpon dishes extremely popular among tourists.

38 | Indo-Pacific tarpon | Megalops cyprinoides | MEGALOPIDAE / TARPONS

Indo-Pacific tarpon (En), Indopazifischer Tarpun, Ochsenauge (D), Tarpón indo-pacífico (E), Tarpon indo-pacifique (F), Tarpone indiano (I), Ossenoog-tarpoen (Nl) • Osoog-tarpon (Afr), Ox-eye herring, ten-pounder (Au), Buwan-buwan, mulan-bulan (Bik), Nga-kun-nya (Bur), Bourgandet, mandecdec (Cree), Hairen, isegoi (J), Seleh, trupang (Jav), Buobuan (Kap), Banang, bulan, pipih (Mal), Abulong (Mara), Buan-buan (Mara, Tag), Buburena (Nen), Bulan-bulan (Pan), Vuvula, yavula (Phi), Puloon (Pi), Bunpis (Pid), Indo-tikhookeanskiy tarpon (R), Bastard mullet (SA), Ana'analagi, fa (Sam), Lubine (Sey), Ileya, mareva (Sin), Cheche, pawale (Swa), Ropa (Tah), Morankenda, morua (Tam), Mana (Tua), Broussonet tarpon (UK), Oxeye (US)

The Indo-Pacific tarpon is native to the Indian and Pacific oceans, from the Red Sea to Natal, South Africa, eastwards to the Society Islands, northwards to South Korea, southwards to the Arafura Sea and New South Wales. Reports from Asia and Africa reveal that it also invades the freshwater of rivers. The Indo-Pacific tarpon grows to 150 cm (59 in) length and 18 kg (40 lb) body weight. Adults mostly inhabit the sea, while juveniles can be found in estuaries, inner bays and mangroves. In freshwater, this species occurs in rivers, lakes, lagoons, as well as marshy dead branches, and preys mainly on fish and crayfish. It spawns far offshore, probably at any time of the year. The larvae are transparent and suggestive of glass eels. The Indo-Pacific tarpon is known to take up atmospheric oxygen when necessary. The young are caught along the coasts and subsequently raised on fish farms. Indo-Pacific tarpons are not specifically harvested commercially, and although edible, not popular.

39 | European eel | Anguilla anguilla | ANGUILLIDAE / FRESHWATER EELS

European eel (En), Europäischer Flussaal (D), Anguila europea (E), Anguille d'Europe (F), Anguilla (I), Aal, paling (Nl) • Njala (Alb), Zmiorka (Bul), Anguila (Cat), Úhor ríční, Úhor obecný (Cze), An eascann (Ga), Angolna (H), Áll (Is), Tzlofach (Isr), Unagi (J), Sallura (Malt), Ål (N, S, Da), Wegorz europejski (Pl), Retschnoi ugor (R), Anguilla europeana (Ru), Úhor obycajný (Slk), Yilan baligi (Tr)

The family Anguillidae consists of members with an unusual, snake-like body. The most common species is the European eel, which has been introduced for propagation purposes to all continents permanently inhabited by man. The mysteries of its life were already studied by ancient scholars, but real answers were not found until the 20th century. A cathadromous, migratory carnivore, it leaves freshwater for the sea in the spawning season. Only a few decades ago were its spawning grounds traced in sufficient detail to 17°C isothermic areas of the Sargasso Sea. Its larvae (known by the name "elvers"), caught on coasts and in rivers, are raised in characteristic, circular tanks on European farms. For the sake of anglers, the European eel has been introduced into numerous natural waters. Although its role is considered contradictory by conservationists, its artificial dispersal cannot possibly be halted, for 90% of its 50–100 cm (20–40 in) long body is considered edible, and is a valuable product very much sought after. Prepared smoked and pickled, it is one of the most expensive delicacies in European cuisine.

40 | New Zealand longfin eel | Anguilla dieffenbachii | ANGUILLIDAE / FRESHWATER EELS

New Zealand longfin eel (En), Neuseeland-Aal (D), Anguila de Nueva Zelanda (E), Anguille de Nouvelle-Zélande (F), Anguilla neozelandese (I), Nieuw-Zeelandse paling (Nl) • Newzealandsk ål (Da), Longfin eel (NZ), Nyzeeländsk ål (S)

Distributed in the southwestern regions of the Pacific Ocean, this endemic species of the eel family chiefly dwells in New Zealand. The New Zealand longfin eel favour the gravel bottom of rivers. They may attain body lengths of 120 cm (47 in) and a weight of 2.5 kg (5.5 lb). Like to their European relatives, New Zealand longfin eel migrate to the sea to spawn, then their young return to their freshwater habitat until they reach sexual maturity. The navigational ability of the young to travel back to their freshwater habitat is still a mystery. A bottom-dwelling predator species, New Zealand longfin eel feed on a diet consisting of smaller fish, crustaceans, insects, worms and insect larvae. Their meat being of exceptionally good quality, both commercial and recreational fishermen are keen on catching them. Marketed fresh, smoked and frozen, meat of the longfin eel is mostly eaten grilled or fried in oil. Smoked in the proper way, it counts as an especially flavoursome delicacy.

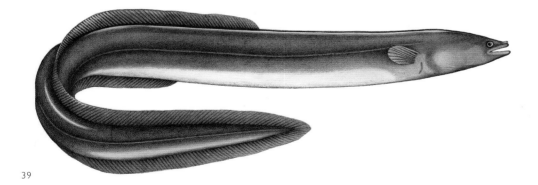

39

40

41 | **Japanese eel** | Anguilla japonica | ANGUILLIDAE / FRESHWATER EELS

Japanese eel (En), Japanischer Aal (D), Anguila japonesa (E), Anguille du Japon (F), Anguilla giapponese (I), Japanse paling (Nl) • Bat sin (Cant), Unagi (J), Paen-jang-o (Kor), Mán lí (Mand), Enguia japonesa (P), Igat (Tag), Freshwater eel (Thai-En)

Japanese eel live in East Asia, in Japan, Taiwan, Korea, China and the northern part of the Philippines. They may attain sizes as large as 150–160 cm (60–63 in) and 8 kg (18 lb). A typically freshwater species, Japanese eel migrate to the sea to spawn, although no particular spawning grounds of the fish are known. Their offspring travel back to their freshwater habitat and they attain sexual maturity there. Bottom-dwelling in habit, they are predators, feeding mainly on smaller fish, crustaceans, insects, insect larvae and worms. They are able to cross the land overnight to other waters. Extensively fished for and bred in fisheries, Japanese eel are held to be the most valuable fish in Japan. They are marketed fresh, smoked, frozen and canned. Popular recipes include various methods of simmering, frying and grilling. They are also used in Eastern medical practices.

42 | **American eel** | Anguilla rostrata | ANGUILLIDAE / FRESHWATER EELS

American eel (En), Amerikanischer Aal (D), Anguila americana (E), Anguille d'Amérique (F), Anguilla americana (I), Amerikaanse paling (Nl) • Common eel (Bar), Anguila (Cub), Silver eel (UK), Freshwater eel (US)

American eel are abundant in the northwestern part of the Atlantic Ocean, in the area stretching from the coastal waters of Canada and the USA as far south as Panama, and also in the greater region of the West Indies as far as Trinidad, especially in the subtropical-tropical climate. They may attain body lengths of 150 cm (60 in) and weights of 7–7.5 kg (16 lb). Of a bottom-dwelling habit, American eel generally occur in perennial streams. In daytime, they hide in burrows or in hollows under the shoreline washed out by the water, while they spend the precious night hours hunting for food. A typically predator fish, American eel feed on insects and their larvae, worms and smaller fish. In the autumn, like their European relatives, American eel start for the Sargasso Sea to spawn. Their young travel back to their freshwater habitat and attain sexual maturity there. Of especially good quality, the meat of American eel is highly appreciated by both commercial and recreational fishermen. Usually it is eaten fried or smoked, the latter being an exceptionally tasty delicacy.

41

42

43

44

43 | **Common pike conger** | Muraenesox bagio | MURAENESOCIDAE / PIKE CONGERS

Common pike conger (En), Hechtmuräne (D), Morenocio común (E), Morénésoce commun (F), Lucciomurena (I), Snoekaal (Nl) • Snoekpaling (Afr), Pike-eel (Au), Kamila (Ben), Suzu-hamo (J), Belut, indong, malong, mong, tuan, tuna (Mal), Safio comun (P), Maguungi (Som), Koe, mkunga (Swa), Silver eel (UK), Obud, ogdok (Vis)

A large bodied eel-like species, common pike conger are distributed in the Indian Ocean and the Pacific. They occur in the vast region stretching from the east coast of Africa to the Philippines and Japan, and also somewhat to the south, around New Guinea, in the Arafura Sea, along the coasts of Australia, New Caledonia and the Fiji islands. They may attain body lengths of 2 m (6 ft) and weights of 28–30 kg (62–66 lb). Common pike conger dwell in the shallow waters of the littoral zone, and they occasionally intrude the brackish waters of river estuaries, too. A night-time predator, the common pike conger feeds on benthic fish and crustaceans. On several occasions they were reported to have attacked fishermen after having been landed. The bite of this aggressive species may cause serious harm to the victim. Widely appreciated by the fishing public, common pike conger are sought for by both commercial and recreational fishermen. The meat of the fish is primarily marketed fresh, although canned products are also popular.

44 | **Conger eel** | Conger conger | CONGRIDAE / CONGERS

Conger eel (En), Congeraal, Meeraal (D), Congrio común (E), Congre d'Europe (F), Grongo (I), Zeepaling, congeraal (Nl) • Grug (Cr), Almindelig havål (Da), Mougri (Gr), Anago (J), Astan-varrey (Manx), Havål (N), Congro, safio (P), Morskoj ugor (R), Migri (Tr), Gringou (Tun), Dieye (Wol)

A species inhabiting the northern half of the Atlantic and adjacent seas. Males and females greatly differ in size, the female reaching about twice as much as the male, in both length and weight, 3 m (118 in) and 10 kg (22 lb), respectively. A reclusive fish, the conger eel usually lurks in rock crevices and shipwrecks. Because of its snake-like, scaleless body, comparatively wide gape and powerful teeth it is feared by many, even though it has never been known to attack humans. Instead, it usually feeds on smaller animals, which it kills and tears to pieces by swiftly rotating itself around its own body, picking up the bits afterwards. It has regularly been observed while scavenging on carrion and garbage in harbours, and places inhabited by man. Almost every coastal fishing village has its own conger eel population. Small farms existed even in ancient Rome, in which young specimens caught from the sea were fattened. This species mates at great depth, and the young larvae gradually drift towards the coasts. The parents die after spawning, but their offspring survive by the millions. The flesh of the conger eel, which is mainly preserved by smoking, is considered reasonably palatable, and is made into different dishes.

45 | Dorab wolf-herring | Chirocentrus dorab | CHIROCENTRIDAE / WOLF HERRINGS

Dorab wolf-herring (En), Großer Wolfshering (D), Arencón dorab, arenque lobo de la India (E), Chirocentre dorab (F), Dorab (I), Indische wolfharing (Nl) • Olfharing (Afr), Haff, huff, hiff (Ara), Balila (Ban, Bik, Kuy, Tag), Voivoi (Fi), Po do (HK), Balbaliga (Ilo), Oki-iwashi (J), Parang-parang (Kap, Tag), Mul-myeol (Kor), Pacal, pachal (Mal), Dahon-tubio (Mara), Biraw-biraw (Pan), Kallaku vallai (Pap), Sabre (Sey), Panu katuvalla, pat katuvalla, podi katuvalla (Sin), Mkonge (Swa), Mullu-valai (Tam), Dorab, dorab wolfherring, Silver barfish (UK), Balira (Vis)

This species of herring inhabits the Pacific and the Indian Oceans. It is found in tropical waters from the Red Sea along the eastern coasts of Africa to the Solomon Islands in the west, to southern Japan in the north, and northern Australia in the south. It has been reported from 26–29°C warm waters off Australia, and it also occurs in brackwater. It lives alone or in small schools in offshore waters. Males grow to 90–100 cm (36–40 in), females to 35–40 cm (14–16 in) in length. The dorab feeds on small fish, and, probably, crustaceans. It is caught in large quantities and is distributed fresh, frozen, dried and/or salted. It also occurs in the catch of anglers, and is prepared according to various recipes, cooked, stewed or fried.

46 | Allis shad | Alosa alosa | CLUPEIDAE / HERRINGS AND SARDINES

Allis shad (En), Maifisch, Alse (D), Sábalo común (E), Alose vraie (F), Elft (Nl), Alosa (I) • Majsild (Da), Gobhar (Ga), Kepa (Gr), Maisild (N), Sável (P), Alosa adevarata (Ru), Pilkkusilli (SF), Tirsi (Tr)

According to palaeontologists, the allis shad is one of the oldest species of herring. Hundreds of thousands of years could not affect it more seriously than has pollution in just the past few decades. This tasty species, reaching approximately 30–60 cm (12–24 in) in length and at most 1–2 kg (2–4 lb) in weight, is nearing extinction today. Its chances of survival are seriously reduced by the fact that the allis shad is anadromous, i.e. migrates into freshwater from the sea for spawning. Once it was so plentiful in western Europe that permanent traps were constructed for catching it in river mouths. This activity is forbidden in most countries today, and even where it is permitted the mesh size of nets is regulated by law, thus giving specimens maturing in two to three years a chance of reproducing at least once in a lifetime. The eggs float freely, and the larvae hatch after 1–2 weeks of embryonic development. They remain in freshwater for about 4–5 months before returning to the sea. The allis shad is considered an excellent fish for frying, but its flesh is also consumed smoked.

47 | Twaite shad | *Alosa fallax* | CLUPEIDAE / HERRINGS AND SARDINES

Twaite shad (En), Finte (D), Saboga (E), Alose feinte (F), Agone (I), Fint (Nl) • Kubla (Alb), Stavsild (Da), Gobhar (Ga), Sardelomana (Gr), Augnasíld (Is), Stamsild (N), Savelha (P), Parposz (Pl), Finta (R), Scrumbie (Ru), Staksill (S), Täpläsilli (SF)

This is the closest relative of the allis shad, from which it can be distinguished by 6–8 black blotches on its back, and somewhat smaller fins. In addition, it grows to a slightly smaller size (30–50 cm / 12–20 in), but is more heavily built and reaches a comparable weight. The number of eggs per kg body mass surpasses 100,000, and larval development is shorter than in the previous species. Their collective spawning has been observed in some river sections, and thus their hybridisation cannot be excluded. The differences mentioned above account for the fact that the size of the twaite shad world population is believed to be considerably bigger, and many thousand tons of specimens are caught annually, mainly in the Mediterranean region. Whole schools are caught mainly by fishermen working with small nets at night or dawn, and individuals are also trapped in brackish coastal waters. In addition to Europe, it is also offered for sale in north and northwest African markets, and is considered a medium-quality fish for frying. In the British Isles and in Germany its flesh used to be preserved by salting, smoking and pickling, but this practice is no longer common.

48 | Alewife | *Alosa pseudoharengus* | CLUPEIDAE / HERRINGS AND SARDINES

Alewife (En), Maifisch, Nordamerikanischer Flusshering (D), Alosa, pinchagua (E), Gapareau (F), Alosa, falsa aringa atlantica (I), Amerikaanse rivierharing, meivis (Nl) • Anadromous alewives, bigeye herring, branch herring, freshwater herring, gray herring, grayback, kyak, river herring, white herring, sawbelly (US)

This member of the herring family dwells in the northwestern part of the Atlantic Ocean, in the vast area covering the stretch of water from the Gulf of St. Lawrence through Nova Scotia to as far south as North Carolina. They also occur in the rivers feeding these seas, and in lakes Seneca and Cayuga. Stock introduced to the Great Lakes do not have any connection with the marine stock. The largest specimens may grow as big as 40 cm (16 in) and 700–800 g (24–28 oz). When sexually mature, they ascend rivers to spawn in the slower stretches of rivers or in lakes. Landlocked stock dwelling in lakes also migrate upstream to their spawning grounds. When young, alewife feed on zooplankton and smaller crustaceans, insect larvae and insects. Later they adopt predatory habits and eat fish and crabs. A widely exploited species, alewife are marketed as food in fresh, salt-dried, smoked and frozen form. It is usually fried for human consumption and is also used as bait for catching crabs. Alewife also constitute an important ingredient of dog and cat food.

47

48

49 | **Araucanian herring** | Clupea bentincki | CLUPEIDAE / HERRINGS AND SARDINES

Araucanian herring (En), Chilenischer Hering (D), Sardina araucana (E), Hareng araucian, hareng du Chili (F), Aringa cilena (I), Chileense haring (Nl) • Sardina anchoa, Sardina común, Sardina da invierno, Sardina del sur (Chi), Bentinku-nishin (J), Espadilena-chilena (P), Chilean herring (UK)

A species of the herring family, araucanian herring dwell in the southeastern region of the Pacific Ocean, along the coasts of Chile, in the subtropical zone. Relatively small in size, they attain maximum body lengths of about 25–30 cm (10–12 in). Araucanian herring live in large groups in the coastal waters, close to the surface. They feed on plankton, mostly on diatom they sieve out of the sea water. Specimens larger than 10 cm (4 in) spawn from June to November, producing pelagic roe which float in the water with the plankton until they hatch. Not only do Araucanian herring often fall prey to other predator fishes, they are also being extensively sought for by fishing fleets. Largely used as an important source for fishmeal, the meat of the Araucanian herring is not particularly valued as food, although it is marketed dried or frozen to some extent.

50 | **Atlantic herring** | Clupea harengus | CLUPEIDAE / HERRINGS AND SARDINES

Atlantic herring (En), Hering, Atlantischer Hering (D), Arenque del Atlántico (E), Hareng de l'Atlantique (F), Aringa (I), Haring (Nl) • Sild (Da, N), Régha (Gr), Nishin (J), Arenque (P), Mongopozvonkavaja seld (R), Gumsill (S), Silli, silakka (SF), Ringa (Tr)

The atlantic herring, distributed in the waters of the Atlantic Ocean and the marginal seas, is one of the most widely utilised food fishes. Fishermen have observed migration routes of herring for centuries and have carefully plotted their spawning grounds. No wonder there are scarcely any areas of herring life that remain hidden from eager anglers. Furthermore, the herring, swimming in huge schools, cannot escape their fate, given the modern fishing methods that employ fleets equipped with satellite fish-finders, echosounders and sonar equipment. Shooting and hauling the trawl is entirely mechanised, too. Fishing for herring is not as romantic an enterprise as it used to be. There have been international fish conservation acts signed which include the limits of waters to be exploited by the nations concerned, a coast-wide commercial quota, recreational harvest limits and minimum size restrictions. Generally, fishing fleets tow drift nets several hundred metres long in the areas where herring school, and a great majority of the schooling fish end up in the ships' freezers. There is a great variety of herring dishes, all nations having their own traditional specialities. Gourmets especially appreciate it smoked, salted or pickled, but the fresh meat of the fish is also widely sought on the market.

49

50

51 | **Pacific herring** | Clupea pallasii | CLUPEIDAE / HERRINGS AND SARDINES

Pacific herring (En), Pazifischer Hering (D), Arenque del Pacífico (E), Hareng du Pacifique (F), Aringa del Pacifico (I), Pacifische haring (Nl) • Iquallux-paq (Inu), Nishin (J), Cheong-eo (Kor), Fei (Mand), Arenque-do-pacífico (P), Sea herring, California herring (US)

The most closely related species of the Atlantic herring, Pacific herring are most abundant in the northern and central parts of the Pacific Ocean. Slightly smaller than their Atlantic relatives, they average about 25–30 cm (10–12 in) in length. Entirely plankton-feeders when young, they filter the tiny animal organisms through long teeth densely but irregularly distributed in the mouth. With the zooplanktonic mass primarily occurring towards the margins of marine currents, where cold and warm waters meet, herring are also most abundant in these regions. The enormous herring shoals can easily be detected and followed by aerial finders. For centuries fishermen have been keeping records of the individual herring groups, each group following a specific trail of their own throughout the year. Asian herring are most popular when fried, nevertheless, a large percentage of the total landings is preserved smoked, in oil or marinated. In the Far East the exploitation of international waters often causes conflicts, since several countries possessing modern technological means and fishing gear have to share the fishery.

52 | **European pilchard** | Sardina pilchardus | CLUPEIDAE / HERRINGS AND SARDINES

European pilchard (En), Pilchard, Sardine (D), Sardina, parrocha (E), Sardine commune (F), Sardina, sardella (I), Sardien, pelser (Nl) • Sardin (Da, S), Sardélla (Gr), Iwashi, maiwashi (J), Sardinha (P), Sredizenomorskaya sardina (R), Sardiini (SF), Sardalyo (Tr), Sardine (US)

Perhaps the best-known species along the shores of the Atlantic Ocean and the Mediterranean Sea, European pilchard barely reach a maximum length of 20–30 cm (8–12 in). They school by the thousand and as filter-feeders, they mainly feed on plankton. Fishing for European pilchard is strictly regulated by the European Union. Nevertheless, disagreements among Atlantic nations are frequent. In some shallow, tidal shore areas European pilchard are trapped, but the more usual fishing method is to attract the fish with a decoy light at night. The high-quality part of the catch is canned in oil, the rest is usually utilised as bait for carnivorous species. Along the Mediterranean shore, on beaches and in marketplaces, European pilchard are very popular among tourists as small fried fish eaten while drinking beer. After all, this relatively small fish is no small beer, especially if your beer is not small!

53

54

53 | **South American pilchard** | Sardinops sagax | CLUPEIDAE / HERRINGS AND SARDINES

South American pilchard (En), Südamerikanische Sardine, Pazifik-Sardine (D), Sardina chilena (E), Sardinops du Chili, sardine chilienne, pilchard du Chili (F), Sardina del Cile (I), Chileense sardine (Nl) • Pilchard (Au, NZ), Peruvian sardine (En), Iwashi (J), Ivasy (R), Pacific sardine (US)

This is a sardine occurring in enormous numbers in the great currents of the Pacific, growing at most to 15–20 cm (6–8 in) in length. Such a size would barely be visible at sea if this fish did not form huge clouds containing several hundred thousands of individuals. However, it thus falls victim to modern techniques, as it can easily be located by satellite radar, and entire schools are dragnetted with methods used by industrial fisheries, raised to deck by high capacity pumps or 'water hoovers' and sorted through a system of sieves. Better quality fish are preserved in oil, while less valuable specimens are turned into animal food by the floating canning factories accompanying the fleets. Less industrialised, traditional fisheries employ fixed nets for catching South American pilchard, while small, lonely ships prefer light trapping. On the market, this species can be distinguished from its European relative by its slightly larger scales, and the more or less regular, dark blotches situated along its lateral line. A comparatively cheap, tasty fish for frying, the South American pilchard is suitable for feeding many people along the Asian as well as the American coast.

54 | **European sprat** | Sprattus sprattus | CLUPEIDAE / HERRINGS AND SARDINES

European sprat (En), Sprotte, Brisling, Breitling (D), Espadín, trancho, sardineta (E), Sprat, esprot (F), Papalina, spratto (I), Sprot (Nl) • Brisling (Da, En), Papalina (Gr), Espadilha, lavadilha (P), Skarpsill, vassbuk (S), Kilohaili (SF)

European sprat, also called bristling or brisling, are distributed in the northeastern waters of the Atlantic and in the adjacent seas. An omnivorous member of the herring family, they form enormous schools. In spite of the fact that they have a better tolerance for changes in salinity than most of their relatives, stocks of European sprat have declined considerably in the past few decades. In some areas, especially in the far north, they may also occur in freshwater. Their attachment to near-shore waters may have contributed to their overfishing. In order to handle the situation, the European Union and the Baltic States have enacted strict regulations regarding the fishing of European sprat. Most of the catch is smoked or canned, and only a lesser quantity is delivered to the food market as frozen, fresh fish. Its Black Sea variant is widely popular among tourists as cheap fish for frying on the Bulgarian, Ukrainian and Turkish beaches.

55 | Argentine anchovy | Engraulis anchoita | ENGRAULIDAE / ANCHOVIES

Argentine anchovy (En), Argentinische Sardelle (D), Anchoíta (E), Anchois d'Argentine (F), Acciuga d'Argentina (I), Argentijnse ansjovis (Nl) • Biqueirão-argentino (P)

The smallest species of the family Engraulidae, Argentine anchovies are low-bodied, slim little fish, merely 10–12 cm (4–5 in) in length, and, on top of all these diminutive proportions, they have pindling fins that no other fish would be proud of. As its name also shows, the species is most abundant along the east coast of Argentina, Uruguay and Brazil, where the stock is thoroughly exploited. Due to the small size they attain, Argentine anchovies are primarily used in processing canned food or are pulverized as ingredients of animal feed additives. They spawn several times a year, especially in warmer waters. They indirectly affect commercial fishing by their enormous stock attracting the more valuable predator fishes to the coastal region, where, in turn, these larger fishes are caught in wide-meshed selective nets. The roe of the Argentine anchovy are slightly elongated and pelagic (floating), and, as such, important constituents of the marine microplankton. Larvae hatch in about 3–4 days, depending on the actual temperature, nevertheless, not only are they in danger because of the larger predator fishes, but also because the condition of the seas may also do great harm to them, since they are exceptionally vulnerable.

56 | European anchovy | Engraulis encrasicolus | ENGRAULIDAE / ANCHOVIES

European anchovy (En), Europäische Sardelle, Anchovis (D), Boquerón, anchoa, bocarte (E), Anchois européen (F), Acciuga, alice, sardone (I), Ansjovis (Nl) • Ansjos (Da, N), Anchooga (Egy), Gavros, antjúga (Gr), Afian (Isr), Katakuchi-iwashi (J), Incova (Malt), Amplona (Mon), Lanvhouba (Mor), Biqueirão, anchova (P), Hamsi (Tr), Anchouba (Tun)

One of the most abundant species of the Atlantic Ocean and the northern seas of Eurasia, European anchovies attain body lengths of a mere 10–20 cm (4–8 in). They have great commercial value and also play an important role in the food chain as the regular prey of larger fishes. On the other hand, as zooplankton feeders, European anchovies contribute to maintaining the biological eco-balance of waters. Their disproportionately large mouth serves for filtering plankton. The mouth of the European anchovy, when open and at work, reminds one of a large scoop net. They travel in huge schools, spawn more than once a year, and on each occasion produce several thousand pelagic roe. The eggs are oval in shape, which is rare among fishes, and they hatch within a few days. European anchovies are landed by specially equipped ships, the more modern ones being factory ships processing the catch on board. Increasing amounts of the catch are used for canned fish in oil, and other canned foods, such as marinated anchovies.

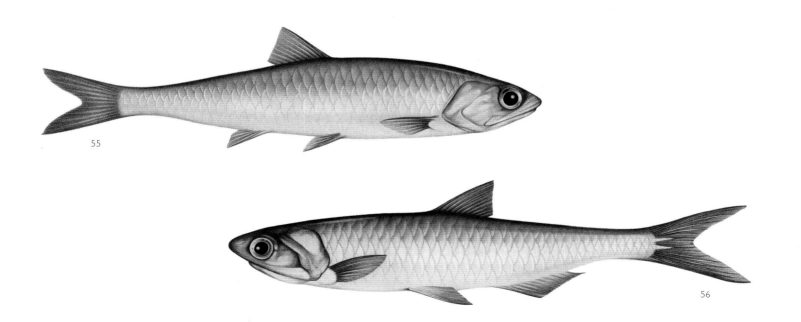

55

56

57 | Japanese anchovy | Engraulis japonicus | ENGRAULIDAE / ANCHOVIES

Japanese anchovy (En), Japan-Sardelle (D), Anchoíta japonesa (E), Anchois japonais (F), Acciuga del Giappone (I), Japanse ansjovis (Nl) • Anchovy (Au, NZ, US), Katakuchi-iwashi (J), Myeol-chi (Kor), Dilis (Tag)

Despite their name, Japanese anchovies not only dwell in Japanese waters, but also in the region covering several millions of square miles at the meeting of the waters of the Indian and Pacific Oceans, extending as far south as the seas east of the Australian continent. Nevertheless, the stock is primarily exploited by the Japanese, along with Russian, Korean and Chinese fishing fleets. A typically marine species, rarely do Japanese anchovies approach the coastline, the only exception being the islands of the Pacific, where they frequently enter the straits between the small islands to feed on the abundant plankton carried there by the currents. Japanese anchovies grow slightly larger than most of the related species, attaining a size of 15–20 cm (6–8 in) and a slightly thicker build. Probably due to their travelling habit in the tropical and subtropical waters, their growth rate is also somewhat better. Besides canned in oil, the greater part of the total landings is marketed frozen. In the north they are pre-served pickled or fermented. Served freshly sautéed, Japanese anchovies are an extremely popular and cheap "fast food", especially in the market-places of Asia.

58 | Northern anchovy, Californian anchovy | Engraulis mordax | ENGRAULIDAE / ANCHOVIES

Northern anchovy, Californian anchovy (En), Amerikanische Sardelle (D), Anchoveta de California (E), Anchois de California (F), Acciuga del Nord Pacifico (I), Noord-Amerikaanse ansjovis (Nl) • Biqueirao-do-Pacifico norte (P), Northern anchovy (US)

Widely distributed in the entire region of the Indian and Pacific Oceans, and most abundant along the west coast of Canada and the United States, northern anchovies are of high commercial value in both aforementioned countries. Landings in the individual fisheries are strictly regulated by a commercial quota and a recreational harvest limit. In the three summer months in most fisheries total closure is also introduced, this period being the spawning season of the northern anchovy. Since anchovies travel in enormous schools, their movement can easily be detected by satellite finders, despite their tiny individual sizes of 10–20 cm (4–8 in). With such modern equipment it is not a tedious task to accurately regulate landings. The amount of their pelagic roe may range from a few thousand to as much as 10,000 per fish. With a very fast rate of development, the fry hatch in about 2 to 4 days and within about the same time-span they quickly take to feeding on zooplankton. A great number of anchovy fry become prey to their own close relatives, since the adult fish, gulping down with their enormous mouths whatever suitable food they find, are hardly able to tell their own larvae (only a few mm large) from other organisms carried by the current.

57

58

59 | Peruvian anchovy, Anchoveta | Engraulis ringens | ENGRAULIDAE / ANCHOVIES

Peruvian anchovy, Anchoveta (En), Peru-Sardelle (D), Chicora (E), Anchois du Pérou (F), Acciuga del Cile (I), Peruaanse ansjovis (Nl) • Anchovy (Au, NZ, US), Biqueirão do Peru (P)

The Peruvian anchovy is perhaps the most thoroughly exploited species of anchovy. Commercial landings had reached a record peak of millions of tons of anchovies in the 1980s, in the heyday of marine fishing in Peru. This enormous amount was supplied by thousands of fishing fleets in the coastal streams, and meant a stable financial resource and job opportunities to perhaps as many as 3 million people. A great part of the commercial landings was usually processed into ground fish-scrap in the coastal localities, 90% of which, in turn, constituted an important ingredient of poultry feed, especially because of its high oleic acid content. With the ocean currents gradually receding further offshore, it became nearly impossible for local fishermen to follow the anchovy stock with their small fishing boats. Due to the same phenomenon, in the second half of the 1980s Peru and Ecuador had to face a considerable loss of the anchovy stock. Nowadays it is mostly the technically more advanced nations that can successfully exploit the stock. Merely 10–15 cm (4–6 in) long, the Peruvian anchovy is a largely plankton-feeder species, therefore they mainly dwell in ocean currents abundant in micro-organisms. The greatest part of total commercial landings are canned in oil, whereas inhabitants of the Andes coastal region chiefly fry them whole, this even counting as a staple food among the locals.

60 | Shorthead anchovy | Encrasicholina heteroloba | ENGRAULIDAE / ANCHOVIES

Shorthead anchovy (En), Kurzkopf-Sardelle (D), Boquerón aduanero (E), Anchois domnier (F), Stoleforus ansjovis (Nl) • Kong Yue (Cant), Mælkefisk (Da), Pa' a pa' a (Fij), Blue anchovy (Guam), Kang hu (Hok), Mizusururu (J), Gon eo ri (Kor), Mairo (Mak), Besin, bilis, bunga air, kenaren, mempinis teri, pula-pula, teri (Mal), Anchovetav aduaneira (P), Mjölkfisk (S), Rahu halmass (Sin), Oh jiau (Teo), Pla bai pai, (Thai), Anchovy (US), Guno, gurayan (Vis)

This small-sized anchovy inhabits tropical waters of the Indian and Pacific oceans. It is found from the Red Sea along the east African coast to the northern part of Madagascar, and occurs in the Bay of Bengal and the southern islands of Japan in the East, the northern coasts of Australia in the South, and the islands of Fiji, Tonga, Samoa, New Caledonia, the Solomons, and Palau Islands in the East. A small fish, the shorthead anchovy grows to a maximum 8–10 cm (3–4 in) in length and 6–8 g (0.2–0.3 oz) in weight. It occurs in huge schools close to the shores, but is also found in deep gulfs to a depth of 20–50 m (22–55 yd). Its food consists of zooplankton. Unusually among marine fish, its eggs are oval in shape, and no protuberance is found at either end. Commercially harvested on a very small scale only, the shorthead anchovy is used mainly as a bait fish. For human consumption, it is dried or made into a sauce after fermentation.

61 | Milkfish | Chanos chanos | CHANIDAE / MILKFISHES

Milkfish (En), Milchfisch (D), Sabalote, chanos (E), Chanidé, chanos (F), Cefalone (I), Melkvis (Nl) • Giant herring (Au), Bandeng (Ind), Sabahii (J), Pisang-pisang (Mal), Pla thu nam jüt (Thai)

Also called bandeng, or bandang, milkfish may often be encountered by holiday-makers in the markets of South Asia and the Pacific Islands. Attaining body lengths of about 1.5 m (60 in), milkfish are often collected when young and raised for food in brackish or freshwater tropical ponds, and these are the specimens most often marketed. The abundance of the species is primarily due to the fact that they tolerate changes in salinity well. This is explained by the fact that they are mainly confined to brackish waters on flat tidal shores, where the schooling milkfish are often trapped when the tide turns. Most local names refer to the light colouring of the body and the swift swirling movement. The tiny but very strong scales help the fish get through areas of very shallow water. Artificial breeding of milkfish had been worked out as early as twenty years ago, in many countries there being a great demand for the young (fingerling) on the food market. Artificial breeding seems to be increasingly essential, since thousands of small-scale fish-farms are engaged in rearing milkfish to supply the food market. The meat of the fish is largely determined by water quality, consumers usually having a preference for the marine form.

62 | Blackfin pacu | Colossoma macropomum | SERRASALMIDAE / PIRANHAS

Blackfin pacu (En), Schwarzer Pacu (D), Pacu (F, I, Nl) • Pacú (Arg), Tambaqui (Bra), Cachama negra (Col), Gamitana (Per), Cachama, Tambagui (US), Morocoto (Ven)

The blackfin pacu, also known as the tambaqui, is native to the Amazon and Orinoco river systems of South America. Due to its herbivorous food habits and its quick development, it is much sought for, and a serious decline in catch has been recorded. It can reach 1 m (40 in) in length, and 30 kg (66 lb) in weight. It usually lives alone, with adults inhabiting flooded forests for five months a year, feeding on fruit and seeds. Young pacus live in flooded plains until reaching sexual maturity, feeding on zooplankton, insects, snails and decaying vegetable matter. A favoured fish on fish farms, the pacu tolerates soft water and is very resistant to disease. Its fishing is of little economic importance, but anglers regularly catch it. It is distributed fresh or frozen.

63 | **Zope** | *Abramis ballerus* | CYPRINIDAE / CARPS ·

Zope (En, D, F, I), Brasemblei (Nl) · Spitzpleinzen (A), Chil kossat (Bul), Pleskac siny (Cze), Brasenflire (Da), Laposkeszeg (H), Brasmeflire (N), Rozpior (Pl), Faren (S), Sukava (SF), Kesega (Slo), Sinets (R), Cosac-cu-bot-scutit (Ru), Blue bream (US)

Also called blue bream in the United States, zope are a species widespread in the clear natural waters of Europe and Asia, averaging about 20–35 cm (8–14 in) in length. Zope populations have considerably decreased in the past few decades. In contrast to the other members of the bream family, zope typically dwell in open waters and only in the spawning season do they migrate in large schools by the thousand toward the shores or, through the feeding rivers, to the spring area. Feeding chiefly on plankton and organic pelagic substance, zope have an important role in maintaining the eco-balance of a given area. Once zope populations start to diminish, the depletion of the waters is to be taken seriously in the respective area. Catches of zope are mainly obtained by trawling in lakes or rivers. Its meat being dry and bony, it is usually eaten fried in oil; in Asia they gut and dry them whole, or they are dried and pulverised. Zope spawn relatively early, when waters are still cold, therefore the incubation period is twice or three times longer (12–14 days) than in other bream species. Because of this, and the aforementioned water-cleansing activity of the fish, zope deserve more attention.

64 | **Common bream, Carp bream** | *Abramis brama* | CYPRINIDAE / CARPS

Common bream, Carp bream (En), Brachse, Brasse (D), Brema común (E), Brème (F), Abramida (I), Brasem (Nl) · Dlešec (Cze), Brasen (Da), Dévérkeszeg (H), Brasme (N), Brema (P), Leshtsch (R), Cârjanca (Ru), Braxen (S), Lahna (SF), Capak baligi (Tr), Common bream (UK, US)

One of the most widespread members of the carp family, common bream average in length up to 40–60 cm (16–24 in), and 0.5–1 kg (1–2.2 lb) in weight. It is constantly gaining in economic importance, since it easily adapts to man-made environments, such as storage lakes and ponds. These bream populations produce hundreds of thousands of fry annually, the survival rate of which is far better than those of other members of the bream species. They generally do well even in changing salinity conditions of waters, thus they also occur in river estuaries. Common bream are appreciated by anglers and are considered a valuable catch. Their meat is of medium quality, the main problem being caused by its being very bony. This may be the reason why bream are chiefly eaten fried thoroughly, or well cooked. In Slavonic regions they are often eaten pickled. The common bream in the early stage of their life swim in schools, but become solitary in habit when growing old, at about 5–10 years of age. But beauty comes with age, it seems, for this is the time when they become colourful – from silvery-green they shift to a brilliant, shiny golden colour.

65 | White-eye bream | Abramis sapa | CYPRINIDAE / CARPS

White-eye bream (En), Zobel, Scheibpleinzen (D), Brema del Danubio (E), Sopa, brème du Danube (F), Brema do Danúbio (I), Donaubrasem (Nl) • Donaubrasen (Da), Danube bream (En), Tsironi sirko (Gr), Bagolykeszeg (H), Beloglazka (R), Klepets (Ukr)

As their most closely related species, young white-eye bream are often mistaken for common bream. White-eye bream are much more common in rivers, and are also more sensitive to the cleanness of the water. They occur in greatest numbers in the Ukraine and Russia, where they represent a great proportion of natural landings. Migrating schools are often observed in the Black Sea and the Sea of Azov. Although fished throughout Europe, white-eye bream are not counted among the most valuable catch. The price of their meat may get very high in the summer season, when it is largely sold as a pleasant and nourishing meal around lunchtime in holiday resort restaurants. White-eye bream average about 25–30 cm (10–12 in) in length and 0.5 kg (1 lb) in weight, but they attain sexual maturity when they are half as big, when they lay approximately 50–100,000 eggs. This is why populations of white-eye bream often fluctuate in numbers. They were often believed to have become extinct in some waters, but a few pairs of fish could always successfully rebuild the stock.

66 | Bleak | Alburnus alburnus | CYPRINIDAE / CARPS

Bleak (En), Ukelei, Laube (D), Alburno (E), Ablette (F), Alborella (I), Alver (Nl) • Laube (CH), Ouklejka obecná (Cze), Küsz (H), Laue (N), Ruivaca (P), Ukleja (Pl), Ukléika (R), Laube (S), Inci baligi (Tr)

Abundant in most regions, bleak reach an average size of a mere 10–15 cm (4–6 in) and weigh no more than a few ounces. In bygone days bleak were called in many countries "breadfish", since in trying times they had often saved humans and animals alike from starvation. Bleak inhabit most European freshwaters, sometimes schooling in numbers of up to several hundred. Angling contests sometimes truly revolve around this tiny fish, since the fisherman of the day often wins the palm by having caught a large amount of bleak. In eastern Europe it is still prepared by the "good old" recipe, i.e. fried or roasted whole, but more importantly, bleak are extensively used in the production of cheap canned fish in oil. Its tiny scales are easy to scrape off and used for obtaining pearl essence ("Essence d'Orient"), the method of which has an age-long tradition. The extracted "essence" is largely used in the making of artificial pearls, fashion jewellery and Christmas decorations.

67 | Asp | Aspius aspius | CYPRINIDAE / CARPS

Asp (En), Rapfen, Schied (D), Aspe (F), Aspio (I), Roofblei (Nl) • Asprogrivado (Gr), Balin (H), Áspio (P), Bolen (Pl), Kocaagiz baligi (Tr)

The unfortunate depletion of the high-quality asp populations in the past few decades is everywhere believed to have been caused by environmental pollution and flood control along rivers. Artificial breeding of this fluvial species averaging in length up to 50–80 cm (20–31 in) and 1–2 kg (2.2–4.4 lb) in weight is widely applied. Asp fishing is especially significant in some areas of central and eastern Europe, for instance, in Transylvania an entire branch of tourism is based on fishing for asp. A notable stock has developed in the Caspian Sea by asp having migrated from the feeding rivers into the sea and its brackish waters. Fillets of asp are of an exceptionally good quality, trimmings and heads are largely used as chowder ingredients. Anglers' associations generally buy specimens of about two years of age, but the fish can be kept for such a long time only in clear-water gravel pit lakes. In contrast to most fishes of the carp family, asp stick their numerous (60–80,000) roe onto the gravel bottom of rivers. When young, they feed on organic detrital material and plankton, but gradually convert to preying on larger and larger animals.

68 | Barbel | Barbus barbus | CYPRINIDAE / CARPS

Barbel (En), Barbe (D, Da), Barbeau fluviatile (F), Barbo (I), Barbeel (Nl) • Rózsás márna (H), Barbo (P), Brzana (Pl), Usatsch (R), Breana (Ru), Jokibarbi (SF)

An omnivorous fish of medium size, reaching a length of 30–60 cm (12–24 in) and a weight of 1 or 2 kg (2.2–4.4 lb), barbel are perhaps the most abundant species of western and central European rivers. They are normally sedentary in habit, sticking to their native habitat, where they dwell in burrows around smaller eddies near the river bed. In the spawning period they migrate further up river, closer to the source. Barbel are highly valued as sport fish, this presumably being the reason for their having been introduced to the waters of some African and Middle-Eastern countries. It has been known for centuries that the barbel's roe is poisonous when eaten raw. This is why those less well-versed in the art of cooking this fish refrain from using it as food, however delicious its meat may be. On the other hand, some claim pickled or smoked barbel meat to be the gourmet's best bet. In central Europe it is very common to bard the fish before frying, i.e. the dorsal muscular flesh of the fish is cut into deeply and is filled with bits of ham, bacon, onion and other vegetables, then the fish is neatly placed into a fireproof dish to be roasted in a pre-heated oven.

69 | White bream | Blicca bjoerkna | CYPRINIDAE / CARPS

White bream (En), Güster, Blicke (D), Brema blanca (E), Brème bordelière (F), Blicca (I), Kolblei (Nl) • Skalák (Cze), Karikakeszeg (H), Flire (N, Da), Gustera (R), Pasuri (SF), Abdalca (Tr)

One of the most common species in European and Mediterranean waters, the white or silver bream averages 25–30 cm (10–12 in) in length. Although white bream are landed by anglers in large quantities and many fishermen entirely rely on the stock, due to their relatively small size and slow growth rate they are not very much liked by aquaculturists, who even try to expel them to natural waters, where they are the main food of larger predator fishes. In southeastern Europe and Turkey white bream shoals have been observed to migrate to estuaries. An omnivorous species feeding on organic detrital material, white bream adapt well to small waters in the vicinity of human settlements. In the pleasant early summer period, despite their small build they produce an enormous number of offspring, generally tens of thousands, to the great delight of other water creatures feeding on them. The meat of the white bream is very lean and bony, therefore it is mainly eaten fried crisp in oil, often in a paprika-seasoned breading. In Asia Minor it is dried, since it can be easily stored in this form.

70 | Silver crucian carp | Carassius gibelio | CYPRINIDAE / CARPS

Silver crucian carp (En), Giebel, Silberkarausche (D), Carassin doré (F), Ciprino dorato (I), Giebel (Nl) • Damkarusse (Da), Goldfish (En), Ezüstkárász (H), Karas srebrzysty (Pl), Serebreanyi karas (R), Crap-caras (Ru)

The species, native to central Asia, can nowadays be found in nearly all corners of the world, reaching body lengths of 20–40 cm (8–16 in). Due to their extraordinary ability to survive in all circumstances and to their genetic characteristics, an extremely large number of breeds of silver crucian carp have developed. Silver crucian carp belong to the carp family (Cyprinidae), differing from the carp in having no mouth barbels. This is an important trait at a younger stage, since it eases the age-selection process in carp-breeding lake fisheries. In many countries, however, silver crucian carp are considered a nuisance, since they oust indigenous fishes. Nevertheless, anglers generally appreciate silver crucian carp, and their specimens over 100 g (3.5 oz) are eaten fried crisp. Specimens weighing more than 500 g (17.6 oz) are a rarity, since silver crucian carp attain sexual maturity at a very early age that may sometimes cause a boom in the number of their offspring, which, in turn, is often the cause of food shortage in their habitat. The silver crucian carp is the wild form of the goldfish.

71 | **Crucian carp** | Carassius carassius | CYPRINIDAE / CARPS

Crucian carp (En), Karausche (D), Carpín (E), Carassin (F), Carassio, carpa à specchi (I), Kroeskarper (Nl) • Karas obecný (Cze), Søkarusse (Da), Széleskárász (H), Pimpão-comum (P), Karas pospolity (Pl), Kruglyi (R), Garasita (Ru), Ruutana (SF)

A tenacious fish, the crucian carp is able to adjust to the most diverse conditions; it may even live through shorter dry seasons by retiring to the mud bottom of temporary lakes. Its short but stout build makes it especially apt, too. Although the crucian carp very seldom weighs more than a pound, in maturity one single fish would surely make a hearty meal even for the less hearty. As a Eurasian species known and appreciated for long as a savoury food ingredient, the crucian carp has even become one of the most sought-after fishes in central Asia and China. Unusual though it may seem to the European taste, the culinary tradition in these parts of the world is to serve the fish while it is alive. Despite having bony meat, its considerably thick dorsal part makes the crucian carp especially fit for roasting. The crucian carp has been gradually spreading all over the world, and it has become the best-known variant of the carp species. In some countries, however, it is regarded as an environmental hazard, in Australia even inducing serious attempts to exterminate it. These, however, will undoubtedly meet with difficulties due to the species' genetic varieties and ability to adapt.

72 | **Nase, Sneep** | Chondrostoma nasus | CYPRINIDAE / CARPS

Nase, Sneep (En), Nase, Näsling (D), Hotu, nase commun (F), Naso (I), Sneep (Nl) • Näsling (A), Savetta (CH), Nosek (Cze), Syrtis (Gr), Márványajkú vagy vésettajkú paduc (H), Boga-do-Danúbio (P), Podust (R), Scobai (Ru), Kababurun baligi (Tr)

The nase belongs to the Eurasian cyprinids most heavily affected by river regulation. A strongly riverine fish, it does not feel at home in reservoirs. It grows to 30–45 cm (12–18 in) in length and 0.5–1 kg (1–2 lb) in weight, and this is the size at which it is commonly caught by anglers. Nase can fairly easily be recognised by their typical, downward oriented mouth, and torpedo-like snout. The species' Hungarian name ("vésettajkú" or "márványajkú" standing for engraved or marbled lip) is derived from its extremely hard, cartilaginous lower jaw, which helps the nase to attack benthic organisms occurring on, or attached to the bottom. Its mixed diet includes plant as well as animal matter. Its flesh is of medium quality, suitable for frying. Due to its comparative rarity in markets, the nase can mostly be obtained from fishermen using trawling nets, or turns up when irrigation ditches are drained. It is artificially propagated only in a few countries in the Carpathian Basin, for the purpose of restocking natural waters.

71

72

73 | **Grass carp** | Ctenopharyngodon idella | CYPRINIDAE / CARPS

Grass carp (En), Graskarpfen, Amurkarpfen (D), Armura blanca, carpa china (E), Amour blanc, carpe herbivore (F), Carpa erbivora, amur (I), Graskarper (Nl) • Waan ue (Cant), Amur bílý (Cze), Graeskarpe (Da), Amúr (H), Sogyo (J), Graskarpe (N), Amur bialy (Pl), Belyi amur (R), Crap alb chinezese (Ru), White amur (US), Cá châm Treng (Vie)

The most widely distributed herbivorous species of the world's lake fisheries, grass carp are – together with other Chinese carp species – the most useful fish of mixed population fishponds and channels, and dead channels lush with vegetation. In most languages it is named after its place of origin, the Amur river. On most continents, except Australia, it is bred under controlled conditions and released into both natural lakes and reservoirs. Some ecologists expressly object to the further spreading of grass carp, therefore in some countries only sterile hybrid specimens are allowed to be released into natural waters. Although grass carp feed exclusively on higher plants (macrophytes), anglers are increasingly reporting catches by live bait and artificial lures. It can be a real experience to catch such a fighting game fish by angling, since the fish, sometimes reaching a length of nearly 1 m (40 in), and a weight of 20–30 kg (44–66 lb) struggles a long time for its life. The meat of grass carp, prepared in various ways, is most delicious.

74 | **Common carp** | Cyprinus carpio | CYPRINIDAE / CARPS

Common carp (En), Karpfen, Schuppenkarpfen (D), Carpa (E), Carpe commune (F), Carpa (I), Karper (Nl) • Krapi (Alb), Lei ue (Cant), Kapr obecný (Cze), Karpe (Da, N), Cyprinos (Gr), Ponty (pikkelyes) (H), Karpar (Is), Karpion (Isr), Koi (J), Pba ni (Lao), Ikan mas (Mal), Sarmão (P), Karp (Pl), Karppi (SF), Sazan (R), Ciortanica, Olocari (Ru), Karpa (Tag), Sazan baligi (Tr), Korop (Ukr)

Perhaps the most well-known freshwater fish, common carp are distributed throughout all the inhabited continents. Native to Eurasia, it has partly spread naturally, but more typically by controlled breeding. It has been bred in lake fisheries for centuries, and it has numerous variants and species. Methods of its controlled breeding and rearing are widely known. A fish of average size, common carp are omnivorous and resistant to environmental degradation. Marketed at a weight of 1–2 kg (2.2–4.4 lb), and 30–50 cm (12–20 in) in length, it is one of the most suitable fishes for family meals. Practically, there is no dish that cannot be prepared from common carp. In Europe it is mostly eaten breaded then fried or is used in fish soups. In Africa and Asia, before frying, the fish are cut through across the flanks so that the bones can perish in the heat, whereas in China they are boiled alive. A special Japanese way of preparing carp is to freeze it alive and shave it into flakes.

73

74

75 | **Mirror carp** | Cyprinus carpio morpha nobilis | CYPRINIDAE / CARPS

Mirror carp (En), Spiegelkarpfen (D), Carpa (E), Carpe-miroir (F), Carpa a specchi (I), Spiegelkarper (Nl) • Bőrponty, tükörponty (H), Sazan (R)

A variant of common carp bred in lake fisheries, mirror carp are characterised by a high back, and partial or total lack of scales that makes them especially easy to handle. This very "artificial" trait has caused several nations not to use it as food, for religious reasons. Nor do anglers entirely approve of this species, since mirror carp are generally held to be lazy and picky. In addition to this, populations released into rivers to supply stock proved to have an inability to survive since they normally drift downstream to the first lake or fall prey to predator fishes. The meat of mirror carp is generally fattier and has a more flaky texture than that of their relatives in the wild. Still, this may be exactly what some appreciate, when they prepare the fish wonderfully simmered with vegetables and sour cream, as in the cuisine of South Slavonic nations. Fish goulash or fish soup Hungarian style is also appealing to the gourmet's taste. Mirror carp attain body lengths of 30–50 cm (12–20 in), and a comparably large weight of 1.5–3 kg (3.3–6.6 lb).

76 | **Wild carp** | Cyprinus carpio morpha hungaricus | CYPRINIDAE / CARPS

Wild carp (En), Wildkarpfen (Stammform) (D), Carpa (E), Carpe (F), Carpa (I), Karper (Nl) • Podoustev říční (Cze), Nyurgaponty (H), Certa (Pl), Syrt (R)

A characteristically elongated fish, wild carp have a low back and may attain body lengths as long as 1 m (40 in). Discovered in the Carpathian basin, it has spread to many countries for purposes of genetic breeding and sport fishing. Since this species is believed to be an original variant of carp, stock bred in diverse regions are re-stocked with wild carp specimens in order to cross back. This breeding method is justified by the wild carp's resistance, swift movement, and its rich, firm-textured and tasty meat. The very same characterics are highly valued by anglers too, thus wild carp are mostly released into lower and middle stretches of rivers and dead channels. Controlled breeding and rearing of wild carp fry have constantly been experimented with, but with poorer results than in the case of variants reared in lake fisheries. The meat of wild carp is much leaner and more muscular, but also bonier than that of the lake fishery hybrid species.

77 | **Silver carp** | Hypophthalmichthys molitnix | CYPRINIDAE / CARPS

Silver carp (En), Silberkarpfen, Tolstolob (D), Carpa plateada (E), Carpe asiatique (F), Carpa argentata (I), Zilverkarpen (Nl) • Tolstolobik obecný (Cze), Sølvkarpe (Da, N), Asimokyprinos (Gr), Fehérbusa (H), Kasaf (Isr), Hakuren (J), Tongsan putih (Mal), Carpa-prateada (P), Tolstolobik (R), Hopeapaksuotsa (SF), Pla pea long (Thai)

The most widely known phytoplankton-feeder belonging to the Chinese carp family, silver carp owe their name in most languages to the fact that they fashion numerous tiny and beautiful scales. It emerged from its native country in the 1960s and has been established in lake fisheries applying carp-based polyculture, i.e. mixed populations of diverse fishes. Nowadays silver carp are found in about one hundred countries. In many areas they are considered undesirable, as they seem to endanger the balance of the local fauna. Making good use of the species' peculiar feeding habits, in many areas they are used as biological waterfilters. In natural waters they may attain a weight of 50 kg (110 lb), but the marketable specimens normally come from controlled fisheries, in sizes of 30–40 cm (12–16 in) and 3–4 kg (6.6–9 lb). The meat of the silver carp is less fatty, but substantially juicy and flaky in texture, and this is why it is especially valued in many areas. It does have a peculiar strong taste though, but this can be removed by soaking the meat in milk or special marinade for a couple of hours prior to cooking. Although not very much appreciated by most, this strong taste is exactly what some people fall for.

78 | **Bighead carp** | Hypophthalmichthys nobilis | CYPRINIDAE / CARPS

Bighead carp (En), Marmorkarpfen, Dickkopfkarpfen (D), Carpa cabeza grande (E), Carpe à grosse tête (F), Carpa testa grossa (I), Grootkopkarper (Nl) • Ballgjeri laraman (Alb), Hak lin (Cant), Tolstolebec pestrý (Cze), Marmorkarpe (Da), Bighead carp (En), Marmarokyprinos (Gr), Pettyesbusa (H), Kokuren (J), Kap kepala besar (Mal), Piostryi tolstolobik (R), Novac (Ru), Marmorkarp (S), Pla song heu (Thai)

Native to the countries of the former Soviet Union, bighead carp were very quickly introduced to Europe and the other continents. Unlike related species, bighead carp primarily feed on zooplankton and organic detrital material. Their colour is rather greyish than silvery. In most languages the name of the fish originates from its disproportionately large head adapted to filter-feeding. Its roe is pelagic, i.e. floating in the surface waters, a fact that has contributed to the successful breeding of the fish in controlled environments. Bighead carp are often cross-bred with related species, thus sometimes very strange, omnivorous hybrid variants may result. In many fisheries bighead carp populations are restricted to a given quota, since feeding habits may get out of control, and in recent years individual growth has apparently declined. It is one of the cheapest freshwater fishes available in the market, therefore it has often been used pulverised as an animal food ingredient. The marketed size is generally 40–70 cm (16–28 in), 4–5 kg (9–11 lb).

79 | Rohu | Labeo rohita | CYPRINIDAE / CARPS

Rohu (En, D, E, F, I, Nl) • Rohiti, rui (As), Rohu, rui (Ben), Tebulit (Ind), Rohi, ruhu (Ori), Dhambra, Tapra (Pun), Dum-bra (Sin), Bocha-gandumeenu (Tel), Pla yee sok tad (Thai), Ruee, Sharkminnow (US)

This large-bodied cyprinid is native to Asia – India, Pakistan, Bangladesh, Myanmar and Nepal. It can reach 2 m (80 in) in length and 45–50 kg (100–110 lb) in weight. A freshwater fish, the rohu is common in larger rivers. It usually lives alone, sometimes burying itself in the bottom. Its spawning is triggered by the southwestern monsoon and it breeds in flooded rivers. It is rather prolific, the females producing as many as 2–3 million eggs at a time, according to their size. An herbivorous species, the rohu feeds on aquatic macrovegetation. It has been introduced into several areas, mainly to populate water reservoirs and for breeding purposes. Besides fishery uses, it is of major importance in controlling plants in reservoirs. It is intensely fished and is farmed throughout its range. Also favoured as an anglers' catch, it is sold fresh, being prepared in various ways in Far Eastern cuisine.

80 | European chub | Leuciscus cephalus | CYPRINIDAE / CARPS

European chub (En), Döbel, Aitel (D), Cacho (E), Chevaine (F), Cavedano (I), Meun, kopvoorn (Nl) • Aitel (A), Cavezzale (CH), Dyblink (Cze), Døbel (Da), Tylinari (Gr), Fejes domolykó (H), Stam (N), Escalo-do-Norte (P), Klen (Pl), Golavl (R), Clean (Ru), Färna (S), Turpa (SF), Kosswig inci baligi (Tr)

A popular sport fish of colder European waters, the omnivorous chub averages about 30–60 cm (12–24 in) in length and 1 kg (2 lb) in weight. Chub populations can usually be easily detected, since they tend to attack from hiding any bait falling into the water. Fly fishermen often try out their collection of flies on chub, in most cases very successfully. Chub belong to those carp-like fish that are active even in wintertime, and are very often observed hunting in large groups. They adapt considerably to man-made environments, therefore they have been successfully launched into several reservoirs. Its meat is tasty, it can be prepared both fried and simmered after having been cut across the flanks against the bone. It is also an indispensable ingredient of the first broth of the chowder or fish soup characteristic of national cuisines of the Carpathian Basin. Chub is widely believed to be native to east European regions, but it has recently been observed in several areas in the Near East and south Caucasus. Chub has become very popular in Turkish cuisine, where it is prepared similarly to the locally abundant barbel.

79

80

81 | Orfe, Ide | Leuciscus idus | CYPRINIDAE / CARPS

Orfe, Ide (En), Aland (D), Cachuelo (E), Ide mélanote (F), Ido (I), Winde (Nl) • Nerfling (A), Jelez jesen (Cze), Rimte (Da), Ide (En), Jász (H), Escalo-prateado (P), Iaz (R), Vaduvita (Ru), Id (S)

Distributed over most of Europe and in the East as far as China, ide average 25–40 cm (10–16 in) in length and grow to a maximum 1 kg (2 lb) in weight. Adapted to withstand environmental depletion, they gradually come to outnumber their related species. One related species called orfe, cross-bred in lake fisheries, differs considerably from the indistinct original in that it has bright colours. The meat of the orfe is more yellowish and also fattier than that of the forms living in natural waters. Both the leaner-meated river-dwelling ide, and the somewhat thicker, but more flaky-textured lake-fishery orfe are sold in large quantities, since both are used as ingredients of different foods. Orfe is sometimes palmed off as smoked salmon to unsuspecting customers, but its meat, being bony, betrays the trick. Like most members of the carp family, ide and orfe are omnivorous, thus anglers easily catch them with diverse natural bait.

82 | Black carp | Mylopharingodon piceus | CYPRINIDAE / CARPS

Black carp (En), Schwarzer Karpfen (D), Carpa negra, caracolera (E), Carpe noire (F), Carpa nera (I), Zwarte karper (Nl) • Hak waam (Cant), Fekete amur (H), Ao-uo (J), Kap hitam (Mal), Amur czarny (Pl), Tscherny amur (R), Scoicar (Ru), Musta-amuri (SF)

A freshwater species, black carp are distributed in the Far East in the area stretching from the water-system of the Amur River down to south China. Specimens may attain body lengths of 1 m (40 in) and weights of 30–35 kg (66–77 lb). They mainly live over the sand and mud bottom of sluggish waters of rivers and lakes. The species was introduced to the European waters of the Volga River as a "plant-feeder" species. Nevertheless, the diet of black carp primarily consists of snails and smaller shellfish. They crush the shells of shellfish and clams with their extremely efficient jugular teeth. Black carp have been introduced into the lakes and canals of Israel in order to eliminate populations of snails known to transmit diseases and vermin. Widely exploited by commercial fishermen, black carp also constitute an important artificially bred species in lake fisheries. In some countries where they have been introduced, black carp populations are reported to have caused serious ecological damage. The meat of black carp is of high quality and is usually eaten fried. In the Far East a vast variety of cooking methods are known.

81.

82

83 | Knife fish, Ziege | Pelecus cultratus | CYPRINIDAE / CARPS

Knife fish, Ziege (En), Ziege (D), Peleco (E), Rasoir (F), Pesce rasoio (I), Sabelbliek (Nl) • Ostrucha krivocará (Cze), Knife (En), Garda (H), Peixe-sabre (P), Ciosa (Pl), Tschékhon (R), Miekkasärki (SF)

Named after the peculiar shape of its body, reminding one of a blade, knife fish migrate in enormous schools between seas and freshwaters. They nearly always stay in the surface zone of the water, where they can easily obtain all sorts of food with their characteristically upward oriented mouth which can function as a sucker. Environmental changes and flood control in rivers have caused the development of purely freshwater stock. Knife fish are especially popular in the kitchen, since even the unskilled can easily free them of their large scales. In central and eastern Europe sweep-net landings of young stock are often used canned in oil. Knife fish produce pelagic roe, i.e. they float in the surface zone of the water. The roe, apart from predators, are also endangered by the swell of waters. Knife fish average 25–40 cm (10–16 in) in length and attain a maximum weight of 1 kg (2.2 lb).

84 | Roach | Rutilus rutilus | CYPRINIDAE / CARPS

Roach (En), Plötze, Rotauge (D), Gardon (F), Triotto rosso (I), Blankvoorn (Nl) • Rotauge (A, CH), Vengeron (CH), Plotice obecná (Cze), Skalle (Da), Bodorka (H), Mort (N), Płoć (Pl), Plotva (R), Babuscă (Ru), Kizilgöz baligi (Tr)

The relatively small roach, growing to a length of 15–30 cm (6–12 in), belongs to the carp family and adapts itself easily to diverse circumstances. It dwells in almost any smaller river or stream, but smaller schools of roach have been observed roaming in southeast European brackish waters and marginal seas. Sometimes they even go as far as to "over spawn" with their sticky roe the nests placed in the fish breeding areas for the walleye and pike stock of the fishery. No wonder aquaculturists do not appreciate their presence. Nevertheless, anglers delight in catching these very lively small fish. True, one cannot possibly transform the bony and thin meat of roach, yet one can always hope for a nice bite when eating them grilled, whole. In Russia roach are caught in fishing nets, and the smaller specimens are used for food, pickled with onions.

85 | **Rudd** | *Scardinius erythrophthalmus* | CYPRINIDAE / CARPS

Rudd (En), Rotfeder (D), Gardí (E), Rotengle (F), Scardola (I), Rietvoorn (Nl) • Lloska-ë (Alb), Perlín rudoploutvý (Cze), Rudskalle (Da), Veresszárnyú keszeg (H), Sorv (N), Wzdrega (Pl), Krasnoperka (R), Rdeceperka (Slo), Kizilkanat baligi (Tr)

Perhaps the most well-known Old World freshwater fish, rudd often feature in the folk songs and tales of many peoples. Frequently landed from the natural waters along the Danube and Volga rivers, rudd is very much liked by anglers, catching a 20–40 cm (8–16 in) long specimen being a rewarding sport. As a species of small build, it takes at least a dozen fish to suffice for a lighter meal for the entire family. The meat of the rudd is dry and bony, thus it is mostly eaten gutted and fried thoroughly. In some countries (e.g. Poland, Belorus and Russia) smaller specimens are pickled or used as ingredients of cabbage and fish soup. In natural waters rudd are consumed by other fish, thus, despite the large number of offspring they produce, the rudd stock is often depleted in certain areas. One reason for this may be the fact that they especially like dwelling near shores, where water insects and their larvae also kill their fry. Rudd especially like warm temperatures, thus in many areas, such as the Carpathian Basin and Turkey, they have been observed in the off-flow waters of thermal springs.

86 | **Tench** | *Tinca tinca* | CYPRINIDAE / CARPS

Tench (En), Schleie (D), Tenca (E), Tanche (F), Tinca (I, P), Zeelt (Nl) • Linë (Alb), Lín obecný (Cze), Suder (Da), Compó (H), Lin (Pl, R), Yesil sazan (Tr)

Most abundant in mud-bottomed quiet waters and lakes, tench are a typically European species. Nevertheless, they also occur in all areas stretching to the Far East. Tench may reach a weight of a few pounds, but they grow at a very slow rate, reaching a length of 30–50 cm (12–20 in). Its main trait, its tiny-scaled stout build, clearly distinguishes tench from other similar fish. Tench exhibit a calm movement, and are rather nocturnal than diurnal animals. The meat is especially flavoursome and is used both for cooking and frying. It is increasingly valued in the European market and can be sold in any quantity. Tench are also widespread in lake fisheries, but the rearing of the young is extremely difficult due to the increased vulnerability of its larvae. Thus it is only recommended for highly experienced fish farmers. Tench have a good ability to survive low oxygen conditions, therefore they are becoming popular as inhabitants of park and garden ponds. In recent years colourful hybrid variants have also spread, sometimes occurring in natural waters, possibly due to the increased interest of anglers.

87 | Vimba | Vimba vimba | CYPRINIDAE / CARPS

Vimba (En), Zährte, Rußnase (D), Vimbe, zaerthe (F), Vimba (I), Blauwneus (Nl) • Russnase (A), Podoustev říční (Cze), Zanthe (En), Szilvaorrú keszeg (H), Strandslabbi (Is), Certa (Pl), Syrt (R), Tiganca (Ru), Vimpa (SF), Kara balik (Tr)

The vimba or zanthe is a member of the carp family, dispersed throughout Europe and Asia. Vimba average 20–30 cm (8–12 in) in length. The largest stocks of vimba occur in the nearshore waters of seas, from where they migrate to the upper stretches of feeding rivers, where they spawn in schools. Rivers where they are totally absent can be assumed to be polluted. As vimba are omnivorous, anglers can successfully use a great variety of bait. Their silvery body becomes colourful in the spawning season, therefore the spawning stock can be a truly amazing sight in clear, gravel-bottomed rivers. Vimba can be easily distinguished from related species by their typically blunt snout and forehead. The meat of the vimba is primarily used for frying, and it is also used as a primary ingredient of the first broth of the famous Carpathian fish soup, hardly ever occurring in the "main" broth due to the bony character of the meat. Otherwise, the meat itself is palatable.

88 | Bigmouth buffalo | Ictiobus cyprinellus | CATOSTOMIDAE / SUCKERS AND BUFFALO FISHES

Bigmouth buffalo (En), Großmäuliger Büffelfisch (D), Búfalo (E), Buffalo (I, Nl), Buffalo à grande bouche (F) • Bredmundet bøffelkarpe (Da), Buffelfisk (S), Isoimukarppi (SF)

This member of the suckers and buffalo fish familiy is an inhabitant of North American freshwaters. It is found from Hudson Bay through the Great Lakes to the Mississippi Basin, from Ontario to Saskatchewan in Canada, and from Montana southwards to Louisiana and Texas in the US. It has been successfully introduced to a number of Californian waters. This bottom-dweller reaches 1 m (39 in) in length and 30–32 kg (66–71 lb) in body mass. It feels itself at home in the main channel and the side arms of rivers, as well as in lakes and ponds, and quickly adapts to conditions present in man-made reservoirs. It resembles the (European) carp in both appearance and habits. An omnivorous species, it feeds primarily on benthic organisms (i.e. minute animals inhabiting the upper level of the water bottom rich in organic matter). Because of its bony flesh, it is not highly valued in North America, but is caught by both commercial and recreational fishermen, and is popular as a sport fish in some regions. The bigmouth buffalo is marketed fresh or frozen, and is prepared fried, roasted or grilled. Attempts to introduce it into Europe have not been very successful.

89 | **Weatherfish** | Misgurnus fossilis | COBITIDAE / LOACHES

Weatherfish (En), Schlammpeitzger (D), Loche d'étang (F), Cobite di stagno (I), Grote modderkruiper (Nl) • Guvori (Alb), Piskoř páskovaný (Cze), Réti csík (H), Dynnsmerling (N), Piskorz (Pl), Viun (R), Cinklja (Slo)

This strange-shaped, elongated fish, reaching a maximum size of merely 10 cm (4 in), was well-known in Europe up to the 1900s. Before any flood control took place, European weatherfish had multiplied by the million during extensive floods, and people living riverbanks and swampy regions fished them in enormous quantities. Weatherfish is a species rare in western Europe and it is only in the east that it is utilised for food. Due to their small size, weatherfish are generally used whole, either fried or marinated and pickled. In southeastern Europe and in northern Asia dried and ground weatherfish is widely used as a basic ingredient of human and animal food. Several of its Far East sub-species are used in the sour fish soups of Chinese and Korean cuisine. In many regions weatherfish are also used as "living barometers", since their complementary respiratory organ makes them especially sensitive to changes in barometric pressure and they "rise and fall" signalling an oncoming storm. Normally weatherfish hide in the riverbed, frequently burrowing themselves into the muddy bottom. They may also occur in small puddles of water only a few inches deep, since it is quite common for weatherfish to sneak inland away from the river through whatever available channel they may find.

90 | **Black catfish, Black bullhead** | Ameiurus melas | ICTALURIDAE / CHANNEL CATS AND NORTH AMERICAN FRESHWATER CATFISHES

Black catfish, Black bullhead (En), Schwarzer Katzenwels (D), Poisson-chat noir, barbotte noire (F), Pesce gatto (I), Zwarte Amerikaanse dwergmeerval (Nl) • Yellow belly bullhead (Can), Sumecek zakrský (Cze), Dvaergmalle (Da), Black catfish (En), Fekete törpeharcsa (H), Bagre (Mex), Sumik czarny (Pl), Amerikanskii som (R), Svart dvärgmal (S)

Like most catfish, this species also originates from the USA, but interestingly it is becoming increasingly widespread in central and southern Europe. In most parts of the world it is considered to be of secondary importance and is used mainly for the entertainment of children as sport fish typically caught at a size of 15–40 cm (6–16 in) and 150–300 g (5.2–10.5 oz). In contrast, in some countries, especially in Mediterranean cuisine, black catfish have become one of the most popular freshwater fish for frying. Its price grows incredibly in the summer tourist season, quite often surpassing that of the trout. Most of the demand is met by intensive lake fisheries, and the hybrid variant obtained by crossbreeding black bullhead and common (brown) bullhead is increasingly common. A truly "cunning" animal, the black bullhead masterfully poaches the nests and offspring of other fishes, but it is its curiosity that makes it a veritable sport fish, since it will take practically any fisherman's bait. Nevertheless, one should be aware of the fact that a dangerous spine in its dorsal fin can cause serious distress if the fish is mishandled.

89

90

91 | **Common (brown) bullhead** | Ameiurus nebulosus | ICTALURIDAE / CHANNEL CATS AND NORTH AMERICAN FRESHWATER CATFISHES

Common (brown) bullhead (En), Katzenwels, Zwergwels (D), Poisson-chat, Barbotte brune (F), Pesce gatto (I), Bruine Amerikaanse dwergmeerval (Nl) • Sumecek americký (Cze), Dvaergmalle (Da), Törpeharcsa (H), Dvergmalle (N), Sumik karlowaty (Pl), Amerikanskii som (R), Dvärgmal (S)

Although not highly appreciated in their native sub-tropical still waters of North America, common bullhead have become extremely popular in Eurasia. One of the reasons is perhaps rooted in the species' habit of taking care of their offspring – one or both of the parents escort the schooling young, extending the period of care by following them for several weeks. Another reason is that the common bullhead is a typically one-portion meal when prepared; thus, the species has become popular in the catering business, especially in the cuisine of countries largely dependent on tourism. Its meat is somewhat more firm-textured and also bonier than that of most catfish, but it is also more flavoursome. This is why it is largely used as both a basic ingredient of fish soups and for eating fried. Almost none of the variants of the famous paprika chowder of the Carpathian Basin will do without a touch of the common bullhead; nor can the Slavonic vegetable fish soups be complete without it. There is a great difference between the 30–50 cm (12–20 in) variants living in North America and those in Europe, which only reach an average length of 15–30 cm (6–12 in).

92 | **Channel catfish** | Ictalurus punctatus | ICTALURIDAE / CHANNEL CATS AND NORTH AMERICAN FRESHWATER CATFISHES

Channel catfish (En), Getüpfelter Gabelwels (D), Coto punteado (E), Poisson-chat tacheté (F), Pesce gatto puntado (I), Channel-dwergmeerval (Nl) • Kanalmalle (Da), Gatópsaro (Gr), Peixe gato pontuado (P), Kanavnaya zubatka (R)

The channel catfish, by reaching even 1 m (40 in) in length in some cases, tend to surpass in size most other members of the catfish family (Ictaluridae). They have been introduced to most continents from the water system of the Mississippi. The species acquired the name "channel" after commercial farming methods were developed about fifty years ago. The method involves the use of very long ponds especially constructed for the purpose. Around 90% of the quantity marketed is bred on fish farms. The fish thus obtained is processed through machines especially designed for this type of fish. Its meat is usually sold ready to cook, in fillets and deep-frozen; other parts of the fish, trimmings and heads, are used as soup ingredients. Apart from the common carp, it is believed that this species will become the most popular fish for cooking in the new millennium.

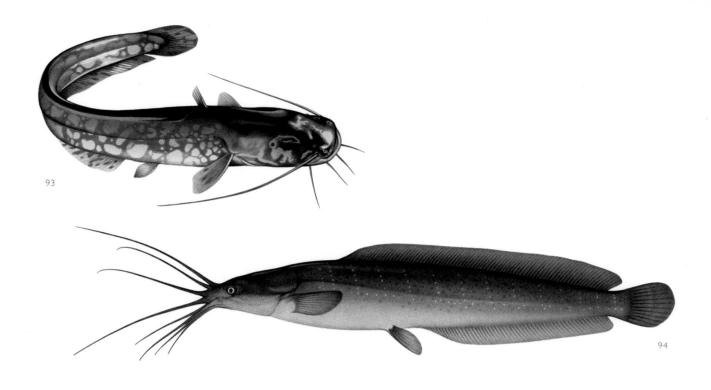

93

94

93 | **Wels catfish** | Silurus glanis | SILURIDAE / SHEATFISHES

Wels catfish (En), Waller, Wels (D), Siluro (E), Silure glane (F), Siluro (I), Meerval (Nl) • Sumec (Cze), Malle (Da, N), Harcsa (H), Siluro-europeu (P), Sum (Pl), Som (R), Moaca (Ru), Mal (S), Monni (SF), Yayin baligi (Tr), Rechnoi som (Ukr), Danube catfish (US)

The best-known member of the sheatfish family, wels have also been experimentally introduced to some lake fisheries in Africa and America. The very palatable meat of the wels and the fact that the species is entirely with scales has given it a high reputation among anglers, with landings of specimens with body lengths of around 1 m (40 in) and a weight of sometimes several tens of pounds having become an especially prestigious challenge. The fish entering the fresh fillet market at an average weight of 3–5 kg (6.6–11 lb) is especially suitable for nearly all kinds of culinary processes, with nearly all regions having their local traditional recipe, such as Hungarian paprika fish fillets, German smoked and fried fillets, Russian cooked or simmered fillets with sour cream, etc.

94 | **Walking catfish** | Clarias batrachus | CLARIIDAE / CLARIDES

Walking catfish (En), Froschwels, Wanderwels (D), Clarias (E), Poissons-chat (F), Afrikaanse meerval (Nl) • Pantat (Ban, Pan, Tag), Magur (Ben), Hito (Bik), Nga-khoo (Bur), Paltat (Ilo), Leleh (Ind), Leleh (Jav), Ito (Kap), Trey andeng (Khm), Kawatsi (Kuy), Pa douk (Lao), Ikan keling, ikan lele, keli (Mal), Freshwater catfish (Mal-En), Mungri (Nep), Klarievyi som (R), Konnamonni (SF), Hitong (Tag), Pla duk dam (Thai), Clarias catfish (US), Cá tren trang (Vie), Alimudan (Vis)

This species of catfish is native to Asia. Originally it inhabited southeast Asian freshwaters, but has meanwhile been established in numerous countries. An extremely popular breed in its homeland, it is not nearly so successful elsewhere, probably due to its small size. With the use of an organ situated near the gills it is able to use atmospheric oxygen. This ability helps it to migrate overland in the dry season from desiccating waters to the nearest suitable habitat. Its name – walking catfish – refers to this feature. A small-bodied fish, it can reach 40 cm (16 in) maximum length and 250–300 g (8–10 oz) weight. A carnivorous species, it feeds on insect larvae, worms, clams and mussels, small fish, plants, as well as organic debris. A very important food source in Asia, it is distributed live, freshly dead or frozen. Its flesh is of good quality and is prepared according to various recipes in Far Eastern cuisine. Reportedly, the walking catfish has become a pest in some areas to which it was introduced in former times.

95 | North African catfish | *Clarias gariepinus* | CLARIIDAE / CLARIDES

North African catfish (En), Afrikanischer Wels (D), Pez gato (E), Poisson-chat nord-africain (F), Afrikaanse meerval (Nl) • Skerptandbaber (Afr), Ambaza (Amh), Mulonge (Bem), Balbout (Cha), Baleewu (Ful), Afrikai harcsa (H), Tarwada (Hau), Arira (Igb), Imunu (Ijo), Sfamnun matzui (Isr), Namazu (J), Kemudu (Kan), Trey andaing afrik (Khm), Eyisombi (Kon), Pet cick (Nue), Ejengi (Nup), Mlamba (Nya), Ambaazaa (Oro), Stawada (Pl), Yuzhnoafrikanskaya zubatka (R), Cogo (Shi), Talage (Son), Abu shanab, garmut, kor (Sud), Kambale, mlamba (Swa), African catfish (UK), Barbel, catfish, sharptooth catfish (US), Bambara, toucouleurs, yess (Wol-S), Aro (Y)

Originally an African freshwater species, this catfish has been introduced through human intervention to almost all continents and is now found in Africa, Asia, as well as in Europe. An inhabitant of the Niger and Nile river systems, it has reached rivers in South Africa: the Okavango, the Limpopo, the Orange-Vaal and the Cunene. While it has been established in many waters, a negative ecological impact has been reported only from a couple of areas. This species can reach 1.5 m (59 in) body length, and 50–60 kg (110–132 lb) body mass. With the use of a supplementary organ it is able to breath atmospheric air and can thus survive critical periods of drought. An omnivorous species, it consumes both animal and plant matter: crayfish, insects, clams and mussels, fish, smaller birds, rotting meat, plants and fruit. Locally, it is of negligible importance to fisheries, but the North African catfish is bred in intense systems and fish ponds for its excellent flesh. It is eaten grilled, roasted or fried.

96 | Big-headed catfish, Broadhead catfish | *Clarias macrocephalus* | CLARIIDAE / CLARIDES

Big-headed catfish, Broadhead catfish (En), Großkopfwels (D) • Trey andaing toun (Khm), Pa douk (Lao), Keli (Mal), Freshwater catfish (Mal-En), Hito (Tag), Duk uey (Thai), Pla duk uey (Thai), Cá tre vrng (Vie), Alimudan (Vis)

A large-bodied Asian representative of the genus Clarias, the range of this species extends from Thailand to Vietnam, but it has also been established in China, Malaysia, the Philippines and Guam. It grows to 120 cm (47 in) in length and 12–13 kg (27–29 lb) in body mass. A freshwater species, it inhabits shallow waters and is able to withstand longer periods of drought by burying itself into the mud. By using its powerful fins it can even climb onto land and migrate to extant waters when necessary. It spawns in minor rivers. This catfish feeds on aquatic insects, young crustaceans and smaller fish, and is in higher esteem in Thailand and Laos than its relative, C. batrachus. In Thailand, the species is often incorrectly identified as the female of C. batrachus. Spawning occurs between May and October in Thailand. The big-headed catfish is marketed alive, freshly killed or frozen, and is prepared fried, roasted or grilled for human consumption. Presently farmed on a small scale in fish ponds, it is likely to become more popular in the future.

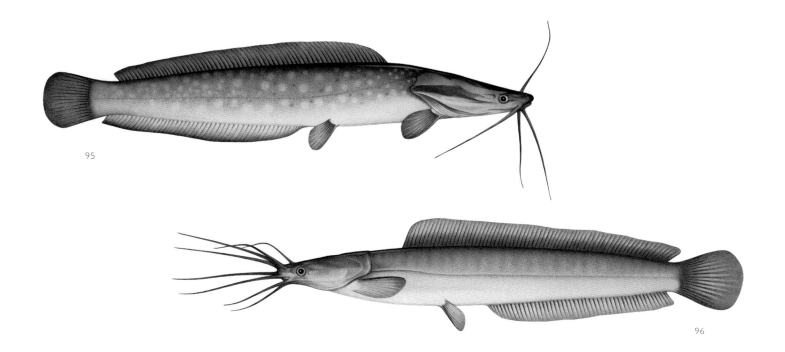

95

96

97 | Giant seacatfish | Arius thalassinus | ARIIDAE / SEA CATFISHES

Giant seacatfish (En), Bagre titán (E), Machoiron titan (F) • Giant salmon catfish (Au), Majung, duri padi (Ind), Manyung (Jav), Trey kaok (Khm), Barukang (Mak), Duri, gagok, goh, ikan duri, jahan (Mal), Marine catfish (Mal-En), Jam (Om), Bagre titánico (P), Kanduli, arahan (Phi), Kann (Q), Mudhu anguluva (Sin), Bacoore (Som), Fumi, hongwe (Swa), Mandai-kaliru, ven keluru (Tam), Pla kot thaleh (Thai), Buunuruu (Tok), Khagga, khangga (US), Cá út (V-Cam)

The foremost area of distribution of the giant seacatfish is the Red Sea and the northwestern part of the Indian Ocean. It has also been reported from the seas surrounding Polynesia, Australia and Japan. Other records have not been confirmed with certainty, as related, similarly looking species are often mistaken for giant seacatfish. It inhabits warm, (sub)tropical waters, also tolerating brackwater conditions, but only temporarily, if at all, can it be found in freshwater. A large-bodied catfish, it reaches 185 cm (73 in) maximum length, and approximately 60 kg (132 lb) maximum weight. Unique to this catfish, the eggs are carried in the mouth of the male, to which the fry retreat for some two months after hatching. When the little fish become independent the male starts to feed avidly, and, considering its own young potential to be prey, occasionally swallows them. A bottom-dwelling carnivore, it mainly consumes different crustaceans, but also fish and gastropods. It is considered an important food item in its area of distribution and is intensely fished. It reaches its consumers chiefly fresh, but is often preserved dried. It is popular both fried and poached.

98 | Northern pike | Esox lucius | ESOCIDAE / PIKES

Northern pike (En), Europäischer Hecht (D), Lucio (E), Brochet du nord (F), Luccio (I), Snoek (Nl) • Qalru (Alu), Tchinouchao, Cinosa (Cree), Štika obecná (Cze), Gedde (Da), Liús (Ga), Toúrna (Gr), Csuka (H), Sjulik, Siilik, Hiulik (Inu), Kawakamasu (J), Gjedde (N), Szczupak (Pl), Shchuka (R), Stiuca (Ru), Gädda (S), Hauki (SF), Scuka (Slo), Turna baligi (Tr)

Arguably the best-known member of the freshwater pike family, northern pike are infamously voracious predators, threatening even animals living near the river banks. It has been observed in many corners of the world that small ducks and even the young of various animals which have slipped into the water have fallen prey to northern pike. This "pike bite" is indeed a plight, at least the ambush of such a "live torpedo", reaching a body length of about 1.5 m (60 in), may well be fatal to littoral animals. The meat of the northern pike is extremely palatable and tender, and is very popular both fried in oil and breaded. Fillets of northern pike contain hardly any bones; portions of about 500 g (17.6 oz) (usually one side of the fish) are normally marketed as first class fresh fillets. In restaurants northern pike is usually served whole, since, remarkably, its huge mouth can hold some fruit – a tablefare especially appealing to the eye. Hungarian and Czech fisheries that have developed the controlled breeding and rearing of northern pike can barely meet the demands of European anglers' associations, since the rearing of the fry is a highly hazardous business due to the species' cannibalism.

97

98

99 | Muskellunge | Esox masquinongy | ESOCIDAE / PIKES

Muskellunge (En), Muskellunge, Amerikanischer Hecht (D), Maskinongé (F), Luccio nordamericano (I), Maskulonge (Nl) • Maskinonge, musky (En), Great pike, muskie, masquinonge (US)

One of the most widespread New World species of the pike family, muskellunge are also very much liked by anglers. Muskellunge are much more sensitive to environmental changes than the northern pike and this is the reason for their not having been stocked in large numbers anywhere but in North American waters, despite all efforts. Methods of controlled rearing of muskellunge were developed several decades ago, and stocks of the species are being bred to meet the demand of fishing associations and to re-stock lake fisheries. The main problem rests with the fish's fabled voraciousness, and so one of the most important technical stages in the rearing of muskellunge is regular selection by size. Muskellunge produce highly valuable meat, its price competing with that of the trout and walleye, and there is a constantly increasing demand for muskellunge in the market. Interestingly, the head of muskellunge is a veritable angler's trophy when prepared or a popular souvenir for tourists.

100 | Atlantic rainbow smelt | Osmerus mordax | OSMERIDAE / SMELTS AND EPERLANS

Atlantic rainbow smelt (En), Amerikanischer Stint, Regenbogen-Stint (D), Eperlano americano (E), Éperlan d'Amérique (F), Sperlano, eperlano (I), Amerikaanse spiering (Nl) • Amerikansk smelt (Da), Iquar-niq (Inu), Eperlano-arco-íris (P), Rainbow smelt (US)

A gradually depleting species of the commercially not very significant Osmeridae family, genus Clupeiformes, Atlantic rainbow smelt dwell in the waters of the Northern Hemisphere. The related species are distinguished by their meat having a particular scent, a fact that has caused local peoples of many regions to name the fish after their garden vegetables. Smelt are fairly small, and like the other salmoniform species, they migrate upstream along rivers to spawn. American rainbow smelt can be distinguished from the other related species by a row of dark adipose finlets along the straight side line. They do not grow bigger than 20 cm (8 in), the growth rate largely depending on the water temperature. This may be the reason for occurrences of specimens spawning at one year of age, whereas it is generally accepted by connoisseurs that they normally do so when they reach the age of 3–5 years. This debate is important also because research shows that at least two-thirds of the total spawning biomass do not survive the depositing of their roe. The meat of American rainbow smelt is not highly appreciated in the food market, it merely counting as cheap fish to fry. The fish is also used as a source of fish-oil and as additives to animal feed.

101 | **Danube salmon** | Hucho hucho | SALMONIDAE / SALMONID FISHES

Danube salmon (En), Huchen, Donaulachs (D), Salmón del Danubio (E), Saumon du Danube (F), Salmone del Danubio (I), Donauzalm (Nl) • Mladica (Cr), Hlavatka podunajská (Cze), Dunai galóca (H), Glowacica (Pl), Dunaiskii losos (R), Sulec (Slo)

The largest Salmoniform species dwelling in waters of central and western Europe, Danube salmon may attain body lengths of 1 m (40 in). However, it is mostly the artificially bred specimens of 30–40 cm (12–16 in) that are marketed as food. Danube salmon stocks have become so depleted that almost throughout the entire Old World they are officially considered an endangered species. As for their migratory habits, Danube salmon occupy a transitional position, since they do not like to wander too far from their permanent habitat, not even in the breeding season. They tend to avoid the sea utterly; it is only along the Bulgarian and Rumanian seashore that some small numbers of huchen have been reported. They produce a very small number of eggs, or roe, a mere 1,000–2,000 by the kilogram, a number that is further reduced by the degrading natural habitats of the fish. The species would have very narrow chances of survival were it not for systematic conservation, and breeding and rearing in controlled fisheries. Specimens of 5–10 years of age and of weights of a few kilograms are sold at an enormous price in the food market. This size provides us with huge fillets of about a pound, enabling cooks to prepare larger and more elaborate dishes instead of the usual one-portion delicacies.

102 | **Taimen** | Hucho taimen | SALMONIDAE / SALMONID FISHES

Taimen (En, D, E), Huchon (F), Taimen (Nl) • Taimen (R)

In recent years, in the heyday of Russian fishing tourism, the pike-like slender taimen have become increasingly popular. A freshwater member of the Salmoniform species, taimen are native to waters of the Upper Volga river and other streams of the sparsely inhabited Ural mountains. In these regions taimen are considered eminent predators, not only because of their respectable size of 1–1.5 m (40–100 in), but also because of the tactical strategies they apply when approaching their prey in large groups. Silvery-grey below, the back of taimen is greenish-grey with discreet patterning in order to blend more easily into the natural environment. In the spawning season, however, the dorsal part acquires a vivid colouring. Taimen inhabit most of their "territorial waters" and they are extremely voracious, not even water birds and smaller mammals entering the respective waters can escape from them. Smaller schools of non-aggressive fishes are usually attacked by taimen in a crescent-shaped "open formation", and they are even followed by their attackers in the air, if necessary. Fishermen can tell veritable legends about this fish, and of catches of voluminous specimens. The most usual fishing method is by artificial bait and spinning.

103 | Cutthroat trout (freshwater form) | Oncorhynchus clarki | SALMONIDAE / SALMONID FISHES

Cutthroat trout (freshwater form) (En), Cutthroatforelle (D), Trucha (E), Truite (F), Trota (I), Purperforel (Nl) • Talaa'ik (Alu), Rødstrubet ørred (Da), Masu (J), Klarka (R), Coastal cutthroat (US)

A member of the Salmonidae family, cutthroat trout dwell in the rivers flowing into the eastern regions of the Pacific Ocean, from Alaska to the Eel River in north California. They have been introduced to several streams and lakes in their native area, but also in the eastern region of North America. In some bodies of water they are extremely abundant, and they count as the most important sport fish, whereas in other regions the stock is relatively thin. The largest specimens may reach sizes of about 1 m (39 in) and 20 kg (44 lb). Specimens staying in freshwater are darker in colour: they are dark green or greenish-blue on the back, olive green on the sides and silvery below. A predator species, they feed on fish, insects and crustaceans in freshwater, whereas in the ocean their diet consists of fish, crustaceans and smaller molluscs. The spawning season is from December to May, being intensive only in spring. Before spawning the female fish builds a nest in the gravel bottom. A special trait of the species is that the sexually mature specimens may spawn several times a year, for the first time at the age of 3–4. After spawning, most of the specimens return to the sea, but some may stay for years in freshwater. The excellent meat of the cutthroat trout is of orange-red hue.

104 | Cutthroat trout (marine form) | Oncorhynchus clarki anadromous | SALMONIDAE/SALMONID FISHES

Cutthroat trout (marine form) (En), Cutthroatforelle (D), Trucha (E), Truite (F), Trota (I), Purperforel (Nl) • Talaa'ik (Alu), Rødstrubet ørred (Da), Masu (J), Klarka (R)

A member of the Salmonidae family, cutthroat trout dwell in the eastern regions of the Pacific Ocean, from Alaska to the Eel River in north California, in the sea near river estuaries, but they return to the upper flow of the rivers to spawn. The largest specimens may attain sizes of about 1 m (39 in) and 20 kg (44 lb). Specimens migrating to the ocean are silvery in colour, only toward the back turning slightly blue. In the sea they prefer river estuaries and coastal waters abundant in smaller fishes that serve as their food, alongside crustaceans. The spawning season is from December to May, being intensive only in the spring. A special trait of the species is that the sexually mature specimens may spawn several times a year, for the first time at the age of 3–4. In late spring, after spawning, most specimens return to the sea, but some may stay for years in freshwater. The excellent meat of the cutthroat trout is of orange-red hue. A very popular sportfish, its meat is marketed for food fresh, and is usually pan-fried, baked in the oven or roasted.

103

104

105 | Pink salmon (freshwater form) | Oncorhynchus gorbuscha | SALMONIDAE / SALMONID FISHES

Pink salmon (freshwater form) (En), Buckellachs (D), Salmón rosado (E), Saumon rose (F), Salmone rosa (I), Pink zalm, roze zalm (Nl) • Amarturpiaq (Alu), Pukkellaks (Da), Humpback salmon (En), Atakak (Inu), Bleiklax (Is), Sepparimasu (J), Pukkellaks (N), Salmão-rosa (P), Gorbusa (R), Kyttyrälohi (SF)

One of the most widely distributed species of the so-called Pacific salmon. It has an anadromous lifestyle (i.e. migrates from the sea to freshwater in the breeding season) in cold coastal waters of the Northern Hemisphere. Its best populations have been successfully preserved in Italy and Scandinavia. As can be seen in the accompanying pictures, freshwater and marine forms can be easily distinguished by external characteristics. In the freshwater form, a so-called salmon hook develops, as well as a huge bulge on the head. Pink salmons reach sexual maturity at 40–50 cm (16–20 in) length, and seldom surpass this size, since for unknown reasons most individuals die shortly after spawning in the upper reaches of rivers. Due to its special quality, salmon flesh is considered extremely valuable. Consumers most often come across it in smoked, thinly sliced fillet form, tinted pink. Its fishing is a traditional sport in North America and Norway, with a tourist industry in the main season.

106 | Pink salmon (marine form) | Oncorhynchus gorbuscha anadromous | SALMONIDAE / SALMONID FISHES

Pink salmon (marine form) (En), Buckellachs (D), Salmón rosado (E), Saumon rose (F), Salmone rosa (I), Pink zalm, roze zalm (Nl) • Amarturpiaq (Alu), Pukkellaks (Da), Humpback salmon (En), Atakak (Inu), Bleiklax (Is), Sepparimasu (J), Pukkellaks (N), Salmão-rosa (P), Gorbusa (R), Kyttyrälohi (SF)

The marine form of pink salmon can most often be encountered in waters close to continental shelves in the Northern Hemisphere. It appears en masse in spring, when the new generations reach the estuaries in large schools. This is the most dangerous period in their lives, since besides having to adapt to marine conditions they also have to face numerous predators. The coloration of the marine type is entirely different from that of the "pinkish" freshwater form, being vaguely marked with red on a bluish-silvery ground. As its scales are extremely small, sometimes a very sophisticated pattern of dark dots or blotches develops on the back. A fast growing species, it usually attains sexual maturity by three years of age, and then starts returning to its "place of birth". There are attempts to raise its fry in sea water in various countries. Keeping it in huge, drifting cages is expensive, but the market price of the flesh is so high that all investments are soon reimbursed. Gourmets vote for the marine form, and specimens caught in the sea are held in high esteem.

105

106

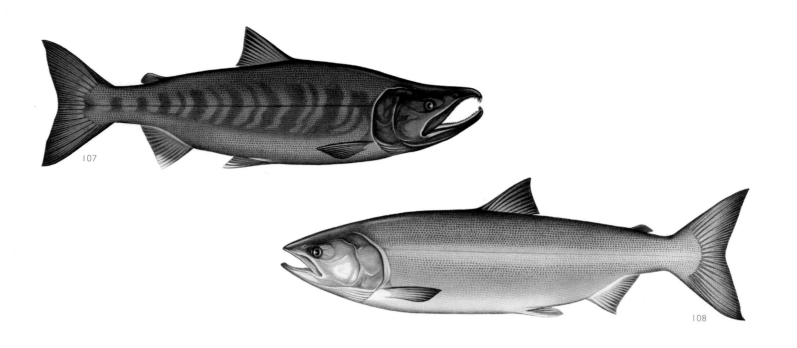

107 | **Chum salmon (freshwater form)** | Oncorhynchus keta | SALMONIDAE / SALMONID FISHES

Chum salmon (freshwater form) (En), Keta-Lachs, Hundslachs (D), Keta (E), Saumon chum, saumon keta (F), Salmone keta (I), Chum zalm, hondszalm (Nl) • Kangitneq (Alu), Keta (Can, Pl, R, S), Hundelaks (Da), Dog salmon, keta salmon (En), Ikalugruak (Inu), Sake (J), Salmão-cão (P), Keta (R), Hundlax (S)

One of the biggest species of salmon, reaching 5–10 kg (10–20 lb) body mass. This relatively large weight arises not only from a 50–100 cm (20–40 in) mean length, but also from a stubbier build, and heavier trunk musculature. The advantages of this anatomical characteristic are most obvious during the long migration in the spawning season. In addition, it is highly valued by the processing industry, as it provides more flesh for fillets. Males grow larger than females, their back turns characteristically olive, and reddish stripes develop on their sides. The chum salmon occurs in most cold water rivers flowing into the sea in the Northern Hemisphere, but is more numerous in the Far East. The female drops its 5,000–20,000 eggs into depressions with a hard bottom, and due to the low water temperatures it can take as long as 100–200 days until they hatch. The larvae slowly drift along with the current, but usually enter the sea in schools only at one year of age. This is the time when the fry are collected for captive propagation.

108 | **Chum salmon (marine form)** | Oncorhynchus keta anadromous | SALMONIDAE / SALMONID FISHES

Chum salmon (marine form) (En), Keta-Lachs, Hundslachs (D), Keta (E), Saumon chum, saumon keta (F), Salmone keta (I), Chum zalm, hondszalm (Nl) • Kangitneq (Alu), Keta (Can, Pl, R, S), Hundelaks (Da), Dog salmon, keta salmon (En), Ikalugruak (Inu), Sake (J), Keta (R), Hundlax (S)

The chum salmon is another anadromous carnivore, i.e. one that migrates from the sea into rivers. The largest numbers are found in the sea, and more and more populations are being forced to stay longer in sea water due to artificial barriers. Perhaps this is the reason for anglers more frequently catching huge, over 1 m (40 in) long specimens. The marine form is much less colourful than the one inhabiting freshwater, with a greyish-silvery, or greenish tinge, depending on the site where it is found during its migration, which often encompasses several thousand kilometres. Research has revealed that specimens of a given population do not usually mix with members of others, as can frequently be observed with other migratory sea fish. The majority of northern fishing nations are attempting to convert the chum salmon into a permanent, basic species in marine aquaculture. Hence they invest capital in developing breeding protocols for this popular fish.

109 | **Silver salmon, Coho salmon (freshwater form)** | Oncorhynchus kisutch | SALMONIDAE / SALMONID FISHES

Silver salmon, Coho salmon (freshwater form) (En), Silberlachs, Coho-Lachs (D), Salmón plateado (E), Saumon argenté (F), Salmone argentato (I), Zilverzalm, cohozalm (Nl) • Caayuaq (Alu), Sølvlaks (Da), Silver salmon (En), Ginzake (J), Kizjuts (R), Silverlax (S)

The marine form is named after its numerous small, silvery scales, but the type migrating in freshwater manifests itself in diverse breeding colours. As it fights its way through rapids towards the upper reaches of rivers its appearance gradually changes. Nuptial teeth develop, i.e. the maxilla and the mandible lengthen, and their tips typically turn inwards. This change in the shape of the jaws is thought to prevent the 60–80 cm (24–31 in) long males weighing several kilograms from hurting each other or the females during mating. This assumption is further substantiated by the fact that the mouth regains its shape in specimens that have survived spawning. As they can return to their carnivorous diet only after this change takes place, the alteration is not simply a question of form. The adaptability of the silver salmon is also shown by the fact that when animal prey is scarce, it can feed on other organic matter as well.

110 | **Silver salmon, Coho salmon (marine form)** | Oncorhynchus kisutch anadromous | SALMONIDAE / SALMONID FISHES

Silver salmon, Coho salmon (marine form) (En), Silberlachs, Coho-Lachs (D), Salmón plateado (E), Saumon argenté (F), Salmone argentato (I), Zilverzalm, cohozalm (Nl) • Caayuaq (Alu), Sølvlaks (Da), Silver salmon (En), Ginzake (J), Kizjuts (R), Silverlax (S)

This is a carnivorous species growing to 50–70 cm (20–28 in) in length, and migrating in schools consisting of several thousand individuals in the cold northern seas. It swims with the current and feeds on small, plankton-eating fish on its way, attacking and swallowing its prey in groups. Besides some obvious advantages, its gregarious hunting habits are at the same time disadvantageous, since the huge silvery mass can easily be detected by fish radar, and followed by satellite tracking systems used by rich fishing nations. There is enormous competition between modern fleets fishing in international waters to snatch a large school of this species, which is much sought after on markets. Thus, it is no coincidence that populations of all Oncorhynchus species have seriously declined over the past few decades, which tendency people are attempting to compensate mainly by raising fry and restocking. Farms also produce hybrids with other, related species, thus contributing to the loss of genetic diversity in salmonids, and to conservation problems associated with this process.

111 | Cherry salmon (freshwater form) | Oncorhynchus masou | SALMONIDAE / SALMONID FISHES

Cherry salmon (freshwater form) (En), Masu-Lachs (D), Salmón japonés, salmón cherry (E), Saumon japonais, saumon masou (F), Salmone giapponese (I), Masouzalm, Japanse zalm (Nl) • Masu salmon (En), Sakuramasu, honmasu (J), Sima (R)

This Salmoniform species dwells in the northwestern part of the Pacific Ocean and in the rivers flowing into the sea along this coast, as well as in the Sea of Okhotsk, in the Sea of Japan, and in the eastern part of the Korean peninsula. In Japan there are several landlocked stocks of the species, the colour of each being different according to its habitat. They may attain sizes of about 60–70 cm (24–28 in) and 10 kg (22 lb), with the strictly freshwater specimens hardly ever exceeding 30–40 cm (12–16 in) in length. Two forms of the species are known: the freshwater form is abundant at the head spring of rivers, and very often they display territorial behaviour. They feed on insects, crustaceans and small fish. They spawn from August to October, over the gravel bottom of the upper flow of rivers. After spawning most specimens die. Cherry salmon are very popular among fly fishermen. The excellent meat of the cherry salmon is marketed for food fresh and frozen, and is usually pan-fried, roasted, or fried in the oven. Eastern cuisine also has recipes involving simmering the meat with spices or frying the meat in oil after dipping it into batter. Sometimes they are eaten smoked.

112 | Cherry salmon (marine form) | Oncorhynchus masou anadromous | SALMONIDAE / SALMONID FISHES

Cherry salmon (marine form) (En), Masu-Lachs (D), Salmón japonés, salmón cherry (E), Saumon japonais, saumon masou (F), Salmone giapponese (I), Masouzalm, Japanse zalm (Nl) • Masu salmon (En), Sakuramasu, honmasu (J), Sima (R)

This Salmoniform species dwells in the northwestern part of the Pacific Ocean and in the rivers flowing into the sea along this coast, as well as in the Sea of Okhotsk, in the Sea of Japan, and in the eastern part of the Korean peninsula. Marine cherry salmon very often attain sizes of about 60 cm (24 in) and 10 kg (22 lb). The catadromous specimens form large schools as they migrate downstream, and when getting into the brackish waters of the estuaries they stay there for a while to get used to the climate before entering the sea. About their migration in the ocean, information is still scarce. In the sea they feed on small fish and crustaceans dwelling in midwater, and small molluscs. After spending several years in the ocean, the marine species also travels to the head-springs of rivers to spawn. Spawning migration and spawning lasts from August to October. After spawning most specimens die. Both freshwater and marine form are popular sport fishes. The excellent meat of the cherry salmon is marketed for food fresh and frozen, and is usually pan-fried breaded or coated in batter, or even without any coating. In some regions the meat is roasted, or fried, baked in the oven or eaten smoked.

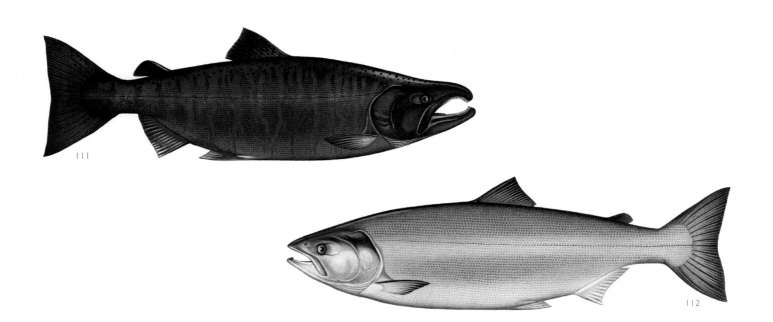

113 | Rainbow trout (freshwater form) | Oncorhynchus mykiss | SALMONIDAE / SALMONID FISHES

Rainbow trout (freshwater form) (En), Regenbogenforelle (D), Trucha arco iris (E), Truite arc-en-ciel (F), Trota iridea (I), Regenboogforel (Nl) • Mayu'artaq (Alu), Pstruh duhový (Cze), Stålhovedørred (Da), Szivárványos pisztráng (H), Regnbogasilungur (Is), Nijimasu (J), Regnbueørret (N), Truta-arco-iris (P), Pstrag teczowy (Pl), Raduznuju forel (R), Pastrav curcubeu (Ru), Alabalik türü (Tr)

The freshwater variant of rainbow trout acquired its name in most languages after its brightly coloured body. Besides having the colours of the rainbow, rainbow trout also sport several small spots that look like perfect circles from a distance. Spots may often occur on the small adipose (fatty) fin situated between the dorsal fin and the tail. Specimens thus decorated for the breeding season can be seen wandering upstream in search of spawning grounds, especially in those few rivers flowing into northern seas where man has not yet upset the eco-balance. Rainbow trout often travel hundreds of miles before depositing a couple of thousand of their roe, which hatch after an incubation period as long as 3–5 months. The majority of rainbow trout populations, however, face a less adventurous fate – man has introduced the species to all continents, thus they are bred and reared in commercial fisheries. Estimates show that rainbow trout and its hybrid variants constitute nearly half of the marketed trout stock, specimens of around 250–300 g (9–10.5 oz) being sold as food fish. Highly praised for its flavour, the meat of rainbow trout is especially suitable for frying.

114 | Rainbow trout (marine form) | Oncorhynchus mykiss anadromous | SALMONIDAE / SALMONID FISHES

Rainbow trout (marine form) (En), Regenbogenforelle (D), Trucha arco iris (E), Truite arc-en-ciel (F), Trota iridea (I), Regenboogforel (Nl) • Mayu'artaq (Alu), Pstruh duhový (Cze), Stålhovedørred (Da), Steelhead (En), Regnbogasilungur (Is), Nijimasu (J), Regnbueørret (N), Truta-arco-iris (P), Pstrag teczowy (Pl), Raduznuju forel (R), Pastrav curcubeu (Ru), Alabalik türü (Tr)

Native to the northern shores of the Pacific, the marine form of rainbow trout, also called steelhead, chiefly dwells in waters of temperatures around 10°C (50°F). Occasionally they migrate in large schools along ocean currents to deeper seas, but they usually stay near the coast, in the vicinity of river estuaries. In contrast to the freshwater rainbow trout, steelhead are much less colourful, adapting perfectly to their environment; almost totally silvery-grey variants have been reported. A voracious predator of about 40–60 cm (16–24 in), the steelhead attacks nearly all animals that are smaller than itself, and larger wounded animals unable to defend themselves are attacked and devoured by entire groups of steelhead. More and more countries are engaged in rearing steelhead in huge cages suspended in the open sea, where they are fed from a young age with fishmeal processed in factories. Specimens of 25–40 cm (10–16 in) thus raised are much sought after by shopkeepers, since customers prefer the species to the freshwater variant because of the characteristically salty flavour of their meat.

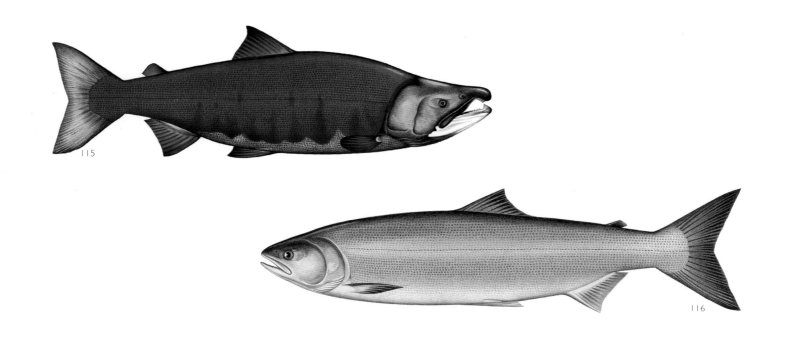

115 | **Sockeye salmon, Red salmon (freshwater form)** | Oncorhynchus nerka | SALMONIDAE / SALMONID FISHES

Sockeye salmon, Red salmon (freshwater form) (En), Rotlachs, Blaurücken (D), Salmón rojo, salmón sockeye (E), Saumon rouge, saumon sockeye (F), Salmone rosso (I), Rode zalm (Nl) • Niklliq (Alu), Rødlaks (Da), Red salmon (En), Kokkinos solomos (Gr), Sgwaagaan (Hai), Rauolax (Is), Benizake (J), Indian-laks (N), Salmao-vermelho-do-Pacífico (P), Krasnaja nerka (R), Indianlax (S), Schaanexw (Saa), Intiaanilohi (SF), Kokanee (US)

The marine type known as "blue-back" is locally named "rosy salmon" after its breeding colours. Somewhat different from other anadromous salmonids, this species migrates for spawning to lakes at the upper reaches of rivers, or at least to inlets with a slow current. It spawns group-wise in these calm waters rich in oxygen, several males courting a single female. As a result, there are populations permanently inhabiting freshwater on both the American and the Siberian sides of the Pacific. Due to its higher adaptability, its fry can easily be raised on farms, both in marine and freshwater aquacultures. It is also restocked for the sake of anglers, not only in the Northern, but also in the Southern Hemisphere, in economically developed but environmentally "healthy" countries.

116 | **Sockeye salmon, Red salmon (marine form)** | Oncorhynchus nerka anadromus | SALMONIDAE / SALMONID FISHES

Sockeye salmon, Red salmon (marine form) (En), Rotlachs, Blaurücken (D), Salmón rojo, salmón sockeye (E), Saumon rouge, saumon sockeye (F), Salmone rosso (I), Rode zalm (Nl) • Niklliq (Alu), Rødlaks (Da), Red salmon (En), Kokkinos solomos (Gr), Sgwaagaan (Hai), Rauolax (Is), Benizake (J), Indian-laks (N), Salmao-vermelho-do-Pacífico (P), Krasnaja nerka (R), Indianlax (S), Schaanexw (Saa), Intiaanilohi (SF), Kokanee (US)

The marine form of the red salmon reaching 50–60 cm (20–24 in) length and 1–3 kg (2–6 lb) weight on average is known as "blue-back" to some fishermen, as if it were a different species when held in the hand. The marine type is a schooling carnivore which grabs small sea creatures and little schooling fish with its densely arranged, pointed teeth. Secondary teeth are located on the palate, and even at the base of the tongue. No wonder that once prey is ingested, its chances of escaping are minimal. A widely distributed species in coastal regions in the entire Northern Hemisphere, the red salmon is of high economic significance on the Russian and Alaskan sides of the Pacific. The largest salmon industries are located in this area, the products of which traditionally find their way to American, Japanese and Korean markets. Smoked red salmon fillet is on sale in virtually all major food markets.

117 | **Chinook salmon (freshwater form)** | Oncorhynchus tschawytscha | SALMONIDAE / SALMONID FISHES

Chinook salmon (freshwater form) (En), Königslachs (D), Salmón real (E), Saumon royale (F), Salmone reale (I), Chinook zalm, koningszalm (Nl) • Iqallugpak (Alu), Spring salmon (Can), Taagun gaaw gaada (Hai), Tarjaxfaq (Inu), Masunosuke (J), Salmao-real (P), Tjavytja (R), Kungslax (S), Sk'wel'eng's schaanexw (Saa), Kuningaslohi (SF), Yee (Tsi), King salmon, king (US)

A large-bodied Salmoniform species, Chinook salmon dwell in the northern region of the Pacific Ocean and in the Arctic Sea, in rivers flowing into the Ocean from Alaska to the Ventura river in California, and on Honshu Island in Japan, and also in the Bering Sea. They may attain body lengths of 160 cm (63 in) and weights of 60 kg (132 lb), with the freshwater forms being considerably smaller. The sexually mature specimens return to the same river where they hatched. The spawning season lasts from July to September. Some of the offspring spend about three months in the freshwater before returning to the sea, whereas some spend as long as three years in freshwater. Chinook salmon are also found in freshwater lakes, the stock never migrating to the sea. They mainly feed on land insects and small crustaceans. A highly valued sport fish, the meat of the chinook salmon is generally reddish, but occasionally it may be white, the red flesh commanding higher prices. The interior organs are said to be very rich in vitamins. The meat of the fish is marketed for food fresh, smoked, frozen and canned. It is usually prepared simmered, boiled, or fried in oil, baked in the oven, or roasted.

118 | **Chinook salmon (marine form)** | Oncorhynchus tschawytscha anadromous | SALMONIDAE / SALMONID FISHES

Chinook salmon (marine form) (En), Königslachs (D), Salmón real (E), Saumon royale (F), Salmone reale (I), Chinook zalm, koningszalm (Nl) • Iqallugpak (Alu), Spring salmon (Can), Taagun gaaw gaada (Hai), Tarjaxfaq (Inu), Masunosuke (J), Salmao-real (P), Tjavytja (R), Kungslax (S), Sk'wel'eng's schaanexw (Saa), Kuningaslohi (SF), Yee (Tsi), King salmon, king (US)

A large-bodied Salmoniform species, Chinook salmon dwell in the northern region of the Pacific Ocean and in the Arctic Sea, and also occur in the Sea of Japan and the Bering Sea. They spawn in the region extending from Alaska to the Ventura river in California, and in rivers on Honshu Island of Japan. They may attain body lengths of 160 cm (63 in) and weights of 60 kg (130 lb). The sexually mature specimens return to the same river where they hatched. The spawning season lasts from July to September. Some of the offspring spend roughly about three months in the freshwater before returning to the sea, whereas some would spend even three years in freshwater. The majority of the anadromous stock normally spend one year in freshwater before returning to the sea. Some of the marine stock stay near the coastline throughout their entire life, whereas others travel long distances. They may go as deep as 300–350 m (980–1150 ft). They feed on fish, crustaceans and other invertebrates dwelling in midwater. A very highly appreciated sportfish, the meat of marine chinook salmon is usually red, but occasionally it may be white, the former being more expensive on the market. The interior organs are said to be very rich in vitamins. The meat of the fish is usually prepared simmered, boiled, or fried in oil, baked in the oven, or roasted.

119 | Atlantic salmon (freshwater form) | Salmo salar | SALMONIDAE / SALMONID FISHES

Atlantic salmon (freshwater form) (En), Atlantischer Lachs (D), Salmón del Atlántico (E), Saumon atlantique (F), Salmone atlantico (I), Zalm (Nl) • Losos atlantsky (Cze), Atlantisk laks (Da), Bradán (Ga), Solomos (Gr), Kapisilik (Inu), Lax (Is, S), Sake masu-rui (J), Braddan (Manx), Laks (N), Salmão do Atlântico (P), Losoś (Pl), Losos (R), Lohi (SF), Alabalik atlantik (Tr)

One of the most widely distributed species of cooler rivers of the Northern Hemisphere, Atlantic salmon average about 50–70 cm (20–27.5 in) in body length. The freshwater variant is distinguished from the marine form by its reddish-yellow body colour and its hooked jaw. It is chiefly during migration to spawning grounds that they fall prey to humans and other animals. One only has to recall vivid scenes from documentaries, where bears are delightfully feasting on salmon wriggling in despair on rocky riverbanks near some waterfall. In this stage of their life, the meat of salmon also undergoes considerable changes in terms of quality. The muscular tissue is richly lined with fat, since only specimens thus "upgraded" are fit enough to make the long journey to the spawning grounds. Animal fat is still considered the most widely used substance among northern peoples; thus no wonder that Atlantic salmon has always been enormously highly prized.

120 | Atlantic salmon (marine form) | Salmo salar anadromous | SALMONIDAE / SALMONID FISHES

Atlantic salmon (marine form) (En), Atlantischer Lachs (D), Salmón del Atlántico (E), Saumon atlantique (F), Salmone atlantico (I), Zalm (Nl) • Losos atlantsky (Cze), Atlantisk laks (Da), Bradán (Ga), Solomos (Gr), Kapisilik (Inu), Lax (Is, S), Sake masu-rui (J), Braddan (Manx), Laks (N), Salmão do Atlântico (P), Losoś (Pl), Losos (R), Lohi (SF), Alabalik atlantik (Tr)

The entire species Salmo salar was named after this marine form. For several centuries Atlantic salmon have been a staple diet among peoples in northwestern Europe. Atlantic salmon normally prey for food in schools fairly close to the coastline, thus they can be equally landed by boat seines, by lining, or, in shallow waters, by trapping. Adult specimens 50–100 cm (20–40 in) long are still highly valued in the market. In former times salmon were chiefly salted, dried or smoked. Thus preserved they were an important item in the stores taken on long sea voyages. Nowadays they are mostly marketed deep-frozen whole or pre-prepared for kitchen use, a method which makes salmon easier to handle and an attractive ingredient of various delicious dishes. A totally silvery-grey fish while in sea water, Atlantic salmon gradually turn bright red when the spawning season comes. The lower jaw protrudes and hooks upward. Thus embellished in red-hued lustrous skin and with the characteristic hooked jaw, Atlantic salmon start off to the river mouths. Disturbing such a wooing gallant being an indecent gesture, fishing for salmon in the breeding season is strictly forbidden in most countries.

119

120

121 | Brown trout | Salmo trutta | SALMONIDAE / SALMONID FISHES

Brown trout (En), Bachforelle (D), Trucha común (E), Truite de rivière (F), Trota, fario (I), Beekforel, rivierforel (Nl) • Trofte mali (Alb), Potočna pastrmka (Cr), Pstruhv potoční (Cze), Bakørred (Da), Sebes pisztráng (H), Bekkaure (N), Truta-comum (P), Pstrag potokowy (Pl), Rutschjevnaja forel (R), Păstrăv (Ru), Bäcköring (S), Puro taimen (SF)

The brown trout, which includes several varieties, is native to the waters of Europe and Asia Minor. In many languages called "common" trout for being the most well-known of trout, brown trout are of relatively small build, average about 20–50 cm (8–20 in) in length, and due to their formidable adaptability, they have been able to survive the environmental changes caused by industrial development and constant environmental degradation. Brown trout also have an immense adaptability in terms of temperature, thus they can thrive in the very warm (15–20°C / 59–68°F) waters of rivers among foothills some hundred metres high in the Mediterranean region. The diet of brown trout is similarly flexible, therefore they can easily be converted from predatory habits to feeding on offal from butcheries or even fish feed. Clearly then, brown trout are a favoured species of modernising commercial fisheries. The English, the French and the Spanish bred and reared them in many of their colonies, on fisheries in mountainous regions. True, brown trout do not produce the most rewarding growth rate. Yet as a species adapted to withstand environmental changes, they have become the most widely distributed freshwater food fish in developing countries.

122 | Sea trout | Salmo trutta anadromous | SALMONIDAE / SALMONID FISHES

Sea trout (En), Meerforelle (D), Trucha marina (E), Truite de mer (F), Salmotrota, trota di mare (I), Zeeforel (Nl) • Havørred (Da), Sjourrioi (Is), Ørret (N), Truta marisca (P), Troć (Pl), Losos taimen (R), Öring (S), Meritaimen (SF)

As the most common of the trout family in European marginal seas of the Atlantic, sea trout were the first species to be confined to highland lake fisheries in the 19th century. Experimenting with the rearing of sea trout in barricaded coastal waters, concrete pools and cages suspended in the open sea led to the wide distribution of trout even in Africa, Asia and South America, especially in the period of colonisation. However, in these areas the species was unable to adapt to coastal waters and the transplanted stock diminished, either because the fish, formerly migratory in habit, died out, or they chose to migrate to the rivers where they could find more suitable waters. Attaining sizes of merely 30–50 cm (12–20 in) and 0.5–1 kg (1–2 lb), "true" marine sea trout can be found in greater numbers around the British Isles, the Scandinavian coastline, in the Baltic Sea and the Arctic Ocean. Gourmets at once recognise the particular taste of specimens reared in sea waters or landed by fishing boats from sea-dwelling stock. Populations of sea trout which still undertake migration to rivers are protected by very strict time and area closures in northern countries. Due to such regulations and to the regular allocation of their fry to river estuaries, a stable sea trout biomass has been rebuilt in Scandinavian waters.

121

122

123 | **Arctic char (freshwater form)** | Salvelinus alpinus | SALMONIDAE / SALMONID FISHES

Arctic char (freshwater form) (En), Seesaibling (D), Trucha alpina (E), Omble-chevalier (F), Salmerino alpino (I), Riddervis, beekridder (Nl) • Wandersaibling (CH), Jezerska zlatovčica (Cr), Awanans (Cree), Fjeldørred (Da), Mountain trout, char (En), Akalukpik (Inu), Bleika (Is), Iwana (J), Arktisk røye (N), Salvelino-árctico (P), Golec zwyczajny (Pl), Arktitjeskij golets (R), Pastrav alpin (Ru), Fjällöding (S), Nieriä (SF)

Having been introduced to nearly all regions of the world, freshwater Arctic char are perhaps the least abundant in their native Alpine water systems. Averaging 30–60 cm (12–24 in) in length, the several sub-species of Arctic char are difficult to classify. There is similar confusion stemming from their anatomy and biological features. Populations confined to various cool-water ponds, lakes and rivers have the most diverse diet: they may feed on microscopic plankton, may be omnivorous, but one may even find predator species among them. Very few populations maintain an anadromous existence, i.e. are apt or willing to undertake migration to sea waters. This great variety and adaptability might have greatly contributed to the fact that in many areas Arctic char are cultivated in fisheries under controlled conditions, despite the fact that their growth rate is considerably inferior to that of any other species of the Salmonidae family. Very small variants of the species are normally released into smaller waters to the great delight of anglers, and they are often used in park ponds. Specimens served in restaurants weigh 300–400 g (10.5–14 oz). When properly fried, the bones of the fish cause no harm.

124 | **Arctic char (marine form)** | Salvelinus alpinus anadromous | SALMONIDAE / SALMONID FISHES

Arctic char (marine form) (En), Seesaibling (D), Trucha alpina (E), Omble-chevalier (F), Salmerino arctico (I), Riddervis, beekridder (Nl) • Jezerska zlatovčica (Cr), Awanans (Cree), Mountain trout, char (En), Aupalijaat (Inu), Bleika (Is), Iwana (J), Arktitjeskij golets (R), Fjällöding (S), Nieriä (SF)

One of those species that still puzzle scientists trying to establish a clear-cut order among the various species of fishes, the marine form of the Arctic char was first observed in the Alps, and it was only much later that the connection with populations wandering in Scandinavian and Russian seas was established. Strangely enough, they are the least distributed in alpine regions, with much larger truly anadromous populations dwelling in the North Atlantic covering areas extending as far as the coasts of Iceland. As is usual with marine forms of fishes in general, marine Arctic char are rather silvery in colour, and due to their habit of following the vast amount of suitable food drifted by ocean currents, their growth rate is also faster than that of the freshwater variant. Marine Arctic char attain body lengths of 50–60 cm (20–24 in), and are predator fishes, except for populations of coastal (littoral) habitats and brackish (semi-saline) waters of river mouths. Being very voracious fish, they are easy to catch, either by live bait or artificial lure. The strong fish hauled into the boat should be handled with care, for their strong teeth and spiny gill-cover can be dangerous. Normally light-coloured while in sea-water, the pelvic fin gradually acquires a reddish hue, signalling the approach of the spawning season, when the sexually mature specimens head for the rivers.

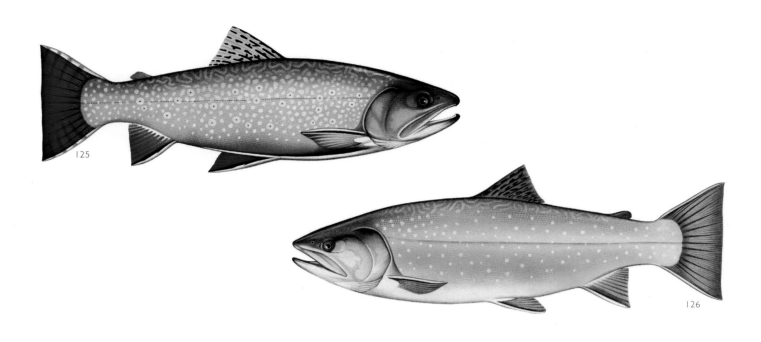

125

126

125 | Brook trout (freshwater form) | Salvelinus fontinalis | SALMONIDAE / SALMONID FISHES

Brook trout (freshwater form) (En), Bachsaibling (D), Salvelino, trucha de fontana (E), Saumon de fontaine (F), Salmerino di fontana (I), Bronforel (Nl) • Giigaq (Alu), Potočna zlatovčica (Cr), Masamekos (Cree), Siven americky (Cze), Pataki szajblin (H), Anokik (Inu), Kawamasu (J), Bekkerøye (N), Truta-das-fontes (P), Amerikanskij goletz (R), Bäckröding (S), Puronieriä (SF)

One of the most widespread members of the genus Salvelinus, freshwater brook trout are native to the mountainous regions of eastern North America and to the colder rivers flowing into the Atlantic Ocean. Specimens attain body lengths of 30–50 cm (12–20 in) and weights of 1–2 kg (2.2–4.4 lb), and are widely favoured for the table. Freshwater brook trout are distinguished from their close relatives by the colour of their double fins and their anal fin, which may be white through or white-rimmed. White specimens speckled with light spots have also been frequently reported. In many languages called "brook" because of their habit of migrating up rivers all the way to the headwaters, brook trout can deposit their eggs or roe even in swift waters only few inches deep. They dig small nests into the gravel river bed and place their roe in packs of hundreds of eggs. Due to their remarkable adaptability, brook trout tolerate man-made environments well, thus they have been introduced to most continents. They can easily be made to abandon their anadromous migrating habit, with many populations restricted to freshwater habitats occurring in several countries. Brook trout appeared in Europe some time in the 19th century, especially in the clear waters of streams at higher altitudes in mountainous regions.

126 | Brook trout (marine form) | Salvelinus fontinalis anadromous | SALMONIDAE / SALMONID FISHES

Brook trout (marine form) (En), Bachsaibling (D), Salvelino, trucha de fontana (E), Saumon de fontaine (F), Salmerino di fontana (I), Bronforel (Nl) • Giigaq (Alu), Masamekos (Cree), Anokik (Inu), Kawamasu (J), Bekkerøye (N), Amerikanskij goletz (R), Bäckröding (S)

In the beginning observed only in Atlantic coastal waters of the United States and Canada, the marine form of brook trout have since occurred in several harbours and bays of the Atlantic. Marine stock of this anadromous species have been depleted dramatically, the main reason being the fact that the polluted estuaries of feeding rivers are becoming increasingly difficult for the fish to ascend, and the way back is also dangerous. Since artificial fertilisation of eggs of marine brook trout has been known for nearly a century, stocks of young trout called "fingerlings" are often released into continental shelf waters. A veritable predator, marine brook trout hunt in schools for smaller fish and other animals of acroplanktonic habit. They easily adapt to being reared in cages suspended in the open sea and can be quickly taught to accept fish food from automatic feeders. The commercial food market is also primarily supplied by fish farms, a fact which by no means devalues the tasty meat of the fish coming from marine stock.

127 | Whitespotted char | Salvelinus leucomaenis | SALMONIDAE / SALMONID FISHES

Whitespotted char (En), Fernöstlicher Saibling (D) • Japansk fjeldørred (Da), Japanese char (En), Amemasu (J), Kundzja (R), Kundsharöding (S), East Asian char (US)

A species related to the trout family, whitespotted char inhabit the northwestern parts of the Pacific Ocean, from Hokkaido Island of Japan to the northeastern part of the Korean peninsula, on Sakhalin Island, the Kuril Islands, as far as the Khamchatka peninsula. Several variants of the species are known in Japan, some of these being of landlocked stock. They may attain sizes of 70 cm (28 in) and 1.7–1.8 kg (3.7–4 lb), with the specimens of the landlocked freshwater stock being much smaller, rarely exceeding body lengths of 30–40 cm (12–16 in). After hatching, the specimens migrate to the sea at the age of two, to return only at the age of four to spawn on the upper stretch of the very same river. Freshwater stock prefer water temperatures below 15°C (59°F). A predator species, the young char feed on insects and zooplankton, while larger specimens also eat fish. They spawn in October, after which the majority of the specimens die. A popular sport fish, whitespotted char are commercially not very significant. Marketed for food fresh, smoked and frozen, the meat of the fish is usually roasted, pan-fried or baked in the oven. When simmered in gravy, it is usually served with flavoursome sauces of ginger or soy.

128 | Dolly Varden trout | Salvelinus malma | SALMONIDAE / SALMONID FISHES

Dolly Varden trout (En), Pazifischer Saibling (D), Salvelino (E), Omble malma, omble du Pacifique (F), Salmerino (I), Malmaforel (Nl) • Giigaq (Alu), Malmaørred (Da), Oshorokoma (J), Salvelino-do-Pacífico (P), Malma (R), Härkänieriä (SF)

Related to the trout family, Dolly Varden dwell in the northwestern parts of the North American continent, in the rivers coastal seas from Alaska to Puget Sound in Washington state. Earlier they were also found in the catchment area of McCloud River in California. They are abundant in the rivers flowing into the northeastern Pacific Ocean, from Korea to the Bering Sea. A usually anadromous species, Dolly Varden may also occur in several landlocked stocks. A large-bodied species, they may attain sizes of about 120–130 cm (47–51 in) and 17–18 kg (37–40 lb). In freshwater they prefer clean, deeper waters of rivers and streams, but may also occur in lakes. After hatching, even the anadromous fish spend 3–4 years in freshwater. In the sea the fish live 2–3 years in the coastal waters. A predator, it feeds on insects, fish and smaller invertebrates, but they also like the roe of salmon. Spawning migration and spawning lasts from September to November in the gravel-bottomed upper flow of rivers. The roe are deposited into nests burrowed by the female fish, and after fertilization they are covered by gravel. Several nests are made in this fashion during one spawning season. Dolly Varden are very popular with both commercial and recreational fishermen. The fish is marketed fresh, and is usually pan-fried, roasted or baked.

127

128

129 | **Lake trout** | Salvelinus namaycush | SALMONIDAE / SALMONID FISHES

Lake trout (En), Amerikanischer Seesaibling (D), Trucha lacustre (E), Omble d'Amérique, truite de lac d'Amérique (F), Trota (salmerino) di lago (I), Amerikaanse meerforel (Nl) • Amerikanische Seeforelle (CH), Namekus (Cree), Canada-rødding (Da), Great Lakes trout, namaycush, salmon trout (En), Col-lic-puk (Inu), Murta (Is), Canadaröye (N), Salvelino-lacustre (P), Canadaröding (S), K'wit'thet (Saa)

Native to northeastern American waters, lake trout or salmon trout were of high commercial value in the Great Lakes until they became nearly extinct in the 1930s. However, lake trout populations were transplanted into waters of Britain and of several other European and Asian countries. They attain body lengths of 50–80 cm (20–32 in) and weights of 5–10 kg (11–22 lb), and in contrast to most related species, lake trout primarily inhabit cold still waters. Dwelling in a relatively calmer habitat, lake trout are stockier, broader and somewhat shorter than their relatives. One of the smallest-scaled of freshwater fish, they display delicately minute patterns on the body, impressing the beholder with their characteristically mottled patterning. Development of the fish in natural waters tends to be extremely slow (mainly because of the low temperature). Larvae of lake trout take more than three months to hatch. The adult fish take almost ten years to attain maturity, so larger specimens are rare. Old specimens gradually become solitary in habit. Devouring even their close family members, they readily prey on any fish they come across. The meat of lake trout is tasty and prepared in various ways. Americans opt for sautéed fillets, whereas in France simmered lake trout fillets are served in a delicious sauce.

130 | **Vendace** | Coregonus albula | SALMONIDAE / SALMONID FISHES

Vendace (En), Kleine Maräne, Zwergmaräne, Zollfisch (D), Coregono blanco (E), Corégone blanc, petite marène (F), Coregone bianco (I), Kleine marene (Nl) • Evropeiskaja riapushka (Bel), Marena mala (Cze), Heltling (Da), Whitefish (En), Lefkokorégonos (Gr), Törpe maréna (H), Lagesild (N), Coregono branco, coregon-bicudo (P), Coregon-mic (Ru), Siklöja (S), Muikku (SF)

The vendace is an extremely tolerant species of salmonid. It occurs in sea and brackwater in the Atlantic and the northern seas, and in cool, oligotrophic, freshwater lakes north of 58° northern latitude in Europe and Asia. Typically, it is a pelagic species forming huge schools. The Baltic population is migratory, but non-migrating freshwater populations are also known. The vendace seeks sandy or stony shallows for spawning. Its maximum length is 45 cm (18 in), maximum weight 1 kg (2.2 lb). A filter-feeder, it consumes exclusively zooplankton, so anglers are unable to catch it due to the lack of a suitable bait. It is caught in substantial numbers by traditional fishing methods in seas and large lakes. In Scandinavian countries it is caught with small gill nets. Its flesh is of good quality, containing few bones, and is prepared in various ways, both fried and cooked. A popular method is to pickle it in salt for one day prior to quickly smoking it. Thus prepared, it is one of the most delicious seafood dishes.

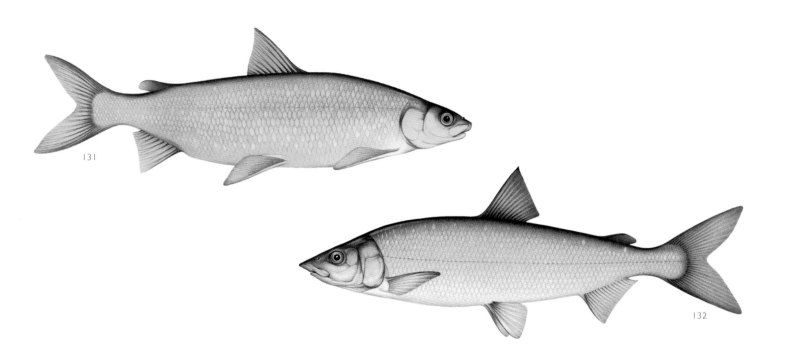

131 | Lake whitefish | Coregonus clupeaformis | SALMONIDAE / SALMONID FISHES

Lake whitefish (En), Heringsmaräne (D), Corégono de lago (E), Coregono de lago (P), Corégone de lac, corégone cisco (F), Coregone dei Grandi Laghi (I), Amerikaanse marene (NI) • Atekamek (Cree), Helt (Da), Koregonos (Gr), Anahik (Inu), Sik (N, S), Kanadasik (S), Siika (SF), Whitefish (US)

The lake whitefish lives in North America, in Alaska and Canada, but occurs southwards in the catchment area of the Great Lakes, New England and the central part of Minnesota. This whitefish species has been introduced in two Latin American countries into high altitude lakes in the Andes. It is possibly conspecific with Coregonus lavaretus. It reaches 1 m (40 in) in length and 18–20 kg (40–44 lb) in maximum weight. Primarily an inhabitant of lakes, it also occurs in large rivers and even brackwater. Twice a year it leaves deep water for the shallows in large freshwater lakes. A bottom-dwelling fish, it feeds on insect larvae, gastropods and gammarideans, but also consumes smaller fish and fish eggs, including its own. Extensive hatching and reproducing programmes are in operation in the Great Lakes area and elsewhere. Due to the high quality of its flesh and its eggs which can be made into caviar, the lake whitefish is of great economic importance. It appears on markets fresh, frozen, as well as smoked. The flesh is prepared stewed, cooked, grilled, or roasted in an oven or microwave, and thus the lake whitefish is a popular catch of anglers.

132 | Houting | Coregonus oxyrhynchus | SALMONIDAE / SALMONID FISHES

Houting (En), Nordseeschnäpel, Edelmaräne, Gangfisch (D), Coregono (E), Outil, bondelle (F), Coregone musino (I), Houting (NI) • Kleine Schwebrenke (A), Snæbel (Da), Pollán (Ga), Sik (N), Coregono bicudo (P), Älvsik, näbbsik, nordsjösik, planktonsik (S), Ozimica (SC), Järvisiika (SF)

The houting is a species of salmonid occurring in both sea and freshwater. It is found in the seas and freshwater lakes of northern Europe, and prefers cooler conditions, growing to a maximum 50 cm (20 in) length and approximately 2 kg (4.4 lb) weight. An anadromous species, marine populations migrate to the upper reaches of rivers to spawn on their stony bottom. However, non-migrating freshwater populations are also known. The houting is a bottom-dwelling fish that forms large schools. Its main food is zooplankton. In some areas its populations have been entirely exterminated or seriously reduced in size, and the houting has been put under legal protection. Elsewhere, in areas having substantial populations, it is fished for, and is sometimes even artificially reproduced. Its high-quality flesh is a popular food both fried and smoked. Special care is taken in the European Union for conserving its populations.

133 | Arctic grayling | Thymallus arcticus | THYMALLIDAE / GRAYLINGS

Arctic grayling (En), Arktische Äsche (D), Ombre Arctique (F), Temolo (I), Vlagzalm (Nl) • Lipan bajkalský (Cze), Arktisk stalling (Da), Kewlook powak (Inu), Harr (N, S), Lipien syberyjski (Pl), Sibirskij kharius (R), Arktisk Harr (S), Pohjanharjus (SF)

A trout-like game fish of the Salmonidae family, Arctic grayling are native to the freshwaters of North America. They dwell in the region extending from Hudson Bay to Alaska, and in the upper stretch of the tributary streams of the Missouri River. Earlier they were abundant in the Great Lakes. They are also found in Asia, in the Siberian territories of Russia. They may attain body lengths of about 70–75 cm (28–30 in) and weights of 2.7–2.8 kg (6–6.2 lb). They form smaller schools in larger and medium-sized rivers and lakes, preferring colder waters. The young feed on zooplankton, mature specimens eat mainly insects fallen into the water, but fish, roe, planktonic crabs and even lemmings may diversify their diet. They migrate to the smaller tributary rivers to spawn in April and May. An immensely colourful fish, the male Arctic grayling assumes a spectacular look in the spawning season. Very popular among fly-fishermen, the fish is eagerly sought by anglers who travel to the northern regions of Canada just to fish it. The flaky-textured meat of the fish is of excellent quality. Marketed for food fresh, it is usually boiled, or sautéed, roasted, or baked in the oven. The Inuit and Native Americans – quite surprisingly – primarily feed their sled-dogs with this fish, only very rarely using it for human consumption.

134 | Grayling | Thymallus thymallus | THYMALLIDAE / GRAYLINGS

Grayling (En), Äsche (D), Ombre commun, oumbre (F), Temolo (I), Vlagzalm (Nl) • Freskori (Alb), Asche (CH), Lipen obycajny (Cze), Europæisk stalling (Da), Pénzes pér (H), Harr (N, S), Peixe-sombra (P), Lipien europejski (Pl), Kharius (R), Lipan (Ru), Harjus (SF), Lipen obycajný (Slk)

Once a widespread fish in almost all cold, montane waters in Europe, its populations are now considerably reduced. However, popular with anglers, a number of farms produce and sell its fry. Growing to 30–50 cm (12–20 in) in length and 1–2 kg (2–4 lb) in weight, the grayling can be distinguished from its carnivorous relatives by its huge dorsal fin. As it is extremely sensitive to low oxygen levels, its disappearance is a certain sign of pollution and reductional processes. The female grayling lays a few thousand eggs at one time. Since it makes a nest for its eggs, which it subsequently covers with a layer of pebbles, the survival rate of the fry is remarkably high. Its flesh is mainly prepared fried. Due to its comparative rarity, it is often more expensive than that of other salmonids. The grayling is protected by law in many European countries, so may be marketed only as farm specimens.

135 | Capelin | Mallotus villosus | OSMERIDAE / SMELTS

Capelin (En), Lodde, Polarstint, Kapelan (D), Capelín (E), Capelan atlantique (F), Capelin (I), Lodde (Nl) • Cikeq, iqalluaq (Alu), Ammassak (Cree), Lodde (Da), Caplin, cock caplin (En), Kapelános (Gr), Amagiak, angmagsak, ko le le kuk, nulilighuk, qulilirraq (Inu), Loðna (Is), Karafuto-shishamo (J), Capelim (P), Gromadnik (Pl), Moiva (R), Lodda (S), Villakuore (SF), Lodde (US)

The capelin is an inhabitant of arctic waters of the Northern Hemisphere, but also occurs in the Atlantic, the northern seas of Europe and the Pacific Ocean. It grows to a maximum of 20–25 cm (8–10 in) in length and 70–80 kg (154–176 lb) in weight. Typically an open-water species, it lives in huge schools. It moves towards sandy beaches for spawning and a substantial portion of the population die after reproducing, with only a small part of the females surviving. The food of the capelin consists of marine zooplankton and small fish, while it is itself an important prey of many larger carnivores. It is caught on an industrial scale. Females containing eggs are a more valuable catch, while males are made into fishmeal and oil. The human consumption of its flesh is substantial. It is distributed both canned and frozen, and is eaten fried and dried. Its fishing is now ceasing due to earlier overfishing.

136 | Ayu | Plecoglossus altivelis | PLECOGLOSSIDAE / AYUS

Ayu (En, D, Da, E, F, I, Nl, S) • Ayu, koayu (J), Eun-eo (Kor), Hai tai yú (Mand), Aiyu (R), Ayu sweetfish, ko-ayu (US)

The ayu inhabits the northwestern part of the Pacific, from the island of Hokkaido (Japan) southwards to the Korean Peninsula, Taiwan and China. It can reach 70 cm (28 in) in length and 4–5 kg (9–11 lb) in weight. It is a member of the salmon family, occurring in both fresh and sea water. Of freshwaters, it prefers clean, cool rivers and lakes. It spawns in the lower reaches of rivers, after which some of the adults die, while others migrate to the sea. The fry lives in the sea for some time after hatching, then moves upstream in rivers, reaching sexual maturity there. Those inhabiting the sea arrive there for spawning. Some specimens spawn two to three times a year, while the majority breed only once, and die subsequently. Specimens of 4–6 cm (1.6–2.4 in) length feed on insects and algae attached to rocks, then switch to a wholly carnivorous diet. The ayu is of great importance to fisheries and is also reproduced in substantial quantities. Anglers much admire it. It is distributed fresh, and is prepared grilled or pan-fried.

135

136

137 | Inanga | Galaxias maculatus | GALAXIIDAE / GALAXIIDS

Inanga (En), Gefleckter Hechtling (D), Raya noruega (E), Bianchetti (I) • Jollytail (Au, US), Almindelig laksegedde (Da), Shirasu (J), Inaka, Inanga (Mao), Inanga (NZ), Galaksiya inanga (R), Täplämeltti (SF), Whitebait (US)

This small-bodied fish occurs in Australia, New Zealand and some islands in Oceania, as well as in the southern part of South America and the Falklands. It is found in temperate zone areas, usually in standing or slowly flowing freshwaters (streams, rivers and lakes close to the sea), but frequently also in brackwater. Its maximum size is 14–15 cm (5.5–6 in). Its food consists of aquatic and terrestrial arthropods, and zooplankton. Although it does not play an important role in fisheries, it often occurs on local markets. It is distributed fresh, and while it is mainly eaten dried, it is also prepared fried and cooked. Anglers use it as a bait. It has no particular economic significance.

138 | Brushtooth lizardfish | Saurida undosquamis | SYNODONTIDAE / LIZARDFISHES

Brushtooth lizardfish (En), Eidechsenfisch (D), Lagarto escamoso (E), Anoli á grandes écailles, poisson-lézard á grandes écailles (F), Pesce ramarro orientale (I), Groteschubbenhagedivis (Nl) • Grootskub-akkedisvis (Afr), Kau kwun (Cant), True lizardfish (En), Daldalag (Ilo), Ma-eso (J), Harmout Balady (Leb), Bekut laut, chonor, hai la, ubi (Mal), Lagarto (Moz-E), Anoli de mer (Moz-F), Banana, mbolopfuma, peixe-banana escamoso (Moz-P), Poleeneen, shijeeah (Om), Hasoum (Om, Q), Lagarto escamudo (P), Basasong (Pan), Large-scaled saury (Pap), Tigbasbay, Largescale lizardfish (SA), Hasoom Anishow (Som), Bumbo, goromwe, mbumbura, (Swa), Bubule, kalaso, kamutihan (Tag), Balanghutan, tiki-tiki (Vis)

This fish is an inhabitant of the Indian and the Pacific oceans. Its range extends from the Red Sea, the Persian Gulf and the coasts of east Africa eastwards to Japan and the Arafura Sea, and southwards to the Great Barrier Reef. It has also reached the eastern Mediterranean through the Suez Canal. Males grow to 50 cm (20 in) in length and 1–1.2 kg (2.2–2.6 lb) in weight, while females approach 25 cm (10 in) in length at most. The brushtooth lizardfish is found along the coasts on a sandy or muddy surface, close to the bottom, to a maximum depth of 300 m (984 ft). A predatory species, it feeds on fish, crayfish and other invertebrates. It spawns in April and May around Japan. A peculiarity of the species is that even its tongue is covered by minuscule, sharp teeth. Usually sold frozen, it is sometimes marketed fresh, or cut into "kamaboko" in Japan.

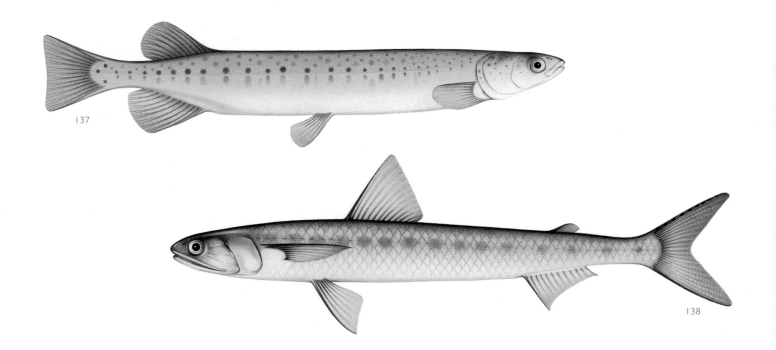

137

138

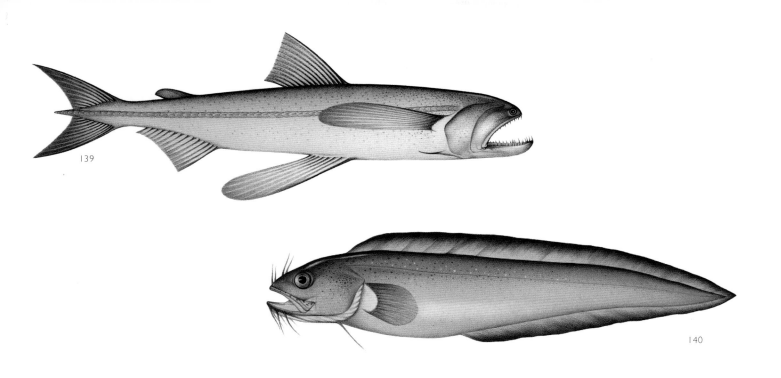

139 | **Bombay-duck** | Harpadon nehereus | HARPADONTIDAE / BOMBAY DUCKS

Bombay-duck (En), Bombay-Ente, Bummalo (D), Bumalo (E), Scopélidé (F), Bumalo (I), Bombay-eend (Nl) • Loitta (Ben), Barega, nga-hnat (Bur), Bombay-and (Da), Bumla (Guj), Tenaga-mizutengu (J), Acang-acang (Jav), Mul-ch'on-gu (Kor), Luli, luli-luli, lumek, lumi-lumi, uli-uli (Mal), Lóng tóu kào (Mand), Bumblim (P), Vangaravasi (Tam), Cucah-sawahri (Tel), Cá khoai (Vie)

This fish species occurs in the Indian ocean and the western Pacific, and reaches 40 cm (16 in) in length and 1.8–2 kg (4–4.5 lb) in body mass. For most of the year, the Bombay-duck inhabits deeper waters far offshore, but can be seen feeding in huge schools in river deltas during the monsoon period. An aggressive predator, it feeds mainly on fish, but takes other aquatic organisms as well. It is caught with bag-nets called "dhols" off Maharashtra. These nets are used in strong in-coming tide currents – they are placed into the currents, and the fish taken up by these currents are unable to escape by swimming against the waves. Consequently, the nets are collected before the end of the high tide. As a unique feature, this fish gives off a strong light in darkness. Since its flesh is of superb quality, the Bombay-duck is intensely harvested. It is distributed salted and dried, and is usually prepared pan-fried.

140 | **Goatsbeard brotula** | Brotula multibarbata | OPHIDIIDAE / OPHIDIUMS

Goatsbeard brotula (En), Riff-Brotula, Vielbart-Schlangenfisch (D), Rape boca negra (E), Fausse anguille, brotule barbe de bouc (F), Brotola (I), Brotola (Nl) • Baardbek brotula (Afr), Bearded brotula (En), Abrótia (P), Tafuti (Sam), Weasel fish, many-whiskered broulid fish (US), Cá Chôn râu (Vie)

Very much resembling catfish, goatsbeard brotula dwell in the Indian and Pacific oceans, from the Red Sea and East Africa as far as Hawaii, in the tropical waters. They probably occur around the islands in the eastern region of the Pacific Ocean, but this is still not proved. They may attain sizes of about 1 m (39 in) in length and 6–7 kg (13–16 lb) in weight. At first sight the brotula can be mistaken for catfish, yet its entire body being covered in small scales immediately eliminates such delusion. They live over the continental shelf, at the deepening edge of it, over the sea bottom, at depths of about 200–600 m (600–2000 ft). Their larvae live far from the coast, in the surface strata of the sea. They are seldom seen, since they usually hide in caves and crevasses in daytime. They come out of hiding for the night to hunt for crustaceans and fish. A commercially not very significant fish, goatsbeard brotula mainly occur as by-catch in bottom trawls, and are regularly landed by deep-sea fishermen. Marketed for food fresh, the meat of the fish is usually simmered, sautéed, or baked in the oven.

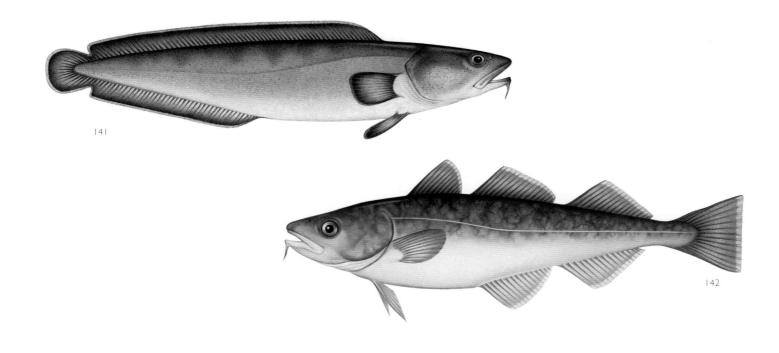

141

142

141 | Tusk | Brosme brosme | GADIDAE / CODS

Tusk (En), Lumb (D), Brosmio (E), Brosme, assiette, tusk (F), Brosmio, brosme (I), Lom, torsk, lomp (Nl) • Brosme (Da, N), Brósmios (Gr), Keila (Is, SF), Bolota (P), Brosma (Pl), Menjok (R), Lubb, brosme (S), Brismak, moonfish, torsk (UK), Cusk (US)

This comparatively large-bodied member of the cod family inhabits the northern Atlantic. It is found from New Jersey to the great riffs of Newfoundland in the west, being rare at the southern end of Greenland, and from Iceland along the Norwegian coasts as far east as Murmansk and the Spitsbergen. The tusk can reach 120 cm (47 in) in length and 30 kg (66 lb) in body mass. It is usually found in deep waters far offshore, up to a depth of 150–450 m (450–1500 ft) in the east, and 200–550 m (600–1800 ft) in the west. It lives alone or in small groups near the bottom. A carnivorous species, it feeds on fish (mainly flounders and gurnards), crustaceans and gastropods, but also on starfish. The tusk itself is a prey of seals. It is intensely harvested and is a favourite catch of deep-sea anglers. Its flesh is marketed fresh, frozen, or as salted and dried filets, and is prepared stewed, cooked, fried, grilled or roasted.

142 | Pacific cod | Gadus macrocephalus | GADIDAE / CODS

Pacific cod (En), Pazifischer Kabeljau (D), Bacalao del Pacífico (E), Morue du Pacifique (F), Merluzzo del Pacifico (I), Pacifische kabeljauw (Nl) • Amutaq (Alu), Gray cod (Can), Bakaliáros (Gr), St'aaydaay (Hai), Madara (J), Dae-gu (Kor), Dà kou yú (Mand), Bacalhau-do-Pacífico-norte (P), Ayet, eyethithen, pk'iken, sheyehl, skim'eth (Saa), K'awts (Tsi), Cod, Alaska cod (US)

The Pacific cod inhabits the northern part of the Pacific, from the Yellow Sea to the Bering Strait, and along the Aleut Islands southwards to Los Angeles. It is rather rare in the southern portion of its range. It grows to 100–120 cm (40–47 in) in length and 20–23 kg (44–51 lb) in weight. Its habitat is the continental shelf and its deepening margin. The Pacific cod occurs in larger groups near the sea bottom, preferring colder waters. An aggressive, fast-moving predator, it exploits available food resources without much discrimination. Young cods feed on copepods and similar organisms, while adults prey on fish, cephalopods and larger benthic crustaceans. This species is of great economic significance and is intensely fished for. It is distributed fresh, frozen, dried, salted and smoked. Its liver is also a valuable product. Humans consume it cooked, stewed, smoked, as well as grilled and roasted in an oven or microwave. Its flesh is much admired for its good quality, and the Pacific cod is thus a popular catch of anglers. It is also used in Chinese medicine.

143 | Atlantic cod | Gadus morhua | GADIDAE / CODS

Atlantic cod (En), Dorsch, Kabeljau (D), Bacalao del Atlántico (E), Morue de l'Atlantique (F), Merluzzo bianco (I), Kabeljauw, gul (Nl) • Bacallà (Cat), Bakalar (Cr), Atlantisk Torsk (Da), Bakaliáros (Gr), Thorskur (Is), Kabliau (Inu), Madara (J), Boiddagh (Manx), Skrei (N), Torsk (N, S), Bacalhau-do-Atlântico (P), Dorsz atlantycki (Pl), Atlanticheskaya treska (R), Turska (SF)

The most widely distributed member of the cod family, Atlantic cod primarily dwell in the northern waters of the Atlantic, and several sub-species and variants have developed. Cod attain body lengths of 1–2 m (40–80 in), and are predator fishes of great commercial value. Like other related species, cod spawn at depths of 50–100 m (150–300 ft), at temperatures of 4–6°C (39–42.7°F). This has been satisfactorily explained by physicists, who have clearly pointed out that at 4–6°C (39–42.7°F) water is of the highest density, thus also the slowest-moving stratum. This allows the fish a fairly peaceful life-style in these areas. Like small marbles of 1.5 mm (0.059 in) in diameter, their roe are of relatively small density, thus they continuously rise to the surface waters. They hatch after an incubation period of one month. Since mature female cod produce several million fry, it is no wonder the species has survived recent technical improvement of fishing methods relatively well. Nevertheless, the danger is looming pretty close, since cod are being "hunted" with all possible means. A very esteemed species in the kitchen, cod are used as food in many countries, some nations even priding themselves on having their own cod specialities. A famous dish to be mentioned is the Spanish "bacalao à la vizcaina".

144 | Burbot | Lota lota | GADIDAE / CODS

Burbot (En), Quappe, Rutte, Trüsche (D), Lota (E), Lotte de rivière (F), Bottatrice (I), Kwabaal (Nl) • Rutte (A), Mihaltza (Bul), Trüsche (CH), Mník jednvoůsý (Cze), Miakoto (Cree), Knude (Da), Menyhal (H), Nätarrnaq (Inu), Lake (N, S), Donzela (P), Mietus (Pl), Nalim (R), Manulet (Ru), Made (SF), Mien obycajný (Slk), Menek (Slo), Myn richkovyi (Ukr)

Reaching 40–60 cm (16–24 in) length on average, the burbot is the only European member of the cod family permanently inhabiting freshwater. Its body shape reminds one of a catfish, and the burbot is often mistaken for one. The single barbel protruding from the middle of its chin, and the absence of an adipose fin are its most important characteristics. From the brackish water of sea coasts to high-altitude lakes (over 1000 m [3300 ft] above sea level) it can be found in various habitats. It consumes small animals in nature, but also takes benthic organic matter. Anglers like it very much, and primarily bait their hooks with earthworms and insects, which it quickly detects thanks to its excellent sense of smell. It is less popular with fish farmers, as it is believed to be one of the most avid consumers of fish fry. It does not eat its own eggs, though, as these contain a fatty granule and are pelagic, i.e. drift with the current until their hatching, like those of most marine fish. Due to this characteristic, their artificial hatching is fairly easy, and is increasingly attempted. Burbot flesh more or less equals trout flesh in price. The liver is considered a superb delicacy, and the medical and cosmetic products made from it are highly valued.

143

144

145 | Haddock | *Melanogrammus aeglefinus* | GADIDAE / CODS

Haddock (En), Schellfisch (D), Eglefino, anon, liba (E), Eglefin (F), Asinello (I), Schelvis (Nl) • Kuller (Da), Ysa (Is), Kolje, hyse (N), Arinca (P), Lupacz (Pl), Piksha (R), Kolja (S, SF)

Haddock got its Latin name from the distinctive dark spot on each shoulder. One of the most important distinguishing marks, however, is its spear-like, sharp dorsal fin, this being very important when telling young haddock from other members of the cod family. They may attain a size of about 50–100 cm (20–40 in) and weight of 4–8 kg (9–18 lb). These figures clearly indicate that they are of a fairly slim build. They spawn at temperatures of 8–10°C (47–50°F), about 50–100 m (150–300 ft) deep and produce millions of pelagic roe. Fry hatch in a few weeks, but only after 6–21 months do they approach the coast. This is when they come to master real predator behaviour, and they practically kill everything they come across, including sea urchins and other echinoderms. Their growth rate is very slow, hence the Atlantic nations have introduced very strict maximum size and age limits to prevent the fishing of specimens which have not yet attained sexual maturity (i.e. specimens younger than five years). In the open sea haddock "rise and fall" in the water when hunting. Thus they can easily be traced from aircraft or even from satellites. Given all the modern appliances, stocks of haddock would have a narrow chance of survival if there were no internationally accepted commercial harvesting limits.

146 | Whiting | *Merlangius merlangus* | GADIDAE / CODS

Whiting (En), Wittling, Merlang (D), Plegonegro, merlán (E), Merlan, valet (F), Merlano, molo (I), Wijting (Nl) • Merlà (Cat), Hvilling (Da), Merling (En), Taouki (Gr), Lysa (Is), Badejo (P), Valkoturska (SF), Mol (Slo), Witlinek czarnomorski (Pl), Mezgit (Tr)

A species attaining relatively small body lengths of about 30–50 cm (12–20 in), whiting are somewhat miniature fish among their related species. It is perhaps due to this small size that instead of an ocean-going habit they prefer dwelling in the marginal seas of the Atlantic and among the eel-grass (or grass-wrack) at the bottom of continental shelf seas. They feed on smaller fish and animals thriving among aquatic plants. Their consuming of organic waste has also been recorded in some areas near human habitation. Even their larvae have peculiar habits, since they shelter under the bells of jellyfish, and when they grow bigger, the fry eat up their generous jellyfish host, out of sheer gratitude. Whiting have several sub-species and variants, these forming increasingly isolated populations. Whiting stock in the Black Sea, for instance, scarcely interbreed with stock in the Mediterranean, and their Scandinavian relatives are even more distant. As a proof of their immense adaptability, several instances have been recorded of whiting intruding into the waters of rivers in search of food.

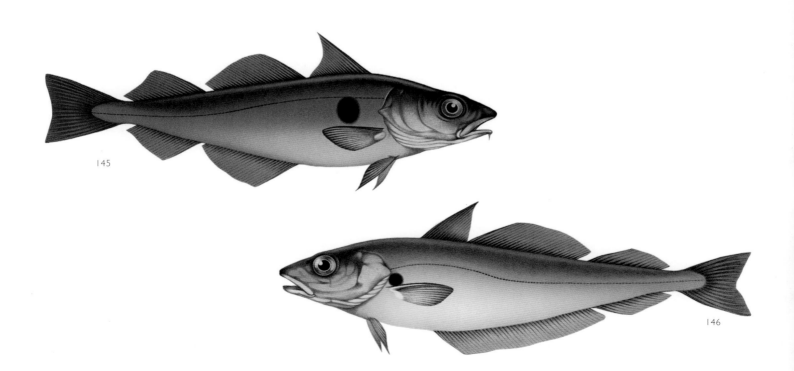

145

146

147 | **Southern blue whiting** | Micromesistius australis | GADIDAE / CODS

Southern blue whiting (En), Südlicher Blauer Wittling (D), Polaca austral (E), Merlan bleu austral, potassou (F), Melù australe (I), Zuidelijke blauwe wijting (Nl) • Polaca (Arg), Merluza de tres aletas, pescada de tres aletas (Chi), Sortmund (Da), Patagonia-minamidara (J), Sydlig blåvitling (S)

This member of the cod family occurs in two distinct populations. One inhabits the Falklands, the southwestern part of the Atlantic along the South American coast, the southeastern part of the Pacific, the vicinity of islands off South Georgia, South Shetland and South Orkney. The other population is found near the South Island of New Zealand. Its maximum body length is 90 cm (36 in). In summer it retreats to the continental shelf, where it is normally found at the deepening margin of the shelf. This whiting lives in huge schools and is found either in open water or near the bottom. A predatory species, it feeds mainly on fish, crustaceans and gastropods. It is very intensely fished, both for human consumption and for other purposes. It is sold either frozen in a block or as fishmeal. In Japan it is used as surimi (minced fish) for making kamaboko (fish cake).

148 | **Blue whiting** | Micromesistus poutassou | GADIDAE / CODS

Blue whiting (En), Blauer Wittling, Stockfisch (D), Bacaladilla, perlita, lirio (E), Merlan bleu, Poutassou, Gros poutassou, nasellu, merlan de Paris, merlus, patafloues, tacaud (F), Melù, potassolo (I), Blauwe wijting (Nl) • Tripendesh, lakuriq, merluc tripendesh (Alb), Ferkh el bajij (Alg), Putasu (Bul), Gourlomata (Cyp), Blåhvilling, Sortmund (Da), Nazeééi (Egy), Couch's whiting (En), Prosfygaki, syko (Gr), Komunni (Is), Shibbut albin (Isr), Abadekho (Mor), Blagunnar, komule blagunnar (N), Bacalhau, pichelim, verdinho (P), Blekitek (Pl), Putassu (R), Blåvitling, komule (S), Pucinca, ugotica (SC), Mustakitaturska (SF), Sinji mol (Slo), Bakalyaro, mezgit, mezit (Tr), Nazalli azraq (Tun), Poutassou (UK)

This species of whiting is an economically important fish of the Atlantic. It is found from the Barents Sea to the western coasts of Africa in the south, while also occurring around Iceland and in the western part of the Mediterranean. In the western Atlantic it occurs from southern Greenland and the southeastern waters of Canada to the northeastern USA. It grows up to 40–50 cm (16–20 in) in length and 250–300 g (8–10 oz) in weight. It lives above and at the deepening margin of the continental shelf to more than 1000 m (3300 ft) depth, but is most common at 300–400 m (1000–1300 ft). Near the bottom and in open waters it is found in groups of various sizes. It feeds mainly on crayfish, but also on smaller fish and cephalopods. It moves vertically in the water in daily cycles – at night near the surface, during the day along the bottom. It is caught in substantial quantities, is distributed either fresh or frozen, but is also made into fishmeal or oil. It is stewed, grilled, roasted or fried.

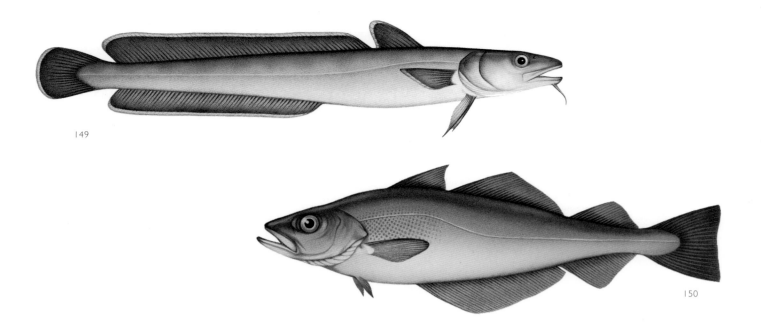

149

150

149 | **Ling** | Molva molva | GADIDAE / CODS

Ling (En), Leng, Lengfisch (D), Maruca, barbada, barruenda, lengua de bacalao (E), Lingue, Elingue, julienne, lingue bleu, lingue franche, morue langue (F), Molva (I), Leng (NI) • Molva (Bul, R, SF), Llenga de bacallà (Cat), Lange (Da, N), Pentiki, pontikópsaro (Gr), Langa (Is), Lipp (Malt), Donzela, maruca (P), Molwa (PI), Långa (S), Manjic morski, mantiz morski (SC), Gelencik (Tr), European ling (UK, US)

The ling occurs in the northeastern Atlantic, from northern Norway, Iceland and the Faroe Islands southwards to the Bay of Biscay and Morocco. It is rare in the north-western part of the Mediterranean. It can reach 2 m (79 in) in length and 30 kg (66 lb) in weight. It occurs in waters 100–400 m (300–1300 ft) deep, and is found above a rocky bottom either alone or in small groups. The ling feeds on fish, crayfish, cephalopods and starfish. It spawns between April and June at a depth of 100–300 m (300–1000 ft) in clearly defined areas. It is intensely harvested, and its prime-quality flesh is distributed fresh, salted and dried, or frozen. For human consumption it is pan-fried, baked in an oven or grilled. The ling is also much admired by recreational fishermen.

150 | **Pollack** | Pollachius pollachius | GADIDAE / CODS

Pollack (En), Pollack, Steinköhler (D), Abadejo, serreta (E), Lieu jaune, colin jaune (F), Merluzzo giallo, pollack (I), Pollak (NI) • Lubbe, blåsej (Da), Green pollack, pollock (En), Kítrinos (Gr), Juliana (P), Bleka, lyrtorsk (S), Lyyraturska (SF)

The most widely distributed species of the cod family, pollack attain body lengths slightly shorter than those of the very similar related species, the saithe or coalfish. Pollack average about 50–80 cm (20–32 in) in size and may weigh 5–10 kg (11–22 lb). They can easily be confused with the saithe when observed from above. Nevertheless, a proper side view would definitely reveal their distinctive mark of paler bands on the body, their much more rounded fins, and their lateral line following the pattern of the spine. Adult pollack travel thousands of miles, and they are of high commercial value. In the European Union regulations impose strict commercial quotas and harvest limits. Thousands of smaller fishing boats off the Atlantic coast are engaged in landing pollack, the main fishing gear being heavy bottom trawls. Members of the cod family constitute 10–15% of world-wide annual fish landings, out of which at least one tenth is pollack. Atlantic cuisine has been using pollack for centuries, especially salted and smoked. Nowadays it is mainly the frozen or pre-prepared products that are commercially marketed, although they are sometimes sold under the slightly confusing name, in some languages, of "marine salmon".

151 | Saithe, Pollock | *Pollachius virens* | GADIDAE / CODS

Saithe, Pollock (En), Seelachs, Köhler, Blaufisch (D), Carbonero, fogonero (E), Lieu noir, colin noir (F), Merluzzo carbonaro (I), Koolvis (Nl) • Sej, gråsej (Da), Coalfish, black cod, saithe, sillock (En), Ufsi (Is), Sei (N), Escamudo, paloco (P), Sajda (R), Gråsej (S), Seiti (SF), Pollack (UK), Black pollock (US)

The saithe, also known as pollock in Europe, range in body length from 50 to 100 cm (20–40 in) and may weigh 5–15 kg (11–33 lb). The various local names ("black cod"; "coalfish", etc.) all refer to the fact that this is the darkest coloured species of the cod family. The underside of the fish is almost totally pale, but the dorsal part and the three dorsal fins are nearly black, sometimes dark bronze. Regarding ecological preferences, saithe is indeed a most flexible fish in habit, a fact especially evident from the various habitats it may choose. Populations occur in practically all possible areas, ranging from the open sea to the not very clear brackish waters of harbours and river estuaries. In the open sea the mature saithe prey on smaller fish in large schools. Another characteristic feature of saithe is that they spawn in large groups at depths of 50–200 m (150–660 ft), at very low temperatures of 5–10°C (41–50°F). Their pelagic roe are typical constituents of marine plankton which reach very gradually the surface strata of the water. The meat of saithe is marketed at medium price, and can be found in the marketplaces of all larger sea ports.

152 | Lesser forkbeard, Tadpole fish | *Raniceps raninus* | GADIDAE / CODS

Lesser forkbeard, Tadpole fish (En), Froschquappe, Froschdorsch (D), Brótola de fango, ranúnculo negro, pez rana (E), Phycis, trident, grenoulle de mer (F), Musdea bianca, mostella (I), Volkswab, vorschkval (Nl) • Sortvels, paddetorsk (Da), Lesser forkbeard (En), Paddetorsk (N), Rainunculo-negra (P), Lyagushkogolov (R), Paddtorsk (S), Mustaturska (SF), Trifurcated hake (UK)

The lesser forkbeard inhabits the northeastern part of the Atlantic. South of Trondheim it occurs along the Norwegian coasts to the Bay of Biscay, but is also found off the British Isles. A small-bodied species, it reaches a maximum 25–30 cm (10–12 in) in length and 400 g (14 oz) in weight. It lives in comparatively shallow coastal waters to a depth of 80–100 m at most. It is found either alone or in small groups above vegetated rocky bottom. Spawning takes place between May and September, along the coast to a depth of 50–70 m (164–230 ft) in the entire range of the species. A carnivorous fish, it preys on starfish and crayfish, gastropods and smaller fish. Economically entirely unimportant, the forkbeard, as a coastal fish, sometimes appears in the catch of anglers. It is eaten mainly cooked or stewed, sometimes also fried.

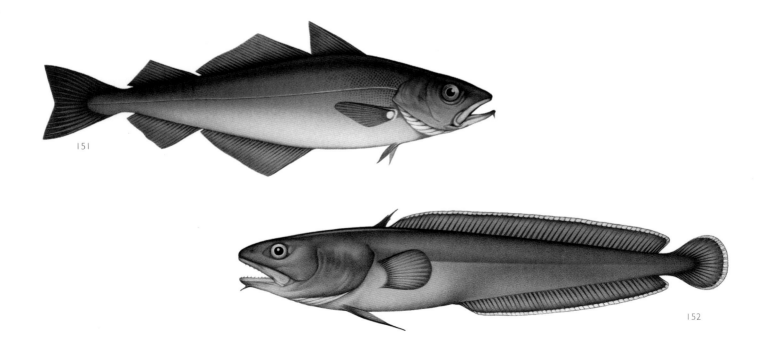

151

152

153 | Alaska pollack | Theragra chalcogramma | GADIDAE / CODS

Alaska pollack (En), Pazifischer Pollack, Alaska-Pollack, Alaska-Seelachs (D), Colín de Alaska (E), Lieu de l'Alaska, morue du Pacifique occidental (F), Merluzzo dell'Alasca (I), Alaskapollak (Nl) • Rririliq (Alu), Whiting (Can), Sukeso-dara, suketodara (J), Mintai (R), Walleye pollock, walleye pullack, walleyed pollock (US)

A member of the cod family, Alaska pollack are distributed in the northern part of the Pacific Ocean. In the eastern waters they are abundant along the American coast as far south as Carmel, California, and in the western seas to the southern coasts of Japan. They may grow as large as 90 cm (35 in) in length and 1.5 kg (3.3 lb) in weight. Mostly dwelling near the bottom, though also observed near the surface, Alaska pollack move up and down along a vertical axis in daytime, while they feed between water strata at night. A predator species, Alaska pollack feed on fish and crustaceans. The stock is largely exploited and is chiefly marketed frozen in fillets. Spawning stock are often landed solely for the sake of their roe. In Japan the meat of the fish is often used in the production of frozen surimi blocks, which is further processed into imitation crab, scallops and shrimp. Simmered, sautéed or fried, the meat is a palatable dish.

154 | Norway pout | Trisopterus esmarkii | GADIDAE / CODS

Norway pout (En), Stintdorsch, Sparling (D), Faneca noruega (E), Tacaud norvégien, mostelle de fond (F), Busbana norvegese (I), Kever (Nl) • Spaerlingur, calypso (Da), Spaerlingur (Is), Øyepål, ogerpal, skellbrose (N), Foneca noruega (P), Okowiel (Pl), Vitlinglyra (S), Havmaaturska (SF)

This member of the cod family inhabits the northeastern Atlantic, from the southwestern part of the Barents Sea southwards to the English Channel, and is also found off the Faroe Islands and Iceland. It prefers cold waters, occurring on the muddy bottom or in open water up to 100–200 m (300–660 ft) in depth. Its maximum length is 35 cm (14 in), maximum weight 300 g (10 oz). A carnivorous species, it feeds mainly on plankton, but also consumes smaller fish, fish eggs and fry. It is caught in huge numbers and is mainly turned into fishmeal. Its flesh is suitable for human consumption, but is rarely eaten. Given its small size, anglers do not admire it much.

155 | **Pouting** | Trisopterus luscus | GADIDAE / CODS

Pouting (En), Franzosendorsch, Bartdorsch (D), Faneca, paneka, palenca (E), Tacaud commun, Gade, Guidon, Plouse (F), Merluzzo francese, merluzzo bruno, busbana fancese (I), Steenbolk (Nl) • Skägtorsk (Da), Bakaliaros, bakallaraki (Gr), Suddrey (Manx), Skieggtorsk, skjeggtorsk (N), Falsos-alabotes, faneca (P), Bielmik (Pl), Lyusca (R), Skäggtorsk (S), Ugotica mala (SC), Partaturska (SF), Bib, pout, pout whiting, whiting-pout (UK)

This member of the cod family is native to the eastern Atlantic, and occurs from the British Isles and Skaggerak to the West African coast and the western Mediterranean. It can also be found off islands far from the continental coast. The pouting reaches 40–45 cm (16–18 in) in length and 1–1.2 kg (2.4–2.6 lb) in weight. A gregarious species, it is mainly smaller specimens which form huge schools. The pouting lives close to the bottom along the outer margin of the continental shelf, but returns to coastal regions for spawning at approximately 50 m (160 ft) depth. It hunts at night in open water. A predatory species, it feeds on bottom-dwelling crustaceans, small fish and gastropods. It occasionally appears in the catch of recreational fishermen, and is also often caught by deep-sea anglers. Distributed fresh or frozen, it is consumed cooked, stewed, grilled, pan-fried or oven baked.

156 | **White hake** | Urophycis tenuis | GADIDAE / CODS

White hake (En), Gabeldorsch, Weißer Gabeldorsch (D), Locha blanca (E), Merluche blanche, phycis blanc (F), Musdea americana (I), Witte heek (Nl) • Mud hake (Can, UK, US), Skægbrosmer (Da), Stóra brosma (Is), Abrótea branca (P), Vitbrosme (S), Boston hake, ling (UK)

The white hake belonging to the cod family inhabits the western part of the Atlantic, from Labrador to North Carolina, but also lives as far as Iceland in the east, and the seas surrounding Florida in the south. A bottom-dwelling species, it is found on the soft, muddy bottom of the continental shelf, mainly at 150–200 m (450–660 ft) depth. It reaches 110–120 cm (43–47 in) in length and 20 kg (44 lb) maximum weight. Adults mass-migrate to coastal waters of the northern part of the Bay of Maine. In autumn, the groups dissolve, and the fish return to deeper waters for the winter. A carnivorous fish, it feeds on small crustaceans, cephalopods and fish. It is intensely fished, being caught in huge numbers in the summer months while mass-migrating. It is sold fresh, smoked and frozen, and considerable numbers are exported to Europe. The flesh is prepared stewed, or roasted. The white hake is a popular catch of anglers, too, for its flesh is of excellent quality.

157

158

157 | **Southern hake** | *Merluccius australis* | MERLUCCIIDAE / HAKES

Southern hake (En), Südlicher Seehecht (D), Merluza austral (E), Merlu austral, merlu magellanique (F), Nasello, merluzzo argentato (I), Australische heek (Nl) • Merluzón (Arg), Maltona, merluza del sur, pescada de los canales (Arg, Chi), Nyujiirando-heiku (J), Tiikati (Mao), Haddock, hake, whiting (NZ), Pescada-austral, pescada-da-Nova Zelándia (P), New Zealand hake (UK, US)

This relative of the cod is found all over the subtropical zone in the Southern Hemisphere. Two main populations are known: one around New Zealand, the other in both the Atlantic as well as the Pacific waters off Patagonia. The southern hake grows to 120–130 cm (47–51 in) in length and 18–20 kg (40–44 lb) in mass. The New Zealand population occurs at depths of 400–1000 m (1200–3300 ft), the South American at 60–800 m (200–2500 ft). Southern hake can be caught both near the bottom and in open water. A predatory species, it feeds chiefly on fish, cephalopods and bottom-dwelling organisms. Adults of the New Zealand population migrate south in summer, possibly following their prey, but move north again for spawning in winter. A species intensely harvested, it is both eaten and made into fishmeal. It is marketed fresh or frozen, and is consumed cooked, stewed, pan-fried or oven-baked.

158 | **Silver hake** | *Merluccius bilinearis* | MERLUCCIIDAE / HAKES

Silver hake (En), Nordamerikanischer Seehecht, Silberhecht (D), Merluza norteamericana, merluza atlántica (E), Merlu argenté (F), Nasello atlantico (I), Zilverhek (Nl) • Lysingur (Is), Pescada-prateada (P), Silverkummel (S), Atlantic hake, New England hake (UK), Whiting (UK, US)

This species is native to the western Atlantic, and occurs along the coasts of Canada and the United States to Belle Isle Channel in the north, and to the Bahamas in the south, but is most abundant between southern Newfoundland and South Carolina. It grows to 70–80 cm (28–32 in) in length and 2.3 kg (5 lb) in weight. It frequents sandy bottoms and regularly enters the shallows. It migrates in an annually returning cycle towards the shores, and then back to the open sea. A greedy predator, it also exhibits cannibalistic behaviour. Specimens longer than 40 cm (16 in) prey on fish, while smaller individuals feed on crayfish and other invertebrates. The silver hake is intensely harvested, being distributed freshly frozen or smoked. It is also exported fresh to Europe. Its flesh is eaten fried in a pan, cooked in an oven or microwave, or grilled.

159 | South Pacific hake | Merluccius gayi | MERLUCCIIDAE / HAKES

South Pacific hake (En), Chilenischer Seehecht, Chile-Seehecht, Peru-Seehecht (D), Merluza chilena, huaycuya, maltona (E), Merlu du Chili, merlu du Pacifique sud (F), Nasello del Cile, merluzzo (I), Chileense heek (Nl) • Pacific hake (Au), Merluza, Merluza común (Chi), Pescada chilena (P), Chilean hake, whiting (US)

This hake occurs in the southeastern part of the Pacific along the Chilean coast. It is found from 100 m (330 ft) depth from the shallow parts of the continental shelf to the deeper areas of the shelf margin. It mostly dwells at the bottom in groups of various sizes, but hunts in open water at night. Its maximum length is 80–90 cm (32–36 in), weight 4.5 kg (10 lb). In summer it moves into shallower southern waters, while it occurs in the deeper (200–500 m) northern waters in winter and spring. A carnivorous species, it preys on smaller fish and cephalopods. It is intensely fished, for its flesh is of high quality. It is marketed either fresh or frozen, and is prepared stewed, cooked, pan-fried or roasted. In addition to human consumption, substantial quantities are also made into fishmeal.

160 | Argentine hake | Merluccius hubbsi | MERLUCCIIDAE / HAKES

Argentine hake (En), Argentinischer Seehecht (D), Merluza argentina (E), Merlu d'Argentine, merlu sud-américain (F), Nasello argentato (I), Argentijnse heek (Nl) • Merluza (Arg, Uru), South Atlantic hake (Au), Pescada-argentina (P), Atlantic hake, Southwest Atlantic hake (UK)

This species of cod is native to the southwestern Atlantic, from southern Brazil to the waters off Argentina and the Falklands. Its maximum length is 90–100 cm (36–40 in), maximum body mass 8–10 kg (18–22 lb). The Argentine hake lives at depths of 100–200 m (330–660 ft) above the continental shelf. Adults consume fish, crayfish and smaller cephalopods, while the food of the young consists of zooplankton. This species occurs near the shores in spring and summer, and migrates after spawning to deeper waters, to its overwintering grounds. It is known to move vertically in a daily cycle: it feeds closer to the surface at night, while sinking to the bottom for the day. It is intensely harvested for its prime quality flesh, which is marketed fresh or frozen.

159

160

161 | European hake | Merluccius merluccius | MERLUCCIIDAE / HAKES

European hake (En), Europäischer Seehecht, Hechtdorsch (D), Merluza europea (E), Merlu européen, colin (F), Nasello, merluzzo argentato (I), Mooie meid, heek (Nl) • Merluci (Alb), Europæisk kulmule (Da), Lysingur (Is), Lysing (N), Pescada-branca (P), Angolsky khek, merluzy (R), Kummel (S), Kummeliturska (SF)

A species widely distributed throughout the entire Atlantic Ocean, including the marginal seas and bays, European hake average about 80–90 cm (32–36 in) and 5–10 kg (11–22 lb) and are of an evenly silvery grey colouring. Specimens have been observed in very deep waters, even as deep as 1000 m (3300 ft), usually rising to the surface waters at sundown. In these upper water zones they split into smaller schools and attack almost every fish smaller than themselves, not even sparing the offspring of related species. European hake variants of the Baltic and Mediterranean regions tend to lead a separate existence. These variants are of considerably smaller build 40–70 cm (16–28 in) than those of the ocean stock. In the summer season the fish are fried whole or in fillets at fish take-aways along beaches for the great pleasure of tourists. Similarly to other cod species, European hake heads are not used as food in most countries, but are processed instead into fishmeal used in domestic animal feed (e.g. for pigs), and for obtaining fish guano (fermented, dried fish). As with the common cod, the liver of the European hake is treated separately in the fish processing industry, since an important basic medicinal component is extracted from it.

162 | North Pacific hake | Merluccius productus | MERLUCCIIDAE / HAKES

North Pacific hake (En), Nordpazifischer Seehecht, Pazifischer Seehecht (D), Merluza del Pacífico norte (E), Merlu du Pacifique nord (F), Nasello del pacifico (I), Pacifische heek (Nl) • Rririliq (Alu), Pacific hake (Can, UK, US), Merluza, merluza norteña (Mex), Pescada-do-Pacífico-norte (P), Balaas (Tsi), Whiting (US)

As its name suggests, this member of its family is found in the northeastern part of the Pacific, from Vancouver Island in the north along the coast of Canada to the northern part of Baja California. Its records from the Gulf of Alaska are questionable. Its maximum length is 90 cm (36 in), maximum body mass 1.2–1.3 kg (2.5–3 lb). This hake is found near the shores and in open waters. It is often described as a bottom-dweller, but its distribution and behaviour suggest that it is a pelagic species instead. Adult specimens can be found in huge schools above the continental shelf and its deepening margin, but move away for several hundred kilometres from the coasts for spawning. A nocturnal predator, it feeds on fish and invertebrates. The North Pacific hake is itself an important food item for seals, smaller cetaceans and sharks. A species intensely harvested, it is marketed fresh or frozen, and is served cooked, stewed, grilled, fried or roasted.

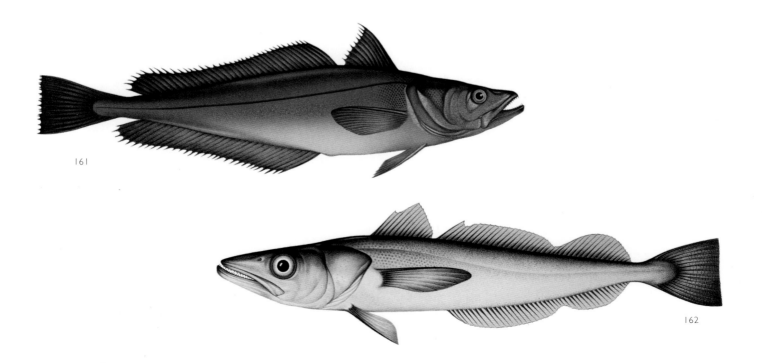

161

162

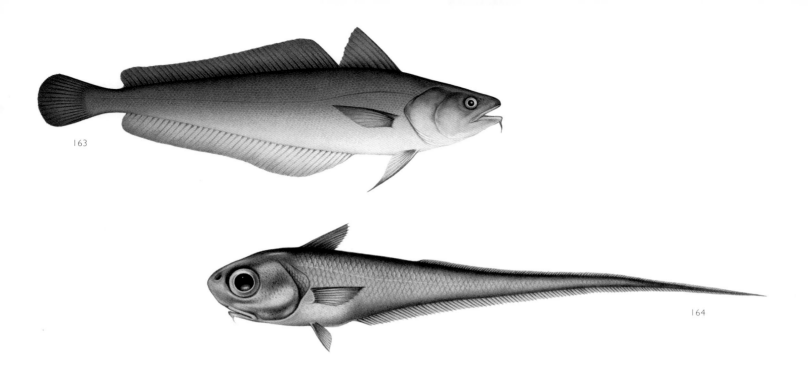

163 | Tadpole codling | Salilota australis | MORIDAE / MORID CODS

Tadpole codling (En), Salilota (D, Nl), Mora renacuajo, bacalao criollo (E), More térard (F) • Bacalao austral (Arg), Renacujo de mar (Chi), Tadpole mora (En), Sarirota (J)

A member of the cod family, tadpole codling are distributed in the southeastern part of the Atlantic Ocean; in the eastern waters they are abundant along the coasts of Chile and Argentina, around the Falkland Islands and in the Magellan Strait. They may grow as large as 50 cm (20 in) in length and 1–1.2 kg (2.2–2.6 lb)in weight. Typically a bottom dwelling species, tadpole codling occur in schools at depths of 200–250 m (660–820 ft). Larger specimens tend to live in even deeper waters. The female fish is larger than the male. Predatory in habit, tadpole codling feed on smaller fish, crustaceans and cephalopods. Commercial landing of the stock is insignificant, the catch being primarily used as a source of fishmeal. When fried, the meat of tadpole codling is a palatable dish.

164 | Roundnose grenadier | Coryphaenoides rupestris | MELANONIDAE / ARROWTAILS

Roundnose grenadier (En), Rundnasiger Grenadierfisch, Langschwanz (D), Granadero (E), Grenadier de roche (F), Granatiere (I), Grenadiervis (Nl) • Almindelig skolæst (Da), Langhali (Is), Nezumi (J), Skolest (N), Lagartixa-da-rocha (P), Lestikala (SF), Rock grenadier, round-nose grenadier, rattail (US)

A most peculiar, club-shaped fish, roundnose grenadiers are very rarely seen in their natural environment, since they generally dwell about 100 m (330 ft) below the surface, rooting about the bottom for food or along the huge, nearly vertical ridges of the continental shelf. Their strong snout is of great help in intruding into crevices and the jungle-like mass of dense vegetation at the sea bottom. The poor light conditions of the deep waters they inhabit have caused the eyes of the fish to be very large. The dorsal and caudal fins are practically joined into a long rat-like tail, hence the name rattail, also used for denoting grenadiers. This construction of the fins is to ease movement in narrow places. Roundnose grenadiers are usually landed as a by-catch from deep-sea bottom trawls. The largest specimens may reach 1 m (40 in) in length and 10–20 kg (22–44 lb) in weight, but only about half the fish is used, usually as ingredients of fish soups and chowders. Fillets of the fish are of medium quality, the taste of the meat being highly improved by the special seasoning applied in Mediterranean cuisine.

165 | Blue grenadier | *Macruronus novaezelandiae* | MACROURIDAE / GRENADIERS

Blue grenadier (En), Langschwanz-Seehecht, Neuseeland-Seehecht, Hoki (D), Merluza azul (E), Hoki, grenadier bleu de Nouvelle-Zélande (F), Nasello azzurro (I), Blauwe grenadier (Nl) • Blue grenadier (Au), Blue hake (Au, NZ), Hoki (J, S, Us, Nz), Granadeiro-azul (P), Whiptail (NZ), New Zealand whiting (US)

A commercially very important fish, blue grenadier dwell in the western regions of the Pacific Ocean, along the southern coasts of Australia and New Zealand. The largest specimens may attain body lengths of about 120–130 cm (47–51 in) and a weight of 1.6 kg (3.5 lb), but landed specimens are normally 60–100 cm (24–39 in) long. They mostly dwell near the sea bottom, in large schools, but they regularly feed in midwater. The mature specimens usually live below depths of about 400 m (1300 ft). Their offspring prefer shallow waters and they are very often observed in larger river estuaries and bays, sometimes even intruding into freshwater. A predatory species, they feed on small fish, crustaceans and Cephalopodae. The spawning season lasts from June to September, the female fish depositing as many eggs as one million per spawning season. The fishing gear used is the bottom trawl dragged at depths of 300–600 m (900–2000 ft), but in the spawning season midwater trawls are also successfully applied. The great bulk of landed fish is marketed for food fresh and frozen in fillets, and all possible methods are used for preparing it.

166 | Pink cusk-eel | *Genypterus blacodes* | OPHIDIIDAE / CUSK-EELS

Pink cusk-eel (En), Leng, Rose Kingklip (D), Rosada, maruca (E), Abadèche rosée, lingue (F), Abadeco (I), Roze koningsklip (Nl) • Dorado (Arg), Abadejo, himakhara (Arg, Chi), Bacalao del sur (Arg, Uru), Australian rockling, kingclip, pink ling, rock ling (Au), Ling (Au, NZ), Congrio dorado (Chi), Kingu, ringu (J), Hokarari (Mor), Northern ling (NZ), Maruca-da-Argentina (P), Congrio colorado (Per), Kingklip (SA)

A common species of the Pacific, pink cusk-eel are found in its southwestern part from the southern coasts of Australia and off New Zealand, in its southeastern part along the Chilean coast, as well as in the southwestern Atlantic off Brazil. The pink cusk-eel reaches 2 m (79 in) in length and 25 kg (55 lb) in weight. A deep-water species, it feeds chiefly on crustaceans and smaller fish. One of its main prey is the hoki (*Macruronus novaezelandiae*), for which it hunts primarily during their spawning. Smaller specimens inhabit shallow regions of the continental shelf, spreading into deeper waters only after maturation. A species intensely harvested, it also occurs in the catch of deep-sea anglers. It is sold fresh, frozen or smoked, and its flesh is served fried in a pan, oven-baked or grilled.

167 | Red cusk-eel | *Genypterus chilensis* | OPHIDIIDAE / CUSK-EELS

Red cusk-eel (En), Roter Kingklip (D), Congribadejo colorado, rosada chilena (E), Abadèche rouge (F), Abadeco rosso (I), Chileense koningsklip (Nl) • Congrio colorado (Chi), Kongurio (J), Maruca-do-Chile (P), Congrio rosado (Per), Kingklip (US)

This eel-like fish is native to the southeastern Pacific, and occurs from southern Peru to south Chile along the South American coast. It reaches 150 cm (59 in) in length and 20 kg (44 lb) in weight. A deep-water species, it occurs in the deeper parts of the continental shelf at its outer margin, mainly above a rock bottom. This carnivore preys chiefly on crustaceans and smaller fish. Although harvested commercially, it is of less importance than its relative, G. blacodes. In South America, it is often wrongly referred to as "sea eel", even though both its body and some part of its head is covered by small scales. Its flesh is of exceptional quality, and thus in high esteem. Sold fresh, frozen or smoked, it is served fried, grilled, or roasted in an oven. During preparation the flesh falls into larger chunks, like cod flesh, and thus it should be treated in the very same way.

168 | Black cusk-eel | *Genypterus maculatus* | OPHIDIIDAE / CUSK-EELS

Black cusk-eel (En), Schwarzer Kingklip (D), Congribadejo negro (E), Abadèche noir (F), Abadeco negro (I), Zwarte koningsklip (Nl) • Congrio, congrio moreno (Per), Kingklip (US)

This species of Genypterus inhabits the southeastern Pacific, off the South American coast in Peruvian and north Chilean waters. It is of smaller size than its congeners, and grows to 60 cm (24 in) in length and 1–1.5 kg (2.2–3.3 lb) in weight. A deep-water species, it occurs in the deeper parts of the continental shelf, at its outer margin, mostly above a rock bottom. A predatory fish, it feeds on smaller invertebrates and fish near the bottom. Like other Genypterus species it is often mistaken for a sea eel due to its snake-like body, although the body and some part of its head is covered by small, cycloid scales. It can be harvested throughout the year and it occurs in the catch of commercial and recreational fishermen alike, but it has no particular economic significance. Distributed fresh or frozen, it is prepared fried, roasted or grilled for human consumption. The flesh resembles that of cod, and should be similarly treated.

167

168

169 | **American angler** | *Lophius americanus* | LOPHIIDAE / GOOSEFISHES AND ANGLERFISHES

American angler (En), Amerikanischer Seeteufel (D), Rape americano (E), Baudroie d'Amérique, lotte (F), Rana pescatrice americana (I), Amerikaanse zeeduivel (Nl) • Amerikansk havtaske (Da), Tamboril-americano (P), Amerikansk marulk (S), Goosefish, monkfish (US)

Although rare in the southern waters of North Carolina, the American angler is distributed along the western coast of the Atlantic from Quebec in Canada to the north-eastern coast of Florida, in the temperate zones. Specimens may grow as large as 120 cm (47 in) in length and 20–22 kg (44–48 lb) in weight. A bottom dwelling species, they mainly occur in mud bottoms where the fish, half-buried in the mud, can easily detect and attack its prey. In the south, the American angler lives in deeper, cooler waters. The diet of the American angler consists of smaller benthic fish it attacks from hiding or approaches carefully by advancing on its arm-like pectoral fins. Despite its frightening appearance, it is not a harmful fish. Its meat being extremely palatable, the American angler stock is widely exploited by commercial fishing fleets, and recreational fishermen indulging in bottom fishing also consider it a good catch. The meat of the fish is usually eaten fried in various ways.

170 | **Anglerfish** | *Lophius piscatorius* | LOPHIIDAE / GOOSEFISHES AND ANGLERFISHES

Anglerfish (En), Seeteufel, Angler (D), Rape (E), Baudroie commune (F), Rana pescatrice, rospo (I), Zeeduivel, hozemond (Nl) • Henez deti (Alb), Rap (Cat), Grdobina mrkulja (Cr), Almindelig Havtaske (Da), Marulk (Da, S), Kott (Egy), Vatrachópsaro (Gr), Skötuselur (Is), Anko (J), Shyt'ân el bah'r (Leb), Petrica (Malt), Guilley-pern (Manx), Zaal ifoundou (Mao), Breiflabb (N), Tamboril (P), Merikrötti (SF), Morska žaba (Slo), Fener baligi (Tr), Bescatris (Tun), Monkfish, goosefish (US)

Anglerfish are distributed in all areas of the Atlantic and the adjacent seas. Its name is derived from the fact that this extremely ugly fish has a lure at the end of the fleshy limb which protrudes from its head, with which the fish is able to attract smaller fish it swallows through an enormous mouth. Due to its horrific appearance, the otherwise palatable meat of the anglerfish is sold pre-prepared, ready for cooking. Larger specimens attain body lengths of 1–2 m (40–80 in), may weigh several tens of pounds, and are very easy to fillet. Along the African shore the meat of anglerfish is also marketed in dried form. The dish "peixe do sol" (sunfish) is also very popular and contains anglerfish mixed with batatas (sweet potato) or other root vegetables. After being neatly transformed into items of folk art, smaller specimens of this "beauty" of a fish are often sold as souvenirs to tourists.

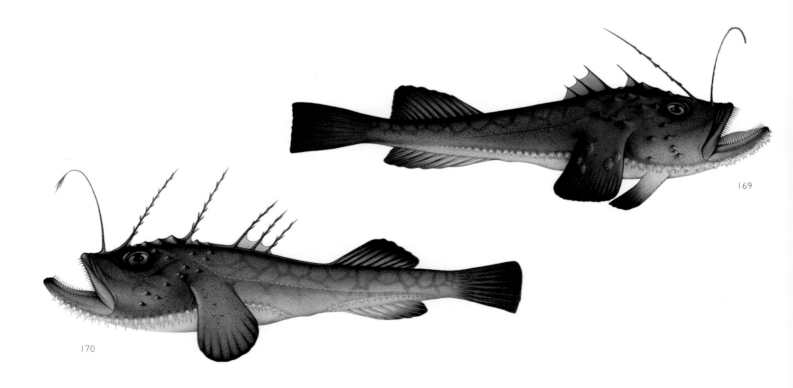

169

170

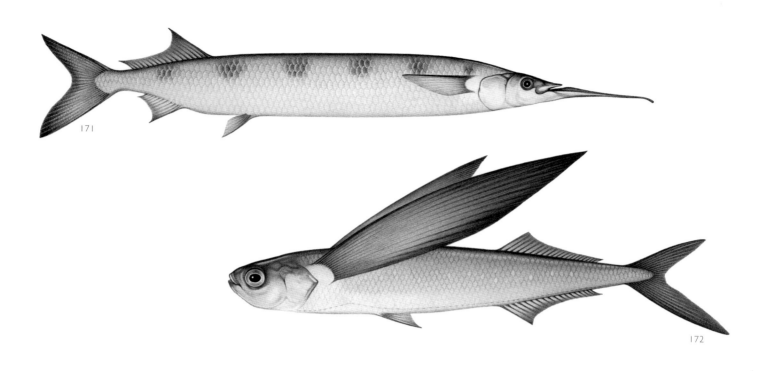

171 | **Blackbarred halfbeak** | Hemiramphus far | HEMIRHAMPHIDAE / HALFBEAKS

Blackbarred halfbeak (En), Gestreifter Halbschnäbler (D), Agujeta manchada (E), Demi-bec bagnard (F), Mezzobecco (I), Halfsnavelbek (Nl) • Gevlekde halfbek (Afr), Bayangban (Ban), Buroy (Bik), Nga-taung-myin (Bur), Balao (Cre), Maminy (Fw), Katjang-katjang (Ind), Hoshi-zayori (J), Sindik, tracas (Jav), Meming (Jaw), Sulwi (Kap), Abou H'arbeh (Leb), Jolong-jolong, puput (Mal), Mwâtéé (Nââ), Maming (Ne), Xaata, thovulu (Nen), Halfbeak (NZ), Sils (Om), Agulha peixe pica, pakanye, zaraganya (P), Buguing, gusa, sise (Phi), Coka-ilo (Pi), Kidau, chuchunge tili, mususa (Swa), Buging babae, kansusuwit (Tag), Mural (Tam), Suwasid (Vis), Fela (Wol)

This fish is native to the Indian Ocean and the western Pacific, but is also found in the Red Sea, along the eastern coasts of Africa, near Samoa, and southwards along the northern part of Australia and off New Caledonia. It has invaded the eastern Mediterranean through the Suez Canal. The blackbarred halfbeak grows to 45 cm (18 in) in length and less than 1 kg (2.2 lb) in body mass. It is characterised by a strongly elongated lower jaw (the length of which is not included in body length measurements). It forms huge schools in coastal shallows and off islands, mainly around reefs. An herbivorous species, it prefers heavily vegetated areas, but it also consumes algae. It spawns in estuaries. It is caught both by recreational and commercial fishermen for its tasty flesh. Equipment employed includes trawl- and draw-nets. This species is marketed fresh or dried-and-salted, and is prepared pan-fried or grilled.

172 | **Tropical two-wing flyingfish** | Exocoetus volitans | EXOCOETIDAE / FLYING FISHES

Tropical two-wing flyingfish (En), Fliegender Fisch (D), Volador, pez volador, liza voladora, golondrina (E), Exocet volant, poison volant (F), Pesce volante, esoceto volante (I), Vligende vis (Nl) • Flyvefisk (Da), Flying fish (En), Chelidonópsaro (Gr), Idaten-tobi-uo (J), Sang-nal-chi (Kor), Belalalang (Mal), Flygefisk (N), Piexe voador (P), Poletusa (SC), Maha piha massa (Sin), Malolo (Sam), Iliw, lawin (Tag), Linne's flying fish (UK)

Widely distributed in the tropical and subtropical waters of all the oceans, tropical two-wing flyingfish also occur in the Mediterranean. They are probably absent from the landlocked seas of southeast Asia. The maximum size they can attain is a body length of 30 cm (12 in) and weight of 150–200 g (5–7 oz). Tropical two-wing flyingfish live near the surface of the water in large groups, both along the coastline and in the open seas. They feed on small crustaceans and zooplankton, whereas large deep sea predators feed on them. When escaping from predators, tropical two-wing flyingfish leap out of water and, using their enlarged pectoral fins as wings, they can float in the air for 8–10 seconds. In this brief time-span they can cover as much as 15–20 m (30–50 ft). A widely fished species, tropical two-wing flyingfish falling onto the ship's deck used to constitute a delicacy for seamen.

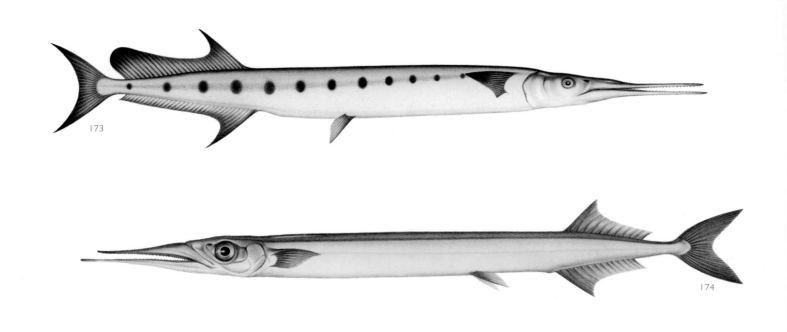

173 | Flat needlefish | Ablennes hians | BELONIDAE / NEEDLE-FISHES

Flat needlefish (En), Carajota, marao machete, agujón sable (E), Orphie plate (F), Balk-naaldvis (Nl) • Agulha (Ang), Hagool, kharam (Ara), Barred longtom (Au, UK), Tambilawan (Ban), Balo, salasa (Bik), Agujón de golfo (Cub), Dayi (Fon), Layalay (Ilo), Hama-datsu (J), Batali (Kap), Anaoróro, te makenikarawa (Kir), Mul-dong-gal-chi (Kor), Subingan (Kuy), Jolong-jolong, todak (Mal), Agulha lisa (Moz), Karkor (Om), Aguja, agulha-da-areia, miriassanga (P), Aku papa (Ra), Barred needlefish (SA), A'u, ise (Sam), Takutér (Sat), Moralla, Valai-mural (Sin), Shoolii (Som), Mkule, ngarara, ngara-ngare (Swa), Bikol, Kambabalo (Tag), Iheraha (Tah), Flat billfish, gaping needlefish, gar fish (UK), Grassfish (Vir), Tagiuteor (Wol)

Inhabiting all tropical and warmer temperate seas of the world, flat needlefish are distributed in the warmer waters along the east and west coasts of the Pacific and the Atlantic Oceans and in all regions of the Indian Ocean. They dwell in the shallow coastal waters around islands and in the brackish water of river estuaries. They may attain sizes of 120 cm (47 in) in length and 1.8–2 kg (4–4.4 lb) in weight. Since their jaws very often break off, body length is usually measured without the head and the caudal fin. A predatory species, they primarily feed on smaller fish. An extensively fished species, they are mostly caught at night, with the help of a decoy light. Marketed fresh, salted, smoked and frozen, the meat of flat needlefish is not a commercially valuable food, since the meat has a greenish hue.

174 | Garfish, Garpike | Belone belone | BELONIDAE / NEEDLEFISHES

Garfish, Garpike (En), Hornhecht, Hornfisch (D), Aguja, agujeta, saltón (E), Orphie commune, aiguille de mer (F), Aguglia, agora (I), Geep, snip (Nl) • Hornfisk (Da), Khirm (Egy), Zargána (Gr), Imsella (Malt), Boulmarayet (Mor), Horngjel (N), Peixe-agulha (P), Obyknovenny sargan (R), Horngädda (S), Nokkakala (SF), Zargana (Tr), M'sella (Tun), Garfish, flat needlefish, garpike hornfish, greenbone (UK)

Garfish are characterised by a distinctly elongated and fragile body, and by long and narrow jaws. The mandibles grow more than the maxillae during development, so the two halves of the beaks often mismatch. The mandible is of particular importance in wounding prey, which is torn to pieces with the aid of the relatively large teeth. Garfish food includes soft-bodied cephalopods as well as pelagic plankton material, and fish fry. With its bluish-greenish colour, the garfish is well camouflaged in its open sea or coastal habitat. Normally growing to 40–80 cm (16–32 in) length, this graceful fish is often seen from motor yachts while jumping out of the waves for its own pleasure, or in the hope of escaping predators. A biological peculiarity is that its some tens of thousands of eggs are attached to coastal vegetation or drifting kelp colonies by fine, flexible filaments. Garfish flesh is much praised since it is not very bony, but due to its comparative rarity, it is mostly found on the menu of coastal restaurants only. Tourists, however, can regularly encounter mounted garfish heads as curios.

175 | **Pacific saury** | Cololabis saira | SCOMBERESOCIDAE / SAURIES

Pacific saury (En), Kurzschnabelmakrelenhecht (D), Paparda del Pacífico (E), Balaou du Pacific (F), Costardella balau (I), Japanse makreelgeep (NI) • Sanma (J), Ggong-chi (Kor), Agulhao-do-Japao (P)

Pacific saury live in the northern part of the Pacific Ocean, east of Japan to Alaska, as far south as Mexico, and tend to migrate very long distances. A small-bodied species, they attain a maximum body length of about 36 cm (14 in). The mature specimens live in large groups far from the shores, in strata near the surface, whereas their offspring dwell in the marine vegetation drifting in the sea. They feed on small planktonic crabs, roe and fish larvae. An important prey of several marine predators, Pacific saury leap above the surface of the water when fleeing from swift enemies. They spawn all year round, but in the California region spawning activity is more intense from February to July. Around Japan they spawn every second month from the age of three to the end of their lives. Their elliptical eggs, or roe, are quite large, 2 mm in diameter. The female fish can produce 100–1800 eggs on one occasion. The roe are attached onto marine plants or rocks. An intensely fished species, Atlantic saury are marketed for food salted and dried, canned or frozen. Large quantities are processed into fishmeal and animal feed. They are usually fried in oil or roasted.

176 | **Atlantic saury** | Scomberesox saurus | SCOMBERESOCIDAE / SAURIES

Atlantic saury (En), Makrelenhecht, Atlantik-Makrelenhecht, Echsenhecht (D), Paparda (E), Balaou atlantique, balaou, aiguille de mer (F), Castaudiellu, costardella, aguglia saira (I), Makreelgeep (NI) • Almindelig makrelgedde (Da), Saury pike (En), Zargána (Gr), Kastardella (Malt), Boulmarayet (Mor), Agulhão (P), Makrillihauki (SF), Zurna (Tr), M'sella (Tun)

One of the most beautiful marine pike-like species, Atlantic saury can very often be observed from the seashore, since members of the species like to wander in large groups near the surface of the water, and in case of danger – or perhaps out of a jocular disposition – they jump and skim above the water with the grace of swallow-fishes. Fishing for saury is difficult even with sweep-nets, for the fish would easily jump over the upper string of buoys of the net. The elongated, slim golden-hued body of the fish is extremely fragile, thus very few specimens per catch remain undamaged. Mature specimens of about 40–50 cm (16–20 in) are marketed well, the beautifully decorated fish fried whole being a tablefare appealing both to the eye and the taste buds of gourmets. The special, unproportionate build of their beaklike jaw makes Atlantic saury popular along the subtropical shores of the Atlantic with holiday-makers, too, who often purchase the head of the fish as a souvenir. Atlantic saury spawn in areas near ocean currents far off the coast, where they attach their roe to seaweed with sticky threads, thus the eggs may sometimes be taken quite far from their native area. The development and evolution of the beaklike jaw has been a preferred topic of scholarly research among ichthyologists.

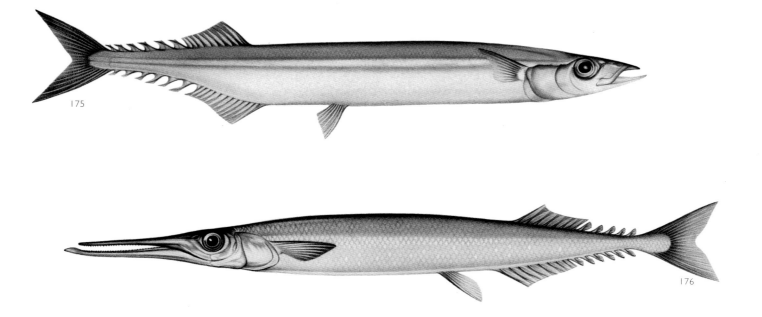

175

176

177 | Sand smelt | Atherina presbyter | ATHERINIDAE / SILVERSIDES

Sand smelt (En), Streifenfisch, Ährenfisch, Priesterfisch (D), Sula, pejerrey, abichón, cabezuda, piarda (E), Prêtre, abusseau, athérine (F), Latterino (I), Kleine koornaarvis (Nl) • Stribefisk (Da), Atherine (En), Bissaria (Egy), Atherína (Gr), Idron (Isr), Kurunella (Malt), Peixe-rei, pirada (P), Aterina (R, Tr), Prästfisk (S), Gavuni, zelenisi (SC), Gümüs (Tr)

The sand smelt lives in the eastern Atlantic, the southern part of the North Sea, the Kattegat, around the British Isles, southwards to Mauritania, the Canary Islands and Cape Verde. It also occurs in the western Mediterranean. A small-sized fish, it reaches 20 cm (8 in) in length and 60–70 g (2–2.5 oz) in body mass at most. It forms huge schools near the coasts, usually above a sand bottom. It is often found in river mouths and brackwater lagoons. Unlike schools of sardines that are constantly on the move, sand smelts commonly remain in a given location for some time. They live near the surface and feed primarily on plankton, but also on fish eggs and larvae. For the winter they sink to greater depths. Spawning occurs between April and July, and the eggs are deposited in heavily vegetated areas, frequently also in brack- or freshwater. The sand smelt is harvested chiefly for direct consumption, seldom reaching markets.

178 | King of herrings | Regalecus glesne | REGALECIDAE / OARFISHES

King of herrings (En), Bandfisch, Riemenfisch (D), Pez remo, rey de los arenques (E), Roi des harengs (F), Re di aringhe (I), Haringkoning (Nl) • Sneesvis (Afr), Sildekonge (Da, N), Oarfish (En), Vasilias regon (Gr), Síldakóngur (Is), Pai-da-sarda, peixe-real, regaleco, regalengo, rei-dos-arenques, relangueiro (P), Sillkungen (S), Airokala (SF), Kurdele baligiv (Tr), Giant oarfish, ribbonfish (UK)

The king of herrings is widely distributed in the Atlantic, and is also found in the Mediterranean. In the Pacific, it occurs in its eastern part from southern California to Chile. The largest specimen on record measured 11 m (43 in) in length and 270 kg (600 lb) in weight. This species is characterised by a thin, ribbon-like body, which can break into two when caught. The first elongated rays of its dorsal fin form a crown-like head ornament typical of this fish. It occurs at a depth of several metres, and feeds on crustaceans, small fish and cephalopods. Spawning takes place between July and December, the larvae living near the surface. An admired catch of anglers for its spectacular appearance, its harvesting is of no particular significance. It is distributed fresh, and is mainly fried, grilled or roasted for human consumption. The king of herrings is listed as the longest bony fish on Earth in the Guinness Book of Records. It sometimes occurs at the surface and ancient tales telling of giant sea snakes may, in fact, have been based on large specimens of this species.

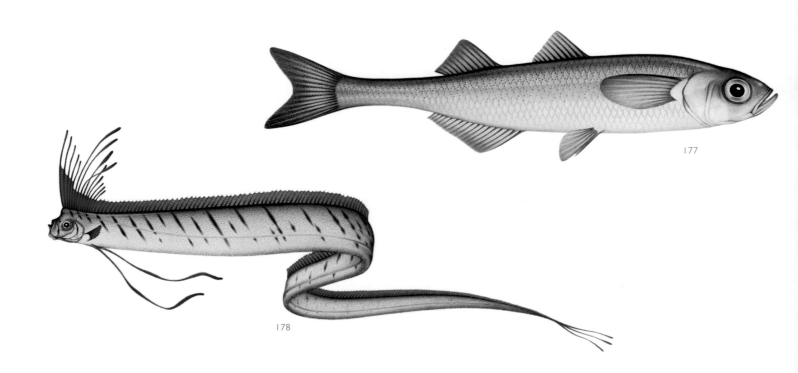

177

178

179 | Opah | Lampris guttatus (L. regius) | LAMPRIDIDAE / OPAHS

Opah (En), Gotteslachs (D), Opa, luna real, brosmio (E), Opah, lampris, assiette (F), Pesce re (I), Koningsvis (Nl) • Glansfisk (Da), Lampropsaro (Gr), Guðlax (Is), Akamanbo, mandai (J), Moonfish (NZ), Peixe-cravo, peixe lua (P), Glansfisk (S)

The most widely distributed species of the family Lampridae, opah may sometimes attain the size of 2 m (80 in) in diameter and 300 kg (660 lb) in weight. They are also called moonfish because of their shining, round body. A specific anatomic trait is the fish's mouth, the upper lip (maxilla) being separately movable forward. This is undeniably essential for this huge creature, since gathering from marine currents and floating macro-zooplanktons the invertebrate organisms that primarily make up its diet would otherwise be a tedious task with less efficient apparatus. Like its lips, the fins of the moonfish are almost all of a reddish hue. The colour of the body varies according to the habitat. The shiny hue also changes with the depth of the water, and the moonfish very often lifts and sinks in the water according to where the actual food-supply is drifting. The meat of the fish is rich in lipids, a trait highly appreciated by customers and very often reflected in the high price many are willing to pay for it. Sometimes the price of moonfish may even exceed that of salmon meat! Moonfish are usually landed as a by-catch in bottom-trawls, but commercially the stock is underexploited.

180 | Splendid alfonsino | Beryx splendens | BERYCIDAE / BERYCIDS

Splendid alfonsino (En), Südlicher Kaiserbarsch (D), Alfonsino besugo, besugo americano (E), Béryx, Béryx long (F), Berice rosso (I), Roodbars (Nl) • Slank beryx (Afr), Pragt-beryx (Da), Slender alfonsino (En), Fagurserkur (Is), Kinmedai (J), Alfonsino comprido (Moz-E), Slender beryx (NZ)

Splendid alfonsino occur world-wide in tropical and subtropical waters, except the northeastern regions of the Pacific and the Mediterranean. They may attain body lengths of 70 cm (28 in). A schooling fish, splendid alfonsino dwell in deeper waters at the margins of the continental shelf, between depths of 180 m and 1300 m (600–4300 ft). They very often ramble in the vicinity of underwater ridges and rocks. They primarily hover over the sea bottom, but at night they may move further up in the water. The young live between water strata. Predatory in habit, splendid alfonsino feed on smaller fish, crustaceans and cephalopods. The scales of the fish are provided with spikes, so the body is very coarse to the touch. After death, the entire body of the fish assumes a reddish hue. Deep-sea fishermen often catch alfonsino. Marketed frozen, the meat of the fish is used for food, being boiled, simmered and fried in various ways.

181 | **Orange roughy** | Hoplostethus atlanticus | TRACHICHTHYIDAE / ROUGHIES

Orange roughy (En), Granatbarsch, Degenfisch (D), Reloj anaranjado (E), Hoplostète orange, poisson-montre (F), Pesce specchio atlantico (I), Atlantische slijmkop (Nl) • Deepsea perch, sea perch (Au), Búrfiskur (Is), Hiuchidai (J)

This eye-catching fish of orange-red hue is found on both sides of the Atlantic, to the west in the Gulf of Maine, in the northeast from Iceland to Morocco, in the southeast from Namibia to South Africa. It is also abundant from the middle region of the Indian Ocean as far south as New Zealand, and along the coast of Chile. They are caught in greatest numbers around New Zealand. The largest specimens may attain body lengths of 75 cm (30 in), and weights of 7 kg (15.4 lb), whereas the landed fish average 30–40 cm (12–16 in) and 1–1.5 kg (1.2–3.3 lb) in size. They prefer deep and cool waters, living on the slopes of the continental shelf, at depths of 200–1800 m (650–6000 ft). Predatory in habit, they feed on crustaceans, fish and cephalopods. Their growth rate is very slow; the species is one of the longest lived, the oldest specimen known was 149 years old. They spawn once a year, in enormous groups. This is the period when the largest numbers of orange roughy are landed with bottom trawls over the spawning grounds. A widely exploited stock, orange roughy have firm-textured, tasty meat of white colour, rich in nutritions fatty acids. The skin of the fish and the layers underneath are rich in oil, used in cosmetics. Marketed for food fresh and frozen, the meat is usually simmered, pan-fried, roasted or baked in the oven.

182 | **John Dory** | Zeus faber | ZEIDAE / DORIES

John Dory (En), Heringskönig, Petersfisch (D), Pez de san Pedro, gallo (E), Saint-pierre, jean doré (F), Pesce San Pietro (I), Zonnevis (Nl) • Jandorie (Afr), Gall (Cat), Sanktpetersfisk (Da, N), Christópsaro (Gr), Matodai (J), Dal-go-gi (Kor), Huta San Pietru (Malt), Hai fáng (Mand), Peixe-galo, galo negro (P), Obyknovennyj solnechnik (R), Dulgher (Ru), Sanktpersfisk (S), Kovaè (Slo), Dülger baligi (Tr), European John Dory (US)

Perhaps the most widely distributed species of the family Zeidae, or dories, the John Dory is found worldwide in warm seas. In the Mediterranean region it is called "Saint Peter's fish" because legend has it that the apostle produced the golden coin from the mouth of this fish. In other regions the traditional story tells us that the distinctive, yellow-ringed black spot on each side of the fish are marks left by the saint's hand. Whatever the truth, there is no mention of any similar legend outside the Christian world. The John Dory mainly dwells in coastal waters, its offspring feeding on a varied diet, very often literally under the feet of swimmers. Mature fish tend to go further from the shore, though, gradually assuming an entirely marine life style. Fishermen do not particularly favour the species because of its enormous head and the spines of their fins, thus rarely does the "useful weight" exceed 50% of live weight. John Dory fillets are dry and not particularly flavoursome. John Dory specimens, rarely exceeding the size of 40 cm (16 in) and 2 kg (4.5 lb), are marketed all year round in some place or another, due to the geographical range of the fish.

183 | **Blackbelly rosefish** | *Helicolenus dactylopterus* | SEBASTIDAE / ROCKFISHES

Blackbelly rosefish (En), Blaumaul (D), Gallineta, rascasio rubio (E), Rascasse du nord, sébaste chèvre (F), Scorfano di fondale (I), Blauwkeeltje (Nl) • Jac, jacopewer (Afr), Akrub (Egy), Blue-mouth, rock fish (En), Sevastos (Gr), Skorfna tal-ghajn (Malt), Cardonniero (Mon), Acantarilho, boca negra, cantarilho legítimo, galinha, papa-jaca (P), Rosefish (US), Teyentan (Wol-M)

The blackbelly rosefish belonging to the family of scorpionfishes is found in the western Atlantic from Nova Scotia to Venezuela, and in the east from Iceland and Norway to South Africa. It has also been recovered from the Mediterranean Sea. It occurs in deep waters in soft-bottomed areas on the continental shelf, on the bottom at depths of 100–500 m (330–1600 ft). Its maximum length is 40–45 cm (16–18 in), maximum weight 1–1.5 kg (2.2–3.3 lb). A carnivorous fish, it preys on either bottom-dwelling or pelagic organisms, such as smaller fish, crustaceans, cephalopods, and echinodermatans. It occurs in large schools, and is a favourite catch of deep-sea fishermen. It is sold in huge numbers in local markets, mainly fresh. It is prepared in various ways, fried or grilled. Deep-sea anglers regularly catch blackbelly rosefish, but it should be handled with caution, as the spinous rays of its fins secrete a poisonous substance.

184 | **Silvergrey rockfish** | *Sebastes brevispinis* | SEBASTIDAE / ROCKFISHES

Silvergrey rockfish (En), Silberrotbarsch (D), Gallineta (E), Sébaste argenté (F), Sebaste (I), Roodbaars (Nl) • Sølvgrå klippefisk (Da), Short-pined rockfish (En)

This pseudo-percoid species dwells in the northeastern regions of the Pacific Ocean, from the Alaskan coast of the Bering Sea to the Mexican stretch of the Gulf of California. They may attain sizes of 71 cm (28 in) and 2.8–3 kg (6–6.6 lb). They live in the vicinity of coasts over the sea bottom at depths of 350–380 m (1150–1250 ft). They occasionally hide in underwater caves and crevasses. They stick to their dwelling grounds, and do not migrate long distances. Generally of predatory instincts, but opportunist in feeding habits, silvergrey rockfish feed on several fishes, crustaceans and worms. Like related species, silvergrey rockfish take 10–20 years to attain sexual maturity, thus the species is in great danger of being overfished. Fertilization is done internally, with the offspring being delivered after hatching in the body of the mother. The most productive fishing gear used to catch silvergrey rockfish is the bottom trawl and "long-line" equipment. They are not very often caught by recreational fishermen. Since they possess a closed swim bladder, the landed fish undergo veritable tortures when dying. The gases in the swim bladder expand and exert great pressure on the internal organs of the fish. The stomach of the fish thus protrudes through the mouth cavity, killing the fish. The tasty meat of the fish is of red hue, the texture being of excellent quality. Generally marketed in fillets, mixed with the meat of other related rockfishes, it is usually pan-fried, roasted or baked in the oven.

183

184

185 | Widow rockfish | Sebastes entomelas | SEBASTIDAE / ROCKFISHES

Widow rockfish (En), Witwenrotbarsch, Witwendrachenkopf (D), Rocote viuda (E), Rocote (F), Scorfano vedova, sebaste bruno (I), Weduweroodbaars (Nl) • Enkerødfisk (Da), Cantarilho-viuvo (P)

This pseudo-percoid species dwells in the northeastern region of the Pacific Ocean, from the Albatross reef in the Alaska Gulf as far south as the Gulf of California. Widow rockfish may attain body lengths of 60 cm (24 in) and weight of 2–2.2 kg (4.4–4.8 lb). Generally an active, freely roaming species, they move about in midwater along rocky reefs and steep rocky coasts, but occasionally they rest motionless in underwater caves and crevices. They mostly prefer rock bottom. Their offspring preferring the shallows, adult species would occasionally go as deep in the sea as 550 m (1800 ft). They form large groups when hunting for prey consisting mainly of small fish and crustaceans. Individuals attain sexual maturity at the age of 3–5. Fertilization is internal, the offspring hatching in the body of the female fish. Larger female individuals may produce as many as 900,000 eggs, or roe, on one occasion. They can be caught all year round. Commercial fishermen use the boat seine, and recreational fishermen also like to catch widow rockfish. One of the most important landed rockfish, widow rockfish yield meat of excellent quality, of pale red hue, with the layers near the skin being somewhat darker. Marketed for food fresh and frozen, the meat of the fish is generally pan-fried, baked in the oven, or boiled.

186 | Yellowtail rockfish | Sebastes flavidus | SEBASTIDAE / ROCKFISHES

Yellowtail rockfish (En), Gelbschwanzrotbarsch, Gelbschwanzdrachenkopf (D), Chancharro cola amarilla (E), Sébaste à queue jaune (F), Scorfano dalla coda gialla, sebaste a pinne gialle (I), Geelstaart roodbaars (Nl) • Gulhalet rødfisk (Da), Green snapper (En), Cantarilho-rabo-amarelo (P), Gulfenad kungsfisk (S)

This pseudo-percoid species dwells in the northeastern region of the Pacific Ocean, in the area extending from Kodiak Island in Alaska to the south of California, but it is most abundant along the middle and northern Californian coasts. They average 66 cm (26 in) in length and 2.5 kg (5.5 lb) in weight. They live in large schools near sheer rocky coasts and rock reefs, but they often hide in underwater caves and crevices, too. Normally they do not go below depths of 500–600 m (1600–2000 ft). Predatory in habit, their diet mainly consists of crustaceans, fish and cephalopods dwelling in midwater, their fry feeding on zooplankton. They generally attain sexual maturity at the age of 4–5. Spawning takes place from January to May. Fertilization is internal, the offspring hatching in the body of the mother and being "delivered" afterwards. Depending on size, a female fish may produce 50,000–500,000 eggs, or roe, in one spawning season. The offspring are often found around the footing of buoys and piers. For catching yellowtail rockfish, commercial fishermen use trawls, whereas recreational fishermen use demersal fishing gear. The excellent, flavoursome meat of the fish, of reddish hue, is usually marketed for food in fillets, mixed with the fillets of other related species. It is fried in oil, baked in the oven or roasted.

185

186

187

188

187 | Canary rockfish | Sebastes pinniger | SEBASTIDAE / ROCKFISHES

Canary rockfish (En), Kanariengelber Felsenfisch (D), Rocote canario (E), Sébaste (F), Scorfano (I), Roodbaars (Nl) • K'aa (Hai)

This pseudo-percoid species dwells in the eastern region of the Pacific Ocean, from the Gulf of Alaska as far south as the Mexican coasts of the Gulf of California. The largest specimens attain body lengths of 76 cm (30 in) and weight of 4.5 kg (10 lb). The fully mature individuals form loose schools over rocky reefs, as deep as 400–450 m (1300–1500 ft). The offspring are found in shallows, in midwater. Predator in habit, they feed on small fish and pelagic crustaceans. They attain sexual maturity only at the age of 5–6. Spawning lasts from January to March. Similarly to related species, fertilization and hatching of the offspring is internal, the fry being "delivered" subsequently. Depending on size, the female specimens produce 250,000–1,900,000 eggs, or roe, in one spawning season. Their larvae live in the plankton. Counting as a good catch any time of the year, canary rockfish are easiest to land from depths of 300–500 m (1000–1700 ft). Due to their large size and spectacular colouring, they are a most appreciated pseudo-percoid species. However, when landed, the fish has to be handled with utmost care, since the sting of the hard fin rays of the fish may be venomous. The meat of canary rockfish is red in colour. In the strata below the skin it is rich in oil, for which reason it is of darker hue. An especially flavoursome type of meat, it is marketed for food fresh and frozen, usually being fried in oil, or roasted.

188 | Yelloweye rockfish | Sebastes ruberrimus | SEBASTIDAE / ROCKFISHES

Yelloweye rockfish (En), Gelbaugenrotbarsch (D), Rocote ojo amarillo (E), Sébaste à l'oeil jaune (F), Scorfano (I), Geeloog-roodbaars (Nl) • Ushmaq (Alu), Guløjet rødfisk (Da), Sgan (Hai), Karmazyn zóltooki (Pl), Gulögd kungsfisk (S)

Yelloweye rockfish dwell in the eastern region of the Pacific Ocean, from the Gulf of Alaska to the Mexican waters of the Gulf of California. A large-bodied species, they may attain body lengths of 91 cm (36 in) and weights of 9.6 kg. They live over rocky reefs and gravel sea bottoms, to depths of 500–550 m (1600–1800 ft), though the young prefer shallow waters. Very spectacular in appearance, they have large yellow eyes; the upper part of the body is orange, and it is yellowish-white below. Predatory in habit, they feed on fish and crustaceans. An ovoviviparous species, with fertilization and hatching of the fry taking place internally, the "delivered" fry are fully developed when they are born. Spawning lasts from January to May. The meat of the fish is red in colour, firm-textured and extremely tasty. Due to the size of the fish, large fillets can be produced from it. The colour of the meat is of darker hue near the skin, due to the layers of blubber there. Commercial fishermen use trawls or longline fishing gear, and demersal fishermen also appreciate the catch. The meat of the fish is usually pan-fried, roasted or baked in the oven, but fish soups, chowders and stew are also delicious with it.

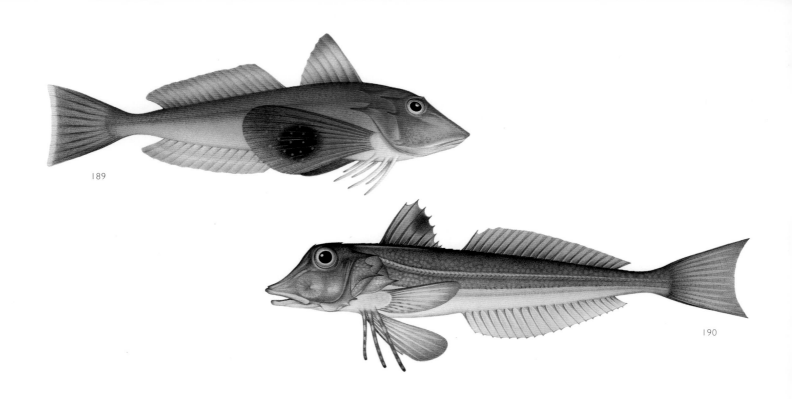

189

190

189 | Bluefin gurnard | Chelidonichthys kumu | TRIGLIDAE / GURNARDS AND GRONDINS

Bluefin gurnard (En), Neuseeländischer Roter Knurrhahn (D), Testolín de aleta azul, rubio kumu (E), Grondin-aile bleue (F), Capone imperiale, gallinella (I), Blauwvinpoon (Nl) • Blouvin-knorhaan (Afr), Kumu gurnard (Au), Red gurnard (Au, NZ), Houbou (J), Seong-dae (Kor), Kumukumu (Mao), Ruivo barbatana azul (Moz-P), Cabra-kumu (P)

A member of the trigla family, bluefin gurnard occur chiefly in the Indian Ocean and in the western region of the Pacific. Also abundant along the southern coasts of Africa and in the waters of Australia and New Zealand, populations of bluefin gurnard have also been reported from Japan, Korea and Hong Kong. The largest size they can attain is 60 cm (24 in) in length and 1.5 kg (3.3 lb) in weight. Bottom-dwelling in habit, they primarily live over sand bottoms, in waters ranging from the brackish waters of river estuaries to the margins of the continental shelf. They have also been observed ascending rivers. Their diet mainly consists of smaller fish and crustaceans. Bluefin gurnard may use the ray of their dorsal fin as a stinging weapon, by which they poison their enemy. Thus when landing, fisherman ought to handle the fish with care. The meat of the bluefin gurnard is of exceptionally good quality and is very popular with both commercial and recreational fishermen.

190 | Grey gurnard | Chelidonichtys (Eutrigla) gurnardus | TRIGLIDAE / GURNARDS AND GRONDINS

Grey gurnard (En), Grauer Knurrhahn (D), Borracho, perlón, cuco de altura, crego (E), Grondin gris, gurnard, trigle gris (F), Anzoleto piccolo, capone gorno, gallinella, pesce cappone (I), Grauwe poon, knorhaan (Nl) • Gjel gri (Alb), Cap d'ase (Cat), Grå knurhane (Da), Kapóni (Gr), Urrari (Is), Kanagashira (J), Djâj Sakhry (Leb), Crodane glass (Manx), Knor, knurr, knurrfisk, vanlig knurr (N), Cabra morena, ruivo (P), Seraya trigla (R), Knorrhane, knot (S), Kokot, lastavica prasica (SC), Kyhmykurnusimppu (SF), Benekli kirlangic (Tr), Searobin (US)

The grey gurnard inhabits the eastern part of the Atlantic from Norway to Morocco, as well as the Mediterranean and the Black Sea. It is found at a depth of 140 m (450 ft) off the coastline, mainly on sandy bottoms, but occasionally occurs on rocky and muddy bottoms. It sometimes occurs alone, but more often in groups of various sizes, growing to 60 cm (24 in) in length and about 2 kg (4.4 lb) maximum weight. A carnivorous species, it preys primarily on crustaceans and fish, mainly sole, young herring and sand eels. It is able to produce a croaking sound, from which its name in some languages is derived. Its fishing is not particularly important, and the grey gurnard is found in local markets either fresh on ice, or frozen. It also occurs in the catch of coastal anglers, or those operating from small boats. The flesh is prepared mainly pan-fried or roasted in an oven.

191 | Yellow gurnard, Tub gurnard | Chelidonichthys lucernus | TRIGLIDAE / GURNARDS AND GRONDINS

Yellow gurnard, Tub gurnard (En), Roter Knurrhahn, Seeschwalbe (D), Bejel, Alfondiga (E), Grondin perlon, gallinette (F), Capone gallinella (I), Rode poon, grote poon (Nl) • Gjel i hirte (Alb), Rød knurhane (Da), Ferakh (Egy), Yellow gurnard (En), Selachi, khelidonás (Gr), Djaj ramyl (Leb), Gallina (Malt), Galinetta (Mon), Rødknurr (N), Cabra-cabaço (P), Morscoj petukh-zhe (R), Fenknot (S), Kokot balavica, lastavica balavica (SC), Isokurnusimppu (SF), Kirlangic baligi (Tr), Djaj (Tun), Sapphirine gurnard, searobin (US)

The yellow gurnard is a typical bottom-dwelling species, inhabiting the eastern part of the Atlantic, from Norway southwards to coastal West Africa. It also occurs in the Mediterranean and the Black Sea. It favours sandy, sandy-muddy and stony bottoms. Found mainly in cold water (8–10°C), it also tolerates warmth (up to 24°C). Its maximum size is 60–70 cm (24–28 in) and 5–6 kg (11–13 lb). This species can be identified by its three long rays, which stand out clearly from the rest of the pectoral fin. The yellow gurnard leans on them while resting, but these stiff rays also help it to locate food on the soft bottom. A predatory fish, it consumes fish, crustaceans and gastropods. It is caught in considerable numbers and is favoured by deep-sea anglers. It is marketed either fresh (on ice) or frozen. Various forms of culinary preparation are known, employing pans, grill, oven or microwave. Thanks to its spectacular appearance, it is also exhibited in show aquariums.

192 | Piper gurnard | Trigla lyra | TRIGLIDAE / GURNARDS AND GRONDINS

Piper gurnard (En), Leierknurrhahn, Pfeifenfisch (D), Garneo (E), Grondin lyre (F), Gallinella cappone, capone lira (I), Lierpoon (Nl) • Peshk gjel (Alb), Knorhaan, lier-knorhaan (Afr), Langpigget knurrhane (Da), Ferakh (Egy), Kapóni (Gr), Urrari (Is), Triglia kenufa (Isr), Gallinetta (Malt), Galinëta cofanu (Mon), Roubiou (Mor), Knurr, lyreknurr (N), Cabra-lira (P), Lyrknot (S), Lastavica-koste jaca (SC), Piikkikurnusimppu (SF), Lirasti krulec (Slo), Öksüz (Tr), Djaje (Tun), Piper (US)

The piper gurnard is a typical deep-sea fish, occurring on the bottom at depths of 100–200 m (350–900 ft) depth. Found in the eastern part of the Atlantic, from the British Isles and the North Sea to Namibia, it also occurs in the Mediterranean, while it is apparently absent from the Black Sea. Reaching 50–60 cm (20–24 in) maximum length, its mass approaches 3–4 kg (7–9 lb) at most. A predator, it feeds on various bottom-dwelling crustaceans. Its name in some languages is derived from the fish's ability to produce sounds. Deep-sea fishermen rarely encounter this species, and it is of no particular economic significance. The ways it is prepared are also poorly known; it is possibly distributed both on ice and frozen. The large head means there is little else left to eat.

191

192

193 | Sablefish | Anoplopoma fimbria | HEXAGRAMMIDAE / GREENLINGS AND COMBFISHES

Sablefish (En), Kohlenfisch, Säbelfisch (D), Bacalao negro (E), Morue noire (F), Merluzzo dell'Alaska, fimbria (I), Zwarte kabeljauw (Nl) • Almindelig fakkelfisk (Da), Skil (Hai), Gindara (J), Peixe-carvão-do-Pacífico (P), Anoplopoma (Pl), Ugolnaya ryba (R)

Sablefish inhabit the northern region of the Pacific Ocean, in the area extending from the Bering Sea, the waters along Kamchatka, Russia and Alaska, as far south as the southern coasts of Japan and the Mexican waters of the Gulf of California. The largest specimens attain sizes of 120 cm (47 in) and 5.7 kg. Mature specimens live over mud and sand bottoms, to depths of 300–1800 m (1000–6000 ft). In the first year of their lives, the offspring are found near the surface and in the shallow coastal waters. They usually remain in their original territory, but some individuals may spend 6–7 years travelling as far as 3–4000 km from their first habitat. Predatory in feeding habits, the diet of sablefish consists of fish, crustaceans and worms. They attain sexual maturity at the age of 5–7. They spawn from January to March over the continental shelf, at depths of 300–400 m (1000–1300 ft). The female fish, depending on size, produce 100,000–1,000,000 in one spawning season. A widely exploited stock, sablefish are very likely to be bred in hatcheries in the future. The greatest proportion of the total landings is marketed in Japan. The meat of the fish is white in colour, oily and of a delicate flavour. The liver of the fish yields oil rich in vitamins A and D. In some countries strips of the meat are fried in batter.

194 | Lingcod | Ophiodon elongatus | HEXAGRAMMIDAE / GREENLINGS AND COMBFISHES

Lingcod (En), Lengdorsch (D), Bacalao largo, lorcha (E), Terpuga buffalo (F), Ofiodonte (I), Lingcod (Nl) • Gjuhez kanali (Alb), Lingtorsk (Da), Ainame (J), Grönfisk (S), Vihersimppu (SF)

Lingcod dwell in the northeastern region of the Pacific Ocean, from the Gulf of Alaska to the Gulf of California. They very likely occur in the Bering Sea, too. They are found from the foreshores to depths of about 500 m (1600 ft), near the sea bottom. Mature specimens prefer a rock bottom, whereas the offspring live over the sand and mud bottom of the coastal waters. They average 152 cm (60 in) and 4.5 kg (10 lb) in size. Both migratory and sedentary stocks are known. A voracious predator, mature specimens feed on fish, crustaceans and cephalopods, their offspring feeding on zooplankton. Lingcod attain sexual maturity at the age of 4–5. Spawning lasts from December to March. In one spawning season a female fish produces 60,000–500,000 roe. The male fish tends the nest until the larvae hatch. A stock widely exploited by both commercial and recreational fishermen, lingcod ought to be handled with care, since they sport very sharp teeth and gill covers, which may cause very painful wounds. Highly appreciated for the extremely palatable meat they yield, lingcod are also caught for their liver, which is rich in vitamin A. The meat may occasionally assume a greenish colour, but this does not mean that it is rotten.

193

194

195 | Okhostk atka mackerel | Pleurogrammus azonus | HEXAGRAMMIDAE / GREENLINGS AND COMBFISHES

Okhostk atka mackerel (En), Atka-Makrele, Terpug (D), Lorcha de Atka (E), Terpuga arabesque (F), Terpugo (I), Atka (Nl) • Atkamakrel (Da), Hokke, im-yeon-su-eo, yase-ainame (J), Línguas-de-cão (P), Yuzhnyi odnoperyi terpug (R), Japanese atka mackerel (US)

The Okhostk atka mackerel inhabits the northwestern part of the Pacific. It lives in temperate waters in the Sea of Okhostk, in the seas off the Kuril Islands and Japan, and can also be found in the Yellow Sea in the south. Its maximum length is 60 cm (24 in), weight 4–5 kg (9–11 lb). Young Okhostk atka mackerels live in huge schools close to the surface, while adults retreat to the bottom. This predatory species feeds in groups on smaller fish. Little is known of its biology. It is intensely fished, and is sold fresh, salted or frozen. It is prepared grilled or fried in a pan.

196 | Atka mackerel | Pleurogrammus monopterygius | HEXAGRAMMIDAE / GREENLINGS AND COMBFISHES

Atka mackerel (En), Einflossiger Terpug (D), Caballa (E), Terpuga atka (F), Maccarello (I), Atka makreel (Nl) • Kitano-hokke (J), Atkafisk (S)

Atka mackerel dwell in the northeastern region of the Pacific Ocean, but are also found in the Yellow Sea, the Bering Sea near Alaska, and they have also been recorded as having travelled as far as Redondo Beach in California. They average 50 cm (20 in) in length and 1 kg (2.2 lb) in weight. They prefer water strata from the lower region of the tidal area to depths of 575 m (1886 ft). They form large shoals and mostly move about in the vicinity of the coastline, over the sea bottom. They do not have a swimbladder, thus they hunt while continuously swimming. Predatory in habit, they feed on smaller fish and crustaceans. They spawn twice a year, the main spawning season being from July to September. They deposit their eggs, or roe, in crevices in the rocks, the male fish tending the nest while continually fanning the water over them with its pectoral fins in order to maintain a permanent change of water. The most productive fishing gear for atka mackerel is the bottom trawl. One of the most important commercially exploited greenling species, atka mackerel are marketed for food fresh, salted and dried, frozen, or sometimes canned. The meat of the fish is usually pan-fried, roasted, or sometimes smoked.

197 | **Lumpfish** | Cyclopterus lumpus | CYCLOPTERIDAE / LUMPFISHES AND MOLLETS

Lumpfish (En), Seehase, Lumpfisch, Lump (D), Lompo, ciclóptero (E), Lompe, mollet (F), Ciclottero, lompo (I), Snotolf, strontvreter (Nl) • Grosse poule de mer (Can-F), Angusalluk, arnarluk, nepisa (Cree), Kulso, kvabso, stenbider (Da), Kotópsaro (Gr), Angusatdluk, angusedlok, arnardlok, arnardluk, lepisuk, nepisa, qorkshuyog (Inu), Hrognkelsi (Is), Dango-uo (J), Kiark-varrey (Man), Rognkall, rognkaeks, rognkjeks (N), Piexe-lapa, galinha do mar (P), Tasza (Pl), Pinagor (R), Sjurygg, stenbit, kvabhso, kvabbso (S), Rasvakala (SF), Lumpsucker (US)

The lumpfish occurs in the Atlantic Ocean and the northern seas of Europe, and favours colder waters. Characteristic flat ossicles arranged in three distinct rows line its sides. Its ventral fins have been modified into a sucker. The maximum size is 60 cm (24 in) in length and 9–9.5 kg (20–21 lb) in mass. A migratory fish species, it covers substantial distances during its annual migration. It returns to the open sea for the winter, but inhabits coastal waters in summer. A bottom-dweller, it favours a rocky bottom, but also occurs in areas with drifting vegetation, and is solitary rather than gregarious. A carnivore, it chiefly consumes ctenophores, smaller crustaceans and fish. The sides of males turn red in the breeding season, while females have a bluish-green colour. Fishermen consider the lumpfish a valuable catch, as its eggs can be made into cheap caviar. Also its flesh is widely consumed.

198 | **Great barracuda** | Sphyraena barracuda | SPHYRAENIDAE / BARRACUDAS

Great barracuda (En), Barrakuda, Amerikanischer Pfeilhecht (D), Picuda barracuda (E), Barracuda, bécune (F), Barracuda maggiore (I), Barracuda (Nl) • Groot barrakuda (Afr), Striped sea-pike (Au), Kutjul (Ind), Oni-kamasu (J), Alu-alu (Jav), Kachang (Mal), Sea pike (NZ), Pilgädda (S), Msusa (Swa)

One of the most feared predators of the Earth's warm seas, the great barracuda is also potentially dangerous for humans. This long, torpedo-shaped, sharp-toothed fearsome fish may attain a body length of 1–2 m (40–80 in). The young typically form schools, and they tend to segregate according to size. They do not normally exceed limit barriers within the groups, since the larger specimens have a cannibalistic instinct. Great barracuda are more feared by divers than are sharks, for they attack their prey very swiftly and unexpectedly, and in such situations everything depends on the fast reaction of the "prey". Typically barracuda are caught by lining, but even the catch has to be handled with care on board the fishing boat, since with its sharp teeth the fish may cause serious harm to the limbs of the less skilful. Highly prized in restaurants, the meat of the barracuda is a rare delicacy. Barracuda is usually served on special occasions, for the huge fish prepared whole is a really spectacular decoration on the table. The head of the fish is often prepared as a trophy and sold to tourists in seaside holiday resorts.

199 | **Thicklip grey mullet** | Chelon labrosus | MUGILIDAE / MULLETS

Thicklip grey mullet (En), Dicklippige Meeräsche, Grauäsche (D), Lisa, mugle (E), Mulet lippu, muge noir à grosses lévres (F), Cefalo boséga, muggine labbrone (I), Diklippige harder (Nl) • Qefulli i dimrit (Alb), Tyklæbet multe (Da), Gröröndungur (Is), Tykkleppet multe (N), Tainha-liça (P), Tolstogubaya kefal (R), Chefal (Ru), Tjockläppad multe (S), Paksuhuulikeltti (SF), Debelousti cipelj (Slo), Lesser grey mullet (UK), Thicklip mullet (US)

This species of mullet occurs in the eastern Atlantic, from Scandinavia and Iceland southwards to Senegal and Cape Verde. It is also found in the Mediterranean and the southwestern part of the Black Sea. Its maximum length is 60 cm (24 in), maximum weight 1.4–1.5 kg (3–3.3 lb). This is a coastal species which also enters brackwater lagoons, and even freshwater. It has sometimes been observed migrating. In summer, it moves north with the increase of temperature, while it spawns in the sea during winter. Its eggs and larvae are pelagic, i.e. they are found drifting in open water. The thicklip grey mullet feeds mainly on epiphytic algae, small invertebrates and detritus. It is harvested for its tasty flesh, marketed fresh and frozen, and mostly served fried, grilled or roasted. This species is regularly exhibited in show aquariums.

200 | **Leaping mullet** | Liza saliens | MUGILIDAE / MULLETS

Leaping mullet (En), Springmeeräsche, Kleine Meeräsche (D), Ilisa, galúa blanca, galúa negra (E), Muge sauteur, mugon, mulet sauteur (F), Cefalo verzelata, musino (I), Springharder (Nl) • Veshverdhi (Alb), Springmulte (Da), Multe (N), Mugem, tainha-de-salto (P), Mugil ostronosy (Pl), Ostronos, ostronosik (R), Hoppmulte (S), Cipli (SC), Dolgin (Slo), Kobar baligi (Tr), Leaping grey mullet (UK)

This species of mullet is native to the eastern Atlantic, from the French coast to Morocco. It is also found in the Mediterranean, the Black Sea and the Sea of Azov. Its maximum length is 45 cm (18 in), maximum body mass 1.2 kg (2.6 lb). This is a coastal fish moving around in relatively small groups. It is frequently found in coastal brackwater areas, entering estuaries in its search for food. An herbivorous species, it filters phytoplankton from the water. It is often caught with gill-nets, and is nowadays bred on fish farms. Also harvested for its eggs, its flesh is marketed fresh, smoked or frozen. It is most often fried, grilled or roasted for human consumption.

199

200

201 | Golden grey mullet | Mugil auratus / Liza aurata | MUGILIDAE / MULLETS

Golden grey mullet (En), Goldäsche, Goldmeeräsche (D), Galupe (E), Mulet doré, mulet daurin (F), Cefalo dorato (I), Goudharder (Nl) • Veshflorini (Alb), Platarina (Bul), Cipal zlatac (Cr), Guldmulte (Da), Myxinari (Gr), Tainha (P), Singhil (R, Ru), Zlati cipelj (Slo), Altinbkefal baligi (Tr)

Native to the eastern region of the Atlantic Ocean, from Scotland to Cape Verde, golden grey mullet are also found in the Mediterranean Sea and the Black Sea, in temperate and sub-tropical waters. They occasionally occur along the southern coast of Norway and in the south around Mauritania. Records of the fish reported from the Accrai Lagoon are probably erroneous. With two golden-coloured spots on the gill covers, they average 59 cm (23 in) in length and 4 kg (9 lb) in weight. A species pertaining to shallow waters, golden grey mullet do not normally go deeper than 10 m (33 ft); they very often occur in the brackish waters of lagoons and river estuaries. They temporarily may intrude into freshwater, too. They move around in large groups. They feed on small demersal organisms and organic detritus, but occasionally eat insects and plankton. They spawn from July to November, in the sea. An important food fish, golden grey mullet stocks are widely exploited and are also bred in aquacultures. Commercial fishermen use surrounding nets and gill nets. The quality of the meat is changeable; it is marketed for food fresh or frozen, and is eaten smoked, pan-fried, roasted or baked in the oven. In some regions fish soup is also made from this fish.

202 | Common grey mullet, Flathead mullet | Mugil cephalus | MUGILIDAE / MULLETS

Common grey mullet, Flathead mullet (En), Großkopf-Meeräsche, Gestreifte Meeräsche, Gemeine Meeräsche (D), Lisa pardete, mugil común (E), Mulet cabot (F), Cefalo, muggune (I), Grootkopharder (Nl) • Sea mullet (Au), Keffal (Bul), Common grey mullet (En), Képhalos (Gr), Gandhia (Guj), Gerita (Ind), Kifon gdol hazosh (Isr), Bora (J), Gereh (Jav), Sung-eo (Kor), Zi yú (Mand), Mugem (P), Loban (R), Chefal (Ru), Juovakeltti (SF), Is barri godeya (Sin), Kasmeen (Tam), Haskefal baligi (Tr), Bouri (Tun, Egy), Striped mullet (US, NZ), Gis (Wol-S)

The common grey mullet is a commercially valuable type of fish widely known and appreciated for its palatable meat from Europe to the Far East. In most countries it is eaten fried in oil. Relatively small in size, the grey mullet reaches an average length of 30–40 cm (12–16 in), and weighs about 600–800 g (21–28 oz). It is widely spread mainly because it can live in any type of water from salt-water to brackish river estuaries. In the warm waters of the open sea they mostly school close to the surface, whereas in coastal waters they may populate an entire area. They may even occur in inshore areas and mangrove swamps. The market has largely benefited from the fact that a substance gained from the fish is believed to be an aphrodisiac. After a preservation process involving drying in the sun and smoking, the reproductive organs of both the male and the female fish are sold in huge quantities in the Far East. An omnivorous fish, the grey mullet is a species easy to breed, and it is largely believed to be a promising future protein repository of the planet.

203 | **Thicklip grey mullet** | Mugil labrosus | MUGILIDAE / MULLETS

Thicklip grey mullet (En), Dicklippige Meeräsche (D), Lisa (E), Muge à grosse lèvre, mulet lippu (F), Cefalo chelone, cefalo bosega (I), Diklipharder (Nl) • Qefulli i dimrit (Alb), Llissa vera (Cat), Mrena (Cr), Tyklæbet multe (Da), Velanitsa (Gr), Gráröndungur (Is), Mulett (Malt), Tykkleppet multe (N), Mugem, tainha-liça, tainha-negrão (P), Tjockläppad multe (S), Paksuhuulikeltti (SF), Kefal baligi (Tr)

Dwelling in the eastern region of the Atlantic Ocean, from Scandinavia and Iceland as far south as Senegal, thicklip greymullet are also found in the southwestern part of the Mediterranean Sea and the Black Sea. They may attain a size of 75 cm (30 in) and 4.5 kg (10 lb), although specimens of about 8–10 kg (17.5–22 lb) in weight have also been recorded. They live very close to the coastline, in schools, in brackish and fresh waters. They occasionally set off on journeys to the north when the warm weather sets in. They feed on algae, smaller invertebrates and organic detritus, over the bottom. Since the greatest part of their diet consists of algae, the stomach of the fish is very muscular and is made up of a long intestinal canal. They spawn in the winter months, from January to April, in the sea; their roe and larvae are pelagic, i.e. they are found floating in midwater. An appreciated sportfish, thicklip greymullet very desperately fight for survival when caught on the hook. They are easily noticed, since when feeding, they very actively move about just below the surface. An important food fish, they are widely sought for by both commercial and recreational fishermen. Marketed for food fresh or frozen, the meat of the fish is simmered or boiled, sautéed, roasted or baked in the oven.

204 | **Thinlip mullet** | Mugil ramada, Liza ramado | MUGILIDAE / MULLETS

Thinlip mullet (En), Dünnlippige Meeräsche (D), Morragute (E), Mulet porc (F), Cefalo calamita (I), Dunlipharder (Nl) • Qefulli i vjeshtes (Alb), Keffal (Bul), Tyndlæbet multe (Da), Milléad (Ga), Mauraki, velanitsa (Gr), Cipal balavac (Hr), Röndungur (Is), Tynnleppet multe (N), Tainha-fataça (P), Kefal (R), Platarin (Ru), Ohuthuulikeltti (SF), Tenkousti cipelj (Slo), Pulatarina baligi (Tr)

This mullet species dwells in the eastern waters of the Atlantic, from the southern coasts of Norway to Morocco, and is also found in the Mediterranean and the Black Sea. It has been reported from tropical waters, too, but most likely these reports were mistakes. They may attain body lengths of 70 cm (27.5 in) and weights of 3.2 kg (7 lb). They live in schools in the shallow coastal waters, but, since they easily adjust to differences in salinity, they are often found in the brackish water of lagoons and river estuaries, and sometimes they even intrude into freshwaters. They never go below depths of 10 m (33 ft). They get on well in slightly salted waters of lakes, but they always travel to the sea to spawn, in October-November. Their eggs, or roe, are pelagic, i.e. they hatch while floating in midwater, and the larvae stay there for a while. The offspring can be observed in the lagoons of the Mediterranean Sea. They grow at a very slow rate, in the natural environment attaining 30–35 cm (12–14 in) in length by the time they are 6 years of age. They feed on demersal algae, organic detritus and small invertebrates on the sea bottom. A widely exploited species, thinlip mullet are also bred in fisheries. The meat of the fish is usually sautéed, roasted, fried in the oven, or boiled in fish soups and chowders.

205 | **Indian threadfin** | *Leptomelanosoma indicum* | POLYNEMIDAE / THREADFINS

Indian threadfin (En), Bastardäsche (D), Barbudo indio (E), Barbure indien (F) • Indiese draadvin (Afr), Lakhua (Ben), Indisk trådfinnefisk (Da), Bahmin (Ma), Kurau, kurau hitam, kurow, mancong, senangin (Mal), Indian tassel fish (Mya), Barbudo do Indico (P), Kupe, mkizi komo maji (Swa), Tahlunkala (Tam), Budathamaga (Tel)

The Indian threadfin is an inhabitant of tropical waters in the Indian and Pacific oceans. It is found from the East African coast through Pakistan and India eastwards to the islands of Sumatra and Borneo. It reaches 140 cm (55 in) in length and 16–18 kg (35–40 lb) in body mass. It frequents sandy and muddy shallows on the continental shelf, but occasionally also enters rivers. It lives either alone or in small groups, feeding chiefly on bottom-dwelling crustaceans and smaller fish. With age, the percentage of fish in its food gradually increases. It is not harvested on a very large scale, but is usually available at markets, and is regularly caught by recreational fishermen for its spectacular appearance. It is distributed fresh, frozen or dried-and-salted, and is stewed, fried, grilled or roasted for human consumption.

206 | **Barramundi** | *Lates calcarifer* | CENTROPOMIDAE / BARRAMUNDIS

Barramundi (En), Barramundi, Riesenbarsch (D), Perca gigante (E), Perche barramundi (F), Barramundi (I), Barramundibaars (Nl) • Cock-up (Au), Giant perch (Au, US), Bhetki (Ben), Bulgan (Bik), Apahap (Bik, Ph, Tag, Vis), Maan cho (Cant), Maang-choe (HK), Kakap (Ind, Mal), Akame (J), Cabeh, pelak, telah (Jav), Apap (Kap), Trey spong (Khm), Pica-pica (Mak), Bukai-bukai, gelungsung, siakap (Mal), Matakatin (Mara), Apaap (Pan), Modha (Sin), Keduwa (Tam), Pla kapong khao (Thai), Murrabal (Tok), Asian seabass (US), Cá vurot (Vie), Bolgan (Vis)

A percid fish of great economic importance, the largest specimens of barramundi reach 2 m (80 in) in length and 60 kg (132 lb) in body mass. A bottom-dwelling fish, it is native to the Indian Ocean and the western part of the Pacific, to the Persian Gulf in the north, and to Papua New Guinea and northern Australia in the south, occurring in tropical freshwaters as well as in the sea. Eastwards it is found as far as Japan. It prefers coastal areas, and can be found both in clear and murky water. Older individuals live in the upper reaches of rivers, and reproduction takes place near river mouths or in the brackwater of lagoons. The fry spend the first part of their life in brackwater, then start migrating upstream in rivers. A predatory species, it feeds on other fish and crustaceans. It is farmed on a large scale in Thailand, Indonesia and Australia. Under favourable conditions it can reach 1.5–3 kg (3–6 lb) within a year in fish ponds. It is sold fresh or frozen, and is eaten smoked, pan-fried, roasted in an oven, or grilled.

207 | Argentine seabass | Acanthistius brasilianus | SERRANIDAE / SEA BASSES AND GROUPERS

Argentine seabass (En), Argentinischer Zackenbarsch (D), Mero sureño (E), Serran argentin (F), Cernia (I), Argentijnse zeebars (Nl) • Senhor de engenho (Bra), Argentinsk havaborre (Da), Serrano-argentino (P)

This medium-sized sea bass inhabits subtropical areas in the southwestern Atlantic, off Brazil, Argentina and Uruguay. It grows to 60 cm (24 in) in length and 2.5–3 kg (5.5–6.6 lb) in weight. This member of reef communities frequents somewhat cooler waters of the continental shelf, and occurs either alone or in small groups near the bottom. It is found to a depth of 30–40 m (100–130 ft) at most, and does not invade brackwater. A predatory species, it attacks bottom-dwelling fish, crustaceans and other invertebrates from its lair. Not harvested on a large scale, only 10–15,000 tonnes are caught annually. Although there are no restrictions, the main harvesting season lasts from August to March. This sea bass is also admired by anglers for its excellent flesh, and is marketed fresh or frozen, both whole and as fillets. It is eaten fried or grilled.

208. | Black seabass | Centropristis striata | SERRANIDAE / SEA BASSES AND GROUPERS

Black seabass (En), Schwarzer Sägebarsch, Schwarzer Zackenbarsch (D), Serrano estriado (E), Fanfre noir, Saint-Pierre (F), Perchia striata (I), Zwarte Zeebaars (Nl) • Sort havaborre (Da), Svart havabbor (N), Serrano-estriado (P), Svart havsabborre (S), Kalliomeriahven (SF), See bass (US)

The black seasbass is an inhabitant of the western part of the Atlantic, from the state of Maine (United States) to northeastern Florida, and is also common in the eastern part of the Gulf of Mexico. In exceptionally cold winters it is also found in southern Florida. It grows to 60 cm (24 in) in length and 4.5 kg (10 lb) in weight. A bottom-dwelling fish, it favours shallow waters, and is a typical member of the fish communities of rock-filled dams, reefs and shallow rocky-bottomed areas. A carnivorous species, it feeds on smaller fish, gastropods and crustaceans. It frequently occurs in the catch of fishermen. It is sold fresh or cooled on ice, and is a popular dish prepared roasted in an oven, grilled or fried in a pan. Anglers admire it for its high quality flesh and its fighting spirit. When caught, it should be handled with caution, as the spinous rays of its fins secrete a poisonous substance. It is regularly exhibited in show aquariums.

207

208

209 | White grouper | Epinephelus aeneus | SERRANIDAE / SEA BASSES AND GROUPERS

White grouper (En), Weißer Zackenbarsch (D), Cherna de ley (E), Mérou blanc (F), Cernia bianca, cernia bronzina (I), Witte zaagbars (Nl) • Kern i bardhe (Alb), Murianga (Ang), Merato, mero (CV), Wakar (Egy), Sphyrida (Gr), Daqqar mazuy (Isr), Louqous Ramly Dyby (Leb), Loukouz (Lib), Fellusa tac cerna (Malt), Fausse morue (Mau-F), Mirou hiad (Mor), Garoupa, garoupa verde (P), Kirnja (SC), Coof (Sen), Fausse morue (Sey), Rékott (Sud), Lahoz (Tr, Tun), Mennani abiad (Tun), Grouper (UK), Loger, tiof (Wol), Khoutch (Wol-M), Xuoo (Wol-S)

This grouper is an inhabitant of the eastern Atlantic, and is found in tropical-subtropical waters off the West African coast to Angola in the south. It also occurs in the southern Mediterranean. Its maximum length is 120 cm (47 in), body mass 7 kg (15 lb). Adults of this species live in rock-, mud- or sand-bottomed areas with equal frequency, while juveniles seem to prefer brackwater areas of coastal lagoons and river mouths. Fully mature specimens are found at a depth of 20–200 m (60–660 ft). The white grouper is a protogynous hermaphrodite. Its migrations off Senegal are triggered by floods of the Senegal, and rivers in Mauritania. A fast-growing, aggressive predator, it feeds on fish, stomatopods, crustaceans and cephalopods. Harvested both by commercial and recreational fishermen for its tasty flesh, it is marketed fresh or smoked, and consumed fried, roasted or grilled. This is one of the most widely available species in West African markets.

210 | Dusky grouper, Itajara | Epinephelus itajara | SERRANIDAE / SEA BASSES AND GROUPERS

Dusky grouper, Itajara (En), Riesenzackenbarsch (D), Cherna mero, mero guasa, mero pintado (E), Mérou géant (F), Cernia gigante, sciarrano (I), Grote zaagbaars (Nl) • Badejo (Bra), Guasa (Cub, Ven), Giant seabass (Cub-En), Havaborre (Da), Tobokogbo (Fon), Muluwaimon (Ga), Rophós (Gr), Vartari (Is), Hata (J), Hamlet (Jam), Havabbor, judefisk (N), Garoupa, itajara zmienna, mero, mero-tigra (P), Southern jewfish (Pa), Tipa (Pali), Mero batata, mero sapo (PR), Fläckig, havsabborre (S), Kirnja, bodeljka (SC), Meriahven, raitameriahven (SF), Gran morgoe, graumurg (Sra), Orfoz, ortoz (Tr), Esonue grouper, giant grouper (UK), Jewfish, spotted jewfish (UK, US), Goliath grouper (US)

Dusky grouper dwell in the Atlantic Ocean and in the Mediterranean Sea, and from the Bay of Biscay, by the southern tip of the African continent as far as Mozambique and Madagascar. Along the western coastline of the Atlantic they inhabit the waters from Guyana to Argentina. The largest bodied percoid fish, they may attain a length of 150 cm (59 in) and weight of 60 kg (130 lb). They are solitary in habit and live over rock sea bottom, to depths of 300 m (1000 ft), but they are most abundant depths of 15–50 m (50–165 ft). They vigorously defend their territory against other specimens. They feed on crustaceans, octopuses and other molluscs, but larger specimens also eat fish. They spawn in summer. A protogynous hermaphrodite species, after hatching all the specimens are female, some of the larger ones later transforming into males. The larger specimens are valued sport fish. The excellent meat is pan-fried or baked. In some countries dusky grouper are an ingredient of fish soups and chowders.

209

210

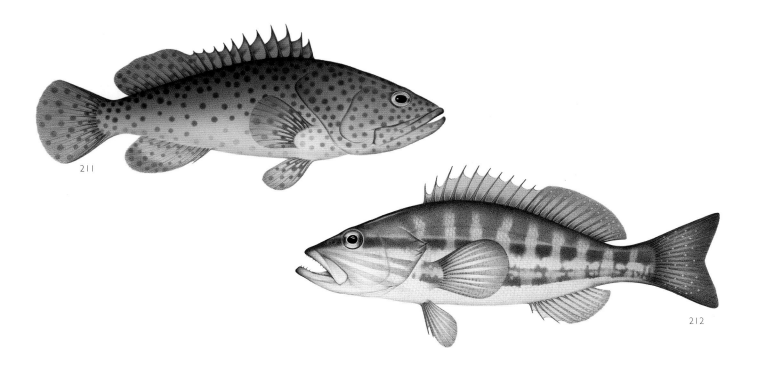

211 | Greasy grouper | *Epinephelus tauvina* | SERRANIDAE / SEA BASSES AND GROUPERS

Greasy grouper (En), Braunflecken-Zackenbarsch (D), Mero lutria (E), Mérou loutre, loche mouchetée (F) • Slym-klipkabeljou (Afr), Hamoor, kushar tooweena, suman (Ara), Rock cod, estuary cod (Au), Nga-tauk-tu (Bur), Kerapu cicak (Chr), Spotted sea bass (FP-En), Fûû-n hago (Fw), Fah-paan (HK), Kerapu lumpur (Ind), Hitomihata (J), Balong, belidra (Jav), Bwaavat pulo (Jaw), Te kuau (Kir), Kerapu hitam, kertang, pertang (Mal), Kalolab (Mars), Garoupa lutra (Moz-P), Gatala (Nie), Tauvina (R), Haroa (Ra), Gatala-tane (Sam), Farey (Som), Pulli kossa (Sin), Chewa (Swa), Lapu-lapu (Tag), Faroa (Tah), Punni-callawah (Tam), Pla karang (Thai), Marrbaarrga (Tok), Faketa (Tua), Te eve (Tuv), Kugtong (Vis), Galiyechosh, maleog (W)

Distributed around coral reefs in the Pacific and the Indian ocean, this sea bass grows to nearly 1 m (40 in) in length. It can be distinguished from its relatives by dark, regular markings of 1–2 cm (0.4–0.8 in) diameter covering its body. All its fins are rounded and densely spotted, the only exception being the anterior, spinous portion of the dorsal fin. The eyes are rather big, slightly oval; the mouth is enormous and can be opened widely to surpass body depth. It contains minute, pointed teeth typical of perciform fishes, and leaves no chance for the prey to escape after it is seized. Young specimens never leave coral reefs, only adults roam any distance. Their foremost enemy are scuba divers hunting with spear-guns, who often exploit the inexperience and curious nature of the greasy grouper. Restaurants pay a small fortune for specimens, as their flesh is regarded as extremely palatable. Production loss is considerable as only 40–50% of the whole can be turned into fillets.

212 | Comber | *Serranus cabrilla* | SERRANIDAE / SEA BASSES AND GROUPERS

Comber (En), Ziegenbarsch, Sägebarsch (D), Cabrilla (E), Serran chevrette (F), Boccaccia, buddaci, canisi, chègnele, donzella, ganele, perchia foretana, perega dalmata, perchia, scirrano (I), Geitenbaars (Nl) • Savbars (Da), Chanos (Gr), Abborrkilling (N), Serrano-alecrim (P), Större medel-havsabborre (S), Asilhani baligi (Tr)

This comber inhabits the eastern Atlantic, from the English Channel southwards to Natal, South Africa, and is also known off Madeira, the Canary Islands and the Azores. It is found in the Mediterranean, the western part of the Black Sea, and, probably, the Red Sea. It grows to 40 cm (16 in) in length and 500–600 g (18–21 oz) in weight. A bottom-dwelling, deep-water species, it occurs on a rocky, muddy or sandy bottom, and on the continental shelf and its deepening side, to a depth of 500 m (1640 ft). It feeds on fish, cephalopods and crustaceans, attacking its prey from its lair. Its commercial harvesting is of minor importance, but it is included in the catch of anglers. Due to its spectacular appearance and its comparatively small size, it is popular also as an aquarium fish. Marketed fresh or frozen, it is fried, roasted or grilled for human consumption.

2I3 | **Painted comber** | Serranus scriba | SERRANIDAE / SEA BASSES AND GROUPERS

Painted comber (En), Schriftbarsch, Buchstabenbarsch (D), Serrano (E), Serran écriture (F), Sciarrano (I), Schritbaars (Nl) • Kerr bilbil (Alb), Sheik (Egy), Toboko (Fon), Perca (Gr), Burqux (Malt), Perca (Mon), Boulamjamar (Mor), Alecrim, garoupa, requeime, serrano riscado (P), Kamenyi okun (R), Pirka (SC), Yazilihani (Tr), Kam'janyi okun (Ukr)

A small species of sea bass, the painted comber grows to a maximum 30–35 cm (12–14 in) in length and 0.5–0.6 kg (1.1–1.3 lb) in weight. It is a bottom-dwelling fish, which occurs at a maximum depth of 100–150 m (300–450 ft) in the eastern part of the Atlantic, the Mediterranean Sea, and the continental shelf of the Black Sea. A solitary species, it defends its territory. It favours warmer subtropical waters and occurs exclusively in the sea. Carnivorous, it preys on smaller fish and crustaceans. Most characteristic are the dark vertical lines irregularly arranged on its sides. As a rather small fish, it does not play a significant role in the catch of fishermen, but occasionally makes it to minor fish markets, either fresh (cooled on ice) or frozen. Rare even in the catch of anglers, it sometimes turns up in areas having a rocky bottom. The flesh of the painted comber is tasty, as is that of percid fish in general, and is prepared in various ways, mostly fried or grilled.

2I4 | **European seabass** | Dicentrarchus labrax | PERCICHTHYIDAE / TEMPERATE WHITE BASSES

European seabass (En), Wolfsbarsch, Seebarsch (D), Lubina (E), Bar européen (F), Spigola (I), Zeebaars (Nl) • Levreku (Alb), Lavrak (Bul), Llobarro (Cat), Almindelig Bars (Da), Bass (En), Doingéan (Ga), Lavraki (Gr), Vartari (Is), Lavraz (Isr), Birrâq (Leb), Lupu (Malt), Havabbor (N), Robalo (P), Labraks (Pl), Lavraki (R), Lup-de-mare (Ru), Havsabborre (S), Meribassi (SF), Brancin (Slo), Çizgili mercan (Tr)

European seabass dwell in the eastern region of the Atlantic Ocean, from Norway to Morocco and Senegal, around the Canary Islands and in the Mediterranean and the Black Sea. Occasional occurrences of the fish have been reported from Iceland, too. They may attain sizes of about 1 m (39 in) in body length and 12 kg (27 lb) in weight. They live in shallow coastal waters at depths of about 10–15 m (33–49 ft), but they are also found in the brackish waters of lagoons and river estuaries, sometimes even in the freshwater of rivers. Often caught by fishermen in the Nile, in the winter months European seabass travel to deeper waters (to depths of 80–100 m or 250–330 ft) in the temperate zone. The young live in relatively large schools, whereas the older specimens form small groups or become solitary in habit. A predatory species, European seabass feed on fish, crustaceans and molluscs, catching them near the surface. They spawn from early spring, in groups. Their larvae hatch in midwater, the offspring urgently migrating to the river estuaries after hatching. Popular with recreational fishermen, European seabass are also bred and reared in fisheries. Marketed for food fresh and smoked, the meat of the fish is usually eaten pan-fried, roasted or baked in the oven. They are also frequently shown in aquariums.

215 | Striped sea-bass | *Morone saxatilis* | PERCICHTHYIDAE / TEMPERATE WHITE BASSES

Striped sea-bass (En), Felsenbarsch (D), Lubina americana, lubina estriada (E), Bar d'Amérique (F), Persico spigola (I), Gestreepte zeebaars (Nl) • Stribet bars (Da), Rockfish (En), Robalo-muge, robalo riscado (P), Polosatyi lavrak (R), Juovabassi (SF), Roccus (US)

One of the most characteristic of its family, striped sea-bass have dense, strong scales, enabling the fish to enter among underwater ridges and coral reefs. The first lobe of the dorsal fin has spines, whereas the back lobe is made up of soft rays, the former serving for coarser, "directional" manoeuvring and the latter for accomplishing more delicate movement. With these and with the pectoral and pelvic fins it can perform practically any kind of manoeuvre even in high seas, from floating to sudden attacks. Larger specimens may attain body lengths of 1 m (40 in) and weights of 20 kg (44 lb). Between the two tropics the members of the species are appreciated as fiercely fighting opponents by divers fishing underwater with spears. Due to the hiding habit of the fish, which usually school in small groups, striped sea-bass are very rarely caught in fishermen's nets, and so they count as a rarity on the food market. The very flavoursome meat of striped sea-bass is best fried, other parts constitute delicious ingredients of fish soup.

216 | Wreckfish | *Polyprion americanus* | PERCICHTHYIDAE / TEMPERATE WHITE BASSES

Wreckfish (En), Wrackbarsch (D), Cherna (E), Cernier commun (F), Cernia di fondale (I), Wrakbaars (Nl) • Wrakvis (Afr), Kerr fundi (Alb), Dot (Cat), Kirnja dubinska (Cr), Vragfisk (Da), Vláchos (Gr), Rekaldsfiskur (Is), Aruzentin-oohata (J), H'afsh dâbby (Leb), Mananni (Malt), Moeone (Mao), Pampanu (Mon), Vrakfisk (N), Cherne (P), Vrakfisk (S), Kirnja glavulja (SC), Globinska kirnja (Slo), Iskorpit hanisi (Tr), Shringi (Tun), Atlantic wreckfish (UK)

Wreckfish dwell in the Atlantic Ocean, in the west from Newfoundland to Argentina, in the east from Norway to South Africa and around the Canary Islands and the Cape Verde Islands. Occurrences have also been reported from the Pacific, from around New Zealand. A percoid species of enormous size, wreckfish may grow as large as 210 cm (83 in) in length and 100 kg (220 lb) in weight. A typical bottom-dweller, they live in caves and crevices of rocks and wreckages. They are found over both hard and soft sea bottoms, between depths of 40 and 1000 m (130–3300 ft). Although most specimens are solitary in habit, the young (under 60 cm – 23.5 in – in body length) may occasionally form small schools below seaweed floating on the surface of the water, or under wrecks. Predatory in feeding habits, their diet consists of large crustaceans, cephalopods and demersal fish. Wreckfish spawn in the summer months. Commercially not particularly significant, they are primarily fished by recreational fishermen and divers.

215

216

217 | Hapuka wreckfish | Polyprion oxygeneios | PERCICHTHYIDAE / TEMPERATE WHITE BASSES

Hapuka wreckfish (En), Neuseeländischer Wrackbarsch, Neuseeländischer Zackenbarsch (D), Bacalo, cherna de Juan Fernández (E), Cernier de Nouvelle-Zélande (F), Cernia Neozelandese, dotto (I), Hapuka-wrakbaars (Nl) • Blue cod, deepwater rock cod, New Zealand grouper (Au), Hapuku (Au, NZ), Newzealandsk vragfisk (Da), Minami-osuzuki (J), Haapuka (Mor), Groper, whapuku (NZ)

The hapuka wreckfish is found in all Antarctic waters, and has been reported from colder waters of the Atlantic, the Indian and the Pacific oceans in the Southern Hemisphere. Its maximum length can reach 150 cm (59 in), and maximum weight as much as 100 kg (220 lb). A deep-water species, it occurs from the central part of the continental shelf, from a depth of 100 m to the deepening margin of the shelf. It usually lives alone or in small schools on a rocky bottom. Young fish occur near the surface, mainly among drifting vegetation. A carnivorous species, the hapuka feeds primarily on sardines and other bottom-dwelling fish. It is caught with hooks at 400 m (1300 ft) depth, but also with drag nets. Due to its large size it is also a favourite of anglers. It is caught for its excellent flesh and is sold fresh or frozen. For human consumption it is stewed, cooked, grilled, pan-fried, or roasted in an oven or microwave.

218 | Largemouth bass | Micropterus salmoides | CENTRARCHIDAE / BLACK BASSES

Largemouth bass (En), Forellenbarsch (D), Perca americana (E), Black-bass à grande bouche, achigan (F), Persicotrota (I), Zwarte baars, forelbaars (Nl) • Tam suy lo ue (Cant), Okounek pstruhový (Cz), Stormundet ørredaborre (Da), Fekete sügér (H), Buraku basu (J), Lakseabbor (N), Achiga (P), Bass wielkgebowy (Pl), Bolsherotnyi amerikanskii tschernyi okun (R), Biban cu gura mare (Ru), Öringsaborre (S), Isobassi (SF), Ostracka lososovitá (Slk)

Native to North America, largemouth bass are now widespread throughout nearly one hundred countries. It was mainly through British colonisers that largemouth bass were introduced to so many different regions, since the species is one of the most favoured sport fishes in the English-speaking world. Angling for and eventually catching the larger specimens, which are nearly 1 m (40 in) long and of several pounds in weight, is a real adventure. In the USA a whole industry is based on fishing and processing largemouth bass. Its excellent meat is highly appreciated everywhere, and it is eaten mainly as grilled fillets. In natural waters it spreads at a very slow rate, since when young largemouth bass are extremely vulnerable to environmental changes. The fact that largemouth bass build nests and protect their fry does not seem to improve the situation either. Thus, this highly prized sport fish is hatched in hatcheries, and only after having been reared for several months in lake fisheries are the fry released into rivers and lakes.

219 | Bulls-eye | Epigonus telescopus | EPIGONIDAE / DEEPWATER CARDINALFISHES

Bulls-eye (En), Teleskop-Kardinalfisch (D), Boca negra (E), Le sonneur commun, apogon noir (F), Re di triglie nero (I), Zwarte kardinalvis (Nl) • Teleskoop-kardinaal (Afr), Salmonete-da-fundura (Ang), Escamuda, escuro, jordão, preto (Az), Black cardinal fish (En), Glymir (Is), Dyphavsabbor (N), Telescope cardinal (Nam, SA), Besoiro, olhudo, robaldo, robaldo-do-alto, robaldo-preto, salmonete-preto (P), Bigeye, deepsea cardinalfish (UK)

Bulls-eye are native to the Atlantic Ocean, from Iceland as far south as the Canaries, and in the south from Walvis Ridge in South Africa to New Zealand, in temperate waters. Only one specimen has been reported from the coasts of South America. Very spectacular in looks, the body of the fish is of an interesting brownish-violet hue, and while alive the colours are iridescent. The largest specimens may attain 75 cm (30 in) in length and 1.5–2 kg (3.3–4.4 lb) in weight. Bulls-eye live at depths of 75–1200 m (246–3937 ft). The mature specimens live at the sea bottom, over the steepening slope of the continental shelf, whereas the young are found in midwater. They tend not to leave their original grounds, but they do not display territorial habits. Predatory in habit, bulls-eye feed on small fish and planktonic invertebrates. They spawn in deep water from March to May. Fished all through the year, bulls-eye are mostly landed with bottom trawls, landed specimens averaging 50–60 cm (20–24 in) and about 1 kg (2.2 lb). Australian fishermen land 2,500–5,000 tons of bulls-eye every year. Mostly marketed frozen, the meat is sautéed, roasted or baked in the oven.

220 | Yellow perch | Perca flavescens | PERCIDAE / PERCHES

Yellow perch (En), Amerikanischer Flussbarsch, Gelbbarsch (D), Perca canadiense (E), Perche canadienne (F), Persico dorato (I), Amerikaanse gelebars (Nl) • American perch (Can), Lake perch, perch (Can, US), Chavoo, osaoeo, osaoeos, osaoes, ukas (Cree), Gul aborre (Da), Perca-americana (P), Okon zólty (Pl), Gul abborre (S), Kelta-ahven (SF)

The yellow perch is an inhabitant of North American freshwaters. It occurs from the east coast westwards to the Mississippi river system, northwards to the Great Lakes and the Great Slave Lake in Canada. The southern limits of its range are the states of Ohio, Illinois and Nebraska. It can reach 50 cm (20 in) in length and 1.5–2 kg (3–4.5 lb) in weight. It inhabits lakes, fish ponds and the slow-flowing sections of streams and rivers, but it also occurs in brackwater and salt lakes. It prefers clean, vegetated waters. In spring it often moves to coastal shallows. It spawns between February and July in the north, and from August to October in the south. A carnivorous species, the yellow perch consumes insects, macro-invertebrates, fish and fish eggs. Young perch themselves fall prey to other fishes and birds. It is caught with pleasure both by fishermen and anglers for its excellent flesh, and is distributed fresh or frozen. It is prepared roasted, grilled or fried.

221

222

221 | **Perch** | Perca fluviatilis | PERCIDAE / PERCHES

Perch (En), Flussbarsch (D), Perche commune (F), Pesce persico (I), Baars (Nl) • Flussbarsch (A), Sharmak (Alb), Okoun říčni (Cze), Aborre (Da), Kostur (Bul), European perch (En), Perki (Gr), Sügér (H), Aborri (Is), Åbor (N), Perca-europeia (P), Okon (Pl), Okun (R), Biban (Ru), Abborre (S), Ahven (SF), Ostriež (Slk), Tatlisulevregi baligi (Tr), Rechnoi okun (Ukr)

One of the most beautiful Eurasian predator fish species, perch can easily be observed even from the water's edge, since they very often chase their prey as far as the bank. Young perch normally swim in large schools, but after a couple of months they shift to a solitary way of life. Anglers often fish for perch, but it is mainly the larger specimens that are appreciated, since the scales are dense and with their fins being very spiny, scaling the average sized (20–30 cm / 8–12 in) fish may be slightly difficult. Aquaculturalists are trying to systematically exterminate perch, since they tend to prey on fry reared in lake fisheries. If perch happen to survive until the age and size suitable for the pot, fillets grilled crisp are a perfect culinary choice. In some arid regions dried perch is a staple food, since in this form the fish can be stored for several months, even in extremely high temperatures. In Europe perch are also kept in park ponds as decorative fish, and at the same time they also rid the park lakes of tadpoles.

222 | **Pike-perch, Zander** | Sander lucioperca | PERCIDAE / PERCHES

Pike-perch, Zander, Hechtbarsch (En), Zander (D), Lucioperca (E), Sandre (F), Sandra (I), Snoekbaars (Nl) • Schill (A), Luci (Alb), Byala riba (Bul), Candát obecný (Cze), Sandart (Da), Potamolavrako (Gr), Fogas süllő (H), Gjørs (N), Lucioperca (P), Sandacz (Pl), Sudak (R), Ciopic (Ru), Gös (S), Kuha (SF), Smuc (Slo), Akbalik (Tr)

The pike-perch, which reaches 50–100 cm (20–40 in) in length, is one of the best tasting and at the same time the most common freshwater fish in Europe and the Near East. As it has been bred in captivity for almost a century, it has been experimentally introduced to some African and American countries. As it is one of the most popular game fishes, fish farms often produce smaller, less-than-one-year-old specimens to suit the needs of anglers, rather than individuals of "edible size". Adult pike-perch are solitary hunters and search for the company of conspecifics only in the spawning season, in spring or early summer. Females attach their eggs to submerged vegetation or tree roots, and it is usually the male that guards them until hatching. A truly beautiful fish, it is offered in restaurants mostly whole (fried and nicely decorated), at a rather high price. In markets, it is commonly sold cooled or frozen, but its dried and smoked varieties are also popular in the East.

223 | Volga pikeperch | Sander volgensis | PERCIDAE / PERCHES

Volga pikeperch (En), Wolgazander (D), Sandre du Volga (F) • Candát volžský (Cze), Kősüllő (H), Sandacz bersz (Pl), Bersh (R), Salaul vargat (Ru), Volgagös (S), Zubác volžský (Slk), Uzunlevrek baligi (Tr)

Distributed mainly in central and eastern Europe, Volga pikeperch reach body lengths of 25–40 cm (10–16 in). As its name implies, they are typically abundant along the upper and middle stretch of the Volga river. Anglers encounter them mainly in slow rivers and the sluggish waters of dead channels. Typically dwelling in natural waters, Volga pikeperch are not profitable for rearing in fisheries, since their growth rate is very slow and they are sensitive to oxygen. In addition, the well-known cannibalism of the species tends to intensify when kept in crowded ponds, and with the only solution being a frequent selective process, the stock normally decreases to a great extent. The meat of Volga pikeperch is sought after in the market primarily because it is an especially savoury dry meat. In restaurants dishes made of this fish count as very expensive delicacies. Generally it is eaten fried, though in eastern countries it is normally dried.

224 | Great northern tilefish | Lopholatilus chamaeleonticeps | MALACANTHIDAE / TILEFISHES

Great northern tilefish (En), Blauer Ziegelbarsch (D), Blanquillo camello (E), Tile chameau (F), Tile gibboso (I), Blauwe tegelvis (Nl) • Gunnet (Bar), Vestatlantisk teglfisk (Da), Peixe-paleta-camelo (P), Plytecznik (Pl), Tilefish (UK, US)

This large-bodied percid inhabits the western Atlantic from Nova Scotia to Florida, as well as the Gulf of Mexico. It probably occurs in the Caribbean, and it prefers subtropical waters along the northern coast of South America. Its body length can reach 120 cm (47 in), weight 30 kg (66 lb). A deep-water bottom-dweller, the great north-ern tilefish is most common at a depth of 200 m (650 ft). It favours a sandy or muddy bottom, but is sometimes found on a hard bottom. Its food consists mainly of crustaceans, but it also feeds on fish, cephalopods, gastropods and holothurians. It is susceptible to cold water. A mass decline in its numbers was recorded in 1882, probably as a result of the unusual cold, and the great northern tilefish could rarely be observed in the subsequent decades. It occurs in the catch of both fishermen and anglers. Marketed fresh or frozen, it is prepared stewed, pan-fried, grilled, roasted in an oven, or microwaved.

223

224

225 | Brasilian sandperch | Pseudopercis semifasciata | PINGUIPEDIDAE / SANDPERCHES

Brasilian sandperch (En), Argentinischer Sandbarsch (D), Chanchito (E), Perche de sable (F), Morate (I), Braziliaanse zandbaars (Nl) • Salmón de mar (Arg), Namorado (Bra), Madara-ootoragisu (J)

This sandperch species is native to the southwestern region of the Atlantic Ocean, from São Paolo in Brazil to the San Jorge Gulf in Argentina. Sandperch may attain body lengths of 1 m (39 in) and 10 kg (22 lb) in weight. They live over the soft mud bottom of the sea. Predatory in habit, they feed on small fish and invertebrates. A protogynous hermaphrodite species, Brasilian sandperch are first female, and when they attain a specific size they all turn into males. The males display strong territorial behaviour, and on their territories preside over a relatively large harem of females. Spawning takes place in midwater, the larvae also hatch from eggs floating in midwater. Not particularly significant commercially, the meat of the Brazilian sandperch is marketed fresh or frozen, and is usually fried in oil or roasted.

226 | Sand sillago | Sillago ciliata | SILLAGINIDAE / WHITINGS

Sand sillago (En), Sandweißling (D), Silago de arena (E), Pêche-madame sable (F) • Blue-nose, silver whiting, summer whiting (Au), Sand whiting (Au, Pap, UK), Bluenose whiting (Au, UK), Yen (Kum)

Sand sillago are found in the western region of the Pacific Ocean, along the eastern coast of Australia, over the Great Barrier Reef, along the northeastern coasts of Tasmania, around Lord Howe Islands, New Caledonia and Papua New Guinea. The maximum body length specimens may attain is 51 cm (20 in), the maximum weight is 1.4 kg (3 lb). They live in schools, near the coast, along sandy beaches, and over underwater sand banks. They may also occur in open bays, river estuaries and lakes near the seaside, or in rivers where the water is brackish. They never go below a depth of 40–50 m (130–165 ft). They keep to sandy bottoms; older specimens usually go farther from the coastline. Their larvae live in river estuaries and mangrove swamps. They feed on crustaceans and worms they dig out from the sand. They spawn from September to February, some tagging experiments suggesting that they spawn twice a year. Spawning takes place during the high tide before the new moon, at night. A widely exploited species, they are mainly caught in lampara nets. There have been attempts at artificially rearing the species, and they are also popular with recreational fishermen. Exceptionally flavoursome, the white meat of the fish is firm-textured, the amount of fat in the meat is low or medium.

225

226

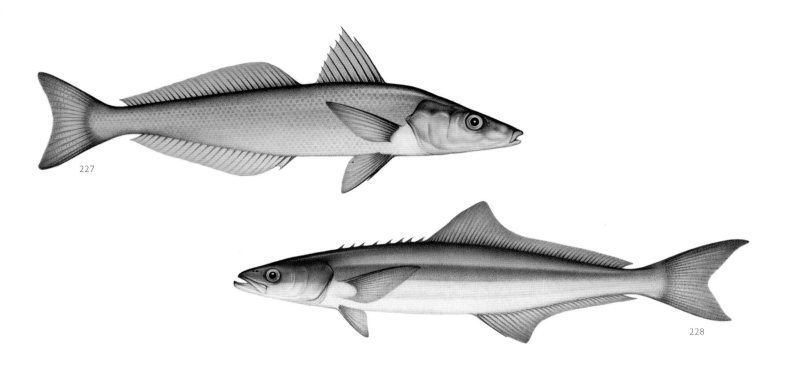

227

228

ᴢᴢ7 | Silver sillago | Sillago sihama | SILLAGINIDAE / WHITINGS

Silver sillago (En), Silberweißling (D), Silago plateado (E), Pêche-madame argenté (F) • Silwer sillago (Afr), Asu-os (Bik), Nga-palwe (Bur), Sillago-whitings, silver whiting (En), Smelt (HK, UK), Osoos (Ilo), Kisu, moto-gisu (J), Bojor, rejun(g), warijung (Jav), Asos (Kap), Awsaos, usaos (Kuy), Amborody, amboso, ambotso, ambotsoka, toholava (Mad), Bebolos, bebulus, besot, bulus-bulus, kedondong-kedondong, punting damar, puntung damar, rejun(g), ubi (Mal), Ili (Moz-E), Muxile, ngulu, pescadinha branca, pescadinha comum (Moz-P), Swam (Om), Northern whiting (Pap), Hasoom (Q), Koryushkovaya sillaga (R), Pêche madame (Sey), Kalanda (Sin), Caanood (Som), Mtambaanchi, sondo, tambanji (Swa), Asuhos (Tag), Culingah, kilaken, kilangan (Tam), Common asohos (UK), Aso-os (Vis)

This small-sized species lives in the Indian Ocean and the western Pacific. From the Red Sea it is found eastwards to Japan, and southwards to Australia, but it has been reported from New Caledonia as well. It grows to 30 cm (12 in) in length and 220–230 g (approx. 8 oz) in weight. The silver sillago forms schools near the coast, among reefs, in mangroves or estuaries, close to the bottom at a depth of up to 60 m (200 ft). It often buries itself in the sand to escape from predators. It feeds primarily on worms and penaeid crayfish. Its commercial harvesting is of little economic importance, but the silver sillago may become a potential species for marine aquaculture in the future. It is marketed fresh and frozen, and is eaten mainly fried, grilled or roasted. In certain regions it is also made into sushi.

ᴢᴢ8 | Cobia | Rachycentron canadum | RACHYCENTRIDAE / BLACK KINGFISHES

Cobia (En), Offiziersbarsch, Königsbarsch, Cobia (D), Bacalao, cobia, pejepalo (E), Mafou, cobio (F) • Cubby yew (Bar), Balisukan, itang, pandauan, sakalan itang (Bik), Bijupirá (Bra), Bonito (Cub), Cabio (Cub, Jam), Lapador (CV), Seekel, segel (Em), Cod (Guy), Sugi (J), Mondoh (Jav), Gabus laut (Ma), Aruan tasek, jaman (Mal), Langlanga (Mar), Bacalhau (Moz-P), Goada, sikel (Om), Agarrador, filho-pródigo, fogueteiro-galego, pegador, pegador-listado, peixe-piolho, peixe-sargento, rémora, sargento (P), Kingfish (Pap), Seheeha (Q), Kobia (SA), Kumi nu'aakhr, sikin (Sau), Cuddul-verari, mudhila, mudhu luhula (Sin), Takho (Som), Bonita (Su), Songoro (Swa), Dalag-dagat, gile (Tag), Pandawan (Tag, Vis), Cuddul-verarl, kadal-viral (Tam), Crabeater, prodigal son, runner, black kingfish (UK), Sergeant fish (UK, US), Black salmon (US), Kume, tayad (Vis)

Cobia are found world-wide in tropical and sub-tropical seas, except the eastern part of the Pacific Ocean. A large-bodied species, cobia may grow as large as 2 m (79 in) in length and 68 kg (150 lb) in weight. They occur over mud, sand and gravel sea bottoms, over coral reefs, along rocky coasts, in mangrove swamps, around stockades or footings of buoys, occasionally around river estuaries and they may go as deep as 1200 m (4000 ft). Solitary in habit, they are landed in small quantities. Cobia feed on fish, crustaceans and cephalopods. In the western part of the Atlantic they spawn in the warm months, their roe and larvae being pelagic, i.e. they float in midwater. The quality meat of the cobia is marketed fresh, smoked or frozen. Sport fishermen highly appreciate the fighting instinct of the fish. Commercial fishermen mostly use the purse seine. Cobia are also bred and reared in marine fish farms. Marketed for food fresh, frozen or in fillets, it is usually pan-fried, roasted or baked in the oven.

229 | **Orange-spotted trevally** | Carangoides bajad | CARANGIDAE / JACKSCADS AND HORSE MACKERELS

Orange-spotted trevally (En), Gelbgefleckte Stachelmakrele (D), Jurel lentejuela (E), Carangue lentigine (F) • Orange spotted trevally (En), Kogane-aji (J), Cermin, demudok, ebek, kwee tutul, putih, rambai landeh (Mal), Butikha, hamam, ka'k, sall (Om), Gold-spotted trevally (Pap), Jesh (Q) Yool (Som), Pampano, trakitilyo (Tag), Talakitilyo, Talakitok (Tag, Vis)

This species of percid inhabits tropical seas in the Indian and Pacific oceans. It is found in the Red Sea, the Gulf of Aden, the Persian Gulf and the Gulf of Oman, Indonesian waters, the Gulf of Thailand, as well as off the Philippines and the island of Okinawa. Its maximum length is 50–55 cm (20–22 in). A predatory member of reef communities, this trevally lives in groups alongside reefs. It is caught with pleasure both by commercial and recreational fishermen for its excellent flesh, which is marketed fresh, and served fried, grilled or roasted.

230 | **Pacific crevalle jack** | Caranx caninus | CARANGIDAE / JACKSCADS AND HORSE MACKERELS

Pacific crevalle jack (En), Pazifischer Makrelenbarsch (D), Cocinero del Pacífico (E), Carangue crevalle (F), Carangidi del Pacifico (I) • Pacific trevally (Au), Pacifisk crevalle (Da), Toro (Mex)

Pacific crevalle jack dwell in the eastern region of the Pacific Ocean, from San Diego, California, as far south as Peru and the Galapagos Islands. Some suppose that the species is identical with the C. hippos species found in the Atlantic Ocean. They may attain body lengths of 1 m (39 in) and weights of 11 kg (24 lb). They can be observed both in the open sea and in coastal waters, though they never go below depths of 350 m (1150 ft). They may also occur in brackish water and occasionally swim up rivers. They form large and medium-sized schools, but the largest specimens maintain a solitary habit. The offspring are often observed in river estuaries. A swift-moving predator fish, Pacific crevalle jack mainly feed on other fishes, but may also include crustaceans and other invertebrates in their diet. In tropical waters they are commercially very important. Recreational fishermen and divers with fish-spears are also keen on catching Pacific crevalle jack. When landed, they often produce a growling sound. The meat of the fish is marketed fresh, smoked, salted and dried, or frozen, and is usually prepared for human consumption fried in oil. Fishmeal and oil are also produced from it.

231 | Indian scad | Decapterus russelli | CARANGIDAE / JACKSCADS AND HORSE MACKERELS

Indian scad (En), Indische Stachelmakrele (D), Macarela de Russel (E), Comète indienne (F), Sugarotto (I), Russels stekelmakreel (Nl) • Indiese skad (Afr), Sibubog (Bik), Nga-gyi-gan (Bur), Tse Yue (Cant), Mamoshig (Car), Indo-maruaji (J), Bengol (Jav), Mi-hong-ga-ra-ji (Kor), Galunggong (Kuy), Basung (Mal), Hóng qí yuán shen (Mand), Baleg (Om), Charro-de-Russel (P), Sadat (Q), Am paratiya (Sin), Buraasow (Som), Lungu (Swa), Moon-dakun-kilichi (Tam), Pula ikog (Vis)

This small-bodied member of the mackerel family inhabits tropical waters in the Indian and Pacific Oceans, from the East African coast to Japan, and from the Arafura Sea to Australia. The Indian scad reaches 45 cm (18 in) in length and 1.2 kg (2.6 lb) in mass. It is the most abundant species of Decapterus in the Indian Ocean, living close to the coasts and in the vicinity of reefs, to a depth of 40–250 m (130–1000 ft). It frequents surface waters in huge schools, feeding on zooplankton. Its breeding is almost continuous, and lasts from February to November. The eggs are pelagic, i.e. they develop while drifting in open water. This species is of major economic significance, intensely harvested for its tasty flesh. Distributed fresh, frozen, or salted-and-dried, it is prepared pan-fried, oven-roasted or grilled. Eaten locally, it is also exported in substantial quantities. Because of its abundance and mass occurrence, the Indian scad is an important prey to larger predatory fish.

232 | Rainbow runner | Elagatis bipinnulata | CARANGIDAE / JACKSCADS AND HORSE MACKERELS

Rainbow runner (En), Regenbogen-Stachelmakrele (D), Macarela salmón (E), Comète saumon, arc-en-ciel (F), Seriolina, cometa (I), Regenboog-stekelmakreel (Nl) • Reënboog-pylvis (Afr), Balilito (Ban), Runner, tabio (Bar), Lapis, salmonon (Bik), Arabaiana norte (Bra), Bagara, songoro (Com), Galate, prodigalson, sorcier (Creo), Drodrolagi (Fij), Kamanu (Haw), Hawaiian salmon (Haw-En), Saleng-saleng (Ilo), Pisang-pisang (Ind), Tsumuburi (J), Sulir (Jav), Te kama (Kir), Sarbassi (Mad), Sinrilli batang (Mak), Sunglir (Mal), Ikaidrik (Mars), Salmão (Moz-P), Samani (Niu), Aifa, gazala, sagla (Om), Fogueteiro-arco-iris (P), Desui (Pal), Cola amarilla, corredores (Per), Tengteng, ulong-ulong, ungong (Phi), Samani (Sam), Niyawmanúr, péyennáy (Sat), Mujlabah, muslabah (Sau), Galati (Sey), Kiharua, kuninga, muhaluwa (Swa), Roe roe (Tah), Kulkul (Tam), Roeroe (Tua), Te kamai (Tuv), Jack, spanish-jack, yellow tail (US), Peje rata, pez rata, zapatero ligereto (Ven), Bansikol, bidbid sa laud, salinao, salindato (Vis), Foafoa (W)

The rainbow runner is found in the western Atlantic from Massachusetts (US) to the northeastern coast of Brazil, in the eastern Atlantic from Ivory Coast to Angola, and even in the Mediterranean Sea at Genoa. It has also been observed around the Cape Verde Islands and the St. Paul Reefs. It is common in the western Indian Ocean, but unknown from the Persian Gulf eastwards. It is abundant in subtropical-tropical waters of the Pacific. It grows to 150 cm (59 in) in length and 15–16 kg (33–35 lb) in weight. Found close to the coasts as well as in the open sea, it hunts near the surface, feeding on invertebrates and smaller fish. It is intensely harvested, and marketed fresh, frozen, or salted-and-dried. While it is eaten mainly fried, roasted or grilled, it is made into sashimi in Japan.

231

232

233 | Double-spotted queenfish | Scomberoides lysan | CARANGIDAE / JACKSCADS AND HORSE MACKERELS

Double-spotted queenfish (En), Doppelpunkt-Makrele (D), Jurel sable (E), Sauteur sabre (F), Talang (I) • Dubbelkol-koninginvis (Afr), Giant dart, leatherskin, skinny fish, white fish (Au), Queenfish (Au, Chr), Yapis (Ban), Talang-talang (Bik, Mal, Tag), Lae (Cha, Haw), Ikan talang (Chr), Carangue leurre (FP), Leatherback (Guam, Haw-En), Leatherback lae (Mic), Lai (Haw, Sam), Kulangit (Ilo), Ikekatsuo (J), Badong (Jav), Te nari (Kir), Lihlah, thelah (Kuw), Dorado, lapis (Kuy), Bekalang, lima jari, seliap, talang, tok pekong hu (Mal), Machope de areia (Moz-P), Lai loa (Nie), Bashkel, bassar, dhela, habes, sain, seunah, zareb (Om), Lari (Pan), Easi, ladi (Pid), Rai (Ra, Tah), Pompre (Reu), Lihia, shirwi (Sau), Tettán (Sat), Votonimoli (SF), Katu bollu kattava, gona kattava, nil kattava, (Sin), Katta (Sin, Tam), Jabto calasey (Som), Pandu (Swa), Dularo, durado, lapis, talapya, talipa, talupak (Tag), Blacktip leatherskin, Blacktip queenfish (US), Tettal (Wol)

The range includes the Indian and the Pacific Oceans, and extends from the Red Sea and the East African coasts to Hawaii and the Marquesas. Its length reaches a maximum of 110 cm (43 in), its weight 11–12 kg (24–27 lb). The double-spotted queenfish prefers clear water, and adults are thus found in quiet lagoons and reefs farther offshore, while the young frequent coastal waters. This species avoids greater depths, and is found to 100 m (330 ft) at most. A fast-swimming, aggressive predator, it feeds on fish and crayfish, with juveniles hunting small schooling fish. Commercial harvesting is of little significance, but it is also caught by anglers. Marketed fresh, frozen, or salted-and-dried, it is served mainly fried or grilled. This fish should be handled with caution, as the spines in its dorsal fin have a venomous sting.

234 | Yellowstripe scad | Selaroides leptolepis | CARANGIDAE / JACKSCADS AND HORSE MACKERELS

Yellowstripe scad (En), Goldband-Selar (D), Chicharro banda dorada (E), Sélar à bande dorée, sélar à razures jaunes (F), Carangidi giallo-legato, suro bandaglia (I), Geelstreep-makrelenbaars, gestreepte selar (Nl) • Atuloy (Bik), Yellow-striped scad (En), Cory (Ilo), Hosohira-aji (J), Salay-salay ginto (Kuy), Haima (Om), Charro-de-riscas-amarelas (P), Balanghay ekol (Pan), Yeneeser (Q), Zeltopolocii selar (R), Ginto-ginto (Tag), Chooparai (Tam), Dalino-an, lambiao (Vis)

This species of scad inhabits the Indian Ocean and the western Pacific, to the Philippines in the east, to Okinawa in the north, and to the Arafura Sea and Australia in the south. Its common name is derived from the conspicuous yellow stripe running on both sides of its blue body. A small-sized fish, it reaches a maximum length of 20–25 cm (8–10 in). It lives in coastal shallows to a depth of 25–50 m (80–160 ft). Forming huge schools, it stays near the soft sand or mud bottom. Its food consists of minute crustaceans and worms, but also of small fish. Harvested on a small scale commercially, it is mainly consumed locally. Although regularly caught by anglers, it is not favoured at all, and is often used as a bait fish. The yellowstripe scad is marketed almost exclusively fresh, and is eaten fried or grilled.

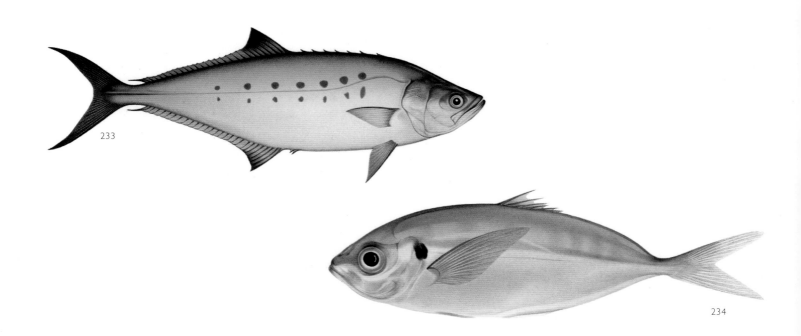

233

234

235 | **Greater amberjack** | Seriola dumerili | CARANGIDAE / JACKSCADS AND HORSE MACKERELS

Greater amberjack (En), Gelbschwanzmakrele, Bernsteinfisch, Bernsteinmakrele (D), Pez de limón, seriola (E), Sériole couronne (F), Ricciola, seriola (I), Grote geelstaart, seriolavis (Nl) • Sailor's choice (AB), Rock salmon (AB, US), Groot geelstert (Afr), Gofa (Alb), Poisson limon (Alg-F), Allied kingfish (Au), Írio (Az), Jibb (Bah), Círvia (Cat), Cola amarilla, machiamarillo (Col), Coronado de ley (Cub), Medregal (Cub, Dom, PR), Esmoregal (CV), Blanquilla (Dom), Inch (Egy), Kpindjikpankpan (Fon), Manali, magiatiko (Gr), Purplish amberjack (HK), Aji-aji, chermin (Ind), Seriol atlanti (Isr), Seriola (E, Isr, N, S), Intias (Isr, Syr), Kanpachi (J), Tsola (Lib), Xaréu coronado (Moz-P), Paanget (Nen), Medregal coronado (Nic), Palu sikava (Nie), Gazala, halwayo (Om), Anchova, charuteiro-catarino, enchova, Lírio (P), Kabiou (Pp), Hamam (Q), Greater yellowtail (SA), Orhan (SC), Sopiikkimakrilli (SF), Gof (Slo), Talakitok (Tag), Sarikuyruk baligi (Tr), Great amberfish, Jenny lind (US), Doronado, madregal (US-E), Fatugerauw (W)

This circumglobal species occurs in tropical-subtropical areas and in the Mediterranean. It grows to 2 m (79 in) and 80–85 kg (176–187 lb). Forming small schools, it occurs near rocky coasts to depths of 60–350 m (200–1200 ft). It hunts smaller schooling fish and crustaceans. It spawns in spring or summer. Its harvesting is of little commercial importance, but the greater amberjack is farmed in marine aquacultures in some parts of the Mediterranean. Marketed fresh or frozen, this species is fried, roasted or grilled. In certain areas it is known to have caused ciguatoxin poisoning, thus the consumption of intestines, head and eggs, in which the toxin is likely to concentrate, should be avoided. Symptoms of malfunctioning of the digestive, nervous and circulatory systems develop within six hours after consuming the fish, but the poisoning is only rarely lethal.

236 | **Almaco jack** | Seriola rivoliana | CARANGIDAE / JACKSCADS AND HORSE MACKERELS

Almaco jack (En), Medregal limón (E), Sériole limon (F) • Langvin-geelstert (Afr), Kamrad (Creo), Boquerón, coronado (Cub), Blanquilla (Dom, Ven), Huayaipe (Ecu), Kahala (Haw), Greater amberjack (Haw-En), Hirenaga-kanpachi, songoro (J), Silvercoat jack (Jam), Aji-aji, chermin (Mal), Esmedregal (Mex), Amberjack (NZ, Tri), Gazala (Om), Fortuna, Fortuno (Per), Escolar (PR), Longfin yellowtail (SA), Palu-kata, tafala, tavai (Sam), Shiiraan (Som), Kolekole (Swa), Talakitok (Tag), Falcate amberjack (US), Amber, crevalle (Vir)

This jack is a circumglobal species found in tropical and subtropical seas. A large-sized species, it reaches 110–120 cm (43–47 in) length and 55–60 kg (121–132 lb) weight. The almaco jack lives in small schools on the outer side of reefs, to a depth of 15–160 m (50–525 ft). A swift predator, the almaco jack feeds mainly on fish, but also takes crustaceans. Breeding occurs between spring and autumn, depending on habitat, in open water far offshore. This species is intensely harvested by commercial and recreational fishermen for its tasty flesh. Sold fresh or salted-and-dried, it is prepared fried, roasted or grilled for human consumption. Occasionally, it can cause ciguatoxin poisoning, especially specimens caught near coral reefs, which manifests itself by malfunctioning of the digestive, nervous and circulatory systems, but is rarely lethal. As an unfortunate consequence, symptoms can re-occur in less serious forms years later. Only fish preying on organisms that feed on certain algae are toxic. The toxin accumulates primarily in the intestines, the head and the eggs, so consumption of these body parts should be avoided.

237 | **Saltwater permit, Snubnose pompano** | Trachinotus blochii | CARANGIDAE / JACKSCADS AND HORSE MACKERELS

Saltwater permit, Snubnose pompano (En), Pompano (D), Pámpano, palometa (E), Pompano (F, I, Nl) • Stompneus-pompano (Afr), Pampano (Bik, Tag), Borung (Jav), Betong (Mal), Busalbukh (Q), Lalafutu (Sam), Kootili (Sin), Madax-dhagax (Som), Sese (Swa), Round pompano, great pompano (US), Kootili (Tam), Ampahan (Vis), Tééréy lemon (Wol)

The range of this species stretches along the western Atlantic coast. It is found from coastal Massachusetts (US) southwards to southeastern Brazil, but also occurs off the Bahamas and most of the West Indian islands, as well as around Bermuda and in the Gulf of Mexico. The permit reaches 114 cm (45 in) in length and 36 kg (79 lb) in body mass. Adult specimens live in channels, by sandbanks, reefs, and, sometimes, above a mud bottom. They usually occur solitarily or in small groups. The young tolerate brack water with a low level of salinity. In summer the fry form huge schools near the coasts, in the tidal zone along sandy beaches. Adults take molluscs, crayfish and small fish, while the young feed on bottom-dwelling invertebrates. Spawning occurs in open water far offshore. An excellent fish for eating, the permit is a favourite catch of anglers fishing with light gear. Attempts have also been made to farm the permit. Sold fresh or frozen, it is eaten fried, grilled, roasted in an oven or microwaved.

238 | **Inca scad** | Trachurus murphyi | CARANGIDAE / JACKSCADS AND HORSE MACKERELS

Inca scad (En), Holzmakrele (D), Jurel del Pacífico Sur (E), Chinchard jurel du Chili (F), Sugarello cileno (I), Chileense horsmakreel (Nl) • Chiri-maaji (J), Slender mackerel (NZ), Carapau-chileno (P), Chilean jack mackerel (US)

This species of scad inhabits the Pacific Ocean. In the southeast it occurs along the Peruvian and Chilean coasts, but it has also been reported from Ecuador. It is known from off New Zealand in the southwest. In the southwestern part of the Atlantic, the Inca scad is found by the southern coast of Argentina. This species is characterized by its large, sickle-like pectoral fins. It can reach 70 cm (28 in) length and 4–5 kg (9–11 lb) in body mass. Found in open sea as well as in coastal shallows, it forms schools to a depth of 300 m (1000 ft). A fast-moving predator, it feeds on small fish and crustaceans. Intensely harvested commercially, it is marketed fresh, but is most frequently canned for human consumption. It is made into surimi in Japan. As it can be caught in masses, it is used in enormous quantities for making fishmeal. It also turns up in the catch of anglers together with the related species T. declivis and T. novaezelandiae.

239 | Yellowtail horse mackerel | Trachurus novaezelandiae | CARANGIDAE / JACKSCADS AND HORSE MACKERELS

Yellowtail horse mackerel (En), Gelbschwanz-Bastardmakrele (D), Jurel (E), Trachures, chinchard (F), Sugarello australe (I), Horsmakreel (Nl) • Cowanyoung, scad, yakka, yellowtail, yellowtail scad (Au), Haature (Mao), Horse mackerel (NZ)

This species of horse mackerel is native to the southwestern Pacific waters off Australia and New Zealand. It probably exists in two subpopulations in the Gulf of Australia and along southeast Australia, and in two subspecies in the southeastern island group. It grows to 50 cm (20 in) in length and 2.7 kg (6 lb) in weight. It inhabits coastal areas and estuaries to a depth of 150 m (500 ft), in waters warmer than 13°C. Hunting close to the bottom as well as in open water, it sometimes appears near the surface. Adult specimens favour underwater cliffs and shelves far offshore, while the young inhabit coastal shallows with a soft bottom. A predatory species, it feeds on smaller fish and crayfish. It is not harvested on a very large scale, but appears in the catch of anglers. Sold fresh, frozen, smoked or canned, it is prepared fried in a pan, roasted in an oven, or grilled.

240 | Atlantic horse mackerel | Trachurus trachurus | CARANGIDAE / JACKSCADS AND HORSE MACKERELS

Atlantic horse mackerel (En), Bastardmakrele, Stöcker (D), Jurel (E), Chinchard d'Europe (F), Suro, sugarello (I), Horsmakreel (Nl) • Stavrid (Alb), Snjur (Cr), Chicharrinho (Creo), Hestemakrel (Da), Sief (Egy), Savrídi (Gr), Brynstirtla (Is), Trakhon gedol moginim (Isr), Muroaji (J), Sawrella catta (Malt), Breac frengagh (Manx), Taggmakrell (N), Carapau (P), Yuzhnoafrikansk stavrida (R), Stavrid mare (Ru), Taggmakrill (S), Sur (Slo), Istavrit (Tr), Shourou (Tun), Scad (US)

A migratory fish of silvery-grey colour living in large schools in the Atlantic Ocean and the marginal seas along the Eurasian coast, the Atlantic horse mackerel averages about 30–50 cm (12–20 in) in length and a couple of pounds in weight. Popular ethnic names attached to it are far from flattering, since a spine in its dorsal fin and two others before the anal fin may be a real nuisance when scaling the fish. They spawn in the open water, their buoyant eggs, or roe, are pelagic, i.e. they drift in the upper zone of the ocean. It is characteristic of the species that, in contrast to other pelagic-egged fishes, before hatching the embryos are kept near the surface with the help of the yolk-sac containing low-density lipids. The offspring are very likely to remain alive, since for the most part of the first stage of their lives they survive by taking shelter between the tentacles of jellyfish. The meat of the Atlantic horse mackerel is widely sought after in the market. It is considered an average quality fish to fry.

241 | Ray's bream | Brama brama | BRAMIDAE / SEA BREAMS

Ray's bream (En), Brachsenmakrele (D), Japuta, palometa negra, castaña, zapatero (E), Brème de mer, grande castagnole (F), Pesce castagna (I), Braam (Nl) • Angelvis (Afr), Castanyola (Cat), Havbrasen (Da), Kastanópsaro (Gr), Bramafiskur (Is), Echiopia (J), Cawlun (Malt), Havbrasme (N), Xaputa, chaputa (P), Merilahna (SF), Kostanjevka (Slo), Pampanong laot (Tag), Atlantic pomfret (US)

This fish with its very strange existence has been given various names by fishermen along the seashores of the Northern Hemisphere. Ray's bream average about 50–60 cm (20–24 in) in length, but as deep-bodied fish they may attain an ample weight, sometimes as much as 4–6 kg (9–13 lb). By extending its pectoral fins, the fish can stay poised in the water. Perhaps it is this particular use of the fins that is reflected in the names given to the fish in Romance languages, most of them calling ray's bream "dove" or "columbine". Ray's bream are usually caught by heavy bottom trawls. Although they travel around in schools, ray's bream are not easy to catch, since they travel up and down at different depths of the ocean. Specimens have been recorded by scientists even as deep as several thousand metres, and the development of the fish is still not entirely researched. A fish with expressly firm-textured meat, its huge fillets often make a substantial portion. Cooks like to prepare it barded, i.e. decorated and grilled with bits of different meat and vegetables tucked into cuts in the flesh of the fish.

242 | Common dolphinfish | Coryphaena hippurus | CORYPHAENIDAE / DORADOS AND DOLPHINFISHES

Common dolphinfish (En), Gemeine Goldmakrele (D), Dorado común (E), Coryphène commune (F), Lampuga, corifena (I), Dolfijnvis, goudmakreel (Nl) • Kynygós (Gr), Lemadang (Indo), Corifena (Isr), Shiira (J), Man-sae-gi (Kor), Belitong (Mal), Lampuka (Malt), Doirado (P), Dhiya vannava (Sin), Delfinka (Slo), Fulusi (Swa), Avlis (Tam), Pla na mawn (Thai), Mahi-mahi (US)

Held by many to be the most beautiful of tropical fishes, common dolphinfish, or mahi-mahi, may reach a length of almost 2 m (80 in) and a weight of 20–30 kg (44–66 lb). Overwhelmed by the glittering beauty of the bright scales of the fish, Spanish seamen discovering America named it "dorado". Preying on smaller fish for food, common dolphinfish hunt in schools, and when so doing their blue or bluish grey, sabre-like long dorsal fin stretching from the head to almost the caudal fin may often catch the attention of the observer. Extremely sensitive to changes in temperature, common dolphinfish do not normally occur in waters colder than 25–26°C (77–78°F). They often rise and fall along these isothermic ranges in order to pick the zone that best suits their preference of temperature. Of high commercial value, fillets of common dolphinfish are easy to detach from the spine. As an especially flavoursome meat, it has a great variety of preparation modes. Since common dolphinfish largely lead a near-surface existence, they are popular game to be hunted in underwater fishing with spears.

241

242

243 | **Eastern Australian salmon** | Arripis trutta | ARRIPIDAE / AUSTRALIAN SALMONS

Eastern Australian salmon (En), Kahawai, Australische Lachsforelle (D), Salmón australiano (E), Kahawai, saumon australien (F), Salmone australiano (I), Australische zalm (Nl) • Salmon trout, native salmon, cocky salmon, colonial salmon, bay salmon, blackbacked salmon, australian salmon, bay trout (Au), Kahawai (Au, NZ, Mor), Østaustralsk laks (Da), Peixe-grosa-australiano (P)

This salmonid is an inhabitant of the southwestern Pacific, and the waters off Australia and New Zealand. It grows to 80–90 cm (32–36 in) in length, and 9.5 kg (21 lb) in weight. A pelagic species, it lives above the continental shelf, including bays and estuaries, occasionally turning up in rivers. Young specimens occur in schools in the shallow water of bays and river mouths. Adults migrate in huge schools along the coasts, but have also been observed above reefs where their body was only barely covered by water. This species feeds mainly on fish, but also on pelagic crustaceans (primarily krill). An intensely caught species, both by fishermen and anglers, it is sold fresh, frozen or canned, and is prepared cooked, stewed, fried, grilled or roasted.

244 | **Schoolmaster** | Lutjanus apodus | LUTJANIDAE / SNAPPERS

Schoolmaster (En), Schnapper (D), Pargo amarillo (E), Vivaneau dent chien, sarde professeur (F), Lutiano nero (I), Berslag (Nl) • Luciano preto (P), Schoolmaster snapper, sea lawyer (US)

Found throughout the entire Atlantic Ocean, this species grows to 40–60 cm in length and 1–2 kg (2–4 lb) in weight. As it prefers warmth, it only occasionally drifts or migrates into colder parts in the summer months. A rather poor swimmer, it avoids open oceans and great depths. A typical coastal fish, the schoolmaster prefers resting on the bottom or on rocks, and moves around mainly after sunset. It can be distinguished from its more colourful relatives by its dull, dark coat, and most local names are derived from this characteristic. Despite its spectacular teeth it is an omnivorous species, which has even been observed to graze on algae. It forages in small schools in the coastal region, and the vicinity of reefs, where zooplankton are concentrated by the currents. Its favourite prey are minute crayfish, small fish and pelagic organic matter. The flesh of this species is considered tasty, but due to certain risks associated with its consumption (true for the entire family), it is usually sought only by "specialists".

245 | Northern red snapper | Lutjanus campechanus | LUTJANIDAE / SNAPPERS

Northern red snapper (En), Roter Schnapper, Nördlicher Schnapper (D), Pargo del Golfo (E), Vivaneau campèche (F), Lutiano rosso (I), Noordelijke rode snapper (Nl) • Luciano do Golfo (P), Chicken snapper, Daytona red snapper, mules, rats (US)

This fish species inhabits the western Atlantic, from the Gulf of Mexico northwards to the coasts of Florida and Massachusetts, but is rarely found north of North Carolina. It grows to 1 m (39 in) in length and 21 kg (46 lb) in weight. Adults occur near the bottom above a rock surface, to a depth of 10–190 m (33–620 ft). The fry is usually found in shallow water on a sand or mud bottom. A carnivorous species, it feeds on fish, crustaceans, worms and cephalopods, but also takes (zoo)plankton. Its breeding occurs between April and December, in open water, but spawning is most intense in the summer months. Eggs are pelagic, i.e. they drift on the water surface until hatching. Since its flesh is of excellent quality, the northern red snapper is the most extensively marketed marine fish in eastern North America, and has become rare (and now protected) along US coasts. Crayfish harvesting has also been banned, as it kills off the fry of this species. Marketed fresh, it is eaten stewed, grilled or roasted. In some cases its consumption can cause ciguatoxin poisoning resulting in the collapse of the circulatory, nervous and digestive systems, but this is only fatal in exceptional circumstances. Anglers especially admire this species, as it can be caught from the coast and fights well once hooked. It can be kept in an aquarium, but grows rapidly.

246 | Grey snapper | Lutjanus griseus | LUTJANIDAE / SNAPPERS

Grey snapper (En), Mangrovenschnapper (D), Pargo prieto, pargo del mangle, caballerote (E), Vivaneau sarde grise (F), Lutiano delle mangrovie (I), Grijze zeebaars (Nl) • Mangrove snapper (En), Nezumifuedai (J), Luciano-do-mangal (P), Gray snapper, mango snapper (US)

One of the best-known species of snapper, it is especially common in the southern seas and bays of the Atlantic. Its local names are mainly derived from its favourite habitat, coastal mangroves. It inhabits mangroves at all depths and levels, and occurs even in the fresh and brackwater of inflowing rivers and channels. The grey snapper is a frequent catch of anglers in the coastal belt, but is not highly valued. Although it is classified as a perciform fish, it is known as an omnivorous, or even scavenging species. Due to this fact, the quality of its flesh is low, and this species, which grows to 40–60 cm in length and 2–3 kg (4–6 lb) in weight, is cheaply available in markets. In addition, it is known to have caused poisoning in man, so tourists are advised to consume its flesh well-done. In nature, the grey snapper can frequently be observed while resting on the air roots of mangrove plants.

247 | **Pacific red snapper** | Lutjanus peru | LUTJANIDAE / SNAPPERS

Pacific red snapper (En), Pazifischer Schnapper (D), Pargo gringo (E), Vivaneau garance (F), Lutiano del Pacifico (I), Pacifische rode snapper (Nl)

This species of snapper inhabits the eastern Pacific from Mexico to Peru. It can reach 95–100 cm (37–39 in) in length and 18–20 kg (40–44 lb) in weight, although the majority of specimens harvested fall in the range of 50–70 cm (20–28 in) in length and 1–4 kg (2–9 lb) in weight. A spectacular fish, its colour is red to pink with a silvery hue. The fins are red. The Pacific red snapper forms large schools near coastal riffs, diving to a maximum depth of 70–80 m (230–260 ft). A voracious predator, it hunts large-bodied invertebrates and fish. It spawns in open water. The eggs are pelagic, i.e. they drift in open water until hatching. Harvested on a small scale, this species is mainly caught for local consumption, but is increasingly popular as a sport fish. Fishermen also take it with hooks, most frequently in winter and spring. Its soft, white flesh is sold fresh or frozen, and is eaten fried, grilled or roasted. It is not allowed to be marketed as red snapper except in California, as this commercial name is reserved for L. campechanus, living in the Atlantic.

248 | **Southern red snapper** | Lutjanus purpureus | LUTJANIDAE / SNAPPERS

Southern red snapper (En), Karibischer Schnapper, Südlicher Schnapper (D), Pargo púrpura, pargo colorado (E), Vivaneau pourpre, vivaneau rouge (F), Lutiano porpora (I), Karibische snapper, zuidelijke rode snapper (Nl) • Sydlig snapper (Da), Southern red snapper (En), Minami-barafuedai (J), Luciano-vermelho (P), Caribbean red snapper (US)

This snapper species lives in the western Atlantic, most of the Caribbean as well as in tropical-subtropical areas from Cuba southwards to northeastern Brazil. Often confused with L. campechanus, it grows to 1 m (39 in) in length and 10–12 kg (22–27 lb) in body mass. It inhabits areas with a rock bottom, at a depth of 26–340 m (85–1115 ft). A voracious carnivore, it preys mainly on fish, crustaceans, cephalopods and planktonic organisms. It spawns between March and August, in open water, and the eggs are pelagic until hatching. Harvested both by commercial and recreational fishermen for its tasty flesh, it is also harpooned by divers. In commerce, the name red snapper is reserved for L. campechanus, so this species is marketed under a different name. The consumption of its flesh may cause ciguatoxin poisoning, thus the head, intestines and eggs should not be eaten, as the toxin tends to accumulate in these parts. Poisoning results in malfunctioning of the nervous, digestive and circulatory systems, and the symptoms may re-occur in a less serious form even years later.

247

248

249 | Lane snapper | Lutjanus synagris | LUTJANIDAE / SNAPPERS

Lane snapper (En), Rotschwanzschnapper (D), Pargo biajaiba (E), Sarde argentée, vivaneau gazou, vivaneau à queue rouge (F), Lutiano striato (I), Roodstaart snapper (Nl) • Kisenfuedai (J), Luciano-riscado (P), Candy snapper, candy striper, redtail snapper (US)

This snapper inhabits tropical-subtropical areas in the western Atlantic, from Bermuda and North Carolina to the northeastern coast of Brazil, including the Gulf of Mexico and the Caribbean. It is most abundant off the West Indies, at Campeche, a sandbank near Panama, and the north coast of South America. The largest specimens approach 50 cm (20 in) in length and 2.6 kg (6 lb) in weight. The lane snapper is found on all bottom types, but prefers coral reefs and densely vegetated sandy areas. It often forms huge schools, primarily at spawning. A nocturnal predator, it feeds on small fish, bottom-dwelling crustaceans, worms and squid. Reproducing all year round, the eggs float in the water until hatching. This fish is harvested by both commercial and recreational fishermen. Marketed mainly fresh, its soft flesh should be adequately cooled. It is eaten fried or grilled. As a toxin is likely to build up in its head, intestines and eggs, which is not broken down even by freezing, frying or roasting, the consumption of these parts should be avoided. Poisoning manifests itself with nervous, circulatory and/or digestive malfunctioning, with symptoms returning even after several years. Although extremely unpleasant, it is rarely fatal. Due to its spectacular appearance, the lane snapper is often exhibited in show aquariums.

250 | Silk snapper | Lutjanus vivanus | LUTJANIDAE / SNAPPERS

Silk snapper (En), Seidenschnapper (D), Pargo de lo alto (E), Vivaneau soie (F), Lutiano di seta (I), Zijden-roodbaars (Nl) • Luciano de seda (P), Chicken snapper, gold-eyed snapper (US)

The silk snapper is native to the Atlantic, and is found from Bermuda and North Carolina southwards to the central Brazilian coast, although it is most abundant off the West Indies and Bermuda. Its largest specimens measure 80 cm (32 in) in length and weigh 8 kg (18 lb). This species is most common at the margins of the continental and island shelves. It can also be encountered at 200–250 m (650–820 ft) depth, and lives near the sea bottom. It moves into shallows at night, for feeding. A predatory fish, the silk snapper takes fish, crustaceans, cephalopods, tunicates and planktonic organisms. In the equatorial part of its range, it spawns nearly all year round, but breeds in spring and summer in more northerly and southerly regions. A delicious tasting fish, it is intensely harvested by commercial and recreational fishermen, as well as scuba divers. According to some it is the best tasting species of snapper. As a toxin tends to build up in its head, intestines and eggs, these should not be eaten. Unfortunately, ciguatoxin does not disappear despite freezing, frying or cooking. Poisoning results in malfunctioning of the nervous, digestive and circulatory systems, and even though these symptoms disappear within a few days after adequate treatment, they sometimes re-occur, though in a less serious form, years later.

249

250

251 | **Yellowtail snapper** | Ocyurus chrysurus | LUTJANIDAE / SNAPPERS

Yellowtail snapper (En), Gelbschwanzschnapper (D), Rabirrubia (E), Vivaneau à queue jaune, sarde cola (F), Lutiano coda gialla (I), Geelstaartsnapper (Nl) • Luciano-cauda-amarela (P)

A fish of the warm seas of the Atlantic region growing to 30–60 cm (12–24 in) in length and 1–2 kg (2–4 lb) in weight. Its name comes from the golden to light yellow colour of its caudal base and caudal fin. Its favoured habitat includes the vicinity of coral reefs and coastal rocks. Thus it is often encountured by people snorkelling or tourists holidaying by the shore. Like its relatives, its body is small compared with its huge mouth, filled with teeth, which it uses literally as a pump. An omnivorous species, it also feeds on organic matter. It takes virtually all types of bait, and anglers having a fixed base can accustom it to a given place. Its flesh is decidedly tasty, but those sensitive to fish should better avoid it. A small percentage of people can be poisoned, and develop a combination of symptoms known as ichthyosarcotoxis maritimus.

252 | **Japanese threadfin bream** | Nemipterus japonicus | NEMIPTERIDAE / NEMIPTERIDS

Japanese threadfin bream (En), Japanischer Scheinschnapper (D), Baga japonesa (E), Cohana japonaise (F), Nemiptero giaponese (I), Japanse vlinderbrasem (Nl) • Bassij (Bah), Bassi (Bah, Kuw), Kolonto (Bal), Kanasi (Bik), Shwe-nga (Bur), Kwa sam (Cant), Melon coat (HK), Nihon-itoyori (J), Krisi (Jav), Bisugo (Kuy, Tag), Koana (Mad, Swa), Geretak lanta, gurisi, kerisi (Mal), Baga japonês (Moz-P), Bitsugo (Pan), Katti (Sid), Huuqle-baraawe (Som), Bakag, bisugong bututan, silay (Tag), Changarah, thullunkendai (Tam), Chalaneera-kanti (Tel), Pla sai dang, pla sai deng hang yai (Thai), Bream, threadfin (US), Ca dong (Vie)

This species inhabits subtropical-tropical areas in the Indian and the Pacific oceans, and is also found in the Red Sea. According to some reports, it has successfully invaded the Mediterranean Sea through the Suez Channel, but these remain to be confirmed. A small-bodied species, it grows to only 32 cm (13 in) in length and 0.6 kg (1.3 lb) in weight. Larger specimens are usually males, as their growth is much more rapid than that of females. Extremely abundant in coastal waters, the Japanese threadfin bream is found to a depth of 5–80 m (16–260 ft), moves around mainly in big schools, and prefers a mud or sand bottom. A predatory species, it feeds primarily on bottom-dwelling fish, crustaceans, gastropods, squid and worms. It spawns with variable intensity through the year, but two clearly defined breeding seasons have been identified from December to February, and in June-July. It is not harvested on a large scale, but is an important target species of local fisheries. Usually marketed fresh, it is eaten fried or grilled. Although very resistant, it is only rarely kept in captivity.

253 | **Common ponyfish** | Leiognathus equulus | LEIOGNATHIDAE / PONY FISHES

Common ponyfish (En), Ponyfisch (D), Motambo común (E), Sapsap commun (F), Pesce pony (I), Glipvis (Nl) • Slymvis (Afr), Lawayan (Ban, Vis), Tak chanda (Ben), Barurog (Bik), Cajao (Cam), Sap-sap (Creo, Sey), Kaikai (Fij), Sapsap (Ilo, Kap), Seitaka-hiiragi (J), Dodok (Jav), Trey sambow hear (Khm), Dexena (Kum), Lawayakan (Kuy), Kedabang, kekek, kekek gedabang, kikeh, kikek, peperek topang, pepetek, sekiki (Mal), Patana comum (Moz-P), Mydliczek ekwula (Pl), Slimy (SA), Mumu (Sam), Chap-chap (Sey), Hotu panna, mas karalla (Sin), Malaway (Tag), Sooro-koo-nam-kare (Tam), Greater ponyfish, narrowbanded ponyfish, slimy soapy, slipmouth (US), Danutan (Vis)

The common ponyfish is an inhabitant of the Indian Ocean and the western Pacific. Its range extends from East Africa (including Reunion, the Comores, the Seychelles, Madagascar and Mauritius) through the Red Sea westwards to Fiji, northwards to the Ryukyu Islands, and southwards to Australia. It occurs exclusively in tropical areas with water temperatures in the range of 26–29°C. A small-sized species, it grows only to 28 cm (11 in) in length and 500–600 g (18–21 oz) in mass. It lives in brackwater areas of river mouths and coastal regions, to a depth of 10–110 m (33–360 ft). It sometimes enters freshwater. Adults form schools and hunt along the bottom or in open water for worms, minute crustaceans and fish. An important fish for eating in the tropics, it is easily caught with drag nets, and along the sandy beaches with drift nets. Marketed fresh or dried, it is either consumed in this form, or prepared fried or grilled.

254 | **Trout sweetlip** | Plectorhynchus pictus | HAEMULIDAE / SWEETLIPS AND POMADASIDS

Trout sweetlip (En), Gelbbrust-Süßlippe, Korodai, Goldwange (D), Burro trucha (E), Diagramme truité (F) • Alatan (Bik), Farsh (Em), Painted sweetlip, sweetlip (En), Gajih, kaci, kaci-kaci (Mal), Cilili, guibata fungo, huwa-huwa, pargo mulato (Moz-P), Khanny, yanam (Om), Yenma (Q), Shahfir, sobaity (Sau), Fute (Swa), Kayubibi (Tag), Grunt, sweetlips (US)

A fish of the Indian and Pacific Oceans, the trout sweetlip is found from the Persian Gulf to Sri Lanka and China to the east. It may reach 70–75 cm (28–30 in) in length and 6–6.5 kg (13–14 lb) in body mass. An inhabitant of tropical waters, it belongs to coastal reef communities, and is found to a depth of 200 m (660 ft). Occasionally it occurs in brackwater. A predatory species, it feeds on smaller animals. Spending the day in its lair, it hunts at night. Its eggs are pelagic, i.e. they develop while drifting in open water. The trout sweetlip is harvested everywhere within its range, but being an uncommon species, it has no particular economic significance. Marketed fresh, it is served fried, roasted or grilled. Due to their spectacular appearance and nice colours, young specimens are sold as aquarium fish, but they need large tanks as adults.

255 | Grey weakfish | Cynoscion regalis | SCIAENIDAE / DRUMS

Grey weakfish (En), Königs-Corvina, Königs-Umberfisch (D), Corvinata real (E), Acoupa royal (F), Ombrina dentata (I), Witte ombervis, koningsombervis (Nl) • Pescada-amarela (Bra), Kongetrommefisk (Da), Corvina, corvinón ocelado (Mex), Havgjørs (N), Corvinata-real (P), Havsgös (S), Veltto (SF), Grey sea trout (UK), Channel bass (UK, US), Seatrout, squeteague (US)

This percid fish occurs in the northwestern part of the Atlantic, from Nova Scotia and Canada southwards to northern Florida, and is also found in subtropical seas. It reaches a maximum length of 60–90 cm (24–36 in) and maximum weight of 2 kg (4.4 lb). It lives in small groups in shallow water, in areas with a sandy or muddy bottom. It also occurs in brackwater, migrating to river mouths in summer for spawning and feeding. A predatory species, it feeds on crustaceans and fish. Due to the high quality of its flesh, it is intensely sought after, and fishermen sell it either fresh or frozen. It is eaten smoked, pan-fried, grilled, roasted in an oven or microwaved. Anglers admire it for its delicious taste, and the grey weakfish is also frequently exhibited in show aquariums.

256 | South American striped weakfish | Cynoscion striatus | SCIAENIDAE / DRUMS

South American striped weakfish (En), Gestreifter Umberfisch (D), Corvinata pescadilla (E), Acoupa rayé (F), Ombrina (I), Gesreepte ombervis (Nl) • Pescadilla (Arg, Uru), Maria-mole, pescada-olhuda, pescadinha (Bra), Shima-nibe (J), Corvinata-riscada (P), Striped weakfish (US)

This species of weakfish is native to the southwestern Atlantic by southern Brazil and along the coast of Argentina. A medium-sized fish, it reaches 60 cm (24 in) in body length. This bottom-dwelling predator feeds on invertebrates and fish. Weakfish are found on various substrates, but seem to prefer a soft bottom. This species spawns in groups in coastal regions and near river mouths. Males call for females with a drumming-like or croaking voice. This sound is produced by a special muscle poorly developed in females. The swimming bladder is of large size and has numerous appendages that serve as resonating chambers in sound production. The fry live near the coasts, in harbours, channels and in the vicinity of river mouths, as they can well tolerate low salinity levels, and they can even be caught in the freshwater sections of rivers. The South American striped weakfish is caught mainly with trawling nets dragged along the bottom. Sold fresh or as frozen fillets or trunk, it is usually fried, grilled or roasted for human consumption. Young specimens are popular aquarium fish, although they are not easily maintained.

255

256

257 | Whitemouth croaker | Micropogonias furnieri | SCIAENIDAE / DRUMS

Whitemouth croaker (En), Weißmaul-Umberfisch (D), Corvinón rayado (E), Tambour rayé (F), Ombrina (I), Witmondombervis (Nl) • Corvina (Arg), Marisqueira (Bra), Verrugato (Cub), West Indian croaker (Hait), Semaru-nibe (J), Rabeta-marisqueira (P), Zoutwatra koebi (Sra), Cro cro, rocando (Tri), Croaker, hardhead (US)

This species of croaker lives in subtropical-tropical waters of the western Atlantic, from the Greater Antilles and Costa Rica to Argentina. It reaches 60 cm (24 in) in length and 1.7–1.8 kg (3.7–4 lb) in body mass. It occurs in coastal regions and estuaries, where it finds suitable conditions for breeding and feeding. It prefers a mud or sand bottom, moves around chiefly in schools, and has been observed to seasonally migrate. Its food is subject to ontogenetic and seasonal change. The fry feed on migrating bottom-dwelling crustaceans and molluscs, while adults consume bottom-dwelling organisms and even attack fish from time to time. The large swimming bladder is lobed, helping it to swim easily and also serve as a resonance chamber. This species breeds all year round, but its reproductive habits are poorly known. An important food-fish, it is marketed fresh or salted, and is eaten fried or grilled, or in its dried form. Young specimens are popular aquarium fish, even though they are not easily maintained.

258 | Atlantic croaker | Micropogonias undulatus | SCIAENIDAE / DRUMS

Atlantic croaker (En), Westatlantischer Umberfisch, Adlerfisch (D), Corbina, corvinón brasileño (E), Tambour brésilien (F), Ombrina (I), Ombervis (Nl) • Corvina, roncadina (Cub), Trommefisk (Da), Guchi, ishimochi, nibe (J), Corvina, rabeta brasileira (P), Havsgös, stubbkväkare (S), Aaltorumpukala (SF), Crocus (UK), Hardhead (UK, US), Croaker (US)

This species of croaker inhabits subtropical and temperate waters in the western Atlantic, from the state of Massachusetts (US) to the northern part of the Gulf of Mexico and the northern coast of Mexico in the north (although absent from Florida), and from southern Brazil to the Argentine coast in the south. Its maximum length is 50 cm (20 in), weight 1.8 kg (4 lb). Found in coastal and brackish estuarine waters above a muddy or sandy bottom, to a depth of 100–120 m (330–400 ft), wherever it encounters suitable conditions for feeding and breeding. The Atlantic croaker is a eurychalinous species, i.e. it is not very susceptible to salinity, with young specimens preferring low salinity levels, and heavily vegetated areas. This bottom-dwelling predator feeds on worms, crayfish and small fish. It is caught with pleasure by both recreational and commercial fishermen for its excellent flesh, and is marketed fresh or frozen. It is prepared fried, grilled or microwaved. Young individuals are popular aquarium fish, although maintaining them in captivity is rather problematic.

257

258

259 | Tiger-toothed croaker | Otolithes ruber | SCIAENIDAE / DRUMS

Tiger-toothed croaker (En), Hundszahn-Umberfisch (D), Bombache tigre mayor, corvina tigre (E), Grande verrue tigrée, otolithe tigre (F), Ombrina tigre (I), Tijgerombervis (Nl) • Snapperkob (Afr), Abo (Bik, Tag), Balat (Ilo), Gelama gigi jarang, jarang gigi, san gaa (Ind), Ganglomo, gelik, grabag, grabah, grabak, melontok (Jav), Alakak (Kap), Gelik, panjang, tengkerong (Mal), Corvina, corvina dentuça, menyuana, pfumbe (Moz-P), Shmahi, yanam (Om), Rainha-dentuda (P), Gulama (Pan), Silver teraglin (Pap), Snapper kob (SA), Annava (Sin), Laqanto (Som), Gufadi, pooza (Swa), Alakaak (Tag), Longtooth salmon, snapper salmon (US), Dulama, lagis (Vis)

The tiger-toothed croaker inhabits subtropical-tropical areas in the Indian Ocean and the western Pacific, from East Africa (including Madagascar) eastwards to the South China Sea and the Queensland coast, Australia. It is absent from the Red Sea. A large croaker, it grows to 90 cm (36 in) in length and 7 kg (15 lb) in weight. Its name is derived from its big teeth. This species lives in schools in coastal regions having a soft bottom, to a depth of 10–40 m (33–130 ft). It often occurs in brackwater areas with a lower salinity level. A bottom-feeder, it consumes fish, crayfish and other bottom-dwelling invertebrates. Similarly to related croaker species, the tiger-tooth has also a large, lobed swimming bladder, which helps it to swim around without much effort. Harvested commercially, it is also caught by anglers. Fishermen catch it with trawling and gill nets. Usually marketed fresh, it is also available salted-and-dried. It is prepared fried, grilled or roasted for human consumption.

260 | Corvina | Sciaena gilberti | SCIAENIDAE / DRUMS

Corvina (En, D), Corvina pampera (E), Courbine blonde (F), Corvina (Nl) • Drum (En), Corvinilla, gringa (Per)

This member of the percid family inhabits tropical waters in the southeastern Pacific. It grows to 60 cm (24 in) in length and 2 kg (4.4 lb) in weight. Found mainly in coastal shallows, the corvina prefers a rocky bottom. It lives alone or in smaller groups, hunting at night. A predatory species, it feeds on fish, crustaceans and gastropods. In South America, it is considered the best quality fish of all, and is thus the favourite catch of both commercial and recreational fishermen throughout its range. It is distributed mainly fresh. Its flesh is regarded as a real delicacy, and is fried in a pan or grilled.

261 | **Brown meagre** | Sciaena umbra | SCIAENIDAE / DRUMS

Brown meagre (En), Meerrabe, Seerabe (D), Corvallo (E), Corb commun, corbeau (F), Corvo, corvina (I), Zeeraaf (Nl) • Korb i zi (Alb), Corball de roca (Cat), Konj (Cr, Slo), Brun ørnefisk (Da), Skios (Gr), Roncadeira preta (P), Kulbak czarny (Pl), Temnyi gorbyl' (R), Brunveka (S), Rumpukala (SF), Eskine baligi (Tr), Gnaw-nekh (Wol)

The brown meagre occurs in the northeastern Atlantic, from the English Channel south to Morocco and Senegal, as well as around the Canary Islands, and, more rarely, in the Mediterranean and the Black Sea. It reaches 70 cm (26 in) in length and 10–11 kg (22–24 lb) in body mass. It inhabits coastal shallows to a depth of 200 m (660 ft). Favouring a rocky or sandy bottom, it is occasionally found in caves and on reefs. It occurs frequently in the brackwater of river mouths. Its large swimming bladder consists of branched chambers that possibly help it to move and manoeuvre swiftly without much effort. A predatory species, it consumes smaller fish as well as bottom-dwelling crayfish and gastropods, which it finds by searching through the bottom. During the day it remains in the vicinity of its hiding place, behaving calmly, while at night it hunts. It is sold fresh or frozen, and prepared cooked, grilled, fried or roasted in an oven for consumption. In Turkey, its exceptionally big otolithes – bones situated in the internal ears serving the sense of balance – are powdered for treating infections of the urinary tract.

262 | **Red drum** | Sciaenops ocellatus | SCIAENIDAE / DRUMS

Red drum (En), Roter Umberfisch (D), Corvinón ocelado (E), Tambour rouge (F), Ombrina ocellata (I), Rode ombervis (Nl) • Corvinão-de-pintas (P), Redfish (US)

This marine percid fish occurs in subtropical waters of the western part of the Atlantic. Its area of distribution includes coastal Massachusetts, southern Florida and coastal northern Mexico. The red drum reaches 155 cm (60 in) in length and 45 kg (100 lb) in weight. A bottom-dweller, it occurs along the coasts on a sandy or muddy bottom, but is also found in brackwater, frequenting the surf zone. This avid predator feeds on fish, gastropods and crustaceans. Although its flesh is of excellent quality, it is not intensely fished. However, it has appeared in marine aquacultures, and is successfully reproduced in gigantic floating cages at sea. Its high-quality flesh is prepared in various ways – fried, grilled, or roasted. Being a coastal species, it is a popular catch of anglers, larger specimens qualifying as excellent sport fish.

263 | Shi drum | Umbrina cirrosa | SCIAENIDAE / DRUMS

Shi drum (En), Umberfisch, Schattenfisch, Bartumber (D), Verrugato (E), Ombrine côtière (F), Ombrina (I), Shi-ombervis (Nl) • Korb i bardhe (Alb), Corball de sorra (Cat), Corvina (CV), Misqâr mlawwan (Leb), Calafate-de-riscas, corvina-marreca, labarda, viuva (P), Svetlana umbrina (R), Korbel (Slo), Gurbell (US), Sea crow (US), Corb (UK), Svetlyi gorbyl (Ukr), Corb (US)

The shi drum inhabits subtropical and temperate areas in the northeastern Atlantic, from the Bay of Biscay south to Morocco, as well as the Mediterranean, the Black Sea and the Sea of Azov. Its occurrence south of Morocco has not been substantiated. It has also reached the Red Sea through the Suez Canal. The shi drum grows to 1 m (39 in) in length and 5–6 kg (11–13 lb) in body mass. Its large and branched swimming bladder enables it to float excellently, and also serves as an organ sensing vibrations. The shi drum occurs above a sandy or muddy bottom, and among rocks, to a depth of 100 m (330 ft). Young specimens can often be found in the brackwater of river mouths and shallow bays. An omnivorous species, its main food consists of bottom-dwelling invertebrates. It lives solitarily, and spawns in June in the Mediterranean. Not harvested commercially on a large scale, it is sometimes caught by sea anglers. Marketed either fresh or frozen, it is prepared grilled, roasted in an oven or fried in a pan. While young drums are popular aquarium fish, keeping them in captivity is problematic.

264 | Atlantic emperor | Lethrinus atlanticus | LETHRINIDAE / EMPERORS

Atlantic emperor (En), Atlantikkehrer (D), Emperador atlántico (E), Empéreur atlantique (F) • Noche, bica-da-rocha, sargo-de-areia (CV), Atlantisk kejserbrasen (Da), Ekpimmèkpaviyii (Fon), Taiseiyo-fuefuki (J), Pelandok (Mal), Argelino, bica, escavador, passarinho (P), Letra okoniak (Pl), Sinapa khamè (Su)

A member of the family Lethrinidae, Atlantic emperors dwell in the eastern part of the Atlantic Ocean, in the area extending from Senegal to Gabon, and in the region around the Cape Verde Islands, São Tomé and Principe and the Rolas Islands. It is almost certain that this is the only Lethrinus species dwelling in the tropical waters of the eastern Atlantic. Specimens may attain body lengths of 50 cm (20 in) and weights of 2.3–2.5 kg (5–5.5 lb). Primarily abundant in shallow coastal waters and near reefs, Atlantic emperors occur to a maximum depth of about 50 m (160 ft). Living near the sea bottom, they mainly feed at night and hide in the daytime. Predatory in habit, they feed on bottom-dwelling invertebrates and tiny fish. In the spawning season they occasionally form enormous groups and travel to the open sea. Like all other Lethrinus species, Atlantic emperors are considered an important food fish and are intensively fished. Larger specimens are particularly popular with sport fishermen and divers. Winter is the most suitable season for fishing Atlantic emperor. Marketed for food chiefly fresh, smoked or salted and dried, the meat of the Atlantic emperor is in most cases pan-fried or roasted, or is alternatively eaten smoked and dried. Sometimes the meat of the fish may smell of iodine after cooking.

263

264

265 | **Pink ear emperor** | Lethrinus lentjan | LETHRINIDAE / EMPERORS

Pink ear emperor (En), Emperador de lentejuelas (E), Empereur lentille (F) • Rooikol-keiser (Afr), Pink-eared emperor, purple-eared emperor (Au), Purple-headed emperor (Au, Pap), Kilawan (Ban), Bukauel (Bik), Metiil, sagiuripiy (Car), Dragi, gwasawa (Creo), Shaari, shekhaili (Em), Pig-face bream (Ind-En), Nisehana-fuefuki, shimofuri-fuefuki (J), Sheiry (Kuw), Tsangou (Mad), Ketambak, landok, mempinang, pelandok (Mal), Ladrão de lentejoulas (Moz-P), Bossu d'herbe (NC), Ngữrê, noo (Num), Bashkhil, khodair, kutam, shari, suli (Om), Metngui (Pal), Shari yaksheena (Q), Shaoor, sheiry (Sau), Maxaaso (Som), Changu, changu n'jana (Swa), Batilya, bukaual, kanuping (Tag), Redspot emperor, saburbir emperor (UK), Helingero, katambak, kilawan (Vis)

A member of the family Lethrinidae, pink ear emperors dwell in the Indian Ocean and in the western region of the Pacific Ocean, from the Red Sea, the Persian Gulf and in the tropical waters from the eastern coasts of Africa to Ryuku and Tonga. The name derives from the bright red spot on each gill cover. Specimens may attain a maximum body length of 50 cm (20 in), and a weight of 1.8–2 kg (4–4.4 lb). They primarily dwell in sand-bottom areas of shallow coastal waters and around coral reefs, but they may also swim up into the brackish waters of river estuaries and lagoons. As predators, pink ear emperors feed on crustaceans and molluscs, but echinoderms, worms and fish are also part of their diet. They spawn throughout the year, but between April and June more intensively. Due to their excellent meat, pink ear emperors are a popular target of both commercial and recreational fishermen. Marketed fresh, the fish is most often pan-fried, baked or roasted.

266 | **Sky emperor** | Lethrinus mahsena | LETHRINIDAE / EMPERORS

Sky emperor (En), Mahsena-Straßenkehrer (D), Emperador mahsena (E), Empéreur mahsena (F) • Bloednek-keier, hemel-keiser (Afr), Capitaine, dame berri, dame berri blanc, lascar (Creo), Mempinang (Ind), Iso-fuefuki (J), Bakoko (Kuy), Angelike, menahelika (Mad), Landok (Mal), Gueule rouge (Mas-F), Ladrão masena (Moz-P), Khutam, shari, suli, (Om), Yellow-tailed emperor (Pap), Cutthroat emperor (SA), Shaoor, sheiry (Sau), Caroole, dhan-guduud (Som), Changu, changu tuku, tukwana (Swa), Bitilya (Tag), Tamure (Tua), Mahsena emperor (UK)

This percoid species is abundant in the western region of the Indian Ocean and dwells in tropical seas in the vast area extending from the Red Sea and the eastern coasts of Africa as far as Sri Lanka. Sky emperors may attain body lengths of 65 cm (26 in) and weights of 7.5 kg (16.5 lb). Predatory in habit, sky emperors feed chiefly on echinoderms, crustaceans and fish, but occasionally also molluscs, porifera and worms are also included on their dietary list. A protogynous hermaphrodite species, the young sky emperors are first female, later transforming into males. They spawn in October-November in the open seas, occasionally forming large groups in the spawning season. In the Red Sea area it is considered an excellent food fish, though the meat of the sky emperor may have an unpleasant "coral" taste and odour in some regions of the Indian Ocean. Due to its excellent meat, sky emperor stock is widely exploited, both by commercial and recreational fishermen, and deep sea divers. Usually marketed fresh, the meat of the fish is eaten fried or roasted.

267 | **Bogue** | Boops boops | SPARIDAE / PORGIES AND PARGOS

Bogue (En), Gelbstriemen, Ochsenauge (D), Boga, catalufa (E), Bogue (F), Boga, boba (I), Bokvis (Nl) • Vopa (Alb), Boca (CV), Moza (Egy), Ox-eye (En), Finouinblc (Fon), Otoe (Gha), Gópa (Gr), Gubus (Isr), Ghoubbous' (Leb), Vopa (Malt), Buga (Mon), Hamrouda (Mor), Okseøyefisk (N), Boga do mar (P), Bukva (SC), Boga (SF), Bukva (Slo), Kupes (Tr), Bouga (Tun), Bream (US)

The bogue inhabits the eastern Atlantic, from Norway to Angola, as well as around the Canary Islands and Cape Verde. It is extremely common in the region stretching from the Bay of Biscay to Gibraltar. Found also in the Mediterranean, it is rare in the Black Sea. It reaches 35–36 cm (14 in) in length and 450–500 g (16–18 oz) in weight. This species lives in coastal areas, and is found in various habitats above a rocky, muddy, sandy or vegetated bottom. It forms huge schools and rises to surface waters at night, but otherwise occurs to a depth of 350 m (1150 ft). An omnivorous species, the bogue takes mainly small crustaceans, but also zooplankton. It spawns in April and May in the western Mediterranean. Intensely harvested commercially, it is caught mainly with nets dragged in open water, but is also hooked by anglers. Marketed fresh or frozen, it is eaten fried, roasted or grilled. It is frequently used as a bait fish, too.

268 | **Santer seabream** | Cheimerius nufar | SPARIDAE / PORGIES AND PARGOS

Santer seabream (En), Nufar-Seebrasse (D), Dentón nufar (E), Denté nufar (F), Dentice nufar (I), Nufar-zeebrasem (Nl) • Santer (Afr), Nufar-havrude (Da), Barred silvery seabream, red stumpnose, soldier (En), Guerreiro-de-barras (P)

This large seabream species is abundant in the western region of the Indian Ocean, in the south as far as the Mossel Gulf and South Africa, in the east to India and Sri Lanka, in the tropical waters. It attains a maximum body length of 75 cm (30 in), and a maximum weight of 7.5–8 kg (16.5–17.5 lb). Santer seabream live over rock sea bottom in coastal waters, at depths of 20–300 m (66–1000 ft). The young specimens live in the protected areas of river estuaries. Larger specimens are easily caught with regular fishing rods from the coast when the seas are rough. Predatory in habit, santer seabream feed on smaller fish, crustaceans and other bottom-dwelling invertebrates. Despite the high quality meat they produce, santer seabream landings are of minor significance. Larger specimens are popular among sport fishermen and divers. Marketed for food fresh and dry-salted, santer seabream are used for food dried or pan-fried, baked or roasted.

269 | **Red seabream** | Chrysophrys major | SPARIDAE / PORGIES AND PARGOS

Red seabream (En), Seebrasse (D), Dorada del Japón, pargo japonés, dorada gigante (E), Spare japonais, daurade japonais (F), Orata del Giappone (I), Japanse zeebrasem (Nl) • Sha lap (Cant), Red pargo (HK), Madai, tai (J), Ch'am-dom (Kor), Zhen diao, jia jí yú (Mand), Dourada do Japão (P), Krasnyi tai (R), Kirmizi fangri (Tr), Japanese seabream (UK), Silver seabream (UK, US), Madai, red porgy, red tail (US)

This seabream species dwells in the northwestern area of the Pacific Ocean, extending from the South China Sea to Japan in the north, but it cannot be found around the Philippines. A large sized species, red seabream may attain body lengths of 100 cm (39 in) and weights of 22 kg (50 lb). They chiefly dwell over rock sea bottom, most often at depths of 10–200 m (33–600 ft), but they are rare below 50 m (160 ft). Mature specimens migrate to shallow waters to spawn in late spring and summer, the young stay in these shallow waters after hatching, only later moving to deeper waters. A protogynous hermaphrodite species, the sexually mature specimens are first female, later transforming into males. Predatory in habit, red seabream feed on bottom-dwelling invertebrates, shellfish, crustaceans and fish. A very popular food fish in the entire area they populate, the meat of the red seabream is extremely expensive in Japan, due to the fact that it is mainly served on special occasions, such as weddings. The stock is widely exploited both by commercial and recreational fishermen, and red seabream are also raised in cages suspended in the sea. Marketed live, fresh and frozen, the fish is cooked or simmered, or fried in oil, roasted or baked. It is also used in Eastern medical practices.

270 | **Squirefish** | Chrysophrys auratus | SPARIDAE / PORGIES AND PARGOS

Squirefish (En), Goldbrasse (D), Daurade de Nueva Zélande (F) • Cockney, pink snapper (Au), Dourada australiana (P)

This seabream species is most abundant in the Indian Ocean and the Pacific, in the tropical-subtropical waters around New Zealand, Australia, the Philippines, Indonesia, China, Taiwan and Japan. Specimens may attain body lengths of 130 cm (51 in) and weights of 20 kg (44 lb). They primarily dwell over rock reefs, up to depths of 200 m (660 ft). The young prefer the protected areas of shallow coastal waters with mud bottom overgrown with marine vegetation. Those smaller than 30 cm (12 in) form schools of about 30 fish. The mature specimens are shy, hence they are seldom observed. They are generally sedentary in habit, but tagging results show that they may occasionally travel a long distance from their home grounds. A predatory species, the squirefish mainly feeds on crustaceans, but marine worms, echinoderms, shellfish and other fishes also rank high in its diet. It spawns from October to December in waters deeper than 50 m (160 ft), when the water temperature is exactly 18°C (64.4°F), forming large groups in the spawning season. It has been observed in New Zealand fisheries that the female fish may transform into males, but transformation is about to start before the fish attain sexual maturity. Due to the excellent meat they provide, squirefish are popular among both commercial and recreational fishermen.

271 | Common dentex | Dentex dentex | SPARIDAE / PORGIES AND PARGOS

Common dentex (En), Zahnbrasse (D), Dentón (E), Denté commun (F), Dentice (I), Tandbrasem (Nl) • Dentali (Alb), Déntol (Cat), Zubatac (Cr), Synagrida (Gr), Samaket Rayyis (Leb), Denci komuni (Malt), Dintos (Ru), Sinagrit baligi (Tr), Dentex (UK, US), Porgy (US)

The common dentex is a fish species inhabiting the eastern Atlantic, from the British Isles south to Mauritania. Sporadically, it occurs as far south as Senegal. It is also found around the Canary Islands and Madeira, as well as in the Mediterranean Sea south of the 40th parallel, i.e. along the Spanish and north African coasts. It reaches 1 m (39 in) maximum length and 10 kg (22 lb) weight. Found above a rocky or stony bottom, to a depth of 200 m (660 ft), it can be encountered much less frequently at depths above 50 m (164 ft). Adults live alone, while juveniles are gregarious. A carnivorous species, the dentex feeds on fish, cephalopods and shellfish. A very active swimmer, young specimens move towards the coasts in spring, and migrate to deeper waters in winter. Spawning occurs between March and May. An important food fish, the dentex is intensely harvested both by commercial and recreational fishermen. The young are caught with traps. Since the dentex is poorly represented at markets, successful attempts have been undertaken to farm it in marine aquacultures, and it is likely to become an important cultured marine fish in the future. It is sold fresh or frozen, and prepared in various ways for human consumption.

272 | White seabream | Diplodus sargus | SPARIDAE / PORGIES AND PARGOS

White seabream (En), Bindenbrasse, Große Geißbrasse (D), Sargo marroquí (E), Sar commun (F), Sarago maggiore (I), Witte ringbrasem (Nl) • Sargu (Alb), Sar rayé (Alg-F, Mau-F), Sarg (Cat), Baraj (Cr), Shargoush (Egy), Sargós (Gr), Taouajtt (Has), Sarghous (Leb), Sargo-legítimo (P), Belyi sarg (R), Blacktail (SA), Crnoprugac, sarag (SC), Isosargi (SF), Karagoz, tahta baligi (Tr), N'gaté en gor (Wol)

The white seabream is an inhabitant of the eastern Atlantic, from the temperate zone to the tropics. It is found from the Bay of Biscay to South Africa, and also occurs in the Mediterranean. The nominate form, D. s. sargus lives in the Mediterranean and the Black Sea. It can reach 45 cm (18 in) length and 1.3 kg (2.9 lb) maximum body mass. This seabream occurs in rocky areas close to the coast, and above Posidonia beds, to a depth of 50 m (160 ft). Like related species, it is extremely agile and is particularly active at dawn in the tidal zone. It feeds on gastropods and other invertebrates, which it collects by rummaging in the mud. It spawns in May and June, and its fry and larvae live among planktonic organisms. While of little importance in commercial fisheries, it often occurs in the catch of recreational fishermen. It is successfully farmed in marine aquacultures. Sold fresh or frozen, it is prepared pan-fried, grilled or roasted in an oven.

271

272

273 | **Common two-banded seabream** | Diplodus vulgaris | SPARIDAE / PORGIES AND PARGOS

Common two-banded seabream (En), Zweibindenbrasse (D), Sargo mojarra (E), Sar á tête noire (F), Sarago testa nera (I), Zwartkop-ringbrasem (Nl) • Sargua (Alb), Variada (Cat), Baraj (Cr), Kampanas (Gr), Kharqoun (Leb), Mojarra, sargo seifa (Mau-E), Sar (Mau-F), Sargo-safia (P), Klyuvoryl (R), Karagoz (Tr), Blacktail bream, Twoband bream (US), N'gaté bu digen (Wol-M)

The common two-banded seabream is native to the eastern Atlantic and is found from the Bay of Biscay to Cape Verde and the Canary Islands, as well as in the Mediterranean and the Black Sea. In the south, it inhabits coastal waters from Angola to South Africa. Its maximum length is 50 cm (20 in), and it weighs up to 3 kg (6.6 lb). It lives alone or in small schools above a rocky, or, less frequently, a sandy bottom, to a depth of 160 m (525 ft), although it is rare below 50 m (164 ft). Young specimens can sometimes be observed in vegetated areas. A predatory species, it feeds on crustaceans, worms and shellfish. Spawning takes place in October and November, and the eggs and larvae live among pelagic planktonic organisms. Juveniles migrate back to coastal areas. An important food fish, it is intensely fished and is also caught by anglers. Marketed fresh or frozen, it is prepared fried in a pan, grilled, roasted in an oven or microwaved. Smaller specimens are popular aquarium fish.

274 | **Striped seabream** | Lithognathus mormyrus | SPARIDAE / PORGIES AND PARGOS

Striped seabream (En), Marmorbrasse (D), Herrera (E), Marbré, dorade marbré (F), Tordo, marmora (I), Zandsteenbraas (Nl) • Murra (Alb), Pageot (Alg-F), Besugo-de-eva, besugo-trombeiro, besugo-trombudo (Ang), Mabre (Cat), Ferreiro, nacho, sargo-de-areia (CV), Stribet blankesten (Da), Ghozailla (Egy), Striped seabream (En), Mourmoura (Gr), Abdhim (Has), Marmour (Leb), Ferreira estriada (Moz-P), Kofer (Om), Ferreira (P), Atlanticheskiy zemleroi (R), Ovčica (SC, Slo), Pageau gris (Sen), Cizgili mercan (Tr), Ring (Wol-S)

The striped seabream is native to the Atlantic, from the Bay of Biscay to South Africa, as well as around the Canary and the Cape Verde Islands. It is found in the Mozambique Channel, the western part of the Indian Ocean, the Red Sea and the Mediterranean. It is not known from tropical waters off East Africa. It can reach 55 cm (22 in) in length and 2.5 kg (5.5 lb) in weight. It is found in equal abundance in sandy, muddy or vegetated areas. A eurychalinous species, it tolerates changes in salinity levels and thus penetrates widely into brackwater sections of river mouths, but also survives in the water of lagoons that have higher salinity levels. A gregarious fish, it sometimes forms huge groups. It preys on worms, shellfish and smaller crustaceans. Specimens take rotting algae from the bottom into their mouth, rise to surface waters, spit out the plants and swallow the little animals inhabiting these plants. Harvested both by commercial and recreational fishermen for its excellent flesh, the striped seabream has no particular economic significance. Offered fresh or dried, it is consumed roasted, fried or grilled, or directly as dried fish.

273

274

275

276

275 | Blackspot seabream | Pagellus centrodotus (bogaraveo) | SPARIDAE / PORGIES AND PARGOS

Blackspot seabream (En), Graubarsch, Nordische Meerbrasse (D), Goraz, pancho, ollomol, besugo del Cantábrico (E), Dorade rose, pageot rose (F), Rovello, occhialone (I), Spaanse zeebrasem, Zeebrasem (Nl) • Spalce e kuqe (Alb), Carapau, peixão (Az), Besuc de la piga (Cat), Arbun okan Grbic (Cr), Almindelig blankesten, spidstandet blankesten (Da), Red bream, sea-bream (En), An deargán (Ga), Sikasikavi, yiyiwa (Gha), Chephalas, phagrí, sparidi, synagrida (Gr), Kólguflekkur (Is), Flekkpagell (N), Besugo, esparideos, goraz (P), Morlesz szkarlatny (Pl), Fläckpagell (S), Ljuskavke, rumenac okan (SC), Pikkupagelli (SF), Okati ribon (Slo), Common sea bream (UK), Gunner, red seabream (US)

The blackspot seabream is a fish of the northeastern Atlantic. Found from Senegal and Madeira, the Azores to Ireland, it is rare in northern regions. It is also known from the Mediterranean. It can reach 70 cm (28 in) length and 4 kg (8.8 lb) weight. Adult specimens live above a muddy bottom at the outer slopes of the shelf to a depth of 400–700 m (1300–2300 ft). The young are found in coastal shallows, above a sandy, rocky or muddy bottom. They are omnivorous, but take mainly crustaceans, gastropods, worms and smaller fish. Like many related seabreams, this species is a protandrous hermaphrodite, i.e. male fish turn into females when they are 20–30 cm (8–12 in) long. The blackspot seabream spawns between January and June, and adults move coastwards in this period. The eggs are distributed along the sea bottom. An important food fish, this species is intensely harvested by commercial and recreational fishermen alike. It is marketed fresh or frozen, and is served fried, roasted or grilled.

276 | Common pandora | Pagellus erythrinus | SPARIDAE / PORGIES AND PARGOS

Common pandora (En), Rotbrasse (D), Breca, pajel (E), Pageot commun, pageot rouge (F), Fragolino, pagello fragolino (I), Rode zeebrasem (Nl) • Pagri, spalce e kuqe (Alb), Pagell (Cat), Rød blankesten (Da), Sika-sika (Fon), Lethrini, lithrini (Gr), Jarbydy (Leb), Bazuga kahla (Malt), Pagell, rødpagell (N), Bica, breca (P), Morlesz szkarlatny (Pl), Krasnyi pagel (R), Rödpagell (S), Arbun, rumenac (SC), Punapagelli (SF), Ribon (Slo), Mandagöz mercan (Tr), Becker, king of the breams, Spanish sea bream (UK), Chervonyi pagr (Ukr), Pandora (US), Tikki (Wol-S)

The common pandora is native to the eastern Atlantic, and is found in subtropical-tropical and temperate zone areas from Norway to Guinea-Bissau, occurring also in the Mediterranean and around Cape Verde and the Canary Islands, and Madeira. It is rare around Scandinavia. It reaches 60 cm (24 in) in length and 4.5 kg (10 lb) in weight. This species lives close to the shore, near the bottom, in rocky, stony and muddy areas. A protogynous hermaphrodite, females turn into males in their third year of age, when approximately 17 cm (7 in) in length. An important food fish, it frequently turns up in the catch of commercial and recreational fishermen alike. Marketed fresh or frozen, it is served fried, grilled or roasted. Consumption may cause ciguatoxic poisoning. Ciguatoxin builds up in fish inhabiting tropical-subtropical areas that feed on certain species of algae. The first symptoms of malfunctioning of the digestive, nervous and circulatory systems may develop within six hours after eating, and can return years after the original poisoning. The toxin usually concentrates in the head, intestines and eggs of the fish, thus consumption of these parts should be avoided.

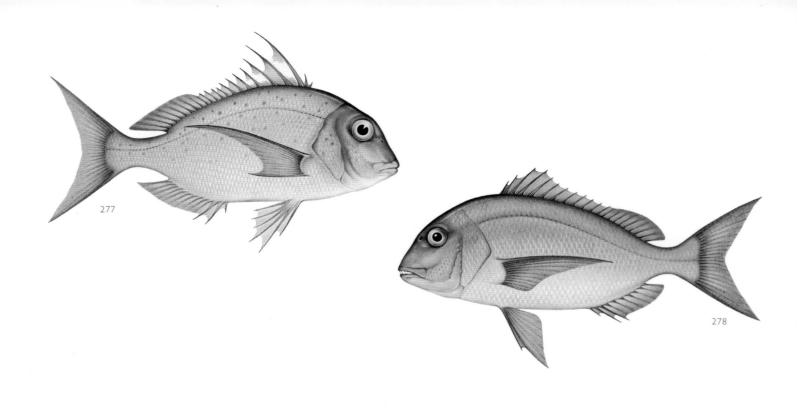

277 | **Blue-spotted seabream** | Pagrus caeruleostictus | SPARIDAE / PORGIES AND PARGOS

Blue-spotted seabream (En), Blaufleckenbrasse, Blaugefleckte Meerbrasse (D), Hurta, pargo zapata (E), Pagre à points bleus (F), Pagro reale maschio, pagro azzurro (I), Blawgevlekte zeebrasem (Nl) • Pargo (Ang, Creo, CV), Pagre reial (Cat), Sikasika (Gha), Stiktofagri (Gr), Sinapa (GuiB, Su), Tamendept Mauritania (Has), Farrydy (Leb), Zapata blanca (Mau-E), Daurade rose, pagre (Mau-F), Pargo-de-pintas-azuis, pargo-boi, pargo-ruço, ruço (P), Pagrus pregacz, pagrus zapata (Pl), Pagar barjaktar (SC), Bluepointed porgy, goldenhead porgy (US), Kibaro Mauritania (Wol-M)

The blue-spotted seabream occurs in subtropical and tropical areas in the eastern Atlantic, from Portugal to Angola, as well as in the Mediterranean Sea. It reaches 90 cm (36 in) in length and 12–13 kg (27–29 lb) in weight. This species lives above a hard – rocky or stony – bottom, to a depth of 200 m (660 ft). Larger specimens usually occur at a greater depth, while smaller, younger individuals inhabit coastal shallows. The blue-spotted seabream has been observed to migrate to soft-bottomed shallows between spring and autumn, for spawning. It reaches sexual maturity in its second year, and, like its relatives, it is a protogynous hermaphrodite, i.e. adult females turn into males with time. This predatory species feeds mainly on seashells, crustaceans and small fish. It is regularly harvested by both commercial and recreational fishermen. Marketed fresh or frozen, larger specimens are also sold as fillets. It is prepared fried in a pan or roasted in an oven for human consumption.

278 | **Common seabream** | Pagrus pagrus | SPARIDAE / PORGIES AND PARGOS

Common seabream (En), Sackbrasse, Gemeine Rotbrasse (D), Pargo (E), Pagre commun (F), Pagro mediterraneo (I), Gewone zeebrasem (Nl) • Pagri (Alb), Besugo, pargo-colorado, (Arg, Uru, Ven), Pagre (Cat), Almindelig blankesten (Da), Sika-sika (Fon), Tsile (Gha), Phágri mertzáni (Gr), Yooroppa-madai (J), Jarbydy mkayyal (Leb), Gejj (Sen), Capatão, pargo, pargo-legítimo, parguete (P), Boneknaap (Pp-B, Pp), Pagar-crvenac (SC), Pagar (SC, Slo), Kirma, mercan (Tr), Couch's sea bream (UK), Red porgy (UK, US), Porgy (US), Xayaay, yennë (Wol-S)

This seabream species is found in the eastern Atlantic, from subtropical areas to the British Isles in the north, and around Madeira and the Cape Verde Islands, as well as the Mediterranean Sea; in the western part of the ocean, it occurs from New York, the northern part of the Gulf of Mexico along the continental coasts south to Argentina. Its maximum length is 90 cm (36 in), weight 15 kg (33 lb). It lives above a hard, stony, rocky or sandy bottom, to a depth of 250 m (820 ft), but is abundant to a depth of 150 m (500 ft) only. Young specimens are frequently found in vegetated areas. A predatory fish, it feeds on crustaceans, fish, and gastropods. A protogynous hermaphrodite, adults become females first, and turn into males with age. The common seabream spawns between January and March. It is regularly caught by both fishermen and anglers, and is also farmed in marine aquacultures. It is popular in show aquariums. Distributed fresh or frozen, larger specimens are marketed as fillets. They are prepared grilled, fried or roasted for human consumption.

279 | **Goldlined seabream** | Rhabdosargus sarba | SPARIDAE / PORGIES AND PARGOS

Goldlined seabream (En), Silberne Stumpfnase (D), Sargo dorado (E), Sargue doré (F) • Natalse stompneus (Afr), Gabit, kabeet (Ara), Tarwhine (Au), Silverbream (Au, US), Gueule pavée (Creo), Natal stumpnose (Ind-En), Ambatovasena, fihampotsy, menaheliky, saifotsy (Mad), Brumbrufuma, xinguende (Moz-P), Gorgofan (Om), Dourada (P), Jerjafan (Q), Vella mattawa (Tam), Yellowfin sea bream, yellowfin bream (US)

This large-bodied percid is widely distributed in tropical waters of the Indian Ocean and the western Pacific. It is found from the Red Sea along the East African coast to Madagascar, and around Australia, as well as the seas of China and Japan. It grows to 80 cm (32 in) in length and 12–13 kg (27–29 lb) in weight. It frequents coastal shallows and is often caught in tidal zones and rocky basins. A solitary species, it has been reported to form schools in Australia. It also appears in brackwater and in mangroves. It feeds on bottom-dwelling invertebrates, primarily gastropods, as well as marine macrovegetation. Harvested by commercial and recreational fishermen for its tasty flesh, the goldlined seabream is artificially reproduced in some areas. It is commonly marketed fresh, and is served pan-fried, oven-baked or grilled.

280 | **Salema** | Sarpa salpa | SPARIDAE / PORGIES AND PARGOS

Salema (En), Goldstriemen (D), Salema, salpa (E), Saupe (F), Salpa (I), Gestreepte bokvis (Nl) • Strepie (Afr), Salpe (Alb), Okseøjefisk (Da), Salema (E, P), Saupe, goldline, bogue, strepie (En), Gwiela (Malt), Okseøyefisk (N), Oxögonfisk, salpa (S), Boga (SF), Salpa (Slo), Sarpan baligi (Tr)

The salema inhabits the eastern Atlantic from the Bay of Biscay and the Straits of Gibraltar to Sierra Leone. It is also found in the vicinity of Madeira, Cape Verde and the Canary Islands, as well as in waters off Congo to South Africa. It is also present in the Mediterranean Sea. This species reaches 50 cm (20 in) in length and 3.6 kg (8 lb) in body mass. It lives in rocky and sandy areas with intense algal growth, to a depth of 50–100 m (160–330 ft). The young are found in very shallow water of only 1 m (3 ft) depth. A gregarious fish, it sometimes forms large groups. These schools are easily identified by their dense, organized swimming formation. Juveniles are carnivorous and feed on small crustaceans, while adults are almost wholly vegetarian. They grow quickly, reaching 10–15 cm (4–6 in) in body length by the end of their first year. A protandrous hermaphrodite, adults are males first and turn into females with time. Spawning occurs from March to April, and from September to November. The eggs and larvae are pelagic. The flesh of the salema is excellent, but easily softens, and is thus not in high esteem. Marketed fresh and frozen, it is prepared fried, grilled or roasted.

279

280

281 | Gilt-head seabream | Sparus aurata | SPARIDAE / PORGIES AND PARGOS

Gilt-head seabream (En), Goldbrasse (D), Dorada, pargo dorado (E), Dorade royale, daurade vraie (F), Orata (I), Goudbrasem (Nl) • Guldbrassen, Guldhovede (Da), Komarca, ovrata (Cr), Tsipoúra (Gr), N'tad (Has), Ajaj (Leb), Awrata (Malt), Zapata morisca (Mau-E), Tamure (Mor), Snapper (NZ), Doirado, dorada, Dourada, douradinha, Safata (P), Kanuping (Tag), Cipura (Tr)

Gilt-head seabream inhabit the eastern part of the Atlantic Ocean, from the British Isles to the Cape Verde islands, but they also occur in the Mediterranean and the Black Sea. Presence of the fish has also been reported from the waters surrounding New Zealand, but it is more likely that the New Zealand stock is a similar species. They may attain sizes of 70 cm (28 in) in length and 17 kg (37 lb) in weight. Dwelling chiefly in shallow waters, gilt-head seabream occur primarily at depths of 5–30 m (16–100 ft), but mature specimens may also be found at depths of 150 m (500 ft). They form small groups in rock and sand bottom areas, but in springtime large schools of gilt-head occur above the sand and mud bottom of brackish waters. Very sensitive to cold temperatures, gilt-head may die when temperatures drop suddenly. Although chiefly predatory in habit, gilt-head seabream also consume plants as supplementary diet. The staple diet of the fish consists of crustaceans and molluscs, including shell-fish. Extensively exploited by commercial fishing fleets, the gilt-head seabream is one of the most important species for aquaculture. Also landed in large quantities by recreational fishermen, gilt-head seabream are available in the food market. The meat of the fish is sold fresh, then boiled, simmered or fried in various ways.

282 | Black seabream | Spondyliosoma cantharus | SPARIDAE / PORGIES AND PARGOS

Black seabream (En), Streifenbrasse (D), Chopa, choupa, pañoso, pargo chopa (E), Dorade grise, griset, canthare gris (F), Tanuta, cantaro (I), Zeekarper (Nl) • Ambua (Ang), Càntera (Cat), Doirada, ruta, viúva (CV), Havrude (Da), Old wife (En), Kperkper (Gha), Skathári (Gr), Kurodai (J), Rayyis (Leb), Havkarudse, havkaruss (N), Havsruda (N, S), Choupa, mucharra, salema, sama (P), Kantar (Pl, SC, Slo), Cantar (Ru), Meriruutana (SF), Sarigöz (Tr), Ursun, wersun (Wol)

The home of the black seabream is the eastern Atlantic, from the Orkney Islands to Morocco, Madeira, the Azores and southwards to Angola. It also occurs in the Mediterranean Sea. It lives above a rocky, sandy, vegetated bottom, to a depth of 300 m (950 ft). It grows to 60 cm (24 in) in length and 2.2 kg (5 lb) in weight. A proto-gynous hermaphrodite, adult females turn into males at a certain size. The black seabream spawns between April and August and lays its eggs onto the bottom. Male and female search for a suitable spawning ground together. The male then makes an oval depression, in which the female deposits her somewhat sticky eggs. The fry hatch from these eggs in 9–10 days and are subsequently guarded by the male for a short while. The young remain in the vicinity of the nest until reaching 7–8 cm (approx. 3 in) in length. A gregarious species, it is sometimes found in enormous schools. An omnivore, it feeds on aquatic plants and small invertebrates, mainly crustaceans. An important food fish, it is often included in the catch of commercial and recreational fishermen. It is sold fresh or frozen, and prepared fried, roasted or grilled.

281

282

283 | **Blotched picarel** | Spicara maena | CENTRACANTHIDAE / PICKARELS

Blotched picarel (En), Gefleckte Schnauzenbrasse, Laxierfisch (D), Chucla (E), Mendole (F), Mennola, menola (I), Mendole-pikarel (Nl) • Meridhe, meridhe e zeze (Alb), Xucla blanca (Cat), Zamrydâ (Leb), Cawla (Malt), Trombeiro choupa (P), Menola (R), Modrak (Slo), Beyazgöz baligi (Tr), Smarida dribna (Ukr), Smarida, marida melkaia (Ukr-R), Picarel (US)

The blotched picarel lives in subtropical-tropical areas in the eastern Atlantic from Portugal to Morocco, as well as around the Canary Islands, but it is also found in the Mediterranean and the Black Sea. A small-sized fish, males grow to 25 cm (10 in) in length and 70–75 g (2.5–2.6 oz) in weight, while females reach 20–21 cm (8 in) in length at most. This bottom-dweller inhabits coastal shallows, and occurs a muddy or sandy surface to a depth of 130 m (430 ft). A gregarious species, its movements are minimal. In favourable habitats it is found in considerable numbers. The sticky eggs are deposited in late summer in very shallow, 20–25 cm (8–10 in) deep water into a nest constructed by the male in the sand. A protogynous hermaphrodite, some females turn into males on reaching a certain age. The food of this species consists of bottom-dwelling organisms and zooplankton. While it is not harvested on a large scale, it is regularly caught by anglers. Sold fresh, it is mainly grilled for consumption.

284 | **Yellowstripe goatfish** | Mulloidichthys flavolineatus | MULLIDAE / GOATFISHES, SURMULLETS AND REDMULLETS

Yellowstripe goatfish (En), Seitenfleck-Meerbarbe (D), Capucina á bande jaune (F) • Geelstreep-bokvis (Afr), Amarilis (Bik, Tag), Ikan jangut kuning (Chr), Pallid goatfish (Chr-En), Bait goatfish, gold-lined goatfish (FP), Kawe (Fw), Oama, weke (Haw), Sand weke (Haw-En), Montsuki-akahimeji (J), Kao (Jaw), Te baweina, te kaira (Kir), Jo, jome, salmonete, tiau (Mars), Salmonete de estria amarela (Moz-P), Petit barbillon, surmulet cordon jaune (NC), Hiilo, kît (Nen), Kaloama (Nie), Chemisech, dech (Pal), Vete (Ra, Sam, Tah, Tua), Afolu, afulu, i'asina (Sam), Wuwérik (Sat), Fangalaato (Som), Sonyo (Swa), Saramulyete (Tag), Ouma, ta'uo (Tah), Kouma (Tua), Samoan goatfish (US), Mwatug, souw, uweshig-uweshig (W)

The yellowstripe goatfish is a fish of the Indian and the Pacific Oceans, and occurs from the Red Sea and the eastern coast of Africa to Hawaii and the Marquesas Islands. It is also found in all tropical waters off Micronesia. It grows to a length of 40–45 cm (16–18 in) and a weight of 1–1.5 kg (2.2–3.3 lb). It lives in shallow water at a depth of 5–35 m (16–115 ft). Usually solitary, it sometimes forms smaller schools. Its habitat includes the shallow sandy areas of lagoons and riffs. Characteristic are the two long barbels under its mouth, which serve to identify chemical signals. These barbels help it to detect its prey in the sand bottom. A predatory species, it feeds on crustaceans, gastropods, worms and echinodermata living in the sand. It spawns in open water, the eggs are pelagic, and the larvae live among planktonic organisms. Its flesh is tasty, so it is caught with pleasure by fishermen and anglers. It is distributed fresh or dried, and is either consumed in its dried form, or prepared grilled, fried or roasted.

285 | **Red mullet** | *Mullus barbatus* | MULLIDAE / GOATFISHES, SURMULLETS AND REDMULLETS

Red mullet (En), Rote Meerbarbe (D), Salmonete de fango (E), Rouget barbet, rouget de vase surmulet (F), Triglia di fango (I), Mull, gestreepte zeebarbeel (NI) • Barbuni (Alb), Moll de fang (Cat), Koutsomoura (Gr), Mulit adduma (Isr), Soultân Ibrahym Ramly (Leb), Trilja zghira (Malt), Salmonete da vasa (P), Bradaè (Slo), Barbunya baligi (Tr), Bluntsnouted mullet, striped goatfish, striped mullet (US)

The red mullet inhabits the Atlantic from the British Isles to Senegal in the south, as well as off the Canary Islands and the Azores. It is also found in the Mediterranean and the Black Sea. The Black Sea subspecies is named M. barbatus ponticus, and is characterized by a depressed snout. A small species, it grows to 30–40 cm (12–16 in) in length and 400–500 g (14–18 oz) in weight. It lives on the stone, sand or mud bottomed areas of the continental shelf, to a depth of 10–270 m (30–900 ft). It moves into coastal shallows for the summer. The fry has been observed in very shallow (1 m or 3 ft deep) water. This species feeds on bottom-dwelling prey, its barbels set with chemoreceptors helping it to locate small bottom-dwelling organisms, crustaceans, worms and molluscs. The red mullet breeds in open water between April and August. The larvae and fry feed on the surface and dive to the bottom with time. Marketed mainly fresh, it is eaten fried, grilled or roasted, but is also made into fish soup.

286 | **Striped red mullet** | *Mullus surmuletus* | MULLIDAE / GOATFISHES, SURMULLETS AND REDMULLETS

Striped red mullet (En), Gestreifte Meerbarbe, Streifenbarbe (D), Salmonete de roca (E), Rouget de roche, rouget-barbet de roche (F), Triglia di scoglio, bottarga (I), Koning van de poon, mul (NI) • Barbuni i shkembit (Alb), Mulle (Da, N, S), An milléad dearg (Ga), Avotáracho, barboúni, koutsomoúra (Gr), Himeji, karasumi (J), Soultân Ibrahym Sakhry (Leb), Ovas secas, salmonete-legítimo, salmonete-vermelho (P), Barabulya (R), Gulstrimmig mullus (S), Butarga, ikra, trlje, trlje odkamena (SC), Keltajuovamullo, mullo, suolatu kuivattu kalanmäti (SF), Progasti bradaè (Slo), Barbunya, nil barbunyasi, tekir (Tr), Surmullet, woodcock of the sea (UK)

The striped red mullet lives in the Atlantic from Scotland to the Canary Islands, in the western part of the Baltic Sea, as well as in the Mediterranean and the Black Sea. Its maximum length is 40 cm (16 in), weight 1 kg (2.2 lb). Adult specimens live above a sandy or muddy bottom to a depth of 3–100 m (10–330 ft), while the fry prefer rock-bottomed shallows with algal growth. It lives either solitarily or in schools consisting of 50 specimens at most. Mating takes place between May and July, and the eggs are pelagic, i.e. they drift in water. The larvae have a blue colour and live among planktonic organisms, only the fry sink to the bottom. Sexual maturity is reached in two years. A predatory species, it feeds on small, bottom-dwelling invertebrates, which it finds by feeling the bottom with long, thick barbels covered by chemical receptors. It catches small fish as well. It is well-known to both commercial and recreational fishermen and is sold fresh or frozen. It is stewed, fried, roasted or grilled.

287 | Mozambique tilapia | Oreochromis mossambicus | CICHLIDAE / CICHLIDS

Mozambique tilapia (En), Mosambik-Buntbarsch, Mosambik-Maulbrüter, Tilapie (D), Tilapia del Mozambique (E), Vivaneau gauloise, tilapia du Mozambique (F), Tilapia del Mozambico (I), Mozambique-tilapia (Nl, S) •
Blou kurper (Afr), Fai chau chak ue (Cant), Mphende (Chc), Mozambique-cichlide (Da). Mozambique cichlid (En), Common tilapia (Fi-En), Java tilapia (Fi-En, US), African mouthbrooder (HK), Fai chau chak ue,
gam san tsak (Hok), Kawasuzume (J), Mujair (Jav), Trey tilapia khmao (Khm), Wu-Kuo yu (Mand), Mojarra, tilapia mozámbica (Mex), Malea (Phi), Valkoleukatilapia (SF), Camel snapper, tilapia, largemouth kurper,
Mozambique mouthbrooder (US)

This species originally inhabited the lower reaches of the Zambezi and the Shire rivers, and waters in the coastal plains south of the Zambezi to the Brak River and the Limpopo catchment area. The Mozambique tilapia grows to 40 cm (16 in) in length and 1 kg (2.2 lb) in weight. Commonly, it occurs in coastal lakes, ponds and river mouths, but is also found in shallow ponds and densely vegetated river sections. It survives even in brackwater, as it is able to tolerate extreme salinity levels. Active during the day, this omnivore takes food ranging from algae to aquatic insects. In the tropics it breeds all year round, while in monsoon areas or those with a dry/wet season, it spawns with the first rains. The eggs number between a few hundred and two thousand, and are hatched in the mouth of the female, which also defends her offspring for some time. Intensely harvested, it is the sole source of animal protein in several areas. Marketed fresh or frozen, it is prepared fried, roasted or grilled.

288 | Nile tilapia | Oreochromis niloticus | CICHLIDAE / CICHLIDS

Nile tilapia (En), Nil-Buntbarsch (D), Tilapia del Nilo (E, I), Tilapia du Nil (F), Nijltilapia (Nl) • Garagaza (Hau), Ifunu (Ig), Amnun yeor (Isr), Chikadai (J), Karwa (Kan), Munruvare (S), Niilintilapia (SF), Ngege (Swa),
Wass (Wol)

Very few freshwater species have spread so fast as the Nile tilapia. Native to the upper region of the Nile in Africa, tilapia attain body lengths of 20–40 cm (8–16 in) and weights of 1 kg (2.2 lb). They are found in natural and artificial waters of all continents, with many states having banned their further introduction, although too late it seems. The only obstacle to the incredible boom of tilapia are the local temperatures, since they do not survive under 15°C (60°F), nevertheless thriving in off-flows of thermal waters in several countries with a colder climate. Definitely beautiful among fishes, the proportionately bodied tilapia have strong scales, making them difficult to handle in the kitchen. Their dry meat is extremely palatable and flavoursome when fried. They produce a relatively small number of offspring, but rear those with great care. They build nests for them and even carry the young in their mouths to protect them from predators, hence the name "cradle-mouthed" attached to the entire genus in many areas, although not all species belonging to the family Cichlidae are such good parents. Tilapia attain sexual maturity after a few months, when they start to spawn. Aquaculturists, in order to reduce this early "pointless loss of energy" and to increase commercial growth, tend to build up unisexed stocks of tilapia.

287

288

289 | Pastel ringwrasse | Hologymnosus doliatus | LABRIDAE / WRASSES

Pastel ringwrasse (En), Colombine pastel (F), Colombina pastel (E) • Geringde lipvis (Afr), Ringed wrasse (Chr, SA, US), Candy cane wrasse, longface wrasse (Guam, Mic), Shirotasukibera (J), Labre cerclé (Mas-F), Candycane (Mic), Ringed rainbowfish (Pap), Sugale-lape (Sam)

A percoid species, pastel ringwrasse dwell in the Indian Ocean and the Pacific from the East African coast to Natal and South Africa, and as far east as Samoa and the Line Islands. They may attain body lengths of 50 cm (20 in) and weights of 3–4 kg (7–9 lb). They mostly prefer areas where sand, coral and gravel-covered territories alternate, to depths of 30–35 m (100–115 ft), around reefs in the open sea. A typical fish of warm tropical waters, pastel ringwrasse dwell in waters at least as warm as 25–28°C (77–82°F). The young live near the bottom in schools, while the mature specimens are found in the higher strata. Predatory in habit, their diet mainly consists of fish and crustaceans, occasionally also starfish and worms. A pelagic-spawning species, the pastel ringwrasse spawn in midwater, the hatching of their larvae also takes place here, and the larvae also live on in the open sea plankton. Commercial exploitation of the stock is of minor importance, it being mainly marketed for food fresh. The fish is prepared mostly pan-fried, oven-baked, or roasted over an open fire.

290 | Green wrasse | Labrus viridis | LABRIDAE / WRASSES

Green wrasse (En), Grüner Lippfisch (D), Bodión verde (E), Labre vert, tourdero (F), Tordo (I), Groene lipvis (Nl) • Peshk bari (Alb), Drozak (Cr), Grøn berggylt (Da), Khoddair (Egy), Chiloú, lapina (Gr), Boxbox (Malt), Scour (Mor), Lâpin (Tr), Kheddir (Tun)

The green wrasse lives in the eastern Atlantic from Portugal to Morocco, as well as the Mediterranean and the Black Sea. It reaches 45 cm (18 in) in length and 1.2 kg (2.6 lb) in weight. It occurs in rocky, vegetated areas to a depth of 2–50 m (7–165 ft), though adults are found mainly below 10–15 m. A peculiarity of this species is that it changes the shade of its green colour and its patterning according to its age, state of development and mood. It sometimes turns into a wine red to orange hue. A bottom-dweller, it mostly lies calmly on its side on the bottom, and is easily approached. This characteristic is (ab)used by fishermen and divers. This predator feeds on worms, crayfish, and smaller molluscs inhabiting the sand bottom. Like other Labrus species, it is able to change its sex: specimens smaller than 25–30 cm (10–12 in) are females, while 35–40 cm (14–16 in) individuals are males. The change in gender is associated with an alteration in colour. True transsexual specimens have never been found. The green wrasse spawns in the winter and spring months. An admired food fish, it is harvested by fishermen and anglers alike. It is sold fresh, and is fried or grilled for consumption.

289

290

291

292

291 | California sheephead | Semicossyphus pulcher | LABRIDAE / WRASSES

California sheephead (En), Lippfisch, Kalifornischer Sheephead (D), Vireja de California (E), Labre californien (F) • Californisk fårehoved (Da)

A member of the Labridae family, California sheephead dwell in the eastern region of the Pacific Ocean, from Monterey Bay in California to the Guadeloupe Islands, in the California Gulf to the coasts of Mexico. They may attain body lengths of 90 cm (36 in) and weights of 15–16 kg (33–35 lb). They largely keep to rock sea bottoms and areas overgrown with sea algae. Their diet consists chiefly of hard-shelled animals, such as sea urchins, shellfish, crayfish and crabs. A long-lived species, California sheephead may survive as long as fifty years. The spawning season is in summer, their eggs, or roe, are pelagic, i.e. they hatch while floating in midwater. A protogynous hermaphrodite species, all specimens of California sheephead are first female, transforming into male specimens when attaining a body length of 30 cm (12 in). The white meat of the sheephead is of exceptionally good quality, for which reason they are a very popular prey of. When sheephead are being landed, they should be handled with utmost care, since they may cause serious wounds with the tough teeth they use for the crushing of their hard-shelled prey.

292 | Tautog | Tautoga onitis | LABRIDAE / WRASSES

Tautog (En), Tautog, Austernfisch (D), Tautoga negra (E), Tautogue noir, matote noire (F), Tautoga (I), Tautog-lipvis (Nl) • Black fish (Can), Bodião da ostra (P)

A relation of the wrasse, tautog live in the western regions of the Atlantic Ocean, from Nova Scotia and the Canadian mainland as far south as the coasts of South Carolina. They are also abundant in the area between Cape Cod and Delaware Bay. They may grow as large as 1 m (39 in) and 10–11 kg (22–24 lb). They largely prefer shallow coastal waters, not going below depths of 60–70 m (200–230 ft). They keep to hard sea bottoms, occasionally intruding into the brackish waters of river estuaries and lagoons. They prefer waters warmer than 10°C (50°F). In the Canadian fishery they spawn in June-July, whereas in the southern waters tautog have been observed spawning as early as April. They spawn in smaller groups, though large males, who avidly defend their territory, spawn in couples after a period of lengthy courtship. Predatory in habit, tautog mainly feed on shellfish, gastropods, other molluscs and crabs. Marketed primarily for food, the market is usually supplied with specimens of 1–2 kg (2.2–4.4 lb), which are sold fresh or frozen. They are usually pan-fried, baked in the oven or roasted.

ᴤ93 | Red morwong | Goniistius fuscus | CHEILODACTYLIDAE / MORWONGS AND HAWKFISHES

Red morwong (En), Roter Morwong (D)

This fish species lives in the western Pacific, and is abundant off eastern Australia and northeastern New Zealand. Growing to medium size, it reaches 65 cm (26 in) in length. This species is easily identified by its coloration and its elongated pectoral fins. Adult specimens prefer solitary cliffs, and are found to a depth of 30 m (100 ft). The fry live near coastal riffs and hide among algae. A predatory fish, the red morwong feeds mainly on bottom-dwelling invertebrates, but larger individuals occasionally attack small fish. Feeding during the day, they retreat to rock crevices or caves for the night. As this species lives near the bottom, it is caught with trawling nets, together with other bottom-dwellers. It is also regularly present in the catch of anglers. An admired food-fish, it is usually marketed fresh or frozen, and is eaten fried, roasted or grilled.

ᴤ94 | Spotted weever | Trachinus araneus | TRACHINIDAE / WEEVERFISHES

Spotted weever (En), Spinnenqueise, Petermännchen, Geflecktes Petermännchen (D), Araña (E), Vive araignée (F), Tracina ragno (I), Gevlekte pieterman (Nl) • Aranhuço, escorpião, peixe-aranha (Ang), Aranha (Ang, CV), Aranya fragata (Cat), Ranj crnac (Cr), Plettet fjæsing (Da), Tracna tat-tbajja (Malt), Peixe-aranha-pontuado (P), Ostrosz sieklik (Pl), Lisasti morski pajek (Slo), Kumtrakonyasi baligi (Tr)

The spotted weever inhabits the eastern Atlantic from Portugal to Angola, as well as the Mediterranean Sea. It reaches 45 cm (18 in) in length and 1.5–1.6 kg (3.3–3.5 lb) in weight. There is a poisonous spine on both opercula, and the first seven spines of its dorsal fin are connected with venom glands, so this fish should be handled with caution. A particular characteristic is the spinous portion of its dorsal fin coloured black on one half. If the fish feels threatened, it may defend itself by using its spines. Sometimes it even attacks swimmers and divers. Harpooning it is a dangerous business, since the wounded weever is extremely aggressive. The sting remains poisonous even after death, and fishermen thus remove the spines before marketing. The spotted weever lives at a depth of 10–150 m (30–500 ft) on a sandy bottom near rocky areas and among vegetation. A bottom-dweller, by day it buries itself in the sand with only its eyes and the spiny portion of its dorsal fin protruding, clearly visible from far away. A predatory species, it feeds on smaller invertebrates and small fish, which it attacks from its den, but at night it is an active hunter. It spawns in the hot summer months. Commercially harvested on a small scale, it is also rarely caught by anglers. It is marketed fresh or frozen, and is eaten stewed, grilled or fried.

Atlantic stargazer (En), Gemeiner Sternseher, Gemeiner Himmelsgucker (D), Rata, miracielo (E), Rascasse blanche, uranoscope (F), Pesce prete, lucerna mediterranea (I), Sterrenkijker (Nl) • Atlantic stargazer (En), Cabeçudo (P)

Atlantic stargazers are mainly abundant in the eastern region of the Atlantic from Portugal to Morocco, in the Mediterranean Sea and the Black Sea. They may attain body lengths of 40 cm (16 in) and weights of 500 g (18 oz). Above the pectoral fin there is a spine directed backwards, supplied with a venomous gland. According to Maltese fishermen, the spine is not poisonous at all. Nevertheless, some caution is necessary. Behind the eyes, in oval shaped sacs, there are electric organs with which the fish can generate electric and acoustic signals for detecting its prey and scare possible attackers. This organ is a transitional form in the evolution of electric organs in fish. They mostly keep to sand and mud bottoms, to depths of 100 m (300 ft). They wait for their prey buried in the sand of the sea bottom, with only the eyes and the obtruding worm-like outgrowth of its mouth showing, which latter acts as a lure for prey. Predatory in habit, the Atlantic stargazer feeds on small fish and crabs. They spawn in the spring and summer, their roe hatch while floating in the water. Although commercial fishing is of minor importance, Atlantic stargazers are occasionally marketed as food, usually being sold fresh. An interesting trait of the species is the fact that it may live for long after landing, even in the fridge. They are usually pan-fried, baked in the oven or roasted.

296 | **Patagonian toothfish** | Dissostichus eleginoides | NOTOTHENIIDAE / NOTOTHENIID FISHES

Patagonian toothfish (En), Schwarzer Seehecht (D), Austromerluza negra (E), Légine australe (F), Austromerluzzo (I), Zwarte Patagonische ijsheek (Nl) • Merluza negra (Arg), Bacalao de profundidad (Chi), Sort patagonisk isfisk (Da), Marlonga-negra (P), Tandnoting (S), Chilean seabass (US)

This species of percid prefers cold water and is native to the Atlantic and the southern Pacific, south of 28 degrees latitude to Antarctic seas. It is found close to the southern coasts of Argentina and Chile, as well as in the vicinity of the Falklands and islands near Antarctica. It grows to 215 cm (85 in) in length and 50–60 kg (110–132 lb) in body mass. This species, like its relatives, lacks a swim bladder. As compensation, its body contains huge amounts of fat, and the mineral salt content of its bones is extremely low, so its density matches that of the water, and the toothfish can float. It lives in the open sea between depths of 70 and 1500 m (230–5000 ft), but is sometimes caught even deeper. It reaches maturity at 10–12 years of age and approximately 70 cm (28 in) in length. A predator, it feeds mainly on squids and crustaceans. It has been intensely harvested commercially from the 1980s, and is most often caught with long-lines set in deep sea. These consist of numerous hooks attached to a fishing line, set by the fishermen at a given depth. The Patagonian toothfish is nowadays threatened by overfishing. Its flesh is of good quality, and retains its snow white colour even after cooking. It is distributed mainly frozen. The flesh is best eaten grilled or fried, but is also excellent when smoked, since it has a high oil content.

295

296

297 | Black cod | Notothenia microlepidota | NOTOTHENIIDAE / NOTOTHENIID FISHES

Black cod (En), Trama (E), Bocasse (F) • Smallscaled cod (NZ), Smallscaled ice cod (US)

A member of the cod family, black cod are distributed in the southwestern part of the Pacific Ocean, along the southern coast of New Zealand and Macquire Islands. The largest specimens attain body lengths of 70 cm (28 in) and weights of 2–3 kg (4.4–6.6 lb). Black cod live in deeper open seas near the sea bottom, in relatively large groups. An omnivorous species, they feed on marine nekton. The meat of the fish is of very good quality, thus it is a sought-after species in its natural habitat. Nevertheless, exploitation of the stock is insignificant. Black cod meat is marketed fresh or frozen, and it is usually eaten fried in various ways.

298 | Bluefish | Pomatomus saltatrix | NOTOTHENIIDAE / NOTOTHENIID FISHES

Bluefish (En), Blaufisch, Blaubarsch (D), Chova, cova, anjora (E), Tassergal, coupe fil (F), Pesce serra (I), Blauwe vis, elwe, blauwbars (Nl) • Elwe, shad (Afr), Chova (Ang), Enchova (Ang, Bra), Tekwa, tekwaya (Ara), Pez azul (Arg), Anchoa (Arg, Uru, Ven), Choppers, jumbos, razorbacks, skipjack, tailor (Au), Elf (Au, Nam, SA), Anjova (Cub), Blabars (Da), Gofári (Gr), Ach'ked (Has), Vígablámi (Isr), Amikiri, okisuzuki (J), Anjova (Mau-E), Coupe-fil (Mau-F), Anchova de banco (Moz-E), Anchova, dzolhwa, tonina, xidanakata, xidzukudzuana, atum (Moz-P), Anchova de banco (Nic), Anchova, xidama (P), Lufar (Ru, Ukr-R), Plitica, strijelka skakusa (SC), Tassergal jeune (Sey), Skakavka (Slo), Kouta (Su), Lüfer (Tr), Ancho (Tri), N'got (Wol-M), Ngal-ngal, rakk (Wol-S)

The bluefish is a widespread species of tropical and subtropical seas, but is absent from the central and eastern part of the Pacific. Its occurrence in the waters off northern Australia and Indonesia remains to be substantiated. Its maximum length reaches 120 cm (47 in), with a weight of 14–15 kg (31–33 lb). An aggressive pelagic predator, the bluefish attacks schooling fish and cephalopods in large groups. It also attacks fish of its own size, and continues to kill even when sated. Its hunt is often revealed by blood and ripped fish bodies (on the surface). It is intensely fished, and is also produced on fish farms. It is also admired by anglers for its strength and agility. It should be handled cautiously, though, for according to reports it can deliver nasty bites. Its flesh is of excellent quality and is generally sold fresh, but also dried, salted or frozen. Like percid fish in general, this species is prepared fried, grilled or roasted for human consumption.

297

298

299

300

299 | Wolffish, Atlantic catfish | Anarhichas lupus | ANARHICHADIDAE / WOLFFISHES

Wolffish, Atlantic catfish (En), Gestreifter Seewolf, Gestreifter Katfisch (D), Perro del norte (E), Loup atlantique (F), Lupo di mare, bavosa lupa, gattomare (I), Zeewolf (Nl) • Stribet havkat (Da), Rockfish, atlantic catfish (En), Peixe-lobo riscado, gata (P),

The most widely known species of the Anarchidadae family, wolffish (known in Europe as catfish) acquired the name because of their frighteningly formidable teeth, a rare quality among fish in general. This heterodox dentition consists of large canines, heavy molars and teeth-like nubs that protrude from most bones lining the oral cavity. With this formidable armour wolffish are able to smash with enormous force nearly anything they come across, be it their regular diet of demersal animals and other prey, or the limbs of a negligent fisherman. In their natural environment, wolffish are not really a great menace to humans, since they mainly feed on demersal crabs, shellfish, snails, sea-urchins and other echinoderms. They may reach body lengths of 60–120 cm (24–48 in) and are highly valued for their tasty meat. Wolffish produce a relatively low number of offspring, only a couple of thousand fry per female. Nevertheless, due to their reclusive way of life, wolffish stock are stable in numbers. An increasing problem of the modern age is the fact that besides being landed in large numbers by trawling, more and more wolffish are caught by diving fishermen. The distasteful craze for acquiring the "ugly" head of a wolffish as a trophy, and its strong skin being used for making souvenirs, also contribute to the widespread exploitation of the fish.

300 | Spotted wolffish, Spotted sea cat | Anarhichas minor | ANARHICHANTIDAE / WOLFFISHES

Spotted wolffish, Spotted sea cat (En), Gefleckter Seewolf (D), Perro pintado (E), Petit loup de mer (F), Bavosa lupa (I), Gevlekte zeewolf (Nl) • Spotted sea cat, spotted catfish (En), Hlýri (Is), Kaerrak (Inu), Flekksteinbit (N), Peixe-lobo-malhado (P), Zebacz pstry (Pl), Fläckig havskatt (S), Kirjomerikissa (SF)

Despite their Latin name, spotted sea cat are not at all minor creatures, being probably the largest of wolffish. Local names also reflect this. The pioneers of ichthyology must have worked with the smaller specimens caught in the Baltic seas. In reality, sea cat may reach body lengths of 1.5 m (59 in) and they indeed inspire fright. The cleaned body and pre-prepared fillets of the spotted sea cat sold by the fishmonger are nevertheless highly appreciated and the impressive head of the fish is often prepared and sold to tourists as a souvenir. Spotted sea cat are distributed throughout the entire area of the Atlantic Ocean, and they retreat to the continental shelves to spawn. They spawn at depths of 100–200 m (330–660 ft), depositing their relatively large eggs or roe of 5–6 mm (0.2 in) in waters of very low temperature. Only after a long period of hatching and incubation, during which they consume all the nutrients in the attached yolk-sac, do the fry swim to the surface zone of the ocean. For a brief period they feed on plankton and smaller fish, afterwards resuming the benthic lifestyle that is to last for the rest of their lives. Since unlike other fish, spotted wolffish do not have a swim bladder, this brief trip to pelagic existence is even nowadays somewhat perplexing to experts.

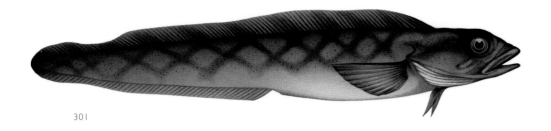

301

302

301 | Eelpout, Viviparous blenny | Zoarces viviparus | ZOARCIDAE / ZOARCOID FISHES

Eelpout, Viviparous blenny (En), Aalmutter (D), Babosa vivípara (E), Loquette, lycode vivipare (F), Blennio viviparo (I), Puitaal (Nl) • Almindelig ålekvabbe (Da), European oceanpout, guffer eel, eelpout (En), Ålekvabbe (N), Beldjuga (R), Tånglake (S), Kivinilkka (SF)

Viviparous fishes (giving birth to live young), Zoarcidae are in most languages named after eels, although biologically speaking they have not much to do with eels. In terms of shape, though, there are considerable similarities, since eelpout have elongated bodies and the dorsal and anal fins are connected around the end of the tail; but with these characteristics the similarity is totally exhausted. Native to the northeastern parts of the Atlantic, eelpout mostly dwell in the coastal regions. Sometimes they occur in river estuaries, but usually do not like to stay away for long from their regular habitats. Eelpout attain body lengths of about 20–50 cm (8–20 in) and they are viviparous, annually giving birth to 100–200 offspring 4–5 cm (1.5–2 in) long. Naturally, this is not true "birth" because fish have no uterus, but science cannot provide us with a better expression. The new-born fry soon hide among rocks and seaweed at the bottom of the sea and they spend the rest of their lives at this depth. They wouldn't be able to rise very far in water anyway, since they do not have a swim bladder. The meat of eelpout is not considered very palatable, though it is used smoked in northern Europe. An interesting trait, due to vivianite, a harmless dye-stuff in the bones of the eelpout, the bones and the surrounding areas turn green while being cooked.

302 | Pacific sand lance | Ammodytes hexapterus | AMMODYTIDAE / SAND LANCES

Pacific sand lance (En), Pazifischer Sandaal (D), Lanzón del Pacífico (E), Lançon du Pacifique (F), Cicerello del Pacifico (I), Pacifische zandspiering (Nl) • Kita-ikanago (J)

Pacific sand lance are abundant in the Arctic seas and the Pacific, in an area extending from Alaska and the Sea of Japan as far south as the coasts of southern California. They are also found in the northwestern region of the Atlantic. A fish of small build, sand lance attain a maximum size of 25–30 cm (10–12 in). They form large schools in the surface waters both near the coast and further in the open sea. Despite the fact that in the open sea they tend to swim in a regular manner, in the shallow coastal waters they quite naughtily bury themselves in the sand bottom. They feed on zooplankton, and they constitute a significant element in the diet of other fish and marine animals, thus playing an important role in the ecological food chain. They spawn in October, when they travel to coastal waters in enormous schools and deposit their roe in the sand bottom. In the spawning season they are harvested in large numbers by marine and non-marine predators alike. The meat of the sand lance is marketed frozen, salted and dried, but large quantities are also used for producing fishmeal. For food, the fish is pan-fried, roasted, baked in an oven or microwaved.

303 | Great sand-eel | Hyperoplus lanceolatus | AMMODYTIDAE / SAND LANCES

Great sand-eel (En), Großer Sandaal, Tobis (D), Pión, sula, lansoya (E), Grand lançon (F), Cicerello, ammodite lanceolato (I), Zandspiering, smelt (Nl) • Tobiskonge (Da), Ammodytis (Gr), Sandsíli (Is), Ikanago (J), Stortobis (N), Galeota-maior (P), Tobis (S), Isotuulenkala (SF), Kum (Tr)

Averaging in length about 20–25 cm (8–10 in), great sand-eel do not belong among true eels. Most abundant along the northern shores of the Atlantic, great sand-eel belong to the family of sand-lances or Ammodytidae. The dorsal and pelvic fins are joined, and the caudal fins form a symmetrical fork-like tail, this latter trait making it possible to distinguish the young from the rest of the fishes swarming at the sea bottom. Another peculiarity of the fish is its protruding lower jaw, and the upper jaw which can be opened as widely as 70–80 degrees from the lower one. With its mouth wide open, the great sand-eel swims into a cloud of macro-zooplankton and picks the larger animals. Over sand bottoms the hard lower jaw is also used as a kind of spade, with which the fish scares the crustaceans hiding in the sand. The usual fishing gear used to catch great sand-eel is the bottom trawl, the meat of the fish being eaten pan-fried especially in the summer when tourists are also abundant. The commercial value of the fish is somewhat higher with fish farms, where they mainly serve as food for larger marine species.

304 | Streaked spinefoot | Siganus javus | SIGANIDAE / RABBITFISHES

Streaked spinefoot (En), Silberstreifen-Kaninchenfisch (D), Sigano ondulado (E), Sigan ondul (F), Sigano (I) • Java rabbitfish (Au, Mic), Safi senefi (Em), Belais, belait, belaris, bliais, debam, debam leban, dengkis, gelibas, ketang lada, lambai, lumban (Ind), Batid (Kuy), Beronang, limaran (Mal), Spinefoot (Mal-En), Safi, seeseege (Om), Streaky spinefoot (Pap), Safi (Q), Nava (Sin), Ottah (Tam), Bluespotted spinefoot (US), Bulawis, tagbago (Vis)

Streaked spinefoot dwell in the Indian Ocean and in the Pacific, from the Persian Gulf to India and south China in the east, the Philippines, Malaysia, Australia, New Guinea and New Caledonia in the south, but also even further afield. They favour tropical waters of at least 25–28°C (77–82°F). The largest attain sizes of about 50–55 cm (20–22 in) and 2–2.5 kg (4.4–5.5 lb). An interesting trait is strong scales on the sides of the head. They school around in small groups of not more than ten individuals. They dwell in shallow coastal waters, in brackish waters of lagoons, and over rock and coral reefs, not exceeding depths of 15–20 m (50–66 ft). A herbivorous species, the streaked spinefoot feeds on algae clinging to the sea bottom and algal detritus floating in midwater. When not feeding, they succumb to the pleasures of idle resting while floating below the surface. They spawn in the open sea, their larvae hatching while floating. Meat is marketed fresh, being pan-fried, roasted or baked in the oven. After landing they have to be handled with care since their thorn-like spines have venomous glands. They are also popular in aquarium shows.

303

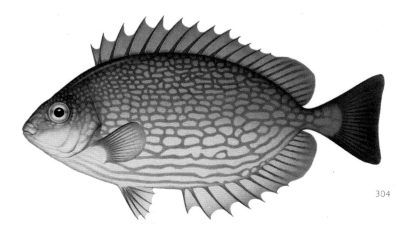

304

305 | Mottled spinefoot | Siganus fuscescens | SIGANIDAE / RABBITFISHES

Mottled spinefoot (En), Kaninchenfisch (D), Sigans (F) • Pin-spotted spinefoot (Au), Rabbit fish (En), Aigo, ae (J), Dog- ga-si-chi (Kor), Danggit (Kuy), Dengkis, debam (Mal), Dusky rabbitfish (Mic), Balawis (Tag), Danggit (Vis)

Mottled spinefoot dwell in the western region of the Pacific Ocean, from South Korea, the southern coast of Japan, south China, Malaysia as far south as Australia, in the tropical waters. They may attain body lengths of 40 cm (16 in) and weights of 1–1.1 kg (2–2.4 lb). The long and thin spines of the fins are poisonous, thus they must be handled with the utmost care. They are able to suddenly change their colour, mature specimens becoming spotted (hence the name "mottled") when scared. They favour shallow waters over territories overgrown with filiform algae and other marine vegetation, usually near coastal reefs and in lagoons; they never go beyond depths of 50 m (166 ft). They are frequently found in the vicinity of larger river estuaries. A herbivorous species, the younger mottled spinefoot specimens feed on algae, the older ones on larger foliaceous algae and seagrass. In the spawning season they form large groups of 30–60 individuals and school around in the shallow waters by the reefs and in the lagoons. The number of roe is as many as 300,000 eggs per female, and the older specimens may spawn more than once a year. This is a popular fish for food and the Japanese have even started breeding and rearing the species. It is usually pan-fried or roasted over an open fire.

306 | Cutlass fish | Trichiurus lepturus | TRICHIURIDAE / FROSTFISHES AND CUTLASS FISHES

Cutlass fish (En), Degenfisch, Haarschwanz (D), Pez sable (E), Poisson-sabre commun (F), Pesce coltello (I), Degenvis, haarstaart (Nl) • Large-head hairtail (En), Bacora (Cat), Hårhale (Da), Baga (Guj), Sablaja ryba (R)

This cutlass fish is abundant in all the seas of the tropical and temperate zones. In different parts of the world they used to be described by different names, but it turned out that they belonged to the same species. The body of the largehead hairtail, as it is also known, is very thin and extremely elongated, the weight of specimens as long as 220–230 cm (87– 90 in) not exceeding 1.5 kg (3.3 lb). The specimens landed fresh are of steel-blue-silvery hue, and after a while they turn into silvery grey. They primarily dwell in shallow coastal waters, no deeper than 370 m (1200 ft), and they may also occur in the brackish waters of river estuaries. Young specimens feed on tiny planktonic crabs and smaller fish, whereas the mature fish mainly feed on fish, occasionally on squid and crabs. The young and the mature specimens have a different orientation in their feeding habits – the mature fish feed near the surface in daytime and tend to the bottom for the night, while the young do the opposite. Since the species is abundant in all parts of the world, the spawning season varies accordingly. Their roe hatch while floating in midwater. Due to the exceptionally good quality of the meat they yield, cutlass fish are landed in huge quantities by both recreational and commercial fishermen. Marketed for food salted and dried or frozen, the fish is most delicious deep-fried in oil or roasted over an open fire, although the meat is very bony. In Japan, used raw, in soya sauce and hot horseradish sauce, it is used for preparing sashimi.

305

306

307 | Wahoo | Acanthocybium solandri | SCOMBRIDAE / SCOMBRIDS

Wahoo (En), Wahoo (D), Peto, sierra canalera (E), Thazard-bâtard (F), Acantocibio, maccarello striato (I), Wahoo (Nl) • Tangigi (Bik), Tenggiri selasih (Ind), Kamasu-sawara (J), B'a'ra (Kir), Ggo-chi-sam-chi (Kor), Kanaad znjebari (Om), Cavala-da-India (P), Guachu (Phi), Paala (Sam), Hera maha (Sin), Yuumbi (Som), Nguru-ngazija (Swa), Palamida-stiuca (Ru), Pla insee lawt (Thai), Cá Thu ngàng (Vie)

In most languages this fish, which attains a size of 80–150 cm (32–59 in) and weight of 100 kg (220 lb), got its name on account of its long snout. Distinguishing itself by being extremely aggressive, wahoo travel in small schools of a couple of dozen specimens, mainly in the vast areas of the Indian and Pacific oceans. Fishermen have reported cases when a wahoo could swallow prey as big as half of its own body, due to its enormous oral cavity. Once hungry, wahoo do not hesitate to eat their own relatives. At great swordfish contests of Asia and Australia, wahoos are regular participants, and they very skilfully approach and devour the bait placed for the 'target group', thus, of course, finding their ultimate end. A very strongly built fish, the wahoo, like most related species, has an elaborate corselet of enlarged scales and bony rings around its eyes. Hauled into the boat either by a scoop-net or by hook, it has to be handled carefully. The meat of the wahoo is exceptionally good, and being firm-textured it is easy to slice. The wahoo is a favourite fish in both Japanese and Korean cuisine. It is eaten raw, frozen, seasoned or unseasoned, usually sliced into paper-thin fillets.

308 | Bullet tuna | Auxis rochei | SCOMBRIDAE / SCOMBRIDS

Bullet tuna (En), Melvera-Fregattmakrele (D), Melva, judío (E), Auxide, bonitou (F), Tombarello, biso (I), Kogeltonijn (Nl) • Skumri i madh (Alb), Fregatmakrel (Da), Frigate mackerel, plain bonito (En), Koponi-Kopanaki (Gr), Chiboh (J), Bizu (Malt), Auxid (N, S), Judeu (P), Auksidi-laj (SF), Eli-choorai (Sin, Tam), Trupec (Slo), Bonito (Tag), Gobene baligi (Tr)

Widely distributed in most warm seas of the world, bullet tuna average about 50–90 cm (20–35 in) in length. In most languages its name contains the adjective "corse-letted", for it has a corselet of enlarged scales in the area in front of the pectoral fins. Otherwise there are hardly any scales on the rest of the body. A characteristic trait is that it has a tapered scaly area along the high lateral line, and it is only in the rear half of the body that typically mackerel-like stripes can be found. It is a truly global fish, although bullet tuna seem to be more sensitive than their related species for they are apparently becoming increasingly restricted to the oceans. In the Mediterranean Sea bullet tuna have become a rare catch, although their pink meat is highly prized. In the Northern Hemisphere the spawning season of the bullet tuna falls at the end of the summer. This is why it is chiefly at this time of the year that they are landed in great quantities, mostly by trawlers. Perhaps this is the only period of the year when one sees meat of the bullet tuna in the European markets. Besides humans, the killer whale is the greatest enemy of the bullet tuna, since often entire schools of bullet tuna, otherwise also a predatory fish, fall prey to plundering groups of killer whales.

309 | **Frigate tuna** | Auxis thazard | SCOMBRIDAE / SCOMBRIDS

Frigate tuna (En), Unechter Bonito (D), Melva tazard (E), Thazard, auxide (F), Motulu, biso, tombarello (I), Fregatmakreel (Nl) • Frigate mackerel (En), Gedar (Guj), Hirasoda (J), Tibban (Om), Judeu (P), Pirit (Phi), Ton negru (Ru), Sehewa (Swa), Gobene (Tr), Mangko (Vis)

Frigate tuna dwell in the Atlantic Ocean, the Indian Ocean and the Pacific Ocean. The stock living in the eastern region of the Pacific has been described as a sub-species bearing the name of A. thazard brachydorax. A tuna-like fish of smaller build, they may attain body lengths of 65 cm (25 in) and weights of 5.8 kg (12.7 lb). They prey on smaller fish in the open sea. Because of the large population of the stock, frigate tuna are held to be an important element in the marine food chain. They feed on smaller fish and planktonic crabs, and they in turn are preyed upon by larger fishes, such as larger tuna species. A quick swimmer, frigate tuna have no swimbladders. Another special trait of the fish is that, like the related tuna species, they can keep the temperature of their muscles somewhat higher than that of the surrounding water by a circulatory system operating on the principle of the countercurrent heat exchanger. Covering a large territory, they spawn at different times of the year. The stock is widely exploited by commercial and recreational fishermen, because the meat of the fish is of exceptionally good quality. Marketed for food fresh, frozen and canned, the meat of frigate tuna is usually pan-fried, baked in the oven or roasted over an open fire.

310 | **Black skipjack** | Euthynnus lineatus | SCOMBRIDAE / SCOMBRIDS

Black skipjack (En), Schwarze Thonine, Schwarzer Skipjack (D), Barrilete negro (E), Thonine noire (F), Tonnetto (I), Zwarte skipjack (Nl) • Bonito, patiseca (Col), Sort thunnin (Da), Pataseca (Ecu), Negra (Ecu, Mex), Bonito negro (Ecu, Per), Merma-negra (P), Macarela (Per)

A tuna-like species, black skipjack dwell in the eastern region of the Pacific Ocean from San Simeon and California as far south as the Galapagos Islands and the northern waters of Peru. Two stray specimens have been caught near Hawaii, showing that they are able to travel long distances. They may grow as large as 85–90 cm (33–35 in), reaching 9–10 kg (20–22 lb). Very keen on a warm climate, black skipjack do not like temperatures below 22–23°C (71–73°F). Their larvae are generally in waters of at least 26°C (79°F). They hunt near the surface in coastal waters, and also in the open sea. They form large schools together with Thunnus albacares and Katsuwonus pelamis. Predatory in habit, black skipjack share their dietary pattern with other tuna species, and they also compete with other marine predators for their prey. Near Mexico they spawn from June to August. As with other related tuna species, black skipjack are also able to keep their muscles at higher temperatures than those of the surrounding water with the help of their special circulatory system. This trait enables the fish to catch its prey at a very high speed. Commercially not particularly important, black skipjack are mostly popular with recreational fishermen.

311 | Skipjack tuna | Katsuwonus pelamis | SCOMBRIDAE / SCOMBRIDS

Skipjack tuna (En), Echter Bonito (D), Listado, bonito de altura (E), Bonite à ventre rayé (F), Tonnetto striato (I), Tonijn, skipjack (Nl) • Anga-rap (Car), Bugstribet bonit (Da), Bonito (En), Palamída, lakérda (Gr), Buslugan (Ilo), Randatúnfiskur (Is), Balamida (Isr), Katsuo (J), Cakalang (Mal), Bukstripet pelamide (N), Atum-bonito, gaiado (P), Polosaty tunets (R), Bonit (S), Èrtasti tun (Slo), Atu (Tah), Çizgiliton baligi (Tr), Bankulis (Vis)

Skipjack tuna are found world-wide in warmer seas. Especially fond of exploring the upper regions of the water, the skipjack tuna is perhaps the most often seen species of tuna. It produces hundreds of thousands of offspring, and there is always some stock of skipjack that is currently spawning somewhere. It largely keeps to waters of temperatures higher than 20°C (68°F), thus it does not wander into deeper waters, not even to spawn. It has a rapid growth rate, attaining sexual maturity in about 3 years, when it is 30–40 cm (12–16 in) long. At its largest, the skipjack tuna is about 60–80 cm (24–32 in). An eye-catching trait in the mature fish is that its typically mackerel-like striping follows the line of the belly in 4–5 rows. Another characteristic of the genus is that the dorsal fins form an almost continuous row up to the homocercal tail fin (i.e. a tail fin having two symmetrical lobes extending from the end of the vertebral column). All in all, skipjack tuna are beautiful and interesting marine-blue fish that justifiably acquired the name of "Latin beauty", as fishermen in many parts of the world tend to call the species. Its meat is very palatable, and fishermen make really great efforts to supply the food market with this wonderfully tender meat.

312 | Butterfly kingfish | Gaterochisma melampus | SCOMBRIDAE / SCOMBRIDS

Butterfly kingfish (En), Großschuppenmakrele (D), Atún chauchera (E), Thon-papillon (F), Palamita squamosa (I), Vlindertonijn (Nl) • Grootskub-makriel (Afr), Big-scaled mackerel, scaly tuna (Au), Butterfly tuna (Au, NZ), Butterfly mackerel (Au, US), Pez chauchera (Chi), Sommerfugletun (Da), Urokomaguro (J), Scaled tunny (NZ), Serra-borboleta (P), Bigscale mackerel (SA, US), Mackerel (US)

Members of this large-bodied tuna species dwell in all the seas of the temperate zone of the Southern Hemisphere. They may grow as large as 165 cm (65 in) in length and 40–50 kg (88–110 lb) in weight. They dwell in the deeper strata of the ocean, but do not go below depths of 200 m (660 ft). In younger specimens the large pectoral fin is longer than the head. Butterfly kingfish have a swim bladder, the two front lobes of which protrude into the rear of the skull. With the help of its circulatory system, the fish is not only able to keep its muscles warmer than the surrounding water, but the retinal nervous tissue of the eyes and the brain are also "heated". This enables the fish to react quickly and to be more efficient in hunting by having good eyesight. A swift-moving aggressive predator fish, butterfly kingfish mainly feed on other fish, but in some specimens caught near Hawaii the content of the stomach has revealed squid and remains of feathers. A commercially not very important fish, in Japanese waters butterfly kingfish are usually landed as a by-catch when fishing for Thunnus maccoyii. Open-sea fishermen are keen on landing the larger specimens. The meat of the fish is generally marketed for food frozen, smoked and canned, and is prepared pan-fried, in the oven or roasted.

313 | **Double-lined mackerel** | Grammatorcynus bilineatus | SCOMBRIDAE / SCOMBRIDS

Double-lined mackerel (En), Zweilinienmakrele (D), Carite-cazón pintado (E), Thazard-kusara (F), Ammoniosgombro (I), Dubbellijnmakreel (Nl) • Scad mackerel (Au), Tangirion (Bik), Salala-ni-toga (Fij), Nijôsaba (J), Aya (Mal), Serra-cação pintada (P), Mokorkor (Pa), Dvukhlinejnaya makrel (R), Atualo (Tok), Mackerel (US), Gaboiu (W)

The double-lined mackerel is a species abundant in the Indian Ocean and the western region of the Pacific. It inhabits the area stretching from the Red Sea as far east as the Andaman Sea, and as far south as the northern coasts of Australia, the Marshall and Fiji Islands, in the tropical and sub-tropical waters. In reference books it is often mistaken for another, related species, G. bicarinatus. Double-lined mackerel may attain a maximum size of 100–110 cm (39–43 in) and 30–35 kg (66–77 lb). They usually form large schools in the shallow areas around reefs, and they do not go below depths of 15 m (56 ft). A swift-moving predator fish, double-lined mackerel feed on crabs and fishes of various genera, but mostly they prefer those belonging to Sardinella and Thrissocles species. Commercial fishing of the stock is of relatively minor importance, the species being more popular with recreational fishermen. The meat of the double-lined mackerel is tender and tasty, although there is an ammonia-like scent to the meat, which can be eliminated by applying lemon juice before cooking. The high oil content of the meat makes it exceptionally suitable for smoking and grilling. Marketed for food fresh and frozen, double-lined mackerel is mostly eaten smoked, pan-fried, baked in the oven, or roasted.

314 | **Short mackerel** | Rastrelliger brachysoma | SCOMBRIDAE / SCOMBRIDS

Short mackerel (En), Indische Makrele (D), Caballa rechoncha (E), Maquereau trapu (F), Sgombro indiano (I), Indische makreel (Nl) • Soeklig-makriel (Afr), Hasa-Hasa (Ban, Tag), Kabalyas (Bik, Tag), Aguma-a (Bik, Vis), Salala (Fij), Bangadi (Hin), A gurukuma (J), Asa-asa (Kap), Luman (Kuy), Au-au (Mak), Kembong, kembung perempuan, rumahan, temenong (Mal), Indian mackerel (Mal-En), Cavala-curta, cava-la-do-Indico (P), Short-bodied mackerel (Pap), Tropjcheskaya skumbriya (R), Spotlight mackerel (SA), Ga (Sam), Pla lung, pla lung tao san (Thai), Pla thu (Thai, Vie), Cá bao ma (Vie), Bonglay, guma-a, hasa (Vis)

Short mackerel dwell in the warm tropical waters of the Indian Ocean and the Pacific Ocean, from the Andaman Sea as far east as Thailand, Indonesia, Papua New Guinea, the Philippines and Fiji. A fish of small build, short mackerel attain a maximum body length of about 35 cm (14 in) and weight of 500 g (18 oz). They mostly prefer waters around river estuaries, where saline levels are low, and where water temperatures near the surface are 20–30°C (68–86°F). They form schools of various sizes, and they segregate by size. An omnivorous species, short mackerel mainly feed on smaller-sized zooplankton, but in the food thus sieved there is a great amount of planktonic ingredients. Fished in large quantities by commercial fleets, the species is also very popular with recreational fishermen. The fishing gear mostly used is the purse seine. Fishing boats look for short mackerel on moonless nights, when the fluorescent body of the fish betrays the location of their schools. The fresh and frozen fish are normally pan-fried, baked in the oven or roasted over an open fire.

315 | **Island mackerel** | Rastrelliger faughni | SCOMBRIDAE / SCOMBRIDS

Island mackerel (En), Insel-Zwergmakrele (D), Caballa isleña (E), Maquereau des îles (F), Sgombro indiano (I), Eilandmakreel (Nl) • Cavala-das-ilhas (P), Avstralijskaya tropjcheskaya skumbraya (R), Bulao-bulao (Vis), Kembong, kembung, mabong, pelaling, rumahan, temenong (Mal), Alumahang Bato (Tag)

Island mackerel dwell in the mid-western region of the Pacific Ocean, from Taiwan to the Philippines, Fiji, Indonesia, Thailand, Malaysia and India, in the warm seas, where water temperatures do not go below 17°C (62.6°F). They may attain a maximum body length of 20–25 cm (8–10 in) and a weight of 250 g (9 oz). They live near the surface, in shallow waters, occasionally going deeper, but never below 100–150 m (330–500 ft). They travel around in large schools, usually segregated according to size. They sieve the largest zooplankton from the water, in this being different from the related species. As with the other mackerel, island mackerel are mainly fished for because of their excellent meat. Before cooking, the ammonia-like scent of the meat can be eliminated by rubbing it through with lemon juice. If inadequately stored, histamine may develop in the meat of the fish, which could lead to "mackerel poisoning". For this reason it is essential to purchase island mackerel only from reliable retailers, where the freezers and storage facilities are of good quality. The meat of the island mackerel is usually marketed frozen, and is eaten smoked or roasted, sautéed or fried.

316 | **Eastern Pacific bonito** | Sarda chiliensis | SCOMBRIDAE / SCOMBRIDS

Eastern Pacific bonito (En), Chilenische Pelamide (D), Bonito del Pacífico oriental (E), Bonite du Pacifique oriental (F), Tonetto cileno (I), Pacifische bonito (Nl) • Bonito (Chi, Col, Mex, Per), Chilensk bonit (Da, S), Bonito-do-pacifico (P), Aguadito, cerrajón, chaucha, chauchilla, monillo, monito, mono (Per), Pelamida pacyficzna (Pl), Chilijskaya pelamida, vostochnaya pelamida (R), Chilensarda (SF), Pasifik uskumrusu (Tr), Pacific bonito (US)

Eastern Pacific bonito dwell in the southeastern region of the Pacific Ocean, from northern Peru to Talcahuano harbour in Chile. Of medium size, Eastern Pacific bonito may attain body lengths of 100–110 cm (39–44 in) and weights of 11 kg (24 lb). They live along the coast, in large schools, segregating by size. Older specimens go further away from the coast. An interesting trait of the species is that they do not have a swim bladder. A swift-moving predator fish, they feed on smaller schooling fish, squid and crustaceans. Due to their special circulatory system, they are able to keep the temperature of their muscles as much as 10°C (21.2 °F) higher than the surrounding water. This difference in temperature doubles muscle performance, by which the fish becomes swifter. They spawn from September to December at various intervals, in the open sea. A female fish averaging 3 kg (6.6 lb) in size is able to deposit several million eggs, or roe, in one spawning season. Eastern Pacific bonito constitute an important catch for recreational fishermen and spear fishing organised from fishing boats and the coast. Commercial fishermen use surrounding nets. Eastern Pacific bonito are marketed for food fresh, frozen and canned, usually being pan-fried, roasted or grilled in the oven.

317 | **Striped bonito** | *Sarda orientalis* | SCOMBRIDAE / SCOMBRIDS

Striped bonito (En), Westpazifische Pelamide, Bonito (D), Bonito mono (E), Bonite de l'Océan Indien, bonite orientale (F), Palamita orientale, tonnetto (I), Gestreepte bonito (Nl) • Bonito sierra (Ecu), Oriental bonito (Ind-En, Pap), Hagatsuo (J), Vari choora (Ma), Aya, tenggiri, tongkol (Mal), Sarda oriental (Moz-P), Stripet pelamide (N), Marmara, sagtana (Om), Bonito-do-Indo-Pacífico (P), Mono (Per), Pelamida wschodnia (Pl), Prodolnopolosaya bonita, vostochnaya pelamida (R), Juovasarda (SF), Thora-baleya (Sin), Jaydar-dhiiglow (Som), Kanangeluthi, kumla (Tam), Mexican bonito, oriental tuna (UK), Ca ngv'o phuo'ng dong (Vie)

The striped bonito inhabits the Indian and the Pacific oceans. It is found in the eastern Atlantic off the Hawaiian Islands, as well as along the entire American coast south to Peru. In the west, it occurs from the island of Honshu (Japan) through Sumatra, Java and Bali, to Australia and the Gulf of Papua. It reaches 1 m (39 in) in length and 11 kg (24 lb). It is usually found 70–80 km from the land. The striped bonito possesses no swim-bladder, and hence swims continuously, hunting in schools in open water. It dives to a depth of 30–40 m (100–130 ft), feeding on fish (mainly herring), cephalopods and crustaceans. Its spawning is triggered by the monsoon rains. Not harvested commercially on a large scale, it is an admired sporting fish. Recreational fishermen employ blinkers for catching it, while commercially it is caught with gill nets. In Japan, it is made into a special dried product named katsuobushi. The fillets are cooked, smoked then dried in the sun and enclosed in a box for a couple of weeks. Fungus grows on the surface of the flesh, which disappears after repeated drying. The treatment is repeated 4–5 times. Thin slices are used in Japanese cuisine.

318 | **Atlantic bonito** | *Sarda sarda* | SCOMBRIDAE / SCOMBRIDS

Atlantic bonito (En), Atlantischer Bonito (D), Bonito atlántico (E), Bonite à dos rayé (F), Palamita, bonnicou (I), Atlantische boniter (Nl) • Atlantiese bonito (Afr), Palamiti (Alb), Rygstribet pelamide (Da), Pelamid, belted bonito, short-finned tunny (En), Ternatav (Gr), Rákungur (Is), Hagatsuo (J), Stripet pelamide (N), Serra, serrajão, bonito-do-Atlântico (P), Atlanticheskaya pelamida (R), Ryggstrimmig pelamid (S), Altiparmak (Tr)

Local names of the Atlantic bonito include such designations as "beautiful", "beauty" and such like. All these names, in fact, are rightly attached to this beautiful light-blue fish. The upper part of its sides is ornamented with strange, criss-cross thin bands. Along the stretch between the belly and the dorsal part there is a line of tiny finlets, which supposedly help the fish navigate the currents of the ocean, the favourite dwelling place of bonitos. There are two large populations recorded, which are increasingly distinct from each other. Bonito stock in the Atlantic primarily dwell around the British Isles, whereas the Mediterranean stock go to the Black Sea and its marginal bays to spawn. They spawn in schools, the number of their pelagic roe reaching as much as half a million per female fish. They have a relatively fast growth rate, attaining sexual maturity in about three years. They have very tiny, cycloid (disc-like) scales, which in the mature specimens accrete to form a corselet under the pectoral fins. The meat of the bonito is flavoursome, it counts as one of the best fried fish. Along the Russian, Georgian and Ukrainian coasts it is popular to eat it marinated or smoked.

319 | Blue mackerel | Scomber australasicus | SCOMBRIDAE / SCOMBRIDS

Blue mackerel (En), Indopazifische Makrele (D), Caballa pintoja (E), Maquereau tacheté (F), Sgombro maculato (I), Gevlekte makreel (Nl) • Common mackerel (Au), Pacific mackerel (Au, NZ), Spotted chub mackerel (Au, Pap, US), Slimy mackerel (Au, US), Gomasaba, marusaba (J), Aya (Mal), Tawatawa (Mao), Macarela azul (Mex), Japanese mackerel (NZ), Southern mackerel (NZ, US), Cavala-pintada (P), Spotted mackerel (US),

An inhabitant of the Pacific, the blue mackerel is found off Australia and New Zealand in the west, north of China and Japan in the north, and among the Hawaiian Islands in the east. It lives off the islands of Socorro and Revillagigedo, and Mexico in the east. It also occurs in the Indian Ocean and the Red Sea. A medium-sized species, it reaches 40–50 cm (16–20 in) in length and 1.5–2 kg (3.3–4.4 lb) in body mass. It is found along the coasts as well as in open sea, and dives to a maximum depth of 200 m (660 ft). It forms huge schools of individuals of about the same size. It often mixes with other species of mackerel and sardine. It mainly feeds on plankton, but also filters out small crustaceans from the water, while adults also take small fish and squid. Spawning occurs in the summer months, but its breeding grounds have not yet been identified. Commercial fishermen catch it with gill nets, and it is also hooked by sea anglers, who use it, in some cases, as a bait fish. It is marketed fresh, salted-and-dried, smoked, frozen or canned. Fresh and frozen blue mackerel are eaten pan-fried, roasted in an oven or grilled.

320 | Chub mackerel | Scomber japonicus | SCOMBRIDAE / SCOMBRIDS

Chub mackerel (En), Mittelmeermakrele, Japanische Makrele (D), Estornino, caballa (E), Maquereau espagnol, hareng du pacifique (F), Lanzardo, scombro cavallo, scombro macchiato (I), Spaanse makreel (Nl) • Kolo (Alb), Makriel (Afr), Common mackerel (Au), Adadangon (Bik), Pacific mackerel (En), Koliós (Gr), Saba (Haw), Kolias (Isr), Honsaba, masaba (J), Go-deung-eo (Kor), Skambary (Leb), Kembong (Mal), Molmol (Mars), Blue mackerel (NZ), Baljeh (Om), Caballa, cavala, cavalinha (P), Afrikanskaya skumbriya (R), Mayikoro (Sat), Bilica, juja, lancarda, plavica (SC), Lokarda (Slo), Alumahan, mata-an, lumahan (Tag), Scomber (UK), Cá thu Nhát-bán (Vie), Aguma-a, anduhau, bulao-bulao, haguma-a (Vis), Ouo (Wol-M), Wo (Wol-S)

Dwelling in the subtropical waters of the Indian Ocean and the Pacific, chub mackerel may attain body lengths of 70 cm (28 in) and weights of 3 kg (6.6 lb). They live in the coastal waters, but they may also occur over the continental shelf. As soon as they attain a length of 3 cm (1 in), they segregate according to size and form large groups, occasionally also joining schools of other species. They spend the day over the sea bottom, coming up to feed near the surface only at night. Their diet consists mainly of fish, crustaceans and squid. In Asian regions they are said to retreat to deeper waters for the winter and remain inactive until spring. The stock is being extensively exploited by commercial fishing fleets, and recreational fishermen are also keen on catching chub mackerel. Chub mackerel are artificially bred in Japan. They are marketed fresh, frozen, smoked, salted and occasionally canned. They are also used in Eastern medical practices.

321 | Atlantic mackerel | Scomber scombrus | SCOMBRIDAE / SCOMBRIDS

Atlantic mackerel (En), Gewöhnliche Makrele (D), Caballa del Atlántico, verdel, sarda (E), Maquereau commun (F), Sgombro, maccarello (I), Makreel (Nl) • Skumbri (Alb), Amindelig makrel (Da), Scoumbri (Gr), Makríll (Is), Marusaba (J), Breac-varrey (Manx), Makrell (N), Cavalla, sarda (P), Makrela atlantycka (Pl), Atlanticheskaya skumbriya (R), Scrumbie albastra (Ru), Makrill (S), Makrilli (SF), Skuša (Slo), Uskumru baligi (Tr)

One of the most popular fishes of the Atlantic region, Atlantic mackerel has been a staple seafood for thousands of years. They do not grow too big, perhaps specimens as old as ten years of age may reach body lengths of 50 cm (20 in). In shops we encounter those of 20–30 cm (8–12 in) length. The main fishing methods used are drift-nets and heavy bottom trawls. Atlantic mackerel can most easily be distinguished from their related species by their vertical dark blue or black stripes. They also have a homocercal tail fin with a row of finlets in front of it, characteristic of mackerels. This small fish produces a huge number of offspring, about 300,000– 400,000, thus there is no particular biological reason for the considerable depletion of their stock. An omnivorous fish when young, Atlantic mackerel do not hesitate to feed on organic detritus and offal along shores near human habitation. The real turning-point is the first spawning season, after this the mackerel becomes entirely predatory. Atlantic mackerel are used for various purposes. Younger specimens end up as canned fish. The larger ones are usually dried, marinated or fried, older specimens being used for nearly everything.

322 | King mackerel | Scomberomorus cavalla | SCOMBRIDAE / SCOMBRIDS

King mackerel (En), Königsmakrele (D), Carite lucio (E), Thazard, maquereau royal, thazard barré (F), Maccarello reale, sgombro reale (I), Spaanse koningsmakreel (Nl) • Cavala (P, Bra), Serrucho (Cub), Atlantisk kongemakrel (Da), Carite (Dom, PR), Sierra (Dom, Ven), Maquereau (FG), Oo-sawara (J), Peto (Mex), Kongemakrell (N), Kungsmakrill (S), Kuningasmakrilli (SF), Kingfish, spanish mackerel (US), Carite sierra, rey (Ven)

The king mackerel is an inhabitant of the Atlantic. It is found in the western part of the ocean, from the coasts of the state of Massachusetts (United States) to Rio de Janeiro in the south, and off the central part of the Saint Paul rocks in the east. It grows to 170–180 cm (67–71 in) body length and 45 kg (99 lb) in mass. It mainly prefers reefs far from the shores, and lives in warm tropical/subtropical waters. It feeds primarily on fish, but consumes Penaeus and other species of crayfish in smaller quantities. Gigantic schools of king mackerel have been observed migrating along the coast of the United States. It is an important species throughout its range from the viewpoints of fisheries, angling and manufacture. The majority of specimens caught are made into steak or sold fresh, but some are occasionally marketed canned, frozen, smoked or salted. Anglers are fond of it for its large size and good quality flesh, which is prepared in various ways for human consumption.

323 | **Narrow-barred Spanish mackerel** | Scomberomorus commerson | SCOMBRIDAE / SCOMBRIDS

Narrow-barred Spanish mackerel (En), Indische Königsmakrele (D), Bonita, carite estriado (E), Maquereau-bonite, thazard de Commerson (F), Maccarello spagnole, maccarello reale (I), Indische konings-makreel (Nl) • Katonkel (Afr), Malaudiyong (Bik), Kau yue (Cant), Seer, leatherskin (En) Tjalong (Ind), Yokoshima-sawara (J), Tenggri, batang (Mal), Dong-gal-sam-chi (Kor), Anjilava (Sin), Nguru (Swa), Konam (Tam), Narrow-barred mackerel (US)

This species of mackerel inhabits the Indian and the Pacific Oceans, and is found from the Red Sea and South Africa to southeast Asia, northwards to China and Japan, southwards to southeast Australia and Fiji. It has established itself in the eastern Mediterranean, entering from the Red Sea through the Suez Canal. A large-bodied mackerel, it grows to a length of 2.5 m (99 in) and a weight of 70–75 kg (154–165 lb). Found from the outer margin of the continental shelf to the coasts, it sometimes occurs in murky waters or in waters with a low level of salinity. It is known to migrate for considerable distances along the coasts, although there are populations that do not undertake such long trips. It hunts in smaller groups, feeding almost exclusively on small fish. Specimens caught off eastern Queensland have been found to contain a fat-soluble toxic substrate called ciguatoxin, and are thus not recommended for consumption. A species intensely harvested, large adults are anglers' favourites. Sold fresh, salted-and-dried, frozen, smoked or canned, it is also frequently made into fish balls.

324 | **Atlantic Spanish mackerel** | Scomberomorus maculatus | SCOMBRIDAE / SCOMBRIDS

Atlantic Spanish mackerel (En), Gefleckte Königsmakrele (D), Carite atlántico (E), Thazard atlantique (F), Maccarello reale maculato (I), Gevlekte koningsmakreel (Nl) • Spaanse makriel (Afr), Plettet kongemakrel (Da), Pintada (Mex), Sierra, carite (Mex, Ven), Serra-espanhola (P), Fläckig kungsmakrill (S), Sierra pintada (Ven)

The Atlantic Spanish mackerel is a fish inhabiting (sub)tropical waters of the western Atlantic, from Cape Cod through Miami southwards through the Gulf of Mexico to the Yucatan Peninsula (Mexico). It is often confused with Spanish sierra, which occurs in the eastern Pacific, with Spanish tritor found in the eastern Atlantic, and with Spanish brasiliensis, which inhabits coastal waters in the Pacific. The Spanish mackerel grows to 80–90 cm (32–36 in) in length and 4.5–5 kg (10–11 lb) in weight. A pelagic species, it moves in gigantic schools for large distances along the coasts. This predator hunts in open water. It feeds mainly on small fish, but also includes Penaeus crayfish and cephalopods in its diet. A species intensely fished, various methods are employed to catch it. Its huge schools are occasionally located by aerial observation. Anglers admire Spanish mackerels, which are distributed fresh, frozen, or smoked, and are fried, roasted or grilled for human consumption.

325 | **Japanese Spanish mackerel** | Scomberomorus niphonius | SCOMBRIDAE / SCOMBRIDS

Japanese Spanish mackerel (En), Japanische Königsmakrele (D), Carite oriental (E), Thazard oriental (F), Maccarello reale giaponese (I), Japanse koningsmakreel (Nl) • Japansk kongemakrel (Da), Sawara (J), Sam-ch'i (Kor), Serra-oriental (P)

Japanese Spanish mackerel wander in the immense waters of the Pacific and Indian oceans. In most languages the name of the fish refers to the fact that Japan is the country which mainly fishes for this type of mackerel with ultramodern fishing fleets. Japanese Spanish mackerel attain sizes of about 50–100 cm (20–39 in) and a weight of 20–30 kg (44–66 lb). The fishermen do not seem to have a very difficult job, since by applying satellite fish-finders they very soon detect the large schools of mackerel, and they can approach them with their ships as close as a few metres. When near enough, they release huge gill nets, sometimes several kilometres long. The nets thus used are similar to the Spanish tonnara in the fact that they end in a large cage where the fish are supposed to get trapped. Japanese Spanish mackerel thus caught end up on board the factory ship and they are processed into deep-frozen mackerel fillets. Popular throughout the Far East, several research institutes are engaged in projects aiming at rearing Japanese Spanish mackerel in controlled environments. The fish do not easily tolerate confinement in concrete pools except when they are young, so the idea is for them to breed and be reared in fish-farms enclosed by a system of nets in marine harbours.

326 | **Pacific sierra** | Scomberomorus sierra | SCOMBRIDAE / SCOMBRIDS

Pacific sierra (En), Ostpazifische Königsmakrele (D), Carite sierra (E), Thazard sierra (F), Sierra-koningsmakreel (Nl) • Sierra (Col, Ecu, Mex, Per), Stillehavskongemakrel (Da), Serrucho, sierra del Pacifico (Mex), Serra-do-Pacífico (P), Verle (Per), Peruanskaya makrel (R)

This species inhabits subtropical-tropical areas in the eastern Pacific, from southern California to the Galapagos Islands and Peru. It was recently recorded from northern Chile as well. Reaching 97 cm (38 in) length and 8.2 kg (18 lb) weight, this pelagic species moves around in large schools and is found near the coast from the surface to the bottom, although it hunts at a depth of 15–20 m (50–66 ft). A fast predator, adults feed on small schooling fish (primarily Anchoa, Cetengraulis, Odontognathus and Opisthonema species). The Pacific sierra is the most abundant fish species along the Pacific coasts of Mexico and central America. It supposedly spawns near the coast within its entire range, breeding between July and September. A delicious food-fish, hence intensely harvested commercially, it is also caught by anglers. Sold fresh, frozen or made into ceviche, it is eaten fried, grilled or roasted.

327 | Long-finned tuna | Thunnus alalunga | SCOMBRIDAE / SCOMBRIDS

Long-finned tuna (En), Weißer Thunfisch (D), Albacora, atún blanco, bonito del norte (E), Germon, thon blanc (F), Alalunga (I), Witte tonijn (Nl) • Langfinnet tun, hvid tun (Da), Long-finned albacore, long-finned tunny, warman, white tuna (En), Tünfiskur (Is), Binnaga (J), Gubad (Om), Albakor (N), Atum voador (P), Albacora (P, S), Dlinnoperyj tunets (R), Tonfisk (S), Jodari (Swa), A'ahi tari'a (Tah), Akorkinoz baligi (Tr)

The long-finned tuna is both the most widespread and the smallest-bodied species of tuna. It may attain body lengths of 1 m (40 in) and weights of about 20–30 kg (44–66 lb). Being typically high-bodied they can be easily distinguished from other species even at a young age. Another important trait of the species is that their huge pectoral fins, which extend to the line of the finlets behind the dorsal and anal fins, can be opened into a fan-like shape. Long-finned tuna prefer warmer waters of seas, and do not normally go below 50 m (155 ft), situating themselves in zones within isotherms linking points where temperatures are above 15–16°C (59–61°F). It shares a distinctive feature of all members of the genus Thunna, defying the heterothermic (changing body temperature) character of fishes by being able to produce body temperatures 10–15°C (20–30°F) higher than those of the waters they are actually in. Specialists unanimously claim that this is because the fish has a huge amount of muscles to move, and this function is performed by an exceptionally strong and well-developed vascular system. Long-finned tuna meat is highly valued and shopkeepers bargain for it by the piece. The layperson usually sees this fish in the freezers of supermarkets as relatively small portions of kitchen-ready fillets.

328 | Yellowfin tuna | Thunnus albacares | SCOMBRIDAE / SCOMBRIDS

Yellowfin tuna (En), Gelbflossenthun, Albakora (D), Rabil (E), Albacore (F), Tonno albacora (I), Geelvintonijn (Nl) • Yellowfin tunny, Allison's tuna (En), Madidihan (Ind), Kihada (J), Tongkol (Mal), Albakor (N), Tambakol (Phi), Albacora (RU, S)

Rarely does naming in the different languages become so variable and diverse as in the case of the yellowfin tuna. Their characteristic fins are distinctively white or cream-coloured. Distributed throughout the Pacific Ocean and the tropical waters of the Atlantic, yellowfin tuna reach enormous sizes of about 80–150 cm (32–59 in) and weights of 150–200 kg (330–440 lb). They are distinctively differentiated from the other, bluish-silvery-grey fishes of the tuna family by their aforementioned golden-yellowish or chestnut-brown fins and gill covers. A typically school predator, a yellowfin tuna will persistently follow the other members of the same school, only to satisfy its tremendous appetite. This great appetite is the fish's nemesis, since a great number of yellowfins end up in the nets of fishing fleets by sticking to the easily attainable "meal" presented by large schools of mackerel. They normally do not go nearer to the coastline than a few tens of miles, thus a usual method is to catch them by bottom longlines, i.e. live bait and big hooks suspended on off-shore buoys, or by trolling. It often happens that participants in swordfish contests are surprised at landing a wonder-fish like this.

329 | Blackfin tuna | *Thunnus atlanticus* | SCOMBRIDAE / SCOMBRIDS

Blackfin tuna (En), Schwarzflossenthun (D), Atún des aletas negras (E), Thon à nageoires noires (F), Tonno pinna nera (I), Zwartvintonijn (NI) • Sortfinnet tun (Da), Monte maguro (J), Albacorinha, atum barbatena negra (P), Svartfenad tonfisk (S)

The blackfin tuna lives in the western Atlantic, from the coast of Massachusetts (USA) southwards to the island of Trinidad, and Rio de Janeiro. It grows to 1 m (39 in) in length and 19–20 kg (42–44 lb) in weight. Usually inhabiting the open sea, it sometimes occurs near the coasts. It hunts in schools at the water surface, and dives to a maximum depth of 50 m (165 ft). It often mixes with other species of tuna. A fast, aggressive predator, it feeds on fish, cephalopods, crustaceans and other pelagic animals. It regularly covers long distances. With the help of its special circulatory system it is able to keep the temperature of its muscles warmer than the surrounding water, which enables it to swim faster. It spawns far away from the coast, but breeding occurs between June and September off Mexico. Its eggs are pelagic, i.e. they float until hatching. This kind of tuna is most intensely harvested off the southeastern coast of Cuba, where it is caught with an angling device baited with live bait. An excellent sport fish, it is the main target of organized angling tours, as it very actively fights once hooked, and its flesh is delicious.

330 | Bigeye tuna | *Thunnus obesus* | SCOMBRIDAE / SCOMBRIDS

Bigeye tuna (En), Großaugenthun (D), Patudo (E), Thon obèse (F), Tonno obeso (I), Grootoogtonijn (NI) • Storøjet tun (Da), Storøyd makrellstørje (N), Albacore-ôlho-grande (P), Tambakol (Phi), Ton bondoc (Ru), Storögd tonfisk (S), Yajdar-baal-cagaar (Som), Irigözorkinoz baligi (Tr)

The bigeye tuna is found in subtropical-tropical waters of the Atlantic, the Indian Ocean, as well as the Pacific, but is absent from the Mediterranean Sea. It occurs in areas where water temperatures are in the range of 13–29°C, although it seems to prefer 17–22°C. A huge species of tuna, it reaches 250 cm in length (99 in) and 210 kg (463 lb) in weight. Its appearance is influenced by seasonal and climatic temperature changes. The fry and the young live in schools near the surface, often mixing with other tuna species. Larger specimens dive to deeper regions, to a depth of 250 m (820 ft). A fast-swimming predator, it feeds on fish, cephalopods and crustaceans, both during the day and at night. It makes extremely long migratory trips. Breeding is continuous in tropical areas, while the bigeye spawns in summer in colder waters. Spawning is most intense at full moon. Adults mate at least twice annually. The eggs are pelagic and develop while floating in water. A species intensely harvested for its excellent flesh, it is also popular as a sport fish. It is mainly marketed canned or frozen, but is also available fresh. In Japan, it is made into sashimi.

329

330

331 | **Northern bluefin tuna** | Thunnus thynnus | SCOMBRIDAE / SCOMBRIDS

Northern bluefin tuna (En), Roter Thun (D), Atún rojo (E), Thon rouge (F), Tonno rosso (I), Tonijn (Nl) • Tuna plava (Cr), Tunfisk (Da), Tónnos (Gr), Túnfiskur (Is), Tunna kehula (Isr), Kuromaguro (J), Thu (Mand), Makrellstjørje (N), Atum rabilho (P), Ton rosu (Ru), Makrillstörje (S), Orkinoz baligi (Tr), Waxandor (Wol)

A giant fish, northern bluefin tuna can attain the remarkable size of about 2–4 m (80–160 in) and a weight of 200–500 kg (440–1100 lb). A schooling fish, nothern bluefin tuna generally wander about in relatively small groups, while for the spawning season, which commences in June they form enormous shoals. The marine-blue colour of the dorsal part blends into a greyish hue towards the sides. One single specimen of bluefin tuna represents very high value and a good catch may supply an entire family for several weeks. A wide array of cunning devices are used to catch them, ranging from hooks and fishing rods to bottom trawls. In waters around the Iberian Peninsula a peculiar fishing method has been developed by applying the so-called "tonnara". This is a net trap of a highly complicated design, at the bottom of which a sack or casket is attached. When these huge fish get stuck in it, large boats especially equipped for tuna fishing remove the catch with the help of power winches and gigantic landing nets. In times past, when there were no such modern conveniences, fishermen could do nothing but wait until the captive fish killed each other in their agony. The meat of bluefin tuna is widely sought after throughout the entire world. Interestingly, countries of the Far East have established themselves as the most influential commercial buyer of this delicacy.

332 | **Longtail tuna** | Thunnus tonggol | SCOMBRIDAE / SCOMBRIDS

Longtail tuna (En), Langschwanzthun (D), Atún tongol (E), Thon mignon (F), Tonno indiano (I), Tongoltonijn (Nl) • Northern bluefin tuna (Au, Pap), Gebab (Em), Kayu, tongkol hitam (Ind), Koshinaga (J), Abu-abu, aya, bakulan, tongkol (Mal), Bonito-oriental (Moz-P), Blue-fin tuna (Mya), Sahwa (Om), Atum-do-índico, atum-tongol (P), Dlinnokhvostyj tunets (R), Yajdar (Som), Jodari (Swa), Indian long-tailed tuna (UK), Oriental bonito (US), Bulis, sobad (Vis), Tulingan (Vis)

The longtail tuna inhabits tropical areas in the Indian and Pacific oceans. Its range extends from southern Japan through the Philippines and New Britain to northern Australia, and it is found along the Indian coast and in southern waters of the Arabian Peninsula, in the Red Sea and off Somalia. The longtail is one of the tuna species with the most restricted range. A comparatively small species, it grows to 136 cm (54 in) in length and 36 kg (79 lb) in weight. It prefers shallow water, but also occurs in open sea. It avoids murky waters or those with a lower level of salinity, and is found chiefly near the surface. The longtail tuna lives in schools consisting of fish of different size. A fast predator, it feeds on fish, cephalopods and crustaceans. Its buoyancy is enhanced by its ability to keep its muscles warmer than the surrounding water thanks to a special circulatory system. It spawns in summer, and reaches sexual maturity when it is 60–70 cm (24–28 in) in length. It is harvested with pleasure by both commercial and recreational fishermen for its palatable flesh. It is prepared fried, grilled or roasted, but is also eaten salted, canned or smoked.

333 | **Sailfish, Indo-Pacific sailfish** | Istiophorus platypterus | ISTIOPHORIDAE / SAILFISHES AND MARLINS

Sailfish, Indo-Pacific sailfish (En), Fächerfisch (D), Pez vela del Indo-Pacífico (E), Voilier de l'Indo-Pacifique (F), Pesce vela (I), Zielvis (Nl) • Faras el bahr (Ara), Malasugi (Bik, Tag), Mbassi kouri (Com), Pacifisk sejlfisk (Da), A'u-lepe (Haw), Dot-sae-chi (Kor), Nolwaro (Mad), Layeran (Mal), Agulháo bandeira (P), Darya-jo-goro (Pak), Kandayan (Phi), Parusnik-ryba (R), Thalapatha (Sin), Daanbeeri (Som), Myl meen (Tam), Dogso, liplipan (Vis)

The sailfish inhabits tropical and temperate areas on both sides of the Pacific, as well as the Indian ocean, and in the Red Sea. Through the Suez Canal it has successfully invaded the Mediterranean Sea. A large species, it reaches 340 cm (134 in) in length and 100–110 kg (approx. 2 cwt) in body mass. The name sailfish is derived from the large dorsal fin. Another characteristic is its sword-like snout. The sailfish is found in open sea and coastal regions, close to the surface above the thermocline level, to a depth of 30 m (100 ft). Sailfish schools are usually formed by individuals of the same size. It feeds on fish, crustaceans and cephalopods. When hunting, it first circles a fish school, then breaks into it and makes sudden rapid turns within it. The sailfish then consumes the fish killed or wounded by this action of its "sword". It is the fastest-swimming fish, reaching 100–110 km/h (62–68 mph) for a short distance (100 m). Breeding is continuous in tropical areas, but peaks in summer. The eggs are pelagic, i.e. they drift in water until hatching. An important fish both commercially and recreationally. In Japan, it is made into sashimi and sushi.

334 | **Striped marlin** | Tetrapturus audax | ISTIOPHORIDAE / SAILFISHES AND MARLINS

Striped marlin (En), Gestreifter Marlin (D), Marlín rayado (E), Makaire strié (F), Marlin striato (I), Gestreepte marlijn (Nl) • Gestreepte marlyn (Afr), Cheong-sae-chi (Kor), Espadim-raiado (P), Haura (Sin), Sa'ula (Sam), Dugso (Vis)

The striped marlin lives in subtropical-tropical areas of the Indian and the Pacific oceans. Occasionally, it is found off the Cape of Good Hope and in the Atlantic Ocean. Its range in the Pacific is unique among marlin and tuna, since it is found in a horseshoe-shaped area stretching from the northwestern Pacific through the eastern side to the southeastern part of the ocean. In the Indian Ocean it lives in the equatorial region, as well as off East Africa, the western part of the Arabian Peninsula, in the Bay of Bengal and off northwestern Australia. A huge species, it reaches 420 cm (166 in) in length and 440 kg (970 lb) in weight. The striped marlin inhabits the open sea far away from the coasts, and dives to a maximum depth of 100 m (330 ft). In coastal regions, it occurs exclusively in areas with a strongly sloping bottom. It lives mainly solitarily, but specimens of the same size congregate into large schools for spawning. Breeding occurs in May and June, in open water, the eggs being pelagic until hatching. Covering long distances, the striped marlin feeds on fish, cephalopods and crustaceans. Harvested commercially and recreationally, it is also harpooned by fishermen, and is popular with marine anglers. Its flesh is the best among marlin for making sushi and sashimi. Marketed mainly frozen, it is sometimes available fresh.

335 | Atlantic blue marlin | Makaira nigricans | ISTIOPHORIDAE / SAILFISHES AND MARLINS

Atlantic blue marlin (En), Blauer Marlin (D), Aguja azul (E), Makaire bleu de l'Atlantique (F), Marlin azzuro (I), Blauwe marlijn (Nl) • Big-ho' (Bik), Atlantisk blå marlin (Da), Makajiki (J), Nog-sae-chi (Kor), Blå marlin (N, S), Espadum-azul, agulhão-preto (P), Chernyi marlin (R), Purjemarliini (SF)

Praised by many as the most beautiful fish in the world, the Atlantic blue marlin has come to be known world-wide, if only on the basis of the many bars and clubs named after it along the Atlantic coast. Atlantic blue marlin are enormous, growing to a size of 2–3.5 m (80–140 in). Soon after being landed, the fish loses its wonderful marine-blue colour. Every tiny piece of it is used. Apart from its flavoursome, tender meat being always a real adventure to taste, its head also makes a good gift for adventure-minded tourists. Those interested in a fashionable look can also find wallets and footwear made from the Atlantic blue marlin's thick but soft skin. Trimmings and fins end up in a casserole; fish soup is delicious when cooked with various vegetables. Atlantic blue marlin have high, dark blue dorsal fins. From a distance this is the only trait by which one can distinguish them from dolphins, since both species are especially keen on leaping spectacularly high above the water. The Atlantic blue marlin overtakes marine motor boats with gracious ease. Contestants on board fishing boats are always overwhelmed when they have to face the Atlantic blue marlin, as it fights really hard when hooked. Usually it is only with huge gaffs and power winches that the beautiful Atlantic blue marlin can be hauled on board.

336 | Atlantic white marlin | Tetrapturus albidus | ISTIOPHORIDAE / SAILFISHES AND MARLINS

Atlantic white marlin (En), Weißer Marlin (D), Aguja blanca del Alántico, marlin blanca (E), Makaire blanc de l'Atlantique (F), Marlin bianco, aguglia imperiale (I), Witte marlijn (Nl) • Hvid marlin (Da, N), Marlinos Atlantikou (Gr), Agulhão-branco, espadim branco do Atlântico (P), Marlin alb (Ru), Spjutfisk (S), Valkomarliini (SF)

This is a carnivorous fish of the warm seas of the Atlantic Ocean, travelling in small schools. It decimates the population of smaller species, mackerel in particular. Extremely fast, it hits its victims like lightning. It is much admired by people angling from yachts, and is also feared, since when it swallows the bait fish, it can drag the rod and line of an inept angler into the deep with ease. The Atlantic white marlin grows to 2–3 m (80–120 in) in length and maximum 250 kg (500 lb) in weight. Because of its long, wing-like pectoral fins, it is locally called "white birdie". From a distance it can be distinguished from other species of marlin by its slightly rounded dorsal fin. The most valuable parts of its body are the two horizontal muscles running along its back, which are put into commercial circulation in large, triangular blocks or slices. The flesh is flexible and easily shaped, and is often compared to that of veal.

337 | Swordfish | Xiphias gladius | XIPHIIDAE / SWORDFISHES

Swordfish (En), Schwertfisch (D), Pez espada, emperador, aguja palar (E), Espadon, poisson-épée, gadiateur (F), Pesce spada (I), Zwaardvis (Nl) • Peshku shtize (Alb), Big-ho' (Bik), Sværdfisk (Da), Broadbill (En), Xiphías (Gr), Tadmachhi (Guj), Dag haherev (Is), Mekajiki (J), Whang-sae-chi (Kor), Sverdfisk (N), Kheil al bahar (Om), Espadarte (P), Malasugi (Phi), Peste-spada (Ru), Kadu kpooara (Sin), Meèarica (Slo), Daanbeeri (Som), Nduwalo (Swa), Ha'ura (Tah), Mayas-pas (Vis)

Perhaps the best-known marine fish in the world, the swordfish has been reported from all warm oceans on Earth. Its scientific name has a long history. The generic name is derived from Greek, the specific name from Latin. Both refer to the swordfish's fierce temperament as well as its huge, elongated snout, a sword-like appendage of the maxillaries. This species can surpass 4 m in length, including sword, and 500 kg (1100 lb) in weight. Marine fishermen regard the swordfish as one of the most valuable trophies. Almost 100 major contests are organised annually with the sole aim of catching swordfish. In addition, the major fishing countries hold special contests to catch it, and the role of fisheries is gradually being taken over by anglers. The swordfish populations are gradually decreasing, so more and more countries are introducing a closed season in their waters. As it mainly inhabits open oceans, these regulations are not particularly effective. Its major reproduction zone is believed to be the Sargasso Sea, where pelagic swordfish eggs can be collected with a plankton net in the spring.

338 | Silver pomfret | Pampus argenteus | STROMATEIDAE / BUTTERFISHES

Silver pomfret (En), Silberne Pampel (D), Palometón platero, palometa plateada (E), Aileron argenté (F), Pampo argenteo (I), Zilverpomfret (Nl) • Pa chong (Cant), Bawai putih (Ind), Managatsuo (J), Dawahan (Jav), Pyong-o (Kor), Byeong-eo, bawal puteh (Mal), Vella vavvel (Tam), Pla jara met khao (Thai)

This fish species is an inhabitant of the Indian and Pacific oceans, from the Persian Gulf eastwards to Indonesia, and northwards to Hokkaido Island of Japan. Occasionally specimens are caught in the Adriatic Sea, the North Sea and in Hawaiian waters. The silver pomfret grows to 62 cm (24 in) in length and 6.5–7 kg (14–15 lb) in weight. It lives in coastal shallows, to a depth of 5–110 m (15–360 ft). It is usually found above a mud bottom, moving around in schools and even mixing with other fish. A carnivorous species, it feeds on ctenophores, tunicates, medusai and zooplankton. Western populations spawn from late winter to summer, with a peak lasting from April to June. A species intensely harvested, the silver pomfret accounts for the majority of catches off Kuwait, where it is caught with gill nets. Sold fresh on local markets, it is transported frozen to nearby cities. It is also used in traditional Chinese medicine.

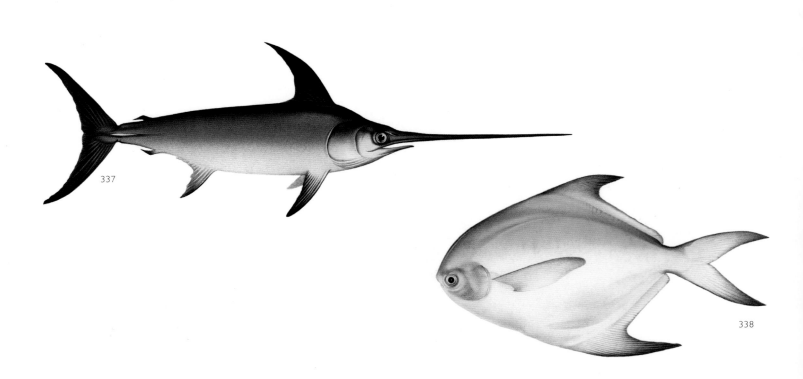

337

338

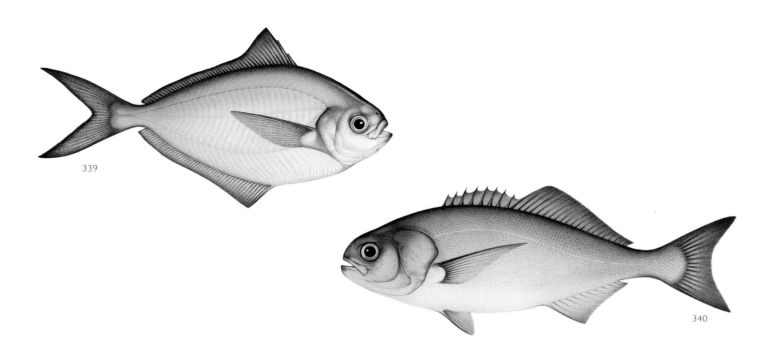

339 | **American butterfish** | Peprilus triacanthus | STROMATEIDAE / BUTTERFISHES

American butterfish (En), Amerikanischer Butterfisch (D), Palometa pintada, pez mantequilla americano (E), Stromaté à fossettes (F), Fieto americano (I), Amerikaanse grootbek (Nl) • Palometa estrecha (Cub), Pâmpano-manteiga (P), Atlantic butterfish, dollar fish, pumpkin scad, sheephead (UK), Butterfish (US)

This butterfish is native to the western Atlantic, its range extending from temperate and subtropical waters of eastern Newfoundland and the St. Lawrence Bay to Palm Beach, Florida, and the Gulf of Mexico. A small-bodied species, it reaches 30 cm (12 in) in length and 500–600 g (18–21 oz) in weight. It lives in large, loose schools above the continental shelf, but migrates to deeper waters for the winter. It is usually found from the bottom to the surface at all water levels. The fry hide among floating vegetation and under medusai. The American butterfish often occurs in brackwater areas. Its food consists primarily of medusai, but also includes minute fish and crayfish. Its spawning season lasts from May to October, with a peak in July and August. Caught by fishermen as well as by anglers, its flesh is of excellent quality. It has a dark colour due to its high fat content, but turns white with cooking. Marketed fresh, smoked or frozen, it is eaten fried, grilled or roasted. It is exported frozen in huge quantities to Japan.

340 | **Antarctic butterfish** | Hyperoglyphe antarctica | CENTROLOPHIDAE / BARREL FISHES AND RUFFS

Antarctic butterfish (En), Antarktischer Schwarzfisch (D), Pez nariz azul antártico (E), Rouffe à nez bleu (F), Ricciola di fondale australe (I), Antarctische ywarte vis (Nl) • Antarktiese bottervis (Afr), Blue eye, deepsea trevalla, big-eye, sea trevally, trevalla (Au), Antarktisk sortfisk (Da), Matiri (Mao), Bluenose warehou (NZ)

This percid fish inhabits waters in the Western Hemisphere, off South America, South Africa, Australia and New Zealand, at the edge of the continental shelf and its deepening margin at depths of 100–300 m. Its maximum size is 120 cm (47 in), with a weight of 20 kg (44 lb). A bottom-dwelling species, it occurs on rocky bottoms or in the vicinity of such areas, and prefers cool waters. It particularly favours the edge of canyons and abysses, and stays close to the bottom during the day, while it rises into shallower waters following its prey. Young individuals live on the surface. A carnivorous species, the Antarctic butterfish feeds primarily on tunicates, but also on cephalopods, gastropods, crustaceans and smaller or larger fish. It is caught for its excellent flesh, being sold fresh or frozen. It is exported to Japan for making sashimi. It is stewed, fried in a pan, grilled or roasted in an oven or microwaved. It very rarely occurs in the catch of anglers.

341 | **Common warehou** | Seriolella brama | CENTROLOPHIDAE / BARREL FISHES AND RUFFS

Common warehou (En), Seriolella (D), Warehou (F), Seriolella (I), Seriolella (Nl) • Sea bream, Snotgall trevally, snotty (Au), Blue warehou, warehou (Au, NZ), Gælleplettet sortfisk (Da), Warehou (Mao)

This percid fish is an inhabitant of the southwestern Pacific, including the seas of Australia and New Zealand. Its maximum length is 75–80 cm (30–32 in), maximum weight 4 kg (9 lb). Adult warehous are found above the continental shelf at its deepening margin. They hunt in large groups mainly on the sea bottom, but have been proved to rise to medium depth at night. The young form schools along the coasts to a depth of 100 m (330 ft), and occasionally dwell in estuaries. A carnivorous species, the common warehou feeds mostly on tunicates, but also takes smaller crustaceans, krill and cephalopods. A fish specifically fished for, it is also caught by anglers. It is sold either fresh or frozen, and is prepared stewed, cooked, roasted in an oven or microwaved, pan-fried or grilled.

342 | **Giant gourami** | Osphronemus goramy | BELONTIIDAE / FIGHTING FISHES AND GOURAMIS

Giant gourami (En), Riesengurami (D), Gurami gigante (E), Gourami géant (F), Gurami (I), Goerami (Nl) • Gurameh (Jav), Pa meng (Lao), Gurami (P, R, S), Seppali (Sin), Sankara (Tam), Pla raed (Thai)

The giant gourami inhabits southeast Asian freshwaters. Originally a native of Sumatra, Borneo, Java, the Malay peninsula and the Mekong River system of Thailand and Indochina, it has been introduced to several regions and countries for farming purposes. An important food-fish, it is widely cultured in tropical Asia. A large species, it grows to 70–80 cm (28–32 in) in length and 8–10 kg (18–22 lb) in weight. The giant gourami occurs in swamps and ponds, as well as rivers. An omnivorous fish, its menu includes water plants, fish, frogs, worms, and even carrion. It is able to "breathe" humid atmospheric air, hence can be kept alive for a long time when taken out of water. As a result, it can easily be transported to areas with no access to electricity for cooling. The male constructs a nest for the eggs and fry. The remains of this species have been recovered from Miocene sediments in central Sumatra.

343 | Snakeskin gourami | Trichogaster pectoralis | BELONTIIDAE / FIGHTING FISHES AND GOURAMIS

Snakeskin gourami (En), Schaufelfadenfisch (D), Gurami piel de serpiente (E), Gourami-peau de serpent (F), Gurami scaglioso (I), Slangenhuidgoerami (NI) • Trey kantho, trey kawnthor (Khm), Pa sa lit (Lao), Sepat siam (Mal), Pla bai mai, pla salid (Thai), Theppili (Sin), Cá sat rang (Vie)

This large species of gourami inhabits Asian freshwaters, from Thailand to southern Vietnam and Malaysia. It has been reported to have a negative ecological impact once introduced. Unlike other, smaller gouramis that are popular aquarium fish, this species can reach 25–30 cm (10–12 in) in length and 500 g (18 oz) in weight, and is thus suitable for human consumption. It lives in ponds and calm rivers with a slow current, and feeds on aquatic plants and zooplankton. Almost uniquely, it is able the breath atmospheric air, but also uses its gills when in the water. A species intensely harvested and farmed, it is also sought by fish hobbyists. It breeds from April to August in Thailand. Its flesh is of exceptional quality, is sold fresh, and is eaten mainly grilled or made into fish soup. In Thailand, it is transported dried to areas in which it does not occur.

344 | Fluke, Summer flounder | Paralichthys dentatus | BOTHIDAE / LEFT-EYED FLOUNDERS

Fluke, Summer flounder (En), Sommerflunder (D), Falso halibut del Canadá (E), Cardeau d'été (F), Rombo dentato (I), Zomervogel (NI) • Sommerhvarre (Da), Carta-de-verão (P), Poskarp letnica (Pl), Calcan de vara (Ru), Sommarvar (S), Northern fluke (US)

Dwelling in the northern regions of the Atlantic, fluke, or summer flounder, average in length up to 70–80 cm (27–30 in) and are fairly heavy. Fluke biomass is on the decrease along the European coast, the food-market is mostly supplied by stock in the western region of the Atlantic. This is why the name "Canadian halibut" is more and more frequently attached to the specimens one encounters in the market. Fluke is one of the most widely researched fishes in the world. Biological research has been conducted in the field of the fluke's exceptional ability to change its colour, the final conclusion of the scientists being that the explanation of this remarkable mechanism is neuro-biological. Ethological research has found that perches are supposedly the direct ancestors of flatfishes, since this is the species whose members often lie on one side while sleeping or resting. This habit could only have been fixed in the course of thousands of years, and this is how the special asymmetrical build of flatfishes could have evolved. The extensive research has definitely contributed to the development and application of the artificial rearing of toothed flatfishes, especially in the English-speaking countries.

343

344

345 | **Turbot** | Psetta maxima | SCOPHTHALMIDAE / TURBOTS AND BRILLS

Turbot (En), Steinbutt (D), Rodaballo, parracho, rémol, corujo, sollo (E), Turbot commun (F), Rombo chiodato (I), Tarbot (Nl) • Gjel i hirte (Alb), Pighvar (Da), Siáki, kalkáni (Gr), Barbun imperiali (Malt), Rombou clavelat (Mon), Piggvar (N, S), Pregado (P), Piikkikampela (SF), Romb (Slo), Kalkan baligi (Tr), Syaks (Tun)

As their Latin name also shows, turbot are the largest species of the family Scophthalmidae, as they may attain body lengthy of nearly 1 m (40 in). A broad-bodied fish, turbot are used very efficiently, often with 70% of the live weight utilised. The fins are mostly soft and spineless, thus it is easy to handle, no wonder that aquaculturists in many areas are engaged in developing methods of artificial rearing the species. This endeavour is also encouraged by the abundant spawning biomass, resulting in the millions of offspring produced, and by the fact that the larvae can easily be fed with artificially processed plankton and other pelagic fish-food substitutes. The rearing of offspring lasts for a few months and is followed by fast growth. The symmetrical fry of swimming habit soon become asymmetrical and assume a benthic existence. Metamorphosis finished, the upper or ocular side of the fish is fully evolved with the grotesquely shaped head and the numerous yellowish brown, often golden tinted spots. Turbot are scaleless, though the head and the body are studded with numerous bony knobs, or tubercles, which further eases the usually tedious task of cleaning the fish before cooking. The meat of turbot is of a pleasantly juicy character, easy to slice and, with good spicing, it makes a delicious supper.

346 | **Brill** | Scophthalmus rhombus | SCOPHTHALMIDAE / TURBOTS AND BRILLS

Brill (En), Glattbutt, Kleist (D), Rémol, rodoballo, rapante, corujo, escamudo (E), Barbue, turbot lisse (F), Rombo liscio, soaso (I), Griet (Nl) • Europæisk slethvarre (Da), Pissi (Gr), Slétthverfa (Is), Barbun lixx (Malt), Slétthverfa (N), Rodovalho (P), Naglad (Pl), Gladkij bril (R), Slätvar (S), Gladki romb (Slo), Çivisizkalkan baligi (Tr)

A characteristic, perhaps the most widely distributed, bottom-dwelling flounder species of the northeastern seas of the Atlantic. It is often called "smooth" or "silky", due to the fact that it possesses few skin appendages, bony ridges and spines. These characteristics might have contributed to the widespread captive breeding projects found in dozens of countries. For similar reasons the brill has been introduced to almost all countries farming marine fish. It produces huge masses of eggs numbering millions, which can easily be hatched under artificial conditions. The fry hatched from these eggs are fed plankton to imitate natural food. Experts consider brill flesh to be excellent, if slightly bony, but easily processed and shaped for culinary use. Thanks to its comparatively easy captive propagation, this species may become a success story in future fish farming.

345

346

347

348

347 | **Arrowtooth flounder** | Atheresthes stomias | PLEURONECTIDAE / RIGHT-EYED FLOUNDERS

Arrowtooth flounder (En), Amerikanischer Pfeilzahnheilbutt (D), Halibut del Pacífico (E), Faux flétan du Pacifique (F), Passera canina (I), Amerikaanse heilbot (Nl) • Stillehavshellefisk (Da), Alabote-dente-curvo (P), Fladra strzalozebna (Pl), Amerikanskij stelozubij paltus (R), French sole, long jaw flounder (US)

This species of flounder lives in the northern Pacific, in the Bering Sea along the Russian coast, and off Alaska southwards to California. It grows to 84 cm (33 in) in body length and 2 kg (4.4 lb) in mass. It occurs on a soft, mud or sand bottom and is found in very shallow, as well as 900 m (3000 ft) deep water. Both of its eyes are situated on the right side of its body, so it can use them while resting on the bottom on its left side. The colour of the pigmented right side can change substantially in order to match the colour of the bottom on which the animal rests. Adult specimens lose their swimming bladder, since they would have little use of it in their bottom-dwelling existence. A carnivorous species, it feeds on small fish and crustaceans. Spawning occurs in open water, from December to February. The arrowtooth flounder is intensely harvested for its tasty flesh, also by anglers. It can be caught any time of the year, but is more common in the catch in the cold winter period. Marketed fresh or frozen, it is eaten fried, grilled or roasted.

348 | **Petrale sole** | Eopsetta jordani | PLEURONECTIDAE / RIGHT-EYED FLOUNDERS

Petrale sole (En), Kalifornische Sole (D), Rodaballo de California (E), Carlottin pétrale (F), Passera della California (I), Californische schol (Nl) • Californisk flynder (Da), Brill sole (US)

This species of sole is native to the northeastern Pacific, from the coast of Alaska in the Bering Sea to the Los Coronados Islands, and the northern part of the Gulf of California. It reaches 70 cm (28 in) in length and 3.6 kg (8 lb) in body mass. Females are usually about 20 cm (8 in) longer than males. The petrale sole occurs on a sand bottom, from very shallow waters to a depth of 550 m (1800 ft). Both of its eyes are located on the right side of its body, as it rests on its left side while awaiting its prey. A carnivorous species, it feeds on bottom-dwelling invertebrates and minute fish. Breeding lasts from November to March. Females spawn once annually, and can lay as many as 1.5 million eggs at a time. The eggs are pelagic, i.e. they drift in water until hatching, and also the fry live a pelagic existence in the first six months of their life. It is harvested with pleasure by both commercial and recreational fishermen, since its high-quality flesh is much sought after, being considered the most delicious sole occurring in the Pacific. The liver of larger individuals contains substantial amounts of Vitamin A. Fishermen catch this species with nets dragged along the sea bottom. Marketed fresh or as frozen fillets, it is prepared stewed, fried in a pan, grilled, or roasted in an oven or microwaved.

349 | Witch flounder | Glyptocephalus cynoglossus | PLEURONECTIDAE / RIGHT-EYED FLOUNDERS

Witch flounder (En), Rotzunge, Hundszunge, Zungenbutt (D), Mendo, falso lenguado (E), Plie cynoglosse, plie grise (F), Passera lingua di cane (I), Witje (Nl) • Skærising (Da), Smørflyndre (N), Rödtunga (S), Grey sole (US)

40–50 cm (16–20 in) long and a few kilograms in weight, witch flounder, or grey sole, primarily dwell in the cold seas of the Atlantic Ocean. The elongated body may occur in various hues from reddish-brown to greyish-brown, and is almost entirely swaddled in the round dorsal, pelvic and caudal fins. While moving, the entire fish gives the impression of a mysterious, undulating creature, with the protuberant side-line giving it an even more suggestive impression. It is primarily the sand and gravel bottom where witch flounder prefer to dwell, where they feed on invertebrate organisms of the benthos. No wonder the main dwelling places of the species occur along the marine shelves a few hundreds of fathoms deep near the fjord-indented coasts of Norway. They do not travel far, usually staying a few miles from the coastline. They are chiefly fished with otter trawls, and are an important feature of Scandinavian fish markets. The meat of witch flounder is highly prized, the methods of preparing and preserving it being immensely varied.

350 | American plaice | Hippoglossoides platessoides | PLEURONECTIDAE / RIGHT-EYED FLOUNDERS

American plaice (En), Doggerscharbe (D), Solla, platija americana (E), Balai de l'Atlantique (F), Passera canadese (I), Lange schar (Nl) • Almindelig Håising (Da), Long rough dab (En), Glossáki-chomatída (Gr), Ikkahnalook (Inu)

Widely distributed in all the cold waters of the Atlantic, American plaice attain body lengths of about 50 cm (20 in) and my grow as large as 4 kg (9 lb). Two large stocks are known to exist, one travelling along the European coast of the Atlantic, the other along the coasts of the USA and Canada. The two stocks tend to be more and more separated, the North American stock even being acknowledged as a distinct species. Like other related species, American plaice prefer mud bottom environments, into which they can perfectly mingle with their greyish brown, yellowish-brown colour. Omnivorous, they practically gulp down all organic matter. American plaice have already been observed in the close vicinity of sea ports, where they usually take to feeding on detritus and waste. Specimens travelling upstream in larger rivers have also been detected. They spawn far off the coast, in the ocean, at depths of about 100–200 m (300–650 ft). They do not take special care of their roe which freely drift in the waters. The meat of the American plaice is especially flaky-textured and juicy, therefore it deteriorates much faster than that of related species. For this reason, it is marketed with special precautions, a fact that shows in the relatively low price of the fish.

351 | Atlantic halibut | Hippoglossus hippoglossus | PLEURONECTIDAE / RIGHT-EYED FLOUNDERS

Atlantic halibut (En), Atlantischer Heilbutt (D), Hipogloso, fletán, halibut, napoleón (E), Flétan de l'Atlantique (F), Ippoglosso atlantico (I), Heilbot (Nl) • Helleflynder (Da), Geiraspjørr (Far), Ippóglossa, hálibat (Gr), Heilagfiski (Is), Kveite (N), Alabote do Atlântico (P), Halibut bialy (Pl), Paltus (R), Halibut (Ru), Hälleflundra (S), Ruijanpallas (SF)

The largest of flatfishes, Atlantic halibut may reach a length of 3–4 m (120–160 in) and a weight of 200–300 kg (440–660 lb). They primarily dwell in cool waters of temperatures below 10°C (50°F), their main habitat being the northern coastline of the Atlantic. They sometimes leave the coast for the deeper waters of the ocean along the isothermic zones (strata of similar temperatures), but this is chiefly undertaken during the spawning season between November and February. They produce 2–4 million eggs, or roe, per female, the larvae emerging at great depths while floating. The incubation period is merely 10–14 days, despite the low temperature and the high pressure, a fact that indicates an exceptional adaptibility to the environment. The mature fish generally prey on anything that moves, attacking from the bottom of the sea. Fishermen usually catch halibut with live bait or by spinning with artificial lures. Skill and good equipment are needed to catch halibut, landing of specimens over 100 kg (220 lb) needs true mastery of the mystery of fishing. Halibut meat is highly appreciated, the delicious fillets of the fish often being of enormous size.

352 | Pacific halibut | Hippoglossus stenolepis | PLEURONECTIDAE / RIGHT-EYED FLOUNDERS

Pacific halibut (En), Pazifischer Heilbutt (D), Fletán del Pacífico (E), Flétan du Pacifique (F), Halibut del Pacifico (I), Pacifische heilbot (Nl) • Sagiq (Alu), Xang (Hai), Ohyô (J), Belokory paltus (R), Thotx (Sal)

The closest relative of the Atlantic halibut (Hippoglossus hippoglossus), the Pacific halibut is regarded by some classifications as a sub-species of the former. The similarity is most obvious in the caudal fins, which are slightly curved inwards, a characteristic that very reliably distinguishes the species even at a young age. Pacific halibut average about 50–60 cm (20–24 in) in size and a couple of pounds in weight, although specimens larger than 1 m (40 in) have also been observed. A voracious fish, the Pacific halibut generally attacks from hiding. Their preferred dwelling is in the coastal waters and the areas around coral reefs and underwater ridges. Along the coastline fishing is rewarding for those using easy equipment, bottom hooks and nets, but once the fish takes the bait, it is difficult to lead the catch out from among the rocks into the landing-net. The meat of the Pacific halibut is chiefly appreciated in the Far East, the main consumer being Japan, where methods of rearing halibut fry are constantly being developed in controlled marine fisheries.

351

352

353 | Yellowtail flounder | Limanda ferruginea | PLEURONECTIDAE / RIGHT-EYED FLOUNDERS

Yellowtail flounder (En), Gelbschwanzflunder (D), Limanda nórdica (E), Limanda à queue jaune (F), Spigola, limanda (I), Geelstaartschar (Nl) • Gulhalet ising (Da), Solha dos mares do norte (P), Zholtokhovostaya kambala (R)

Distributed in the northern cold waters of the Atlantic, especially in the Baltic area, yellowtail flounder attain body lengths of about 40–50 cm (15–20 in) and weights of a few pounds. Like related species, the upper part of the body has a rough surface, as can be easily felt when stroking it from the caudal fin to the front. This is the usual movement applied by customers at the market when testing the fish for freshness. Local names usually refer to the yellowish, rusty-brown colour of the fish, by which hues they brilliantly adapt to the seabed of a similar colour. Delta estuaries of larger rivers are also a preferred dwelling-place of yellowtail, where they have been observed to travel several miles upstream. Their diet mainly consists of invertebrate organisms gathered on the sea bottom, but on mud bottoms they have also been observed collecting organic waste. Because of their omnivorous tendency, methods of artificial breeding and rearing are being researched in the Baltic area. The meat of yellowtail flounder is marketed at medium price, it is generally sold fresh, in ground ice.

354 | **Common dab** | Limanda limanda | PLEURONECTIDAE / RIGHT-EYED FLOUNDERS

Common dab (En), Kliesche, Scharbe (D), Limanda nórdica, gallo (E), Limande commune (F), Limanda (I), Schar (Nl) • Ising (Da), Limánta (Gr), Sandkoli (Is), Karei (J), Solha escura do mar do Norte (P), Limanda, ershovatka (R), Sandflyndre (N), Sandskädda (S), Hietakampela (SF), Pisi baligi (Tr), Flounder (US)

One of the most widely distributed species of the northern waters and cold marginal seas of the Atlantic, dab (also called flounder in the US) attain body lengths of about 30–50 cm (12–20 in) and weights of a couple of pounds. In several countries there are strict minimum size restrictions requiring specimens under 20 cm (8 in) to be discarded. The blind (lower) side is generally cream-coloured, whereas the colour of the ocular (upper) side adapts to the environment they are in. They chiefly dwell over the sand bottom of coastal areas, where they hide by causing a sand curtain with the movement of the pelvic fin and the long dorsal fin which extends from the head to the caudal fin. Thus hidden on the bottom, the fish then skilfully catches its prey passing overhead. Dab mainly feed on smaller fish and macroplanktonic organisms and small crabs. As with other flounders, the symmetrical larvae of dab also hatch from pelagic (floating) roe, to metamorphose after a few weeks' development into asymmetrical specimens and to assume a benthic (bottom-dwelling) existence. During this short time span they dramatically decrease in numbers, partly due to the good appetite of the other, mature members of the family. The meat of the dab is of medium quality and eaten fried or in vegetable fish soups.

353

354

355

356

355 | **Lemon sole** | Microstomus kitt | PLEURONECTIDAE / RIGHT-EYED FLOUNDERS

Lemon sole (En), Limande, Echte Rotzunge (D), Mendo limón, falsa limanda (E), Limande sole (F), Sogliola limanda (I), Tongschar (Nl) • Rødtunge (Da), Lomre (N), Solha-limao (P), Bergtunga (S), Pikkupääkampela (SF)

One of the most widely distributed flatfish of the cold northern Atlantic seas, lemon sole dwell in deep waters, on gravel bottoms, their fry dwelling chiefly in the crevices of rocks along the coastline. Apart from the colour shades they may assume, in many areas local names given to the species reflect the appearance of the fish: they have a small head and extremely sensitive and nimble, snappy lips. This latter trait is due to the special diet lemon sole feed on, primarily consisting of minor invertebrate organisms. Nature documentaries have often shown the way this fish detects crustaceans, molluscs, worms hiding in mud or under rocks, and voraciously dissecting their prey. Maybe because of the cold environment, lemon sole grow at a very slow rate, 5–6 years being needed for the fish to attain the marketable size of 30 cm (12 in) and 0.5–1 kg (1–2 lb), lengths of 50 cm (20 in) being considered a rarity. Its meat is highly appreciated in the English speaking world and in German cuisine, it is chiefly marketed as food in countries around the English Channel. The body of the fish is of varied shades of yellow, ranging from yellowish-brown through orange to bright yellow, a fact which clearly shows its adaptibility to environmental conditions and to the quality of the sea bottom.

356 | **Dover sole** | Microstomus pacificus | PLEURONECTIDAE / RIGHT-EYED FLOUNDERS

Dover sole (En), Pazifische Rotzunge, Pazifische Limande (D), Mendo del Pacífico (E), Dover-sole (F), Tong (Nl) • Stillehavsrødtunge (Da), Doverkoli (Is), Solha-de-Dover (P), Zlocica pacyficzna (Pl), Stillahavsbergskädda (S), Ihémek'we (Sal), Chinese sole (US)

This species of sole is native to the northeastern Pacific, from Navarin Canyon in the Bering Sea to Stalemate Shoal in the Aleutian Islands, south to the Gulf of California. It grows to 76 cm (30 in) in length and 3.5–4 kg (8–9 lb) in weight. Occurring above a mud bottom at a depth of 10–1200 m (33–4000 ft), it withdraws to deeper regions for the winter. Both of its eyes are situated on the right side of its body, as it rests on its left side on the bottom, and even swims around in this position. The upper side is pigmented, and is able to change its coloration substantially in order to match that of the sea bottom. Since they are bottom-dwellers, adults lose their swimming bladder. A predatory species, it feeds on bottom-dwelling invertebrates and small fish. It produces huge amounts of slime, which can cover other species confined within the same net when caught. Regularly harvested both by commercial and recreational fishermen, it can be caught the whole year. Its excellent flesh is sold for feeding mink, or as fillets for human consumption. Animals are fed mainly with soles caught at 300 m (660 ft) or deeper, as their flesh is of inferior quality.

357

358

357 | **Flounder** | Platichthys flesus | PLEURONECTIDAE / RIGHT-EYED FLOUNDERS

Flounder (En), Flunder (D), Platija europea, acedia (E), Flet d'Europe (F), Passera pianuzza (I), Bot, ijbot (Nl) • Ushojze e zeze (Alb), Skrubbe (Da), Kalkáni, chamatída (Gr), Flundra (Is), Karei (J), Barbun (Malt), Liehbage (Manx), Sola (Mon), Skrubbe (N), Solha das pedras (P), Stornia (Pl), Baltiiskaya rechnaya kambala (R), Cambula (Ru), Skrubba (S), Kampela (SF), Iverka (Slo), Derepisisi (Tr)

One of the most widely distributed species of northern and northeastern seas of the Atlantic, flounder were once extremely abundant along the German and Danish coasts, sometimes even occurring several hundred miles upstream in larger rivers. The explanation of this is that flounder, especially at a younger age, can tolerate changes in salinity, and due to their omnivorous nature, they easily find their dietary preferences along the seashore and near human habitation. The upper part of the fish is hard to the touch, and densely covered with spots, whereas the lower part is of a light, cream colour. Except for the spawning season, they are rather solitary in habit, hunting and gathering their food on their own. They do not normally travel very far from their usual habitat, therefore stocks do not usually mix. Caught chiefly along marine coasts by fishermen using otter trawls, flounder are regularly marketed as food, to the delight of many people who certainly appreciate this meat for its low price and reasonable quality.

358 | **Starry flounder** | Platichthys stellatus | PLEURONECTIDAE / RIGHT-EYED FLOUNDERS

Starry flounder (En), Sternflunder (D), Platija del Pacífico (E), Plie du Pacifique (F), Passera stellata (I), Sterschol (Nl) • Ggagtuliq (Alu), Stjerneflynder (Da), Ikkahnalook (Inu), Numagarei (J), Gang-do-da-ri (Kor), Solha-estrelada-do-Pacífico (P), Zvezdchataya kambala (R), P'ewi (Sal)

A well-known species of flatfish dwelling in the middle and northern Pacific Ocean, starry flounder are thus called in most countries because when resting on the sea bottom, the fish looks very similar to a bright star, due to the intricate visual effect of the striped patterns of the fins. One of the largest of its genus, starry flounder may grow as large as 1 m (40 in). Their meat is highly appreciated in the Far East, and because of the high price, the artificial rearing of the fish is also being researched. In natural environments they spawn over the sand bottom. Their roe are pelagic, the newly hatched symmetrical larvae feed on plankton. In a few month they shift to a benthic (bottom-dweller) existence and turn to a diet mainly consisting of organic materials. Very few specimens – about 2–3% – live to be one year of age. This low survival rate is due not least to the young being abandoned by their parents to the perils of life on the sea-bottom.

359 | European plaice | Pleuronectes platessa | PLEURONECTIDAE / RIGHT-EYED FLOUNDERS

European plaice (En), Scholle, Goldbutt (D), Solla, platija (E), Plie d'Europe, carrelet (F), Passera di mare, plattessa (I), Schol (NI) • Rødspætte (Da), Glossáki-chomatída (Gr), Skarkoli (Is), Liehbage spottagh (Manx), Rødspette (N), Solha avessa (P), Gladzica (PI), Morskaya kambala (R), Rödspätta (S), Punakampela (SF), Beneklipisi baligi (Tr), European plaice (US)

One of the commonest flatfish, also frequently met by holiday makers along the sea shore, European plaice average about 30–50 cm (12–20 in) in length, 1 m (40 in) long specimens being a rarity. Specimens that are marketed are of about 2–5 kg (4–11 lb) in weight, larger ones are quite rare even with fishermen specialized in catching plaice. One of those rare species that have both right and left-eyed specimens, European plaice can be distinguished from the other related species by the orange or light red spots scattered over the entire body, and by the hard protuberances behind their eyes. They have been observed in the entire region of the Atlantic of the Northern Hemisphere and in the adjoining seas. With the species' remarkably high tolerance for variations in temperature, more and more countries are engaged in conducting research into the artificial breeding and rearing of European plaice. This endeavour is greatly facilitated by the fact that European plaice feed primarily on small organisms, and can thus be induced to accept processed fish-feed. Of high commercial value, European plaice are marketed as food; in many regions the meat of the fish is a staple diet and also of a reasonable price.

360 | English sole | Parophrys vetulus | PLEURONECTIDAE / RIGHT-EYED FLOUNDERS

English sole (En), Englische Seezunge (D), Mendo limón (E), Bar commun (F), Sogliola limanda del Pacifico (I), Tongschar (NI) • Solha-inglesa (P), Jodnica (PI), Ihémek'we (Sal), California -, pointed nose -, lemon sole (US)

The English sole lives in the northern Pacific and is found from the Bering Sea to the Gulf of California. Females reach 57 cm (23 in) in length and 2–2.5 kg (4.4–5.5 lb) in body mass, while males are slightly smaller. This species is known to hybridise with Platichthys stellatus, their bastard offspring being scientifically described as Inopsetta ischyra. The English sole lives on a mud or sand bottom, to a depth of 550 m (1800 ft), but young specimens also occur in the tidal zone. As in other sole species, the eyes are located on the same, pigmented right side of the fish. The colouration of this side can be changed substantially, in order to match that of the sea bottom. Adults lose their swimming bladder, since they become bottom-dwellers. Their food consists mainly of smaller bottom-dwelling invertebrates and fish. Spawning occurs in coastal regions between September and April. Off California, the English sole breeds in January and February. It is harvested with pleasure by both commercial and recreational fishermen, since its flesh is of good quality. Caught with drag nets, specimens are 35–40 cm (14–16 in) long and weigh 300–350 g (11–12 oz) on average. Their flesh is mostly marketed frozen.

359

360

361 | Winter flounder | Pseudopleuronectes americanus | PLEURONECTIDAE / RIGHT-EYED FLOUNDERS

Winter flounder (En), Winterflunder, Amerikanische Scholle (D), Solla roja (E), Plie rouge (F), Limanda americana (I), Amerikaanse winterschol (Nl) • Solha-de-inverno (P), Vinterflundra (S), Georgia bank, black-backed flounder (US)

A flounder species of the western Atlantic, its range extends from Labrador, Canada, to coastal Georgia, USA. It grows to 64 cm (25 in) in length and 3.6 kg (8 lb) in weight. It lives in coastal shallows upon a sand or mud bottom, to a depth of 35–40 m (115–130 ft). Occasionally it occurs in brackwater. Its left eye migrates to the right side, as the fish spends its life resting on its left side on the sea bottom. The lower (left) surface is white, the upper pigmented, and is able to change its tone substantially in order to match that of the bottom. The winter flounder migrates seasonally, wandering into deeper waters for the summer and returning to coastal shallows for the winter. A carnivorous species, it usually feeds during the day on bottom-dwelling crustaceans, worms, sea cucumbers and snails. Spawning lasts from April to June in northern regions, while it occurs between November and June in the south. This species is considered one of the tastiest coastal fish, and is thus admired by fishermen and anglers alike. Mainly caught in winter months.

362 | Greenland halibut | Reinhardtius hippoglossoides | PLEURONECTIDAE / RIGHT-EYED FLOUNDERS

Greenland halibut (En), Schwarzer Heilbutt (D), Hipogloso negro, halibut negro (E), Flétan noir, halibut noir (F), Halibut di Groenlandia, ippoglosso nero (I), Groenlandse heilbot, zwarte heilbot (Nl) • Almindelig hellefisk (Da), Kaleralik (Inu), Karasu garei (J), Blåkveite (N, S), Alabote-da-Gronelândia (P), Grönlanninpallas (SF), Black halibut, Greenland turbot (US)

Dwelling in one thousand metres depth in the coldest seas of the Northern Hemisphere, Greenland halibut, or black halibut, may grow to nearly 1 m (40 in). They do not stick to the sea bottom, but often venture to leave it for upper zones, sometimes occurring even one hundred metres higher. Fishermen do not hesitate to exploit the predator instinct of the species, and fishing tours are often organized to the coasts of Canada, Alaska and Greenland, aiming at landing this game fish. Landing Greenland halibut needs great physical strength and very good equipment, for the bait has to be lowered several hundred metres deep. Authorities have introduced a strict commercial quota and recreational harvest limit. Commercial fishermen are allowed to use buoyed lines. Lines are stretched between buoys, and thousands of hooks are hung from the individual stretches of lines. The meat of Greenland halibut is fervently sought after by the food market and the catering industry, it being considered among the best types of meat to fry.

361

362

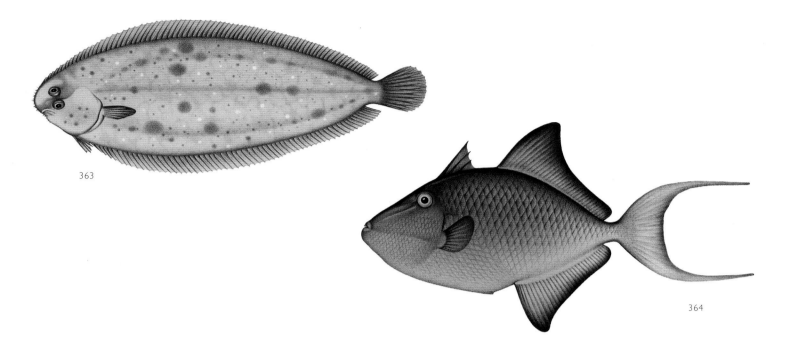

363

364

363 | **Common sole** | Solea solea | SOLEIDAE / SOLES

Common sole (En), Seezunge (D), Lenguado común (E), Sole commune (F), Sogliola (I), Tong (Nl) • Tunge, søtunge (Da), Gjuhez kanali (Alb), Almindelig tunge (Da), Samak moussa (Egy), Dover sole (En), Glóssa (Gr), Sóikoli (Is), Sulit mezuya (Isr), Ingwata tar-rig (Malt), Sola (Mon), Hout-moussa (Mor), Tunge (N), Linguado legítimo (P), Morskoi yazyk (R), Kielikampela (SF), Dil baligi (Tr), Mdass (Tun)

Mainly distributed in the northern region of the Atlantic Ocean and the adjoining seas, common sole average 30–50 cm (12–20 in) in size and 1.5–3 kg (3.3–6.6 lb) in weight. They lie on the bottom, covered by sand or mud, with only their eyes protruding. They adapt well to environmental degradation and lower-quality waters, and specimens travelling upstream along larger rivers have been observed several miles inland. Common sole often fall prey to boat fishermen near the coast, since they cannot resist the temptation which small live bait or hooks embellished with worms or snails may offer. When caught, the fish cannot find refuge anywhere on the sand bottom, therefore, it is easily landed even by recreational fishermen after some fight. Commercial fishermen have a similar strategy, but they hang a large number of hooks along a line of several hundred metres stretched out on buoys. The harvest is hauled in during the early morning hours, since common sole generally get caught while hunting for smaller fish at night. Its meat is of average quality, most of the fish being used as food: apart from the fillets, trimmings and other parts are largely used as ingredients of fish soup.

364 | **Redtoothed triggerfish** | Odonus niger | BALISTIDAE / TRIGGERFISHES

Redtoothed triggerfish (En), Rotzahn-Drückerfisch (D), Pejepuerco dentirojo (E), Baliste dents rouges (F) • Rooitand-snellervis (Afr), Ngüngü (Car), Jebong (Ind), Akamongara (J), Vaalan rondu (Mald), Blue triggerfish (Mald-En, Mas-En), Baliste bleu (Mald-F, Mau-F), Bub mej (Mars), Bourse manne (Mas-Creo), Porco dentes vermelhos (Moz-P), Himarah hamra'a sin, karkamba (Om), Epet (Phi), Redfang triggerfish (SA), Sumu-pe'a (Sam), Mwáánni weneyité, ppwukusaf (Sat), Kalu pothypora, valla (Sin), Kiin-koy (Som), Kikande, tundu, vidui (Swa), 'O'iri ave (Tah), Karuppu-klathi (Tam), Bbugesaf (W)

This species of triggerfish is an inhabitant of the Indian and Pacific oceans, and is found in the Red Sea, in the south to Durban, South Africa, in the east to the Marquesas and the Society Islands, as well as at the Great Barrier Reef, Australia, off New Caledonia, and the whole of Micronesia. It grows to 50 cm (20 in) in length and 2.5–3 kg (5.5–6.6 lb) in weight. A reef fish, it is most abundant on the outer side of coral reefs affected by currents, to a depth of 5–40 m (15–130 ft). It is usually found in schools, the fry inhabiting stony-rocky areas, where they find shelter in crevices. Triggerfish feed on zooplankton and sponges. The eggs are laid into a nest constructed on the sand bottom, which is aggressively protected by the parents, which occasionally attack swimmers and divers. It is not harvested on a substantial scale for human consumption, and is sold fresh or salted-and-dried mainly on local markets. Fresh triggerfish are eaten fried or grilled. This species is extremely popular as an aquarium fish for its spectacular appearance. It is easily maintained, but can be rather aggressive.

365

365 | Puffer | Takifugu vermicularis | TETRAODONTIDAE / PUFFERS

Puffer (En), Fugu (D, E, F, I), Kogelvis (Nl) • Shosaifugu (J), Kuk-mae-ri-bok (Kor), Fú ban chóng wén dong fang tún (Mand), Sea squab, fugu (US)

This marine puffer species is native to the northwestern Pacific and occurs from Japan to the East China Sea. A small-sized fish, it grows to 30 cm (12 in) in body length. It lives in coastal shallows, on various bottom types. Although an omnivorous species, it feeds mostly on bottom-dwelling invertebrates. The eggs are deposited in a self-constructed nest and are probably guarded against other fish. Although its skin, reproductive organs, intestines, liver and even blood contain a lethal toxin (tetraodotoxin), the puffer is considered a delicacy in Japan. It is prepared exclusively by specially trained cooks, and gourmets pay high prices for a fugu dinner, when it is eaten raw. Should the cook make a mistake and the guests die, he often commits ritual suicide. The powerful neurotoxin causes death by blocking muscle function, lowering blood pressure and disturbing circulation, and at present there is no treatment against it. The import of all fugu species is prohibited in the European Union. The flesh is used in traditional Chinese medicine.

{ index }

INDEX   Key 196 | Fish (English names) 197 | Fish (Latin names) 199

Key

A — German in Austria
AB — English in Antigua Barbidua
Afr — Afrikaans
Alb — Albanian
Alg — Arabic in Algeria
Alg-F — French in Algeria
Alu — Alutiiq (Alaska)
Amh — Amharic (Ethiopia)
Ang — Portuguese in Angola
Ara — Arabic
Arg — Spanish in Argentina
As — Assamese in India
Au — English in Australia
Az — Portuguese in Azores Islands
Az-En — English in Azores Islands
Bah — Arabic in Bahrain
Ban — Banton
Bar — English in Barbados
Bel — Russian in Belarus
Bem — Bemba (Zambia)
Ben — Bengali
Bik — Bikol
Bra — Portuguese in Brazil
Bul — Bulgarian
Bur — Burmese (Myanmar)
Can — English in Canada
Can-F — French in Canada
Cant — Cantonese
Car — Carolinian (Caroline Island)
Cat — Catalan
CH — Switzerland
Cha — Arabic in Chad
Cham — Chamorro (Guam)
Chc — Chicewa in Malawi
Chi — Spanish in Chile
Chr — Christmas Island
Chr-En — English in Christmas Island
Com — Comoros (Comoro)
Col — Spanish in Columbia
Cr — Croatian
Cree — Cree (Canada)
Creo — Creole
Club — Spanish in Cuba
Cub-En — English in Cuba
Cyp — Turkish in Cyprus
CV — Portuguese in Cape Verde
Cze — Czech
D — German
Da — Danish
Dom — Spanish in Dominican Republic
E — Spanish
Ecu — Spanish in Ecuador
Egy — Arabic in Egypt
Em — Arabic in the Arab Emirates
En — English
F — French

FG — French in French Guiana
Fi-En — English in Fiji
Fij — Fijian
Fon — Fon (Benin)
FP — English in French Polynesia
Ful — Fulfulde, Pulaar (Senegal)
Fw — Fwâi (New Caledonia)
Ga — Gaelic
Gha — Ghana
Gr — Greek
Gu — English in Guadelope
Guam — English in Guam
GuiB — Portuguese in Guinea Bissau
Guj — Gujarati (India)
H — Hungarian
Hai — Haida (Canadian British Columbia)
Hait — English in Haiti
Has — Arabic, Hassaniva in Mauritania
Hau — Hausa (Nigeria)
Haw — Hawaiian
Haw-En — English in Hawaii
Hin — Hindi
HK — English in Hong Kong
Hok — Hokkien (China Main)
I — Italian
Ig — Igbo (Nigeria)
Ijo — Ijo (Nigeria)
Ilo — Ilokano
Ind — Indonesian
Ind-En — English in India
Inu — Inuktitut
Ire-En — English in Ireland
Is — Icelandic
Isr — Hebrew
J — Japanese
Jam — English in Jamaica
Jav — Javanese
Jaw — Jawe (New Caledonia)
Kan — Kanuri (Nigeria)
Kap — Kapampangan
Khm — Khmer
Kir — Kiribati
Kon — Konjo (Uganda)
Kor — Korean
Kuw — Arabic in Kuwait
Kuy — Kuyunon/Tagbanwa
Lao — Laotian
Leb — Arabic in Lebanon
Lib — Arabic in Libya
Ma — Malayalam (India)
Mad — Malagasy (Madagascar)
Mak — Makassar (Indonesia)
Mal — Malay
Mald — Maldivian (Maldives)
Mald-En — English in Maldives
Mald-F — French in Maldives
Mal-En — English in Malaysia

Malt — Maltese
Man — English in Isle of Man
Mand — Mandarin Chinese
Manx — Manx (Isle of Man)
Mao — Maori
Mara — Maranao/Samal/Tao Sug
Mars — Marshallese (Marshall Island)
Mart — English in Martinique
Mas-Creo — Creole in Mauritius
Mas-En — English in Mauritius
Mas-F — French in Mauritius
Mau-E — Spanish in Mauritania
Mau-F — French in Mauritania
Mex — Spanish in Mexico
Mic — English in Micronesia
Mon — Monaco
Mor — Arabic in Morocco
Moz-P — Portuguese in Mozambique
Moz-E — Spanish in Mozambique
Mya — English in Myanmar
N — Norwegian
Nââ — Nââ Kvényi (New Caledonia)
Nam — English in Namibia
NC — French in New Caledonia
Ne — Nemi (New Caledonia)
Nen — Nenema (New Caledonia)
Nep — Nepali
Nic — Spanish in Nicaragua
Nie — Niuean
Nl — Dutch
Nue — Nuer (Sudan)
Num — Numee (New Caldonia)
Nup — Nupe (Nigeria)
Nya — Nyanja (Malawi)
NZ — English in New Zealand
Om — Arabic in Oman
Ori — Oriya (India)
Oro — Oromo (Ethiopia)
P — Portuguese
Pak — English in Pakistan
Pal — Palauan
Pal-En — English in Palau
Pan — Pangasinan
Pa-US — Panjabi in United States
Pap — English in Papua New Guinea
Per — Spanish in Peru
Phi — Philippines in Philippine Islands
Pi — Pie in New Caledonia
Pid — Pidgin in Papua New Guinea
Pl — Polish
Pp — Papiamento in North Antilles
Pp-B — Papiamento in Barbados
PR — Spanish in Puerto Rico
Q — Arabic in Qatar
R — Russian
Ra — Rapan (French Polynesia)
Ru — Romanian
S — Swedish

SA — English in South Africa
Saa — Saanich (Canadian British Columbia)
Sai — Saipanese Carolinian
Sal — Salish
Sam — Samoan
Sat — Satawalese Carolinian (North Marianas)
Sau — Arabic in Saudi Arabia
SC — Serbo-Croat
Sen — French in Senegal
Sey — French in Seychelles
SF — Finnish
Shi — Shilluk (Sudan)
Sid — Sindhi (Pakistan)
Sin — Sinhalese (Sri Lanka)
Slk — Slovak
Slo — Slovene
Som — Somalia
Sra — Sranan (Surinam)
Su — Susu (Guinea)
Sud — Arabic in Sudan
Syr — Arabic in Syria
Swa — Swahili
Tag — Tagalog (Philippines)
Tah — Tahitian
Tam — Tamil
Tel — Telugu (India)
Teo — Teochew (China)
Thai — Thai
Thai-En — English in Thailand
Tok — Tokelauan
Tr — Turkish
Tri — English in Trinidad and Tobago
Tsi — Tsimshian (Canadian British Columbia)
Tua — Tuamoto Island
Tun — Arabic in Tunisia
Tuv — Tuvaluan (Kiribati)
UK — English in United Kingdom
Ukr — Ukrainian
Ukr-R — Russian in Ukraine
Uru — Spanish in Uruguay
US — English in the United States
US-E — Spanish in the United States
Ven — Spanish in Venezuela
Vie — Vietnamese
V-Cam — Vietnamese in Cambodia
Vir — English in US Virgin Islands
Vis — Visayan (Philippines)
W — Woleaian (Micronesia)
Wol — Wolof
Wol-M — Wolof in Mauritania
Wol-S — Wolof in Senegal
Y — Yoruba (Nigeria)

Fish in English names

Alaska pollack 153
Alewife 48
Allis shad 46
Almaco jack 236
American angler 169
American butterfish 339
American eel 42
American plaice 350
Anchoveta 59
Angelshark 5
Anglerfish 170
Antarctic butterfish 340
Araucanian herring 49
Arctic char (freshwater form) 123
Arctic char (marine form) 124
Arctic grayling 133
Argentine anchovy 55
Argentine hake 160
Argentine seabass 207
Arrowtooth flounder 347
Asp 67
Atka mackerel 196
Atlantic blue marlin 335
Atlantic bonito 318
Atlantic catfish 299
Atlantic cod 143
Atlantic croaker 258
Atlantic emperor 264
Atlantic halibut 351
Atlantic herring 50
Atlantic horse mackerel 240
Atlantic mackerel 321
Atlantic rainbow smelt 100
Atlantic salmon (freshwater form) 119
Atlantic salmon (marine form) 120
Atlantic saury 176
Atlantic Spanish mackerel 324
Atlantic stargazer 295
Atlantic sturgeon 28
Atlantic white marlin 336
Ayu 136
Barbel 68
Barramundi 206
Beluga 33
Big skate 22
Bigeye tuna 330
Bighead carp 78
Big-headed catfish 96

Bigmouth buffalo 88
Billfish 34
Black bullhead 90
Black carp 82
Black catfish 90
Black cod 297
Black cusk-eel 168
Black seabass 208
Black seabream 282
Black skipjack 310
Blackbarred halfbeak 171
Blackbelly rosefish 183
Blackfin pacu 62
Blackfin tuna 329
Blackspot seabream 275
Blacktip reef shark 13
Blacktip shark 12
Bleak 66
Blotched picarel 283
Blue grenadier 165
Blue mackerel 319
Blue shark 14
Blue skate 21
Blue whiting 148
Bluefin gurnard 189
Bluefish 298
Bluespotted seabream 277
Bogue 267
Bombay-duck 139
Bowmouth guitarfish 18
Brasilian sandperch 225
Brill 346
Broadhead catfish 96
Brook trout (freshwater form) 125
Brook trout (marine form) 126
Brown meagre 261
Brown trout 121
Brushtooth lizardfish 138
Bullet tuna 308
Bulls-eye 219
Burbot 144
Butterfly kingfish 312
California sheephead 291
Californian anchovy 58
Canary rockfish 187
Capelin 135
Carp bream 64
Caspian lamprey 2
Channel catfish 92
Cherry salmon (freshwater form) 111

Cherry salmon (marine form) 112
Chinook salmon (freshwater form) 117
Chinook salmon (marine form) 118
Chub mackerel 320
Chum salmon (freshwater form) 107
Chum salmon (marine form) 108
Cobia 228
Coho salmon (freshwater form) 109
Coho salmon (marine form) 110
Comber 212
Common bream 64
Common (brown) bullhead 91
Common carp 74
Common dab 354
Common dentex 271
Common dolphinfish 242
Common grey mullet 202
Common pandora 276
Common pike conger 43
Common ponyfish 253
Common seabream 278
Common skate 21
Common sole 363
Common two-banded seabream 273
Common warehou 341
Conger eel 44
Corvina 260
Crucian carp 71
Cutlass fish 306
Cutthroat trout (freshwater form) 103
Cutthroat trout (marine form) 104
Danube salmon 101
Danube sturgeon 26
Dolly Varden trout 128
Dorab wolf-herring 45
Double-lined mackerel 313
Doublespotted queenfish 233
Dover sole 356
Dusky grouper 210
Dusky smooth-hound 9
Eastern Australian salmon 243
Eastern Pacific bonito 316
Eelpout 301
English sole 360
European anchovy 56
European chub 80
European eel 39
European hake 161
European pilchard 52
European plaice 359

European seabass 214
European sprat 54
Flat needlefish 173
Flathead mullet 202
Flounder 357
Fluke 344
Frigate tuna 309
Fringebarbel sturgeon 27
Garfish 174
Garpike 174
Giant gourami 342
Giant guitarfish 19
Giant seacatfish 97
Gilt-head seabream 281
Goatsbeard brotula 140
Golden grey mullet 201
Goldlined seabream 279
Grass carp 73
Grayling 134
Greasy grouper 211
Great barracuda 198
Great northern tilefish 224
Great sandeel 303
Greater amberjack 235
Green wrasse 290
Greenland halibut 362
Grey gurnard 190
Grey snapper 246
Grey weakfish 255
Haddock 145
Hapuka wreckfish 217
Honeycomb stingray 25
Houting 132
Ide 81
Inanga 137
Inca scad 238
Indian scad 231
Indian threadfin 205
Indo-Pacific sailfish 333
Indo-Pacific tarpon 38
Island mackerel 315
Itajara 210
Japanese anchovy 57
Japanese eel 41
Japanese Spanish mackerel 325
Japanese threadfin bream 252
John Dory 182
King mackerel 322
King of herrings 178
Knife fish 83

Ladyfish 36
Lake trout 129
Lake whitefish 131
Lane snapper 249
Largemouth bass 218
Leaping mullet 200
Lemon sole 355
Lesser forkbeard 152
Ling 149
Lingcod 194
Little skate 24
Long-finned tuna 327
Longnose gar 34
Longtail tuna 332
Lumpfish 197
Machete 35
Milkfish 61
Mirror carp 75
Mottled spinefoot 305
Mozambique tilapia 287
Muskellunge 99
Narrow-barred Spanish mackerel 323
Narrownose smooth-hound 11
Nase 72
New Zealand longfin eel 40
Nile tilapia 288
North African catfish 95
North Pacific hake 162
Northern anchovy 58
Northern bluefin tuna 331
Northern pike 98
Northern red snapper 245
Norway pout 154
Okhostk atka mackerel 195
Opah 179
Orange roughy 181
Orangespotted trevally 229
Orfe 81
Pacific cod 142
Pacific crevalle jack 230
Pacific halibut 352
Pacific herring 51
Pacific ladyfish 35
Pacific red snapper 247
Pacific sand lance 302
Pacific saury 175
Pacific sierra 326
Painted comber 213
Pastel ringwrasse 289
Patagonian smooth-hound 11

Patagonian toothfish 296
Perch 221
Peruvian anchovy 59
Petrale sole 348
Pike-perch 222
Piked dogfish 4
Pink cusk-eel 166
Pink ear emperor 265
Pink salmon (freshwater form) 105
Pink salmon (marine form) 106
Piper gurnard 192
Pollack 150
Pollock 151
Porbeagle 16
Pouting 155
Puffer 365
Rainbow runner 232
Rainbow trout (freshwater form) 113
Rainbow trout (marine form) 114
Ray's bream 241
Red cusk-eel 167
Red drum 262
Red morwong 293
Red mullet 285
Red salmon (freshwater form) 115
Red salmon (marine form) 116
Red seabream 269
Redtoothed triggerfish 364
Roach 84
Rohu 79
Roundnose grenadier 164
Rudd 85
Sablefish 193
Sailfish 333
Saithe 151
Salema 280
Saltwater permit 237
Sand sillago 226
Sand smelt 177
Santer seabream 268
Scalloped hammerhead (shark) 6
Schoolmaster 244
Sea lamprey 1
Sea trout 122
Sharpnose sevengill shark 3
Shi drum 263
Ship 27
Short mackerel 314
Shortfin mako 15
Shorthead anchovy 60

Silk snapper 250
Silver carp 77
Silver crucian carp 70
Silver hake 158
Silver pomfret 338
Silver salmon (freshwater form) 109
Silver salmon (marine form) 110
Silver sillago 227
Silvergrey rockfish 184
Skipjack tuna 311
Sky emperor 266
Smooth dogfish 9
Smooth hammerhead 7
Smooth-hound 10
Snakeskin gourami 343
Sneep 72
Snubnose pompano 237
Sockeye salmon (freshwater form) 115
Sockeye salmon (marine form) 116
South American pilchard 53
South American striped weakfish 256
South Pacific hake 159
Southern blue whiting 147
Southern hake 157
Southern red snapper 248
Splendid alfonsino 180
Spiny dogfish 4
Spotted sea cat 300
Spotted weever 294
Spotted wolffish 300
Squirefish 270
Starry flounder 358
Starry sturgeon 30
Sterlet 29
Streaked spinefoot 304
Striped sea-bass 215
Striped seabream 274
Striped bonito 317
Striped marlin 334
Striped red mullet 286
Sturgeon 31
Summer flounder 344
Swordfish 337
Sydney skate 20
Tadpole codling 163
Tadpole fish 152
Taimen 102
Tarpon 37
Tautog 292
Tench 86

Thicklip grey mullet 199
Thicklip grey mullet 203
Thinlip mullet 204
Thintail thresher 17
Thornback ray 23
Tiger-toothed croaker 259
Tope shark 8
Thresher shark 17
Tropical two-wing flyingfish 172
Trout sweetlips 254
Tub gurnard 191
Turbot 345
Tusk 141
Twaite shad 47
Vendace 130
Vimba 87
Viviparous blenny 301
Volga pikeperch 223
Wahoo 307
Walking catfish 94
Weatherfish 89
Wels catfish 93
White bream 69
White-eye bream 65
White grouper 209
White hake 156
White seabream 272
White sturgeon 32
Whitemouth croaker 257
Whitespotted char 127
Whiting 146
Widow rockfish 185
Wild carp 76
Winter flounder 361
Witch flounder 349
Wolffish 299
Wreckfish 216
Yellow gurnard 191
Yellow perch 220
Yelloweye rockfish 188
Yellowfin tuna 328
Yellowstripe goatfish 284
Yellowstripe scad 234
Yellowtail flounder 353
Yellowtail horse mackerel 239
Yellowtail rockfish 186
Yellowtail snapper 251
Zander 222
Ziege 83
Zope 63

Fish in Latin names

Ablennes hians 173
Abramis ballerus 63
Abramis brama 64
Abramis sapa 65
Acanthistius brasilianus 207
Acanthocybium solandri 307
Acipenser gueldenstaedti 26
Acipenser nudiventris 27
Acipenser oxyrinchus 28
Acipenser ruthenus 29
Acipenser stellatus 30
Acipenser sturio 31
Acipenser transmontanus 32
Alburnus alburnus 66
Alopias vulpinus 17
Alosa alosa 46
Alosa fallax 47
Alosa pseudoharengus 48
Ameiurus melas 90
Ameiurus nebulosus 91
Ammodytes hexapterus 302
Anarhichas lupus 299
Anarhichas minor 300
Anguilla anguilla 39
Anguilla dieffenbachii 40
Anguilla japonica 41
Anguilla rostrata 42
Anoplopoma fimbria 193
Arius thalassinus 97
Arripis trutta 243
Aspius aspius 67
Atheresthes stomias 347
Atherina presbyter 177
Auxis rochei 308
Auxis thazard 309
Barbus barbus 68
Belone belone 174
Beryx splendens 180
Blicca bjoerkna 69
Boops boops 267
Brama brama 241
Brosme brosme 141
Brotula multibarbata 140
Carangoides bajad 229
Caranx caninus 230
Carassius carassius 71
Carassius gibelio 70
Carcharhinus melanopterus 13
Carcharhinus limbatus 12
Caspiomyozon wagneri 2

Centropristis striata 208
Chanos chanos 61
Cheimerius nufar 268
Chelidonichthys kumu 189
Chelidonichtys (Eutrigla) gurnardus 190
Chelidonichthys lucernus 191
Chelon labrosus 199
Chirocentrus dorab 45
Chondrostoma nasus 72
Chrysophrys auratus 270
Chrysophrys major 269
Clarias batrachus 94
Clarias gariepinus 95
Clarias macrocephalus 96
Clupea bentincki 49
Clupea harengus 50
Clupea pallasii 51
Cololabis saira 175
Colossoma macropomum 62
Conger conger 44
Coregonus albula 130
Coregonus clupeaformis 131
Coregonus oxyrhynchus 132
Coryphaena hippurus 242
Coryphaenoides rupestris 164
Ctenopharyngodon idella 73
Cyclopterus lumpus 197
Cynoscion regalis 255
Cynoscion striatus 256
Cyprinus carpio 74
Cyprinus carpio morpha hungaricus 76
Cyprinus carpio morpha nobilis 75
Decapterus russelli 231
Dentex dentex 271
Dicentrarchus labrax 214
Diplodus sargus 272
Diplodus vulgaris 273
Dipturus batis 21
Dissostichus eleginoides 296
Elagatis bipinnulata 232
Elops affinis 35
Elops saurus 36
Encrasicholina heteroloba 60
Engraulis anchoita 55
Engraulis encrasicolus 56
Engraulis japonicus 57
Engraulis mordax 58
Engraulis ringens 59
Eopsetta jordani 348
Epigonus telescopus 219
Epinephelus aeneus 209
Epinephelus itajara 210

Epinephelus tauvina 211
Esox lucius 98
Esox masquinongy 99
Euthynnus lineatus 310
Exocoetus volitans 172
Gadus macrocephalus 142
Gadus morhua 143
Galaxias maculatus 137
Galeorhinus galeus 8
Gasterochisma melampus 312
Genypterus blacodes 166
Genypterus chilensis 167
Genypterus maculatus 168
Glyptocephalus cynoglossus 349
Goniistius fuscus 293
Grammatorcynus bilineatus 313
Harpadon nehereus 139
Helicolenus dactylopterus 183
Hemiramphus far 171
Heptranchias perlo 3
Himantura uarnak 25
Hippoglossoides platessoides 350
Hippoglossus hippoglossus 351
Hippoglossus stenolepis 352
Hologymnosus doliatus 289
Hoplostethus atlanticus 181
Hucho hucho 101
Hucho taimen 102
Huso huso 33
Hyperoglyphe antarctica 340
Hyperoplus lanceolatus 303
Hypophthalmichthys molitrix 77
Hypophthalmichthys nobilis 78
Ictalurus punctatus 92
Ictiobus cyprinellus 88
Istiophorus platypterus 333
Isurus oxyrinchus 15
Katsuwonus pelamis 311
Labeo rohita 79
Labrus viridis 290
Lamna nasus 16
Lampris guttatus (L. regius) 179
Lates calcarifer 206
Leiognathus equulus 253
Lepisosteus osseus 34
Leptomelanosoma indicum 205
Lethrinus atlanticus 264
Lethrinus lentjan 265
Lethrinus mahsena 266
Leuciscus cephalus 80
Leuciscus idus 81
Leucoraja erinacea 24

Limanda ferruginea 353
Limanda limanda 354
Lithognathus mormyrus 274
Liza aurata 201
Liza ramado 204
Liza saliens 200
Lophius americanus 169
Lophius piscatorius 170
Lopholatilus chamaeleonticeps 224
Lota lota 144
Lutjanus apodus 244
Lutjanus campechanus 245
Lutjanus griseus 246
Lutjanus peru 247
Lutjanus purpureus 248
Lutjanus synagris 249
Lutjanus vivanus 250
Macruronus novaezelandiae 165
Makaira nigricans 335
Mallotus villosus 135
Megalops atlanticus 37
Megalops cyprinoides 38
Melanogrammus aeglefinus 145
Merlangius merlangus 146
Merluccius australis 157
Merluccius bilinearis 158
Merluccius gayi 159
Merluccius hubbsi 160
Merluccius merluccius 161
Merluccius productus 162
Micromesistius australis 147
Micromesistus poutassou 148
Micropogonias furnieri 257
Micropogonias undulatus 258
Micropterus salmoides 218
Microstomus kitt 355
Microstomus pacificus 356
Misgurnus fossilis 89
Molva molva 149
Morone saxatilis 215
Mugil auratus 201
Mugil cephalus 202
Mugil labrosus 203
Mugil ramada 204
Mulloidichthys flavolineatus 284
Mullus barbatus 285
Mullus surmuletus 286
Muraenesox bagio 43
Mustelus canis 9
Mustelus mustelus 10
Mustelus schmitti 11
Mylopharingodon piceus 82

Nemipterus japonicus 252
Notothenia microlepidota 297
Ocyurus chrysurus 251
Odonus niger 364
Okamejei australis 20
Oncorhnynchus kisutch 109
Oncorhynchus kisutch
  anadromous 100
Oncorhynchus clarki 103
Oncorhynchus clarki
  anadromous 104
Oncorhynchus gorbuscha 105
Oncorhynchus gorbuscha
  anadromous 106
Oncorhynchus keta 107
Oncorhynchus keta anadromous 108
Oncorhynchus masou 111
Oncorhynchus masou
  anadromous 112
Oncorhynchus mykiss 113
Oncorhynchus mykiss
  anadromous 114
Oncorhynchus nerka 115
Oncorhynchus nerka anadromus 116
Oncorhynchus tschawytscha 117
Oncorhynchus tschawytscha
  anadromous 118
Ophiodon elongatus 194
Oreochromis mossambicus 287
Oreochromis niloticus 288
Osmerus mordax 100
Osphronemus goramy 342
Otolithes ruber 259
Pagellus centrodotus (bogaraveo) 275
Pagellus erythrinus 276
Pagrus caeruleostictus 277
Pagrus pagrus 278
Pampus argenteus 338
Paralichthys dentatus 344
Parophrys vetulus 360
Pelecus cultratus 83
Peprilus triacanthus 339
Perca flavescens 220
Perca fluviatilis 221
Petromyzon marinus 1
Platichthys flesus 357
Platichthys stellatus 358
Plecoglossus altivelis 136
Plectorhynchus pictus 254
Pleurogrammus azonus 195
Pleurogrammus monopterygius 196
Pleuronectes platessa 359

Pollachius pollachius 150
Pollachius virens 151
Polyprion americanus 216
Polyprion oxygeneios 217
Pomatomus saltatrix 298
Prionace glauca 14
Psetta maxima 345
Pseudopercis semifasciata 225
Pseudopleuronectes americanus 361
Rachycentron canadum 228
Raja australis 20
Raja binoculata 22
Raja clavata 23
Raniceps raninus 152
Rastrelliger brachysoma 314
Rastrelliger faughni 315
Regalecus glesne 178
Reinhardtius hippoglossoides 362
Rhabdosargus sarba 279
Rhina ancylostoma 18
Rhynchobatus djiddensis 19
Rutilus rutilus 84
Salilota australis 163
Salmo salar 119
Salmo salar anadromous 120
Salmo trutta 121
Salmo trutta anadromous 122
Salvelinus alpinus 123
Salvelinus alpinus anadromous 124
Salvelinus fontinalis 125
Salvelinus fontinalis anadromous 126
Salvelinus leucomaenis 127
Salvelinus malma 128
Salvelinus namaycush 129
Sarda chiliensis 316
Sarda orientalis 317
Sarda sarda 318
Sardina pilchardus 52
Sardinops sagax 53
Sarpa salpa 280
Saurida undosquamis 138
Scardinius erythrophthalmus 85
Sciaena gilberti 260
Sciaena umbra 261
Sciaenops ocellatus 262
Scomber australasicus 319
Scomber japonicus 320
Scomber scombrus 321
Scomberesox saurus 176
Scomberoides lysan 233
Scomberomorus cavalla 322
Scomberomorus commerson 323

Scomberomorus maculatus 324
Scomberomorus niphonius 325
Scomberomorus sierra 326
Scophthalmus rhombus 346
Sebastes brevispinis 184
Sebastes entomelas 185
Sebastes flavidus 186
Sebastes pinniger 187
Sebastes ruberrimus 188
Selaroides leptolepis 234
Semicossyphus pulcher 291
Seriola dumerili 235
Seriola rivoliana 236
Seriolella brama 341
Serranus cabrilla 212
Serranus scriba 213
Siganus fuscescens 305
Siganus javus 304
Sillago ciliata 226
Sillago sihama 227
Silurus glanis 93
Solea solea 363
Sparus aurata 281
Sphyraena barracuda 198
Sphyrna lewini 6
Sphyrna zygaena 7
Spicara maena 283
Spondyliosoma cantharus 282
Sprattus sprattus 54
Squalus acanthias 4
Squatina squatina 5
Sander lucioperca 222
Sander volgensis 223
Takifugu vermicularis 365
Tautoga onitis 292
Tetrapturus albidus 336
Tetrapturus audax 334
Theragra chalcogramma 153
Thunnus alalunga 327
Thunnus albacares 328
Thunnus atlanticus 329
Thunnus obesus 330
Thunnus thynnus 331
Thunnus tonggol 332
Thymallus arcticus 133
Thymallus thymallus 134
Tinca tinca 86
Trachinotus blochii 237
Trachinus araneus 294
Trachurus murphyi 238
Trachurus novaezelandiae 239
Trachurus trachurus 240

Trichiurus lepturus 306
Trichogaster pectoralis 343
Trigla lyra 192
Trisopterus esmarkii 154
Trisopterus luscus 155
Umbrina cirrosa 263
Uranoscopus scaber 295
Urophycis tenuis 156
Vimba vimba 87
Xiphias gladius 337
Zeus faber 182
Zoarces viviparus 301